2014
The Supreme Court Review

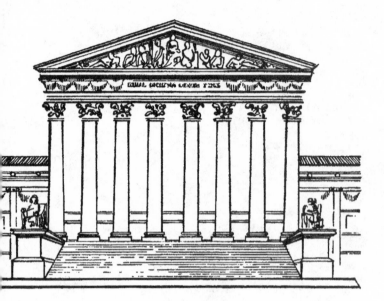

2014
The

"Judges as persons, or courts as institutions, are entitled to no greater immunity from criticism than other persons or institutions . . . [J]udges must be kept mindful of their limitations and of their ultimate public responsibility by a vigorous stream of criticism expressed with candor however blunt."
—*Felix Frankfurter*

". . . while it is proper that people should find fault when their judges fail, it is only reasonable that they should recognize the difficulties. . . . Let them be severely brought to book, when they go wrong, but by those who will take the trouble to understand them."
—*Learned Hand*

THE LAW SCHOOL

THE UNIVERSITY OF CHICAGO

Supreme Court Review

EDITED BY

DENNIS J. HUTCHINSON

DAVID A. STRAUSS

AND GEOFFREY R. STONE

 THE UNIVERSITY OF CHICAGO PRESS

CHICAGO AND LONDON

INTERNATIONAL STANDARD BOOK NUMBER: 978-0-226-26906-1

LIBRARY OF CONGRESS CATALOG CARD NUMBER: 60-14353

THE UNIVERSITY OF CHICAGO PRESS, CHICAGO 60637

THE UNIVERSITY OF CHICAGO PRESS, LTD., LONDON

© 2015 BY THE UNIVERSITY OF CHICAGO, ALL RIGHTS RESERVED, PUBLISHED 2015

PRINTED IN THE UNITED STATES OF AMERICA

The paper used in this publication meets the minimum requirements of American National Standard for Information Sciences–Permanence of Paper for Printed Library Materials, ANSI Z39.48-1984. ∞

TO ABNER J. MIKVA

For half a century:
Public servant in every branch of government,
teacher, mentor, cheerful skeptic

"Healthy skepticism is necessary to the
continuation of our democracy [but a] nation
where cynicism toward government prevails cannot
function effectively." (1995)

CONTENTS

CURTIS A. BRADLEY AND
NEIL S. SIEGEL

AFTER RECESS: HISTORICAL PRACTICE, TEXTUAL AMBIGUITY, AND CONSTITUTIONAL ADVERSE POSSESSION

The Supreme Court's decision last Term in *NLRB v Noel Canning* contains an especially strong and sustained endorsement of the relevance of historical practice to discerning the Constitution's distribution of authority between Congress and the President.[1] In interpreting the scope of the Recess Appointments Clause,[2] the Court gave significant attention to how governmental actors had understood and applied the clause throughout history. The Court did so, moreover, as part of a self-conscious approach to constitutional interpretation. When construing "constitutional provisions regulating

Curtis A. Bradley is the William Van Alstyne Professor of Law, Duke Law School, and Neil S. Siegel is the David W. Ichel Professor of Law, Duke Law School.

Authors' note: For their helpful comments and suggestions, we thank Will Baude, Stuart Benjamin, Joseph Blocher, Guy Charles, Richard Fallon, Darrell Miller, Jeff Powell, Jed Purdy, Stephen Sachs, Jim Salzman, Chris Schroeder, Peter Spiro, David Strauss, and Jonathan Wiener, as well as participants in the inaugural Yale-Duke Foreign Relations Law Roundtable.

[1] See 134 S Ct 2550 (2014).

[2] US Const, Art II, § 2, cl 3 ("The President shall have Power to fill up all Vacancies that may happen during the Recess of the Senate, by granting Commissions which shall expire at the End of their next Session.").

1

the relationship between Congress and the President," the Court explained, "great weight" should be given to "'[l]ong settled and established practice.'"[3] In large part because of the practice, the Court concluded that the Recess Appointments Clause conferred broad recess appointments authority upon the President. The Court invalidated, however, the particular appointments at issue in the case, which in the Court's view lacked historical support.

The Court was unanimous as to the result, but four Justices concurred only in the judgment.[4] Writing a de facto dissent for that group, Justice Scalia objected, first, to the way in which the majority had relied on historical practice. He accepted that "where a governmental practice has been open, widespread, and unchallenged since the early days of the Republic, the practice should guide our interpretation of an ambiguous constitutional provision."[5] In this case, however, Justice Scalia argued that the relevant text was clear, and that the historical practice relied upon by the majority neither dated to the early days of the Republic nor was uncontested. Justice Scalia also characterized the majority as applying "an adverse-possession theory of executive power," which he feared would "have the effect of aggrandizing the Presidency beyond its constitutional bounds and undermining respect for the separation of powers."[6]

The majority, by contrast, invoked James Madison for the proposition that the meaning of some constitutional provisions could be "liquidated" through "a regular course of practice" after the constitutional Founding, and it contended that "our cases have continually confirmed Madison's view."[7] The majority did not explain the contours of this "liquidation" concept, however, and its reasoning about the scope of the Recess Appointments Clause seemed to be based on a potentially distinct and broader concept of "historical gloss"—a concept most famously articulated by Justice Frankfurter in his concurrence in the *Youngstown* steel seizure case.[8] Indeed, judging

---

[3] 134 S Ct at 2559, quoting *The Pocket Veto Case*, 279 US 655, 689 (1929).

[4] *Noel Canning* was one of several decisions in the 2013–14 Term in which the Court was unanimous as to the result but deeply divided on the reasoning. See also *Bond v United States*, 134 S Ct 2077 (2014), and *McCullen v Coakley*, 134 S Ct 2518 (2014).

[5] 134 S Ct at 2594 (Scalia, J, concurring in the judgment).

[6] Id at 2592, 2617–18.

[7] Id at 2580.

[8] See *Youngstown Sheet and Tube Co. v Sawyer*, 343 US 579, 610–11 (1952) (Frankfurter, J, concurring) ("[A] systematic, unbroken, executive practice, long pursued to the knowledge of

from the way in which the concept of liquidation has been developed by originalist scholars, it would seem to accord more closely with Justice Scalia's views in *Noel Canning* than with those of the majority.

Justice Scalia also disagreed with the majority about the clarity of the relevant constitutional text. Justice Scalia and the majority did agree that if the text of the Recess Appointments Clause was clear, it controlled the outcome regardless of other considerations. The majority maintained, however, that "the Clause's text, standing alone, is ambiguous,"[9] and that it was therefore appropriate to consider other sources of constitutional authority, including historical practice. Justice Scalia, by contrast, argued that the text was clear, and he insisted that "[t]he historical practice of the political branches is, of course, irrelevant when the Constitution is clear."[10]

This article engages these two disputes in *Noel Canning* by examining the relationship between interpretive methodology and historical practice, and between historical practice and textual ambiguity. We begin in Part I by describing the historical background and issues in *Noel Canning*. In the next two parts, we consider the relationship between historical practice and constitutional methodology. In Part II, we explain how a reliance on historical practice fits with various nonoriginalist and originalist approaches to constitutional interpretation. In Part III, we critique the idea of "liquidation" of constitutional meaning to the extent that it is something separate from—and narrower than—reliance on historical gloss more generally.

We turn in Part IV from the relationship between methodology and practice to the relationship between practice and ambiguity. We explain that historical practice was relevant not only to the majority's effort in *Noel Canning* to resolve perceived ambiguities in the constitutional text, but also to the majority's very perception of ambiguity in the first instance. As a result, the decision is an example of how the constitutional text is often interpreted through a process that we have described elsewhere as "constructed constraint."[11] Finally, in Part V we assess Justice Scalia's contention that crediting historical

---

the Congress and never before questioned, engaged in by Presidents who have also sworn to uphold the Constitution, making as it were such exercise of power part of the structure of our government, may be treated as a gloss on 'executive Power' vested in the President by § 1 of Art. II.").

[9] 134 S Ct at 2577.

[10] Id at 2600.

[11] See Curtis A. Bradley and Neil S. Siegel, *Constructed Constraint and the Constitutional Text*, 64 Duke L J (forthcoming 2015).

gloss licenses a form of adverse possession by the President. We conclude that Justice Scalia's analogy to adverse possession usefully suggests caution in crediting historical practice, but that the analogy obscures more than it clarifies because it misses critical differences between the values underlying the adverse possession doctrine in property law and those animating a historical gloss approach to the separation of powers. In responding to Justice Scalia, we also offer thoughts on how best to define a historical gloss approach, including how to specify its limits.

I. Historical Practice and Recess Appointments

A. A BRIEF HISTORY OF RECESS APPOINTMENTS

The Constitution provides that federal officers are to be appointed through nomination by the President with the advice and consent of the Senate.[12] It also provides, however, that the President may "fill up all Vacancies that may happen during the Recess of the Senate, by granting Commissions which shall expire at the End of [the Senate's] next Session."[13] Alexander Hamilton explained in *The Federalist Papers* that the Framers had included this Recess Appointments Clause in the Constitution because "it would have been improper to oblige [the Senate] to be continually in session for the appointment of officers" and because "vacancies might happen *in their recess*, which it might be necessary for the public service to fill without delay."[14]

Each Congress has a two-year term, which traditionally has been divided into two yearly sessions.[15] The break between those sessions is referred to as an intersession recess. By contrast, breaks during a session are referred to as intrasession recesses. The Constitution provides that neither chamber of Congress may take a break for more than three days without the consent of the other, which gives the

---

[12] US Const, Art II, § 2, cl 2.

[13] Id, cl 3.

[14] Federalist 67 (Hamilton) in Clinton Rossiter, ed, *The Federalist Papers* 410 (Penguin, 1961).

[15] See generally Henry B. Hogue, *Recess Appointments: Frequently Asked Questions* (Cong Res Serv, June 7, 2013), online at https://www.senate.gov/CRSReports/crs-publish.cfm?pid='0DP%2BP%5CW%3B%20P%20%20%0A. The President can also call one or both houses of Congress into session "on extraordinary Occasions," see US Const, Art II, § 3, and this has happened at various times. Congressional leadership can also call the houses of Congress into special session during a recess.

House of Representatives substantial ability to affect the length of Senate breaks.[16]

Historically, there have been three principal issues concerning the scope of the Recess Appointments Clause: first, whether the clause's reference to "the Recess" covers only intersession recesses, or whether it also encompasses at least some intrasession recesses; second, whether the clause's reference to vacancies "that may happen during the Recess" limits the clause to vacancies that *occur* during the recess or whether it also encompasses vacancies that *exist* during the recess; and, third, whether there is a minimum time period required in order for a break in Senate operations to be considered a "recess" for purposes of the clause.[17]

1. *"The Recess."* There was no sustained practice of making intrasession recess appointments before the twentieth century. Prior to the Civil War, presidents apparently made no intrasession recess appointments at all. There was relatively little opportunity to do so, however, because this was a period in which Congress took very long breaks between sessions—typically at least half a year—and no more than short breaks (of about a week) during the sessions.[18] When Congress took long intrasession breaks during the presidency of Andrew Johnson, he made a number of intrasession recess appointments. After this episode, Congress soon returned to having only short intrasession recesses, and there were apparently no more intrasession recess appointments until 1920.

In 1901, Attorney General Philander Knox advised President Theodore Roosevelt that the Recess Appointments Clause did not apply to intrasession recesses.[19] Knox reasoned that, although a

---

[16] See US Const, Art II, § 3. If the houses of Congress cannot agree on an adjournment, the President "may adjourn them to such Time as he shall think proper." Id. Under Senate practice, Sundays are not counted for purposes of the Adjournments Clause.

[17] For discussions of the relevant post-Founding history, see Edward A. Hartnett, *Recess Appointments of Article III Judges: Three Constitutional Questions*, 26 Cardozo L Rev 377 (2005); Michael B. Rappaport, *The Original Meaning of the Recess Appointments Clause*, 52 UCLA L Rev 1487 (2005); Jonathan Turley, *Constitutional Adverse Possession: Recess Appointments and the Role of Historical Practice in Constitutional Interpretation*, 2013 Wis L Rev 965; and Michael A. Carrier, Note, *When Is the Senate in Recess for Purposes of the Recess Appointments Clause?*, 92 Mich L Rev 2204 (1994).

[18] In the post-Founding period, intersession recesses typically lasted six months or longer. See Rappaport, 52 UCLA L Rev at 1498 (cited in note 17). When the Senate took intrasession recesses in this period, they were typically around the Christmas holiday and lasted only about a week. See Hartnett, 26 Cardozo L Rev at 408 (cited in note 17).

[19] 23 Op Atty Gen 599, 601 (1901).

break during a session "may be *a* recess in the general and ordinary use of that term," it is not "*the* Recess" referred to in the Recess Appointments Clause.[20] Controversy subsequently developed when, in December 1903, Roosevelt made 160 recess appointments (mostly involving military officers) as the Senate transitioned without break from a special session (which had been convened after adjournment of the prior regular session) to a new regular session. Roosevelt claimed that there was a "constructive recess" between the two sessions that triggered his appointments authority.[21] In 1905, the Senate Judiciary Committee published a report criticizing the appointments and arguing that "the Constitution means a real recess, not a constructive one."[22] Although the committee's functional definition of a recess potentially could have been applied to an intrasession recess as well as an intersession recess,[23] Roosevelt had not claimed an intrasession recess appointments power, and the report did not specifically consider that issue.

In 1921, Attorney General Harry Daugherty concluded that, contrary to the Knox opinion, the President has the authority to make recess appointments during an intrasession recess.[24] Daugherty explained that the appointments provisions in the Constitution are designed "to prohibit the President from making appointments without the advice and consent of the Senate whenever that body is in session so that its advice and consent can be obtained."[25] The relevant question as he saw it, therefore, was "whether in a *practical* sense the Senate is in session so that its advice and consent can be obtained."[26] Daugherty also reasoned that a contrary interpretation of the clause could lead to "disastrous consequences."[27]

---

[20] Id.

[21] See T. J. Halstead, *Recess Appointments: A Legal Overview* 10 (Cong Res Serv, July 26, 2005), online at http://fpc.state.gov/documents/organization/50801.pdf.

[22] S Rep No 4389, 58th Cong, 3d Sess, p 4.

[23] The Committee explained that a recess is "the period of time when the Senate is *not sitting in regular or extraordinary session*[;] . . . when its members owe no duty of attendance; when its Chamber is empty; when, because of its absence, it can not receive communications from the President or participate as a body in making appointments." Id at 2.

[24] 33 Op Atty Gen 20 (1921).

[25] Id at 21.

[26] Id at 21–22.

[27] Id at 23. See also id ("If the President's power of appointment is to be defeated because the Senate takes an adjournment to a specified date, the painful and inevitable result will be measurably to prevent the exercise of governmental functions.").

Since 1921, executive branch lawyers consistently have interpreted the clause to apply to intrasession recesses. Particularly since the 1940s, moreover, presidents have made numerous recess appointments during intrasession recesses.[28] In 1948, the Comptroller General, an officer of Congress, cited Daugherty's opinion as representing "the accepted view" on the question.[29] At various times, however, individual senators have disagreed with this view.[30]

2. *"Vacancies that may happen during the Recess."* President Washington's Attorney General, Edmund Randolph, opined that the recess appointments power was limited to executive branch positions that become vacant during a recess. Instead of focusing on the semantic meaning of the text of the clause, Randolph reasoned that "[t]he Spirit of the Constitution favors the participation of the Senate in all appointments" and that the recess appointments power should be viewed as "an exception to the general participation of the Senate" and "interpreted strictly."[31] Despite this opinion, presidents since at least the Madison administration (and perhaps earlier) have used the recess appointments power at various times to fill posts that became vacant before the relevant recess.[32]

In 1823, President Monroe's Attorney General, William Wirt, reached a conclusion contrary to Randolph's, reasoning that the phrase "may happen" "seems not perfectly clear," because it could mean either "happen to take place" or "happen to exist."[33] Wirt

---

[28] See Carrier, 92 Mich L Rev at 2212 (cited in note 17) (noting that "[f]requent presidential use of the recess appointment power during intrasession recesses began in 1947" with appointments by Truman).

[29] 28 Comp Gen 30, 34 (1948).

[30] In 1993, for example, the Senate Legal Counsel drafted an amicus brief, to be filed in a pending case, *Mackie v Clinton*, arguing that the recess appointments power applied only during intersession recesses. The brief, which was prepared at the request of Senator George Mitchell, was never filed due to objections from Senate Republicans. See 139 Cong Rec 15266–74 (July 1, 1993). Similarly, in 2004 Senator Edward Kennedy filed an amicus curiae brief arguing that the President's recess appointments authority is limited to intersession recesses. See Brief for Sen. Edward M. Kennedy as Amicus Curiae in *Franklin v United States*, OT 2004, No 04-5858 (Oct 12, 2004).

[31] Edmund Randolph, *Opinion on Recess Appointments* (July 7, 1792), reprinted in John Catanzariti et al, eds, 24 *The Papers of Thomas Jefferson* 165–67 (1990).

[32] See, for example, Hartnett, 26 Cardozo L Rev at 400 (cited in note 17) ("While there is good reason to believe that both President Adams and President Jefferson made recess appointments that were inconsistent with Randolph's interpretation of the Recess Appointments Clause, I am confident that President Madison did so.").

[33] William Wirt, *Executive Authority to Fill Vacancies*, 1 Op Atty Gen 631, 631–32 (Oct 22, 1823).

thought that the first reading would be more consistent with the "letter of the constitution," but that the second would be "most accordant with its reason and spirit."[34] He observed that the purpose of the recess appointments power was to ensure that offices could remain filled and that if the President could not use this power to fill positions that remained vacant when the Senate went into recess, "the powers are inadequate to the purpose, and the substance of the constitution will be sacrificed to a dubious construction of its letter."[35] After some inconsistency of views within the executive branch on this issue through the mid-nineteenth century, the President's legal advisers since that time have consistently agreed with Wirt's conclusion and have treated the question as settled.[36]

In 1863, the Senate Judiciary Committee issued a report concluding that the recess appointments power applies only to positions that become vacant during the recess.[37] The committee expressly disagreed with Wirt's reasoning, pointing out that keeping governmental offices filled is not the only constitutional interest at issue, and that another interest is ensuring that the offices are filled by well-qualified individuals. The committee also expressed the concern that, if a President could fill preexisting vacancies during recesses, he could deliberately bypass the senatorial process of advice and consent.[38]

Shortly thereafter, Congress enacted the Pay Act, which prohibited paying recess appointees who were filling vacancies that preexisted the recess until the Senate confirmed their appointments.[39] The act was enacted in the context of disputes over President Lincoln's appointment of military officers during the Civil War. The legislation was introduced by Senator Trumbull, who said that he did not think that the President had the constitutional authority to make recess appointments for preexisting vacancies but that "some other persons think he has that power."[40] Senator Harris questioned

---

[34] Id at 632.

[35] Id.

[36] See Halstead, *Recess Appointments* at 5–6 (cited in note 21).

[37] See S Rep No 80, 37th Cong, 3d Sess (Jan 28, 1863). The committee also expressed the view that the recess appointments power applied only to intersession recesses. See id at 3.

[38] Id at 6. See also id ("In the hands of an ambitious, corrupt, or tyrannical executive, this use of the power would soon bring about the very state of things which the Constitution so carefully guards against, by requiring, in express terms, that the advice of the Senate shall first be taken, and its consent obtained, before an appointment shall be made.").

[39] See Act of Feb 9, 1863, ch 25, § 2, 12 Stat 642, 646.

[40] Cong Globe, 37th Cong, 3d Sess 565 (Jan 29, 1863).

Trumbull's constitutional claim, noting, among other things, that "however we may read the Constitution, for forty years the precedents have been against that theory."[41]

Notwithstanding the act, the executive branch continued to endorse Wirt's conclusion about the scope of the Recess Appointments Clause, and presidents continued to make occasional recess appointments to preexisting vacancies. Congress paid those appointees retroactively after they were confirmed, and sometimes voted to pay them even if they were not confirmed. In 1927, the Comptroller General expressed the view that "there is no question but that the President has authority" to make those appointments.[42] In 1940, Congress amended the Pay Act to allow for the payment, under various conditions, of recess appointees who were filling preexisting vacancies.[43]

3. *Duration of the Senate break.* The duration of the break taken by the Senate generally has not been a significant issue for intersession recess appointments. The one exception is the controversy, noted above, about Theodore Roosevelt's appointments in 1903 during an instantaneous transition between Senate sessions. On other occasions, there has not been much controversy over intersession appointments even when the breaks have been fairly short, including when they have been less than ten days.[44]

The length of the break has been an issue, however, for intrasession recess appointments. Attorney General Daugherty addressed that issue in the 1921 opinion discussed above. Although the recess in question there was almost a month long and thus seemed long enough, Daugherty thought it important to address the required length of the break "so as to avoid any misconception as to the scope of this opinion."[45] "If the President is empowered to make recess appointments during the present adjournment," he asked, "does it not necessarily follow that the power exists if an adjournment for

---

[41] Id.

[42] 7 Comp Gen 10, 11 (1927).

[43] See Act of July 11, 1940, ch 580, 54 Stat 751 (codified, as amended, at 5 USC § 5503).

[44] For example, as the majority noted in *Noel Canning*, "President Truman also made a recess appointment to the Civil Aeronautics Board during a 3-day inter-session recess. . . . President Taft made a few appointments during a 9-day recess following his inauguration, and President Lyndon Johnson made several appointments during an 8-day recess several weeks after assuming office." 134 S Ct at 2567.

[45] Memorandum from Harry M. Daugherty, *Executive Power—Recess Appointments*, 33 Op Atty Gen 20, 24 (1921).

only 2 instead of 28 days is taken?"[46] Daugherty "unhesitatingly answer[ed] this by saying no."[47] He also disputed that "an adjournment for 5 or even 10 days can be said to constitute the recess intended by the Constitution."[48] Beyond that, Daugherty doubted that one could specify a precise "line of demarcation," and he suggested that the President "is necessarily vested with a large, although not unlimited, discretion to determine when there is a real and genuine recess making it impossible for him to receive the advice and consent of the Senate."[49]

Subsequent executive branch legal opinions considered the minimum length of time that was needed before an intrasession break would trigger the President's recess appointments authority. In 1992, for example, the Justice Department's Office of Legal Counsel (OLC) concluded that "[p]ast practice is consistent with exercise of the recess appointment power during an intrasession recess of eighteen days."[50] In 2004, it advised the Counsel to the President that the recess appointments power could be exercised during an eleven-day recess.[51]

Starting in 2007, when Democrats assumed control of the Senate, they began a practice of conducting pro forma sessions during intrasession recesses in an effort to block President George W. Bush from making recess appointments during those periods. The practice ended in 2008 but was revived by congressional Republicans during the Obama administration.[52] Although the Republicans did not control the Senate, they did control the House of Representatives, and the House insisted on the pro forma sessions as a condition

---

[46] Id.

[47] Id.

[48] Id at 25.

[49] Id.

[50] Memorandum Opinion for the Deputy Counsel to the President, *Recess Appointments During an Intrasession Recess*, 16 Op OLC 15, 16 (1992).

[51] Memorandum for Alberto R. Gonzales, Counsel to the President (Feb 20, 2004) (heavily redacted), at 2, online at http://www.documentcloud.org/documents/369213-redacted-goldsmith-olc-memo-recess-appointments.html. Without deciding the issue, the memorandum also observes that "[a]rguably, the three days set by the Constitution as the time during which one House may adjourn without the consent of the other, US Const. art. I, § 5, cl. 4, is also the length of time amounting to a 'Recess' under the Recess Appointments Clause." Id at 3.

[52] See Jennifer Steinhauer, *Sometimes a Day in Congress Takes Seconds, Gavel to Gavel*, NY Times (Aug 6, 2011), at A12.

of the House's constitutionally required consent to Senate adjournments of longer than three days.[53]

Shortly after President Obama made the appointments at issue in
Noel Canning, OLC issued an opinion concluding that the appointments were valid. OLC took the position that "while Congress can
prevent the President from making any recess appointments by remaining continuously in session and available to receive and act on
nominations, it cannot do so by conducting pro forma sessions during
a recess."[54] OLC reasoned that the purpose of the Recess Appointments Clause is to allow the President to fill positions when the
Senate is unavailable to consider nominations, and that this purpose is
implicated even when a long Senate break is interrupted by pro forma
sessions, because as a practical matter the Senate is not available to
give its advice and consent during such a period.

B. TREATMENT OF HISTORICAL PRACTICE IN NOEL CANNING

On December 17, 2011, the Senate adjourned, subject to an order
adopted by unanimous consent providing that it would reconvene
"for pro forma sessions only, with no business conducted," on four
dates between December 17 and the end of the congressional session
on January 3, 2012.[55] The order further provided that when the new
congressional session began on January 3, the Senate would reconvene "for pro forma sessions only, with no business conducted," on
five dates between January 6 and January 20. Although the order
stated that no business would be conducted during the pro forma
sessions, it was still possible for the Senate to act in those sessions
through unanimous consent, and some minor business was conducted during this period.[56]

---

[53] See US Const, Art I, § 5, cl 4 ("Neither house, during the Session of Congress, shall,
without the Consent of the other, adjourn for more than three days, nor to any other Place
than that in which the two Houses shall be sitting.").

[54] Memorandum Opinion for the Counsel to the President, *Lawfulness of Recess Appointments During a Recess of the Senate Notwithstanding Periodic Pro Forma Sessions* 4 (Jan 6, 2012),
online at http://www.justice.gov/sites/default/files/olc/opinions/2012/01/31/pro-forma-sessions
-opinion.pdf.

[55] 157 Cong Rec S8783 (daily ed, Dec 17, 2011).

[56] On December 23, 2011, the Senate agreed, by unanimous consent, to a process for
passing the Temporary Payroll Tax Cut Continuation Act of 2011. See Sen. Harry Reid,
"Unanimous Consent Agreement" Remarks in the Senate, 157 Cong Rec S8789 (daily ed,
Dec 23, 2011).

On January 4, 2012, during a three-day gap between pro forma sessions, President Obama announced that he was using his recess appointments authority to fill three of the five positions on the National Labor Relations Board (NLRB).[57] The Noel Canning Corporation, a Pepsi-Cola distributor, subsequently challenged a decision of the NLRB finding that it had committed an unfair labor practice, arguing that the board had lacked a quorum because the President had exceeded his authority in making the appointments. The U.S. Court of Appeals for the D.C. Circuit agreed, ruling broadly that the President's recess appointments power applies only during intersession recesses, and only to positions that become vacant during the recess.[58]

The Supreme Court unanimously affirmed, but it was sharply divided on the rationale. In large part based on historical practice, the five-Justice majority (consisting of Justice Breyer writing also for Justices Kennedy, Ginsburg, Sotomayor, and Kagan) concluded that the President had the authority to make appointments during intrasession recesses and to fill vacancies that predated the recess, but that there was an insufficiently long recess in this case because of the pro forma sessions. Justice Scalia, writing for himself, the Chief Justice, and Justices Thomas and Alito, concurred only in the judgment.

1. *"The Recess."* The majority reasoned that the phrase "the Recess" was ambiguous. Based on Founding-era dictionaries, the majority noted, the phrase might refer only to the recess between sessions of the Senate, or it might refer to any break of substantial length, regardless of whether it is during a session or between sessions. Because the text is ambiguous, the majority reasoned, it was

---

[57] See Press Release, President Obama Announces Recess Appointments to Four Key Administration Posts (Jan 4, 2012), online at http://www.whitehouse.gov/the-press-office/2012/01/04/president-obama-announces-recess-appointments-key-administration-posts. The same day, President Obama invoked his recess appointments authority to fill the position of director of the new Consumer Financial Protection Bureau.

[58] See *Noel Canning v NLRB*, 705 F3d 490 (DC Cir 2103). The Third and Fourth Circuits subsequently agreed that the recess appointments power was limited to intersession recesses, see *NLRB v New Vista Nursing & Rehabilitation*, 719 F3d 203 (3d Cir 2013), and *NLRB v Enterprise Leasing Co. Southwest, LLC*, 722 F3d 609 (4th Cir 2013). These three decisions conflicted with a 2004 decision from the Eleventh Circuit, *Evans v Stephens*, 387 F3d 1220, 1224–26 (11th Cir 2004) (en banc), a case that involved an intrasession recess appointment of a federal judge. Several circuits also had concluded, unlike the D.C. Circuit in *Noel Canning*, that the President's recess appointments authority extended to vacancies that preexisted the recess. See *Evans*, 387 F3d at 1226–27; *United States v Woodley*, 751 F2d 1008, 1012–13 (9th Cir 1985); *United States v Alloco*, 305 F2d 704, 712–13 (2d Cir 1962).

appropriate to consider the purpose of the clause. This purpose, according to the majority, is to "ensure the continued functioning of the Federal Government when the Senate is away,"[59] a purpose that the majority thought is served by applying the clause to lengthy intrasession recesses. "The Senate is equally away during both an inter-session and an intra-session recess," the majority observed, "and its capacity to participate in the appointments process has nothing to do with the words it uses to signal its departure."[60]

In support of that conclusion, the majority placed significant weight on historical practice. The majority acknowledged that there was not much supportive practice in the period before the Civil War, but it said that this was so because Congress did not take significant intrasession breaks during that era. It pointed to the intrasession appointments made by President Johnson in the 1860s as well as appointments made in 1921 and 1929. In addition, it observed that "[s]ince 1929, and particularly since the end of World War II, Congress has shortened its inter-session breaks as it has taken longer and more frequent intra-session breaks" and that "Presidents have correspondingly made more intra-session recess appointments."[61]

The majority also emphasized the repeated view of presidential legal advisers since Daugherty's opinion in 1921 that intrasession recess appointments were valid. While the majority acknowledged that individual senators had sometimes taken a contrary view, it noted that "neither the Senate considered as a body nor its committees, despite opportunities to express opposition to the practice of intra-session recess appointments, has done so."[62] The majority recognized that "the Senate cannot easily register opposition as a body to every governmental action that many, perhaps most, Senators oppose."[63] But it noted that the Senate had at various times been actively engaged with the issue of recess appointments and that, in those situations, it had tended to adopt a functional approach to the nature of a "recess" without questioning the authority of the President to make intrasession recess appointments.

---

[59] 134 S Ct at 2561.
[60] Id.
[61] Id at 2562.
[62] Id at 2563.
[63] Id at 2564.

Justice Scalia responded by emphasizing the lack of intrasession appointments early in history and the scarcity of such appointments before the 1920s. He also emphasized the change of position by presidential legal advisers, from the Knox opinion to the Daugherty opinion. He observed that "[n]o Presidential legal adviser approved th[e] practice [of intra-session recess appointments] before 1921, and subsequent approvals have rested more on precedent than on independent examination."[64] Justice Scalia further noted that individual senators at various times have disputed the claim.

Turning from historical practice to the purpose of the Recess Appointments Clause, Justice Scalia disputed the majority's argument that its purpose favored the broader reading of the phrase "the Recess." In his view, the majority "disregards another self-evident purpose of the Clause: to preserve the Senate's role in the appointment process."[65] He also pointed out that changes in travel and communications mean that it is now much easier than it was historically for the Senate to reassemble in order to consider nominations—a change, he suggested, that renders the recess appointments power an anachronism.[66]

2. *"Vacancies that may happen during the Recess."* The majority concluded that the phrase "vacancies that may happen" in the Recess Appointments Clause also is ambiguous. It acknowledged that the word "happen" in the phrase most naturally seems to refer to vacancies that occur during a recess. But it insisted that this was "not the only possible way to use the word."[67] Rather, the majority reasoned, the word can be read more broadly to refer to vacancies that exist during a recess, and such a broader reading would be more consistent with the purpose of the clause, which the majority thought was "to permit the President to obtain the assistance of subordinate officers when the Senate, due to its recess, cannot confirm them."[68]

---

[64] Id at 2604.

[65] Id at 2597.

[66] See id at 2598. During oral argument, Justice Kagan asked the Solicitor General whether the Recess Appointments Clause was "essentially an historic relic, something whose original purpose has disappeared and has assumed a new purpose that nobody ever intended it to have." Transcript of Oral Argument, *NLRB v Noel Canning*, No 12-1281, at 19 (Jan 13, 2014), online at http://www.supremecourt.gov/oral_arguments/argument_transcripts/12-1281 _3d9g.pdf. The Solicitor General responded by suggesting that, although not its original purpose, the Recess Appointments Clause might operate today as a "safety valve" to address political intransigence in the Senate in the appointments process. See id at 20.

[67] 134 S Ct at 2567. See also id at 2573 (noting that there was "some linguistic ambiguity").

[68] Id at 2568.

In addition, the majority again emphasized long-standing historical practice, this time with a lineage dating back much closer to the
constitutional Founding. From as early as the Madison administration, the majority noted, presidents have used the recess appointments power for vacancies that occurred prior to the recess, and executive branch legal advisors since the Monroe administration have
advised presidents that they have such authority. Although conceding
that the precise numbers of such appointees are unknown, the majority thought it apparent that a large proportion of recess appointments throughout American history have involved vacancies that
predated the recess. As for the Pay Act, the majority argued that it did
not clearly reflect a congressional judgment that the President lacked
constitutional authority to use the Recess Appointments Clause to fill
preexisting vacancies and that, in any event, Congress's amendment
of the act in 1940 showed that the Senate had "in effect supported
the President's interpretation of the Clause."[69]

Justice Scalia responded by noting that appointments for prere-
cess vacancies did not become common until the mid-nineteenth
century, and only after much uncertainty and inconsistency of position within the executive branch on the issue. He also contended
that the Senate Judiciary Committee's report in 1863, as well as Congress's enactment of the Pay Act, showed that the Senate did not
acquiesce in the executive branch's claim about the meaning of the
word "happen." As for the amendment of the Pay Act in 1940, Justice
Scalia argued that it simply reflected Congress's desire not to punish
appointees caught in the dispute between the branches over the scope
of the recess appointments power, not an acquiescence in the President's constitutional claim.

The majority and Justice Scalia had differing views about the
consequences of reading the clause to be limited to vacancies occurring during a recess. The majority thought, like Attorney General
Wirt, that it was problematic to interpret the clause in a way that
"would prevent the President from making any recess appointment
that arose before a recess, no matter who the official, no matter how
dire the need, no matter how uncontroversial the appointment, and
no matter how late in the session the office fell vacant."[70] Justice Scalia
responded that Congress has allowed "acting" officers to carry out

---

[69] Id at 2573.

[70] Id at 2569–70.

the duties associated with vacant offices, and that the President has the power to call Congress into special session to consider a nomination. As for the majority's view that those mechanisms were "inadequate expedients," Justice Scalia argued that inefficiency associated with separation of powers "is not a bug to be fixed by this Court, but a calculated feature of the constitutional framework."[71]

For his part, Justice Scalia expressed the concern that the majority's interpretation of the clause might allow the President to evade the Constitution's advice and consent requirement for appointments. "On the majority's reading," Justice Scalia said, "the President would have had no need *ever* to seek the Senate's advice and consent for his appointments: Whenever there was a fair prospect of the Senate's rejecting his preferred nominee, the President could have appointed that individual unilaterally during the recess, allowed the appointment to expire at the end of the next session, renewed the appointment the following day, and so on *ad infinitum*."[72] The majority acknowledged this concern but noted that Congress had tools for responding to abuses, such as staying in session or enacting laws like the Pay Act. It also noted that "the Executive Branch has adhered to the broader interpretation for two centuries, and Senate confirmation has always remained the norm for officers that require it."[73]

3. *Duration of the Senate break.* Turning to whether the recess in this case was long enough, the majority reasoned that, "for purposes of the Recess Appointments Clause, the Senate is in session when it says it is, provided that, under its own rules, it retains the capacity to transact Senate business."[74] The majority made clear that this deference to the Senate "cannot be absolute," and thus that if "the Senate is without the *capacity* to act, under its own rules, it is not in session even if it so declares."[75] But the majority reasoned that the Senate did have such capacity here, because under Senate rules it could have conducted (and, in fact, did conduct) business by passing a unanimous consent agreement. As a result, the majority concluded

---

[71] Id at 2610.

[72] Id at 2607.

[73] Id at 2569.

[74] Id at 2574.

[75] Id at 2575.

that the appointments in this case were made during what amounted to a three-day recess between the pro forma sessions.[76]

The majority also held that in order to constitute a sufficient recess for purposes of the Recess Appointments Clause, the Senate break must in all cases be more than three days in length and presumptively must be at least ten days in length.[77] Based on the fact that the Constitution does not require a chamber of Congress to obtain the consent of the other to adjourn unless the break is for more than three days, the majority reasoned that a break of three days or less is de minimis and thus insufficient to trigger the President's recess appointments authority. The majority also noted that it had not found a single instance in which an intrasession recess appointment had been made during a break of less than ten days. "The lack of examples," the majority inferred, "suggests that the recess-appointment power is not needed in that context."[78]

Justice Scalia objected that the majority's three- and ten-day limitations lacked support in the constitutional text. He also complained that the majority had failed to establish any clear standard for when a break of longer than three days will be too short to qualify as a recess, and had failed to make clear whether there will ever be circumstances in which a break of more than ten days will not be long enough. Justice Scalia argued more generally that the majority had engaged in "judicial fabrication of vague, unadministrable limits on the recess-appointment power . . . that overstep the judicial role."[79]

II. Historical Gloss and Constitutional Theory

Noel Canning revealed methodological agreements and disagreements between the majority and Justice Scalia. This part begins

---

[76] During the oral argument, Justice Kagan suggested how a reliance on historical practice would lead to this result, explaining to the Solicitor General that "if you are going to rely on history and on the development of an equilibrium . . . then it seems to me that you also have to look to history and the development of an equilibrium with respect to Congress's definition of its own power to determine whether it is in recess or not." Transcript of Oral Argument at 25–26 (cited in note 66).

[77] The majority deemed the presumption rebuttable in emergencies. See 134 S Ct at 2567.

[78] Id at 2566. The majority acknowledged that there had been a few instances of recess appointments made during *intersession* recesses of fewer than ten days, but it said that it regarded "these few scattered examples as anomalies." Id at 2567.

[79] Id at 2595.

by briefly noting them, and then describes the "historical gloss" approach to discerning the separation of powers. Finally, it identifies some ways in which the historical gloss approach overlaps with various nonoriginalist theories of constitutional interpretation, such as Burkeanism and common law constitutionalism, as well as with variants of originalism that emphasize the distinction between interpretation and construction.

A. METHODOLOGICAL DISPUTES IN NOEL CANNING

The *Noel Canning* majority maintained that the Court should give "significant weight" to historical practice when resolving issues concerning "the allocation of power between two elected branches of the government."[80] Justice Scalia did not deny that historical practice might be relevant to some separation of powers issues, but he argued that this is true only when the constitutional text is ambiguous, and the Recess Appointments Clause, he said, was clear. The majority accepted Justice Scalia's premise but insisted that the text was ambiguous.[81]

The majority and Justice Scalia also disagreed about the conditions under which historical practice should be considered to help resolve the meaning of ambiguous text. Justice Scalia would consult historical practice only when it has been "open, widespread, and unchallenged since the early days of the Republic."[82] The majority, by contrast, read the precedents as "show[ing] that the Court has treated practice as an important interpretive factor even when the nature or longevity of that practice is subject to dispute, and even when that practice began after the founding era."[83] The majority emphasized that, regardless of how one reads the nineteenth-century practice, the modern practice supported its conclusions.[84]

---

[80] Id at 2559.

[81] See id at 2561, 2568, 2577.

[82] Id at 2594.

[83] Id at 2560.

[84] See id at 2564 ("[T]hree-quarters of a century of settled practice [of intrasession recess appointments] is long enough to entitle a practice to 'great weight in a proper interpretation' of the constitutional provision."), quoting *The Pocket Veto Case*, 279 US at 689; id at 2573 ("The Senate as a body has not contested this practice [of filling preexisting vacancies] for nearly three-quarters of a century, perhaps longer.").

Justice Scalia criticized the majority's approach to historical practice on several related grounds. First, he suggested that it involved
an abdication of judicial responsibility. In cases that are justiciable,
Justice Scalia wrote, the judiciary has a duty to determine the meaning of the Constitution's structural provisions, so it should not defer
to the resolutions of those questions by other branches.[85] Second, he
contended that the majority's approach amounted to an "adverse-
possession theory of executive power," whereby the President could
gain constitutional authority simply by acting in a certain way without sufficient congressional opposition.[86] Such an approach, Justice
Scalia contended, "will systematically favor the expansion of executive power at the expense of Congress."[87] Finally, Justice Scalia argued that even if the Senate had acquiesced in the historical practice, it lacks the constitutional authority to give away its institutional
power. Structural constitutional provisions, he argued, exist in large
part to protect individual liberty. As a result, Justice Scalia said, "the
Senate could not give away [the limitations in the Recess Appointments Clause] even if it wanted to."[88]

In support of those arguments, Justice Scalia emphasized the
Court's 1983 decision in *INS v Chadha*.[89] In *Chadha*, the Court held
that a "legislative veto" provision violated the bicameralism and
presentment provisions of Article I, Section 7, of the Constitution
even though Congress had enacted hundreds of similar provisions
since the 1930s. According to the Court in *Chadha*, "the fact that a
given law or procedure is efficient, convenient, and useful in facilitating functions of government, standing alone, will not save it if it is
contrary to the Constitution."[90] Moreover, in rejecting the application of the political question doctrine in that case, the Court observed
that "[n]o policy underlying the political question doctrine suggests
that Congress or the Executive, or both acting in concert and in
compliance with Art. I, can decide the constitutionality of a statute;

---

[85] See id at 2593.

[86] Id at 2617; see also id at 2592.

[87] Id at 2605.

[88] Id; see also id at 2594 ("[T]he political branches cannot by agreement alter the constitutional structure.").

[89] 462 US 919 (1983).

[90] Id at 944.

that is a decision for the courts."[91] Relatedly, the Court emphasized that the mere fact of an agreement by Congress and the President to enact legislative veto provisions did not immunize them from judicial review.[92]

The majority in *Noel Canning* responded to those points primarily by suggesting that, at this late date, the judiciary should accord deference to long-standing arrangements worked out by the coordinate branches of government: "We have not previously interpreted the [Recess Appointments] Clause, and when doing so for the first time in more than 200 years, we must hesitate to upset the compromises and working arrangements that the elected branches of Government themselves have reached."[93] The majority also expressed concern about disturbing expectation interests surrounding the practice. With respect to the filling of preexisting vacancies, for example, the majority said that it was "reluctant to upset this traditional practice where doing so would seriously shrink the authority that Presidents have believed existed and have exercised for so long."[94]

Those methodological disagreements between the majority and Justice Scalia in *Noel Canning* invite an examination of how reliance on historic governmental practices relates to various nonoriginalist and originalist approaches to constitutional interpretation. We begin with a description of the "historical gloss" approach.

B. THE HISTORICAL GLOSS APPROACH

Invocations of historic governmental practices are common in debates and decisions concerning the constitutional separation of powers.[95] Giving weight to such practices is sometimes referred to as the "historical gloss" approach to constitutional interpretation, following Justice Frankfurter's oft-quoted statement in the *Youngstown* steel seizure decision that "a systematic, unbroken, executive practice, long pursued to the knowledge of the Congress and never before

---

[91] Id at 941–42. For similar reasoning about the political question doctrine, see *Zivotofsky v Clinton*, 132 S Ct 1421, 1427–28 (2012).

[92] 462 US at 942 n 13. The Court also observed, however, that "11 Presidents, from Mr. Wilson through Mr. Reagan, who have been presented with this issue have gone on record at some point to challenge congressional vetoes as unconstitutional." Id.

[93] 134 S Ct at 2560.

[94] Id at 2573.

[95] See Curtis A. Bradley and Trevor W. Morrison, *Historical Gloss and the Separation of Powers*, 126 Harv L Rev 411, 417–24 (2012).

questioned, engaged in by Presidents who have also sworn to uphold the Constitution, making as it were such exercise of power part of the structure of our government, may be treated as a gloss on 'executive Power' vested in the President by § 1 of Art. II."[96] There are differing accounts of when such gloss should be credited and some of them do not precisely track Justice Frankfurter's articulation, especially his reference to practice "never before questioned."

There are additional issues that must be confronted in determining the contours of the historical gloss approach. Those issues include what kind of history counts, how unequivocal the history must be in order to count, what the relationship of that history is to the constitutional text, and whether the gloss approach is limited to separation of powers questions or instead applies more broadly. One of us has previously explored some of those issues,[97] and we will offer additional thoughts about how best to conceive of the historical gloss approach in responding to Justice Scalia's "adverse possession" complaint in Part V. For now, it suffices to note the basic idea of historical gloss, which is that long-standing practices by one political branch that are acquiesced in by the other political branch should be given weight in discerning whether governmental conduct is consistent with the separation of powers.[98]

The Supreme Court has long invoked historical gloss in construing the constitutional authority of both Congress and the President. An early example is *McCulloch v Maryland*.[99] In affirming Congress's authority to establish a national bank, Chief Justice Marshall invoked historical practice near the outset of his opinion:

> [A] doubtful question, one on which human reason may pause and the human judgment be suspended, in the decision of which the great principles of liberty are not concerned, but the respective powers of those who are equally the representatives of the people, are to be adjusted; if not put at

---

[96] *Youngstown Sheet and Tube Co. v Sawyer*, 343 US 579, 610–11 (1952) (Frankfurter, J, concurring). See also id at 610 ("It is an inadmissibly narrow conception of American constitutional law to confine it to the words of the Constitution and to disregard the gloss which life has written upon them.").

[97] See Bradley and Morrison, 126 Harv L Rev (cited in note 95).

[98] Although not the focus of this article, historical gloss is also likely relevant to discerning the judicial power. See, for example, Charles G. Geyh, *Judicial Independence, Judicial Accountability, and the Role of Constitutional Norms in Congressional Regulation of the Courts*, 78 Ind L J 153, 157 (2003) ("To understand judicial independence and its limits, then, we must look beyond 'doctrinal' independence as divined by courts, and examine the historical development of 'customary' independence as it has emerged in Congress.").

[99] 17 US (Wheat) 316 (1819).

rest by the practice of the Government, ought to receive a considerable impression from that practice.[100]

Marshall also explained that, in interpreting "a Constitution intended to endure for ages to come, and, consequently, to be adapted to the various crises of human affairs,"[101] great weight should be given to "[a]n exposition of the Constitution, deliberately established by legislative acts, on the faith of which an immense property has been advanced."[102]

Given when *McCulloch* was decided, the historical practice to which Marshall referred necessarily dated from the early post-Founding period. When the Court has had more history with which to work, it has not always insisted on such lineage. In *The Pocket Veto Case*,[103] for example, the Court considered whether a law presented by Congress to the President less than ten days before an intersession recess becomes a law if it is neither signed nor returned by the President. Article I, Section 7 of the Constitution provides that "[i]f any Bill shall not be returned by the President within ten Days (Sundays excepted) after it shall have been presented to him, the Same shall be a Law, in like Manner as if he had signed it, unless the Congress by their Adjournment prevent its Return, in which Case it shall not be a Law."[104] In concluding that an intersession recess qualifies as an adjournment and so prevents the return of a bill to Congress for purposes of this provision, the Court emphasized not only the constitutional text and structure, but also the historical practice concerning how presidents and Congresses had treated bills in that situation. The Court observed that "[l]ong settled and established practice is a consideration of great weight in a proper interpretation of constitutional provisions of this character."[105] The Court also quoted from a state court decision for the proposition that "a practice of at least twenty years' duration 'on the part of the executive department, acquiesced in by the legislative department, while not absolutely binding on the judicial department, is entitled to great regard in determining the true

---

[100] Id at 401.

[101] Id at 415.

[102] Id at 401.

[103] 279 US 655 (1929).

[104] US Const, Art I, § 7, cl 2.

[105] 279 US at 689.

construction of a constitutional provision the phraseology of which is in any respect of doubtful meaning.'"[106]

Practice-based reasoning has been especially common in debates and decisions concerning foreign relations.[107] In *United States v Curtiss-Wright Export Corporation*, for example, the Supreme Court upheld a congressional delegation of authority to the President to criminalize arms sales to countries involved in a conflict in Latin America, based in part on the fact that Congress already had established a pattern of delegating broad authority to the President in the area of foreign affairs.[108] The Court explained that "[a] legislative practice such as we have here, evidenced not only by occasional instances, but marked by the movement of a steady stream for a century and a half of time, goes a long way in the direction of proving the presence of unassailable ground for the constitutionality of the practice, to be found in the origin and history of the power involved, or in its nature, or in both combined."[109]

Similarly, in *Dames & Moore v Regan*, the Court invoked historical practice in upholding a presidential suspension of legal claims as part of the resolution of the Iranian hostage crisis. The Court reasoned that, although Congress had not "directly authorize[d]" a presidential suspension of claims in that situation, the presidential action was supported by "inferences to be drawn from the character of the legislation Congress has enacted in the area," as well as "the history of [congressional] acquiescence in executive claims settlement."[110] The Court explained that "[p]ast practice does not, by itself, create power, but 'long-continued practice, known to and acquiesced in by Congress, would raise a presumption that the [action] had been [taken] in pursuance of its consent. . . .'"[111] Finally, the Court made clear that even if the practice of executive claims settlement prior to 1952 should be disregarded because it occurred during a time when foreign

---

[106] Id at 689–90, quoting *State v South Norwalk*, 77 Conn 257, 264, 58 A 759, 761 (1904). The state case concerned the interpretation of a Connecticut constitutional provision providing that a bill would become law if the governor did not return it to the state legislature within three days of being presented with it.

[107] Bradley and Morrison, 126 Harv L Rev at 420–21 (cited in note 95).

[108] See 299 US 304 (1936).

[109] Id at 327–28.

[110] 453 US 654, 678, 686 (1981).

[111] Id, quoting *United States v Midwest Oil Co.*, 236 US 459, 474 (1915).

sovereigns could not be sued in U.S. courts, "congressional acqui-escence in settlement agreements since that time supports the Pres-ident's power to act here."[112]

Dames & Moore illustrates the connection between the historical gloss approach and Justice Jackson's famous tripartite categorization of presidential power in *Youngstown*. Under that categorization, the President's power is at its highest when supported by express or im-plied congressional authorization, and is at its lowest when expressly or implicitly opposed by Congress. When Congress has neither sup-ported nor opposed presidential action, the President's power is in an intermediate "zone of twilight."[113] That intermediate zone, Justice Jackson explained, is one in which the President and Congress "may have concurrent authority, or in which its distribution is uncertain."[114] Historical practice is especially pertinent in cases arising in that zone (although, as *Dames & Moore* illustrates, the pertinence of historical practice is not limited to the intermediate zone).

The Court, however, does not inevitably credit historic govern-mental practices. Probably the most famous example in which it did not do so is *Chadha*. In *Chadha*, part of the Court's disinclination to credit practice appears to have stemmed from its conviction that the text and structure of the Constitution were clear. The Court stated, for example, that "[e]xplicit and unambiguous provisions of the Con-stitution prescribe and define the respective functions of the Con-gress and of the Executive in the legislative process."[115] The Court also seemed to view claims about modern practice as methodologi-cally inconsistent with its self-described originalist approach to in-terpretation in that case. It wrote, for instance, that it was applying the "choices we discern as having been made in the Constitutional Convention,"[116] rather than by "Congress or the Executive, or both acting in concert."[117]

The significance of gloss is not limited to judicial reasoning. In particular, this approach to constitutional interpretation is a staple of legal reasoning in the executive branch. To take one relatively recent example, the Justice Department's Office of Legal Counsel (OLC)

---

[112] Id at 684.

[113] See *Youngstown*, 343 US at 635–38 (Jackson, J, concurring).

[114] Id at 637.

[115] 462 US at 945.

[116] Id at 959.

[117] Id at 942.

issued an opinion in 2011 concluding, based largely on historical practice, that President Obama had the constitutional authority to direct U.S. military forces to take part in bombing operations in Libya without first seeking congressional authorization.[118] Quoting from an earlier legal opinion concerning a military intervention in Haiti, OLC asserted that "the pattern of executive conduct, made under claim of right, extended over many decades and engaged in by Presidents of both parties, evidences the existence of broad constitutional power."[119]

C. RELATIONSHIP TO OTHER INTERPRETIVE METHODOLOGIES

There is overlap between the historical gloss approach and a variety of nonoriginalist approaches to constitutional interpretation. Reliance on historical practice fits well with "Burkean" approaches,[120] which emphasize long-standing traditions and understandings, although most invocations of the gloss approach focus on the separation of powers rather than on other aspects of constitutional structure[121] or on individual rights.[122] Reliance on historical practice also fits well with non-judge-centered versions of "common law constitutionalism," which involves an incremental interpretation of the Constitution in light of both judicial precedent and tradition.[123] Like Burkeanism, this approach is deferential to the "accumulated wisdom

---

[118] See Memorandum Opinion from Caroline D. Krass, Principal Deputy Assistant Att'y Gen, Office of Legal Counsel, to the Att'y Gen, *Authority to Use Military Force in Libya* (Apr 1, 2011), online at http://www.justice.gov/sites/default/files/olc/opinions/2011/04/31/authority -military-use-in-libya.pdf.

[119] Id at 7.

[120] For discussions of Burkean approaches to constitutional interpretation, see, for example, Cass R. Sunstein, *Burkean Minimalism*, 105 Mich L Rev 353 (2006), and Thomas W. Merrill, *Bork v. Burke*, 19 Harv J L & Pub Pol 509 (1996).

[121] Notwithstanding the quotation in the prior section from *McCulloch*, there may be concerns with relying on historical practice to determine the expanse and limits of Congress's enumerated powers, especially when reliance on state practice or on the *lack* of federal practice would thwart the ability of Congress to solve multistate collective action problems that previously did not exist or previously went unaddressed for any number of reasons. See Neil S. Siegel, *Distinguishing the "Truly National" from the "Truly Local": Customary Allocation, Commercial Activity, and Collective Action*, 62 Duke L J 797 (2012). More generally, historical practice may have less of a role to play when an interpreter has a more developed sense of the appropriate division of authority between different government institutions.

[122] Compare Sunstein, 105 Mich L Rev at 400 (cited in note 120) ("Under some constitutional provisions, above all the Equal Protection Clause, the Burkean [tradition-based] approach is hard or perhaps impossible to square with entrenched understandings in American constitutional law. . . .").

[123] See David A. Strauss, *Common Law Constitutional Interpretation*, 63 U Chi L Rev 877 (1996).

of many generations" and to judgments that "have been tested over time, in a variety of circumstances, and have been found to be at least good enough."[124] Both Burkeanism and common law constitutionalism, like the historical gloss approach, allow for the possibility that constitutional law can adapt to changing circumstances.[125] A consideration of historical gloss is also consistent with more general "pluralist" theories of interpretation, which are open to a variety of kinds of constitutional authority.[126]

In addition, historical gloss arguments partially overlap with approaches to constitutional law that emphasize decisive moments in history, such as Bruce Ackerman's account of constitutional "moments" and Eric Posner and Adrian Vermeule's account of "constitutional showdowns."[127] Those accounts of constitutional law are similar to practice-based arguments in that both place special weight on the actions of the political branches. Such approaches, however, tend to focus on critical turning points, whereas invocations of the historical gloss method tend to emphasize longer-term accretions of practice.

Similarly, the gloss approach is related to, but distinct from, the claim that some discrete nonjudicial acts can come to be viewed as "precedent." Michael Gerhardt has developed the idea of nonjudicial precedent,[128] and Keith Whittington's emphasis on "constitutional construction" (discussed below) includes discussion of various nonjudicial events that are asserted to qualify as precedent.[129] The proposition that discrete nonjudicial actions can have precedential effect is not the same as gloss's focus on long-standing practices, but the ideas are complementary in that long-standing practices are likely to have their roots in particular precedents. As is the case with gloss,

[124] Id at 892.

[125] See id at 905 (arguing that common law constitutionalism helps explain why "the most important changes to the Constitution—many of them, at least— . . . have come about either through changes in judicial decisions, or through deeper changes in politics or in society"); Ernest Young, *Rediscovering Conservatism: Burkean Political Theory and Constitutional Interpretation*, 72 NC L Rev 619, 664 (1994) (explaining that, under a Burkean approach, "institutions become effective in meeting the needs of society through a continuing process of adaptation that may or may not be consistent with the original intentions of the founders").

[126] See, for example, Richard H. Fallon, Jr., *A Constructivist Coherence Theory of Constitutional Interpretation*, 100 Harv L Rev 1189 (1987).

[127] See Bruce Ackerman, 1 *We the People: Foundations* 22 (Belknap, 1991); Eric A. Posner and Adrian Vermeule, *Constitutional Showdowns*, 156 U Pa L Rev 991 (2008).

[128] See Michael J. Gerhardt, *The Power of Precedent* ch 4 (Oxford, 2008).

[129] See Keith E. Whittington, *Constitutional Construction: Divided Powers and Constitutional Meaning* (Harvard, 1999).

moreover, there is nothing inherent in the idea of nonjudicial precedent that would limit it to a particular period of U.S. history, or that
would preclude it from being overtaken by later developments.[130]

Historical gloss also can be relevant to "functional" approaches
to the separation of powers. Functional approaches evaluate not
whether governmental arrangements are consistent with certain categorical distinctions between different kinds of government power,
but rather whether those arrangements are beneficial and consistent
with the values underlying the system of separation of powers and
checks and balances.[131] Long-standing historical practice may show
that an arrangement is working well, or at least that it is not unduly
problematic. As *Chadha* illustrates, gloss might be harder to reconcile with "formal" approaches, which attempt to discern whether
arrangements are consistent with the Constitution's separation of
authority into executive, legislative, and judicial categories. That said,
historical practice might shed light on what falls within the different categories—or on when to allow exceptions to the categorization.
For example, the Supreme Court's formalist opinions concerning
the permissibility of non-Article III tribunals allow for exceptions
based on historical practice, and even self-identified originalist Justices like Justice Scalia have accepted those exceptions.[132]

As *Chadha* also illustrates, it is more difficult to reconcile the
historical gloss approach with many originalist theories of interpretation, particularly (but not exclusively) those that were developed
in the 1970s and 1980s.[133] To be sure, some originalists are likely to
credit early post-Founding practice as evidence of the Constitution's
original meaning, based on the idea that the governmental actors in

---

[130] Some nonjudicial precedents also may help to establish "constitutional conventions,"
which involve norms about proper conduct by governmental actors but that do not necessarily entail understandings of what is constitutionally required or permissible. For discussions of the idea of constitutional conventions, see Keith E. Whittington, *The Status of
Unwritten Constitutional Conventions in the United States*, 2013 U Ill L Rev 1847, and Adrian
Vermeule, *Conventions of Agency Independence*, 113 Colum L Rev 1163, 1181–94 (2013).

[131] For a discussion of functional versus formal approaches to the separation of powers, see
M. Elizabeth Magill, *Beyond Powers and Branches in Separation of Powers Law*, 150 U Pa L Rev
603 (2001).

[132] See *Northern Pipeline Construction Co. v Marathon Pipeline Co.*, 458 US 50 (1982) (plurality opinion); see also *Stern v Marshall*, 131 S Ct 2594, 2621 (2011) (Scalia, J, concurring)
("[A]n Article III judge is required in *all* federal adjudications, *unless* there is a firmly established historical practice to the contrary." (second emphasis added)).

[133] For a discussion of first- and second-generation originalism, see Keith E. Whittington,
Originalism: A Critical Introduction, 82 Fordham L Rev 375 (2013).

that period had a particularly good sense of that meaning.[134] But such a rationale would not justify looking to modern governmental practice, as, for example, the majority did in *Noel Canning*.[135]

There are, however, certain variants of originalism that are potentially compatible with the consideration of historical practice for reasons other than as evidence of original meaning. In particular, in recent years a number of theorists associated with the "new originalism" have distinguished between "constitutional interpretation" and "constitutional construction,"[136] a distinction we discuss in greater detail in Part III. It is not clear that those theorists all have precisely the same concepts in mind when they make that distinction. In general, however, they aim to distinguish determinations that are closely linked to the constitutional text (which they call "interpretation") from those that supplement the text (which they call "construction").

Adding the idea of "construction" to the originalist's tool kit closes the gap between originalist and nonoriginalist approaches, which may be why certain originalists resist it.[137] Given the existence of "the construction zone," the new originalism seems receptive to at least some historical gloss on the separation of powers. While new originalists believe that the original semantic meaning of the constitutional text must be applied when that meaning is discernible regardless of historical practice, they also allow other legal materials to be brought to bear—presumably, including historical practice—when "interpretation" does not yield an answer. Nothing about the distinction between interpretation and construction would appear to

---

[134] See Rappaport, 52 UCLA L Rev at 1487, 1498, 1537 (cited in note 17) ("Early interpretations evidence the original meaning of the Constitution because it is thought that early interpreters were likely to understand the meaning of the constitutional language and the context in which it was enacted.").

[135] See Jack M. Balkin, *The New Originalism and the Use of History*, 82 Fordham L Rev 641, 657 (2013) ("The practices of the Washington Administration immediately after adoption of the Constitution are generally thought relevant to understanding the original meaning of Article II. But the practices of the Roosevelt, Truman, and Eisenhower Administrations—which did far more to shape the actual presidency we have and the actual powers that contemporary presidents enjoy—are not relevant to the originalist model of authority.").

[136] See Thomas B. Colby, *The Sacrifice of the New Originalism*, 99 Georgetown L J 713, 714 (2011); Lawrence B. Solum, *Originalism and Constitutional Construction*, 82 Fordham L Rev 453, 467–69 (2013).

[137] See, for example, John O. McGinnis and Michael B. Rappaport, *Originalism and the Good Constitution* ch 8 (Harvard, 2013). See also Peter J. Smith, *How Different Are Originalism and Non-Originalism?*, 62 Hastings L J 707, 710 (2011) ("Given modern originalism's origins as a response to the perceived excesses of non-originalism, it is not surprising that many originalists have resisted refinements to the theory that would tend to collapse the distinction between originalism and non-originalism.").

commit new originalists to rejecting long-standing historical practices as building materials for construction, and theorists like Whittington are expressly receptive to that possibility. Likewise, Balkin's
invocation of the full array of modalities of constitutional argument
suggests that historical gloss is a legitimate part of constitutional
construction,[138] and his robust construction zone seems especially
compatible with regular consideration of historical practice.[139] Even
versions of originalism that posit a smaller construction zone do not
seem incompatible with the historical gloss approach so long as one
is operating within the construction zone because original meaning
has run out.

III. Madisonian Liquidation

A variant of originalism, known as "liquidation," would allow
initial post-Founding practice to resolve ambiguities in the Constitution's original meaning and thereby "fix" the meaning against
subsequent change. This idea is frequently ascribed to James Madison, based on statements he made in *The Federalist* and in later
writings. Madison never presented a detailed explanation of the idea,
and it has received only limited attention in the academic literature.
As a result, it is not entirely clear whether and to what extent it differs
from the historical gloss approach. Indeed, the majority in *Noel
Canning* seemed to treat liquidation and gloss as the same phenomenon.[140]

Among the uncertainties with the liquidation concept are whether
the settlement of constitutional meaning may occur only through
early post-Founding practice, or whether it also may occur through
later practice long after the Founding—and, if the latter, how likely
it is that a settlement long after the Founding could take place. It
is also unclear whether, under the liquidation theory, an initial settlement through liquidation may be undone by a subsequent settlement through a new liquidation. How one answers those questions

---

[138] For a discussion of six "modalities" of constitutional argumentation that are common in
U.S. constitutional decisions and debates, see generally Philip Bobbitt, *Constitutional Fate:
Theory of the Constitution* ch 6 (Oxford, 1982), and Philip Bobbitt, *Constitutional Interpretation*
(Blackwell, 1993).

[139] See, for example, Neil S. Siegel, *Jack Balkin's Rich Historicism and Diet Originalism:
Health Benefits and Risks for the Constitutional System*, 111 Mich L Rev 931, 952 (2013) (emphasizing the thinness of Balkin's version of originalism).

[140] See 134 S Ct at 2580 (citing a variety of decisions, including some that have endorsed
gloss, for the proposition that "our cases have continually confirmed Madison's view").

will go a long way toward determining how much difference in practice there is between the liquidation approach and the historical gloss approach.

Judging from the limited extent to which the liquidation concept has been explored in the literature—most notably by Caleb Nelson—it appears to be narrower in various ways than the historical gloss approach. Our best sense, which informs the following analysis, is that the liquidation concept turns on initial practice, which typically although not necessarily will be early practice, and that the liquidation may not be undone through subsequent liquidation. These limitations, moreover, are what make liquidation potentially compatible with some versions of originalism. Not surprisingly, therefore, it is Justice Scalia's opinion in *Noel Canning*, not the majority's, that seems receptive to an understanding of liquidation that would be narrower than, and distinct from, gloss. In this part, we question whether this narrower conception is properly attributed to Madison, and we argue that it is in any event normatively unattractive as an alternative to gloss.

A. THE "LIQUIDATION" THEORY

Instead of looking to early practices as evidence of original meaning, and instead of embracing the idea of constitutional construction, some originalist scholars attribute to the Founders the recognition that the constitutional text did not settle certain questions of constitutional meaning and that the answers to those questions would need to be worked out, or "liquidated," through decisions and practices.[141] Once liquidated, the argument goes, the meaning of the Constitution on those questions would become "fixed" and so not

---

[141] See, for example, Caleb Nelson, *Originalism and Interpretive Conventions*, 70 U Chi L Rev 519, 525–53 (2003), and Philip A. Hamburger, *The Constitution's Accommodation of Social Change*, 88 Mich L Rev 239, 309 (1989) (suggesting that Madison "expected vagueness in the Constitution to be resolved and made certain rather than that it would be an opportunity for flexibility and judicial adaptation of the Constitution to changing exigencies"). Without specifically endorsing the liquidation thesis, Akhil Amar has argued that a number of the institutional practices of the Washington administration have had lasting precedential effect on understandings of presidential authority. See Akhil Reed Amar, *America's Unwritten Constitution* ch 8 (Basic, 2012). Our colleague Stephen Sachs reads Amar's argument as embracing the idea of liquidation through early practice. See Stephen E. Sachs, *The "Unwritten Constitution" and Unwritten Law*, 2013 U Ill L Rev 1797, 1806–08. In the next chapter of his book, however, Amar goes on to discuss how institutional practices of Congress, the Supreme Court, and administrative agencies, including practices long after the Founding, "gloss and clarify the text, inducing interpreters to read the otherwise indeterminate text in a highly determinate way." Amar at 335.

subject to change. This idea of liquidation through initial practice is most frequently associated with a statement made by James Madison in *Federalist No. 37*. "All new laws," he wrote in that essay, "though penned with the greatest technical skill and passed on the fullest and most mature deliberation, are considered as more or less obscure and equivocal, until their meaning be liquidated and ascertained by a series of particular discussions and adjudications."[142] As this passage makes clear, Madison was not tying liquidation specifically to constitutional interpretation; he was simply observing that it was something that one should expect with all new laws (including statutory law and the common law). Hamilton also made references to "liquidation" in *The Federalist*, similarly without suggesting that it was something specific to the Constitution.[143]

Caleb Nelson has developed the most detailed account of the liquidation concept. Nelson argues that, when Founders such as Madison referred to the possibility that post-Founding practice would "fix" constitutional meaning, they were using that term in a manner similar to those who, like the famous satirist Jonathan Swift, had advocated "fixing" the English language so that its meaning would not change over time.[144] The possibility of preventing change in the meaning of language was controversial, and Nelson notes that many Americans of the Founding generation probably assumed that change in language was inevitable. But Nelson observes that "[w]hatever their position on this issue . . . Americans certainly were familiar with the idea of 'fixing' the language, and they associated this concept with permanence and immutability."[145] Madison's references to "fixing" the meaning of the Constitution, Nelson contends, must be understood in that context: "[a]lthough Madison conceded that the words used in the Constitution might well fall out of

---

[142] Federalist 37 (Madison) at 229, in *The Federalist Papers* (cited in note 14). Madison also referred to the liquidation idea in later writings, albeit decades after the Founding. See, for example, Letter to Spencer Roane (Sept 2, 1819), in G. Hunt, ed, 8 *The Writings of James Madison* 450 (1908).

[143] Alexander Hamilton observed in *Federalist No. 78* that, when two statutes conflict, "it is the province of the courts to liquidate and fix their meaning and operation." Federalist 78 (Hamilton) at 468, in *The Federalist Papers* (cited in note 14); see also Federalist 22 (Hamilton) at 150, in *The Federalist Papers* (cited in note 14) ("Laws are a dead letter without courts to expound and define their true meaning and operation."); Federalist 82 (Hamilton) at 491, in *The Federalist Papers* (cited in note 14) ("'Tis time only that can mature and perfect so compound a system, can liquidate the meaning of all the parts, and can adjust them to each other in a harmonious and consistent WHOLE.").

[144] See Nelson, 70 U Chi L Rev at 530–35 (cited in note 141).

[145] Id at 534–35.

favor or acquire new shades of meaning in later usage, he was suggesting that their meaning *in the Constitution* would not change; once
that meaning was 'fixed,' it should endure."[146]

Under that account, the Founders were delegating to governmental actors, and to the courts, the task of resolving ambiguities
in the original meaning of the Constitution. As Nelson explains,
regardless of whether the Founders viewed the liquidation process
as part of the original meaning of the Constitution (thus binding
originalists today) or something associated with the background
"general" law in existence at the time (thus not binding originalists today), the basic idea of liquidation remained the same:
"reasonable members of the founding generation . . . might con-
ceivably have read each indeterminate provision in the Constitution not only to define a range of permissible interpretations,
but also to delegate power to the provision's initial interpreters to
make an authoritative selection within that range."[147]

It is easy to see why the liquidation account would be attractive to
some originalists. For one thing, it tells interpreters where to look for
evidence of constitutional meaning when ambiguities in the text
render it impossible to discern the original meaning—typically, in
early post-Founding deliberations or decisions. For another thing,
by "fixing" the meaning, the account avoids the possibility that constitutional meaning might change over time. Upon close examination, however, it is not clear that either of the two elements of the
approach—looking only to initial practice and decisions, and disal-
lowing a subsequent interpretation that contradicts the one reflected
in initial practice—follows from Madison's statements. In any event,
a showing that Madison or other Founders had this view would not
establish that it should be followed (as Nelson is careful to acknowledge), and it is normatively problematic along a number of
dimensions.

B. MADISON'S VIEWS

To understand what Madison was getting at in *Federalist No. 37*, it
is necessary to put Madison's reference to liquidation in context. This
Federalist Paper responds to criticisms about the proposed Constitution by emphasizing the extraordinary difficulties that the Framers

---

[146] Id at 535 (emphasis added).
[147] Id at 551.

had confronted in attempting to draft a new framework for government. Madison noted that federalism was a novel constitutional arrangement, so that the Framers had scant previous experience from which to draw.[148] He added that the convention faced great difficulties even in the area of separation of powers, where previous experience was more substantial.[149] "Among the difficulties encountered by the convention," Madison explained, "a very important one must have lain in combining the requisite stability and energy in government, with the inviolable attention due to liberty and to the republican form."[150] In emphasizing the challenging nature of those efforts, Madison pointed to the long experience of Great Britain in attempting to work out differences in categories of law and jurisdiction, a process that he noted was still ongoing.[151] He then made the statement about liquidation.[152]

Liquidation was required, Madison wrote, for three reasons. The first was "the obscurity arising from the complexity of objects" needing to be distinguished, including the distinction between federal and state power, and the lines separating the executive, legislative, and judicial authorities. The second reason concerned "the imperfections of the human faculties," which make it even more difficult to perceive those objects. The third reason involved the limits of language, which Madison characterized as "inadequateness of the vehicle of ideas."[153] "Hence, it must happen," Madison wrote, "that however accurately objects may be discriminated in themselves, and however accurately the discrimination may be considered, the definition of them may be rendered inaccurate by the inaccuracy of the terms in which it is delivered."[154] As Madison must have known, none of those justifications would ever disappear, even after what he referred to as "particular discussions and adjudications" took place in the early years of life under the new Constitution—or even many decades hence.[155]

---

[148] Federalist 37 (Madison) at 226, in *The Federalist Papers* (cited in note 14).

[149] Id at 228.

[150] Id at 226.

[151] Id at 228.

[152] Id at 228–29.

[153] Id at 229.

[154] Id.

[155] Id.

It also bears mention that Madison referred both to practice
and to judicial decisions as involved in liquidation.[156] It seems unlikely, however, that he was referring only to initial judicial decisions,
because it would not have been reasonable to expect all—or even
most—issues of textual ambiguity to be resolved by the courts in the
immediate aftermath of the Constitution's ratification, or even over
the Constitution's first century. Given the common law tradition that
Madison referenced in *Federalist No. 37*, it is also unlikely that he
thought that a judicial decision would fix constitutional meaning in
a way that would disallow subsequent reconsideration of the decision. There are differing accounts of how strongly the Founders conceived of stare decisis, but none of those accounts suggests that they
thought judicial decisions never could be revisited absent an Article V
amendment.[157]

For those reasons, Madison need not be read in *Federalist No. 37*
as suggesting either that initial practice would freeze the meaning
of the Constitution going forward or that only such practice was
relevant to constitutional interpretation. Instead, as historian Jack
Rakove notes, Madison can reasonably be understood as referring
broadly to "the ongoing process of resolving 'obscure and equivocal'
ambiguities through 'particular discussions and adjudications'—in a
word, interpretation."[158] Such a process of interpretation logically
would include frequent consideration of practice long after the

---

[156] See Peter J. Smith, *The Marshall Court and the Originalist's Dilemma*, 90 Minn L Rev
612, 634 (2006) ("That Madison believed that congressional deliberation or popular action
could fix constitutional meaning does not mean that he rejected the notion that the courts
could fix it in appropriate cases, as well. Indeed, his discussion in The Federalist No. 37 and
in other sources suggests that he saw both as viable means of liquidating the meaning of
constitutional ambiguities."). The same can be said of Hamilton in *Federalist No. 78*, which
specifically references the courts.

[157] See, for example, Thomas R. Lee, *Stare Decisis in Historical Perspective: From the Founding
Era to the Rehnquist Court*, 52 Vand L Rev 647 (1999); John O. McGinnis and Michael B.
Rappaport, *Reconciling Originalism and Precedent*, 103 Nw U L Rev 803, 809–23 (2009); Lee J.
Strang, *An Originalist Theory of Precedent: Originalism, Nonoriginalist Precedent, and the Com-
mon Good*, 36 NM L Rev 419 (2006); see also Henry Paul Monaghan, *Stare Decisis and
Constitutional Adjudication*, 88 Colum L Rev 723, 757 (1988) ("In the American common law,
stare decisis states a conditional obligation: precedent binds absent a showing of substantial
countervailing considerations.").

[158] Jack N. Rakove, *Original Meanings: Politics and Ideas in the Making of the Constitution* 159
(Vintage, 1996) (emphasis in original). See also H. Jefferson Powell, *The Original Understanding of Original Intent*, 98 Harv L Rev 885, 910 (1985) ("Madison's argument, which
Hamilton had anticipated in *The Federalist* No. 22, was of course a restatement in somewhat
abstract terms, of the old common law assumption, shared by the Philadelphia framers, that
the 'intent' of any legal document is the product of the interpretive process and not some
fixed meaning that the author locks into the document's text at the outset.").

Founding. As Rakove points out, "only knowledge created by intervening developments could supply the 'want of antecedent experience' felt by the framers."[159]

To be sure, Madison did tell his colleagues in the first Congress that their decision regarding the power of the President to remove executive branch officers unilaterally "will become the permanent exposition of the Constitution."[160] That statement, however, could be read simply as a prediction of the probable precedential and path-dependent consequences of the decision. Madison surely knew that whether Congress's decision would in fact "become the permanent exposition of the Constitution" would depend on whether future interpreters would accept the decision as authoritative. In that regard, it is noteworthy that Congress subsequently insisted on a greater role in the removal process, and, despite resisting some of those efforts in *Myers v United States*,[161] the Supreme Court ultimately has allowed Congress the ability to limit presidential removal of a variety of officials.[162]

Another example commonly cited as evidence of Madison's embrace of the liquidation idea is his shift in public position concerning the constitutionality of the national bank. In December 1790, Alexander Hamilton submitted a plan for a national bank that would be chartered by Congress. Madison, who had been elected to the first Congress from Virginia, opened the debate in the House by declaring the bank beyond the scope of Congress's enumerated powers.[163] By 1815, however, Madison was now President, and in vetoing on policy grounds a bill to reauthorize the bank, he "[w]aiv[ed] the question of the constitutional authority of the Legislature to establish an incorporated bank as being precluded in my judgment by repeated recognitions under varied circumstances of the validity of such an institution in acts of the legislative, executive, and judicial branches of

[159] Rakove, *Original Meanings* at 159 (cited in note 158). See also Charles A. Lofgren, *The Original Understanding of Original Intent?*, 5 Const Comm 77, 110 (1998) (interpreting Madison to mean that "[e]arly and continued practice" would serve as "a check on (but not an invariable barrier to) subsequent reinterpretation").

[160] 1 Annals of Cong 514 (1789). For a description of different scholarly views about what, if anything, was actually agreed upon in this "Decision of 1789," see Bradley and Morrison, 126 Harv L Rev at 477 (cited in note 95).

[161] 272 US 52 (1926).

[162] See, for example, *Humphrey's Executor v United States*, 295 US 602 (1935), and *Morrison v Olson*, 487 US 654 (1988).

[163] James Madison's Speech in Congress Opposing the National Bank (Feb 2, 1791), in Jack N. Rakove, ed, *James Madison: Writings* 480–90 (Library of America, 1999).

the Government, accompanied by indications, in different modes, of a concurrence of the general will of the nation."[164] In that veto message, Madison did not appear to be saying that initial practice had fixed the meaning of the Necessary and Proper Clause for all time absent a formal amendment. Instead, he seemed to be suggesting that, because the political branches and the general public had long agreed that the bank was constitutional, he no longer felt entitled to insist on his own view of the constitutional text and the original understanding in considering whether to sign the bill into law. Such a view is consistent with historical gloss.[165]

Moreover, even if Madison had been suggesting that post-Founding practices and beliefs had fixed constitutional meaning in favor of the permissibility of the bank, it would not have been an example of liquidation as that concept has been described by scholars like Nelson. The liquidation theory posits that certain issues of constitutional meaning were left unresolved at the Founding. Madison, however, did not believe that the meaning of the Constitution was ambiguous with respect to the permissibility of the national bank. On the contrary, he continued to believe that the text supported his previous view.[166] But because too many other institutions and individuals had disagreed with him over an extended period of time, he "'did not feel [him]self, as a public man, at liberty to sacrifice all these public considerations to [his] private opinion.'"[167]

---

[164] James Madison, Veto Message on the National Bank (Jan 30, 1815), online at http://millercenter.org/president/madison/speeches/speech-3626. See also Richard S. Arnold, *How James Madison Interpreted the Constitution*, 72 NYU L Rev 267, 286–90 (1997).

[165] Historian Drew McCoy views Madison's change regarding the bank as an application of "one of his cardinal rules of interpretation," which "was to respect the authority of 'early, deliberate and continued practice under the Constitution.'" Drew R. McCoy, *The Last of the Fathers: James Madison and the Republican Legacy* 80 (Cambridge, 1989), quoting Letter from James Madison to Martin L. Hurlbert (May 1830). Notably, Madison's principle required practice that was continued. When the bank again became controversial during Madison's retirement, McCoy notes, Madison proclaimed that declaring the bank unconstitutional in the 1830s would constitute "a defiance of all the obligations derived from a course of precedents amounting to the requisite evidence of the national judgment and intention." Id at 81, quoting Madison. Such statements suggest that Madison was not insisting upon liquidation only by initial practice.

[166] See Powell, 98 Harv L Rev at 940 (cited in note 158) ("His own 'abstract opinion of the text' remained unchanged: the words of the Constitution did not authorize Congress to establish the bank."), quoting Letter from James Madison to C. E. Haynes (Feb 25, 1831), reprinted in 4 *Letters and Other Writings of James Madison* 164, 165 (1865).

[167] Powell, 98 Harv L Rev at 940 (cited in note 158), quoting Letter from James Madison to Marquis de LaFayette (Nov 1826), reprinted in 3 *Letters and Other Writings of James Madison* 538, 542 (1865).

The majority in *Noel Canning* seemed to interpret some of Madison's statements on liquidation as consistent with the historical gloss approach. In explaining the propriety of looking to practice, the majority quoted a letter from Madison referring to liquidation, and then said that "our cases have continually confirmed Madison's view."[168] Many of the decisions that the majority cited, however, endorsed historical gloss.[169] Indeed, the majority correctly described those precedents as "show[ing] that this Court has treated practice as an important interpretive factor even when the nature or longevity of that practice is subject to dispute, and even when that practice began after the founding era."[170] Thus, the majority—reasonably, we think—interpreted Madison's reference to liquidation differently from how it has been interpreted by some originalist scholars.

To be sure, the majority never clearly committed to a potential feature of the historical gloss approach, which is the possibility that constitutional meaning might change over time. It is precisely the possibility of change in meaning over time that leads many originalists, including those who subscribe to the liquidation idea, to reject gloss and to limit liquidation to the resolution of textual ambiguities. Moreover, the majority emphasized the modern practice relating to recess appointments over the earlier practice, and it made clear that three-quarters of a century of practice is enough to merit substantial weight in interpreting the separation of powers.[171] The majority insisted, however, that the earlier practice did not establish a contrary understanding of the recess appointments power. Regarding the issue of intrasession recess appointments, for example, the majority described the pre–Civil War history as simply "not helpful" to resolving the question one way or the other, rather than as contradictory.[172] Regarding the issue of appointments to preexisting vacancies, the majority suggested that there simply were differing

---

[168] 134 S Ct at 2560.

[169] See 134 S Ct at 2560, citing *Mistretta v United States*, 488 US 361, 401 (1989); *Dames & Moore v Regan*, 453 US 654, 686 (1981); *Youngstown Sheet & Tube Co. v Sawyer*, 343 US 579, 610–11 (1952) (Frankfurter, J, concurring); *The Pocket Veto Case*, 279 US 655, 689–90 (1929); *Ex Parte Grossman*, 267 US 87, 118–19 (1925); *United States v Midwest Oil Co.*, 236 US 459, 472–74 (1915); *McPherson v Blacker*, 146 US 1, 27 (1892); *McCulloch v Maryland*, 17 US (4 Wheat) 316, 401 (1819); and *Stuart v Laird*, 5 US (1 Cranch) 299 (1803).

[170] 134 S Ct at 2560.

[171] Id at 2564, 2573.

[172] Id at 2562.

views about the issue prior to Attorney General Wirt's 1823 opinion.[173]

The majority's silence about the possibility of changes in constitutional meaning outside of the Article V amendment process is characteristic of the Court's other decisions that have endorsed historical gloss. It is also consistent with the Court's constitutional law decisions more generally, even in areas in which it might seem obvious that constitutional meaning has shifted, such as with respect to certain individual rights. The Court's silence likely reflects anxieties about the countermajoritarian difficulty, especially in areas in which there is significant public debate.[174] Despite the Court's reluctance to acknowledge it openly, there is nothing inherent in the logic of the historical gloss approach that would disallow a constitutional interpreter from crediting a shift in practice over time.

C. PROBLEMS WITH THE LIQUIDATION CONCEPT

Even if it could be shown that Madison did have in mind an approach whereby ambiguities in original meaning could be settled by, and only by, initial practice, and even if it could further be shown that some (or many or most) other Founders shared Madison's view, those demonstrations would not themselves establish that constitutional interpreters today should accept such an approach. As careful originalists acknowledge, originalism cannot establish its own validity.[175] A normative defense of the liquidation approach would need to address substantial objections.

---

[173] See id at 2570.

[174] Justice Scalia sometimes exploits those anxieties. See, for example, Transcript of Oral Argument at 38 ll.3–8, *Hollingsworth v Perry*, 133 S Ct 2652 (2013) (No 12-144) ("I'm curious, when . . . did it become unconstitutional to exclude homosexual couples from marriage? 1791? 1868, when the Fourteenth Amendment was adopted? [S]ome time after Baker [v Nelson, 409 US 810 (1972)], where we said it didn't even raise a substantial Federal question? When . . . did the law become this?").

[175] See, for example, Nelson, 70 U Chi L Rev at 547–48 (cited in note 141). Modern variants of originalism, unlike the first generation of originalist scholarship, focus on the original meaning of the Constitution rather than on original intent. See, for example, Whittington, 82 Fordham L Rev (cited in note 133). That shift in focus further complicates any claim that a liquidation approach to the Constitution should be followed because Founders such as James Madison intended it. To be sure, considerations of intent and meaning may not be neatly separable, so it might be argued (for example) that liquidation was part of the background understandings about how the Constitution would operate and thus was part of its original meaning. See Sachs, 2013 U Ill L Rev at 1807 (cited in note 141). Again, however, even if that could be shown, it would not establish that liquidation should be followed. Some justification external to originalism would be needed.

The theory behind the liquidation idea, to reiterate, is that the Founders delegated the settlement of ambiguities in constitutional meaning to subsequent governmental actors.[176] It is unclear, however, why it would have made sense for the Founders to decide that constitutional meaning should be determined dispositively by the particular political alignment that happened to exist whenever the issue first arose. In attempting to determine constitutional meaning, the initial generations presumably would be no less self-serving and potentially short-sighted than later generations, and they would have much less experience in apprehending the needs of American governance. Moreover, those initial generations obviously would lack knowledge of subsequent changes in conditions and values that could dramatically affect the implications of adopting one interpretation of the Constitution instead of another. Notwithstanding those substantial limitations, the liquidation approach would license earlier generations to bind more experienced successors through simple majoritarian politics.

Those objections are not overcome by positing that liquidation should be limited to situations in which the earlier generations deliberated with unusual seriousness.[177] Even if one could identify a way to solve the practical problem of distinguishing different levels of congressional or executive branch seriousness, the more fundamental problem would remain that subsequent generations might deliberate at least as seriously and they would necessarily possess substantially more knowledge and experience. The net effect of widespread acceptance of the liquidation idea would be a regime that possesses many of the "dead hand" disadvantages of originalism, but few of the asserted upsides of originalism beyond limiting interpretive discretion—namely, preventing constitutional change outside the demanding supermajoritarian process of Article V, and conferring democratic legitimacy upon the institution of judicial review by limiting it to enforcement of the original supermajoritarian act of higher lawmaking.[178]

---

[176] See Nelson, 70 U Chi L Rev at 551 (cited in note 141).

[177] See id at 528.

[178] One common justification for *Chevron* deference to administrative agencies rests on a similar delegation account. "Deference under *Chevron* to an agency's construction of a statute that it administers," the Court has explained, "is premised on the theory that a statute's ambiguity constitutes an implicit delegation from Congress to the agency to fill in the statutory gaps." *FDA v Brown & Williamson Tobacco Corp.*, 529 US 120, 159 (2000), citing *Chevron*

Another problem with originalist efforts to distinguish between liquidation and historical gloss is that such a distinction is in tension with the acceptance by many originalists of judicial precedent. Justice Scalia, for example, has made clear that he accepts the presumptively binding force of precedent in a number of areas of constitutional law.[179] Justice Scalia describes his approach to precedent as a pragmatic "exception" to his originalism that is based on interests in stability.[180] Similarly, Robert Bork accepted that a decision "may be clearly incorrect but nevertheless have become so embedded in the life of the nation, so accepted by the society, so fundamental to the private and public expectations of individuals and institutions, that the result should not be changed now."[181] But interests in stability and related rule-of-law considerations, such as consistency, predictability, reliance, and transparency, also can be advanced by adhering to long-standing practices, regardless of whether they date to the early post-Founding period.[182] Madison, it is worth repeating, grouped judicial precedent and political practices together.[183]

There are, to be sure, statements in a number of Supreme Court decisions suggesting that practices dating back to near the Founding

---

U.S.A. Inc. v Natural Resources Defense Council, 467 US 837, 844 (1984). Under *Chevron*, however, agencies are not precluded from changing their interpretations (and, indeed, *Chevron* itself involved a revised agency interpretation). See, for example, *National Cable & Telecommunications Association v Brand X Internet Services*, 545 US 967, 981 (2005) ("Agency inconsistency is not a basis for declining to analyze the agency's interpretation under the *Chevron* framework.").

[179] See, for example, *McDonald v City of Chicago*, 130 S Ct 3020, 3050 (2010) (Scalia, J, concurring) ("Despite my misgivings about Substantive Due Process as an original matter, I have acquiesced in the Court's incorporation of certain guarantees in the Bill of Rights 'because it is both long established and narrowly limited.' *Albright v Oliver*, 510 U.S. 266, 275 (1994) (Scalia, J., concurring).").

[180] See Antonin Scalia, *A Matter of Interpretation: Federal Courts and the Law* 139–40 (Princeton, 1997).

[181] Robert H. Bork, *The Tempting of America: The Political Seduction of the Law* 158 (Free Press, 1990).

[182] See Bradley and Morrison, 126 Harv L Rev at 427–28 (cited in note 95); Posner and Vermeule, 156 U Pa L Rev at 999 (cited in note 127); Cass R. Sunstein, *Originalism v. Burkeanism: A Dialogue Over Recess*, 126 Harv L Rev F 126, 128 (2013). Compare Richard H. Fallon, Jr., *Stare Decisis and the Constitution: An Essay on Constitutional Methodology*, 76 NYU L Rev 570, 588 (2001) (noting that stare decisis "promotes stability, protects settled expectations, and conserves judicial resources").

[183] Some originalists accept judicial precedent not as a pragmatic exception to originalism but as part of Article III judicial power, and so in that way might be able to reconcile an acceptance of judicial precedent with a rejection of nonjudicial precedent, depending on their grounds for accepting certain judicial precedents and not others. See McGinnis and Rappaport, *Originalism and the Good Constitution* (cited in note 137).

can "fix[] the construction" to be given to constitutional provisions.[184] Those statements, however, do not contend that this is the only way in which constitutional meaning may legitimately be affected by practice. Moreover, those statements do not envision that meaning would become fixed merely as a result of the initial practice; rather, they expressly require long-standing acquiescence in the interpretation that was adopted. This is also true of Justice Scalia's acknowledgment in *Noel Canning* that it would be appropriate to look to practices "unchallenged since the early days of the Republic."[185] As a result, those statements do not appear to share the premise of the liquidation approach (as understood by scholars like Caleb Nelson) that the initial post-Founding generation was delegated the authority to fix constitutional meaning. Instead, the statements in those decisions suggest that meaning would become fixed only if later generations continued to accept the early interpretation. The idea of fixation through long-standing acceptance of a practice, however, is fully consistent with a historical gloss approach to constitutional interpretation.

IV. HISTORICAL PRACTICE AND THE CONSTITUTIONAL TEXT

Arguments based on historical practice are common in the area of separation of powers, but the constitutional text is almost always treated as controlling when it is perceived to be clear, even in the face of contrary historical practice. Indeed, it is generally agreed that when the text is clear, it controls. As we will explain, however, historical practice can affect perceptions about the clarity or ambi-

---

[184] See *Myers v United States*, 272 US 52, 175 (1926) ("[A] contemporaneous legislative exposition of the Constitution, when the founders of our Government and framers of our Constitution were actively participating in public affairs, acquiesced in for a long term of years, fixes the construction to be given its provisions."); *McGrain v Daugherty*, 273 US 135, 174 (1927) ("So, when their practice in the matter is appraised according to the circumstances in which it was begun and to those in which it has been continued, it falls nothing short of a practical construction, long continued, of the constitutional provisions respecting their powers, and therefore should be taken as fixing the meaning of those provisions, if otherwise doubtful."); *Stuart v Laird*, 5 US (1 Cranch) 299, 309 (1803) ("[P]ractice and acquiescence under it for a period of several years, commencing with the organization of the judicial system, affords an irresistible answer, and has indeed fixed the construction."). Although the Court in *Stuart v Laird* referenced acquiescence only for a period of several years, it is worth remembering that there were not many years to speak of in 1803.

[185] 134 S Ct at 2594.

guity of the text. This phenomenon, which we have referred to elsewhere as "constructed constraint,"[186] is evident in *Noel Canning*.

A. THE MODALITY OF TEXTUAL ARGUMENTATION

It is widely accepted that the constitutional text is controlling when it is perceived to be clear. More precisely, it is widely agreed that the constitutional text must be followed when it is understood to be (i) clear, (ii) applicable to the constitutional question under consideration, and (iii) comprehensive in the sense that the text says all that there is to be said about the question. It is almost never an acceptable move in constitutional practice to argue for a disregard of the text.[187]

Only occasionally does one encounter suggestions to the contrary. For example, during the oral argument in *Noel Canning*, Justice Scalia repeatedly asked the Solicitor General whether long-standing practice ever could trump clear constitutional text.[188] The Solicitor General replied that such practice, at least if it extended back to the Founding, could trump clear text.[189] He also stressed, however, that it would be "extremely unlikely" for long-standing practice to develop in a way that is contrary to clear text.[190] Unlike the Solicitor General, neither the majority nor Justice Scalia in *Noel Canning* suggested that practice—or any other modality for that matter—could trump clear text.[191] Instead, the majority repeatedly stated that it was relying on nontextual modalities only because it concluded that the text of the

---

[186] See Bradley and Siegel, 64 Duke L J (cited in note 11).

[187] For example, Jack Balkin and David Strauss, two prominent constitutional theorists, disagree about *why* clear text possesses that degree of interpretive authority, but emphatically agree that it does. See Jack M. Balkin, *Living Originalism* 3, 55 (Belknap, 2011), and David A. Strauss, *The Living Constitution* 102–03 (Oxford, 2010).

[188] See Transcript of Oral Argument at 6–8 (cited in note 66).

[189] Id at 6, 8.

[190] See id at 8. Not surprisingly, when Justice Alito asked counsel for Noel Canning the same question, he said that in such a situation "the language has to govern." Id at 42. Justice Kagan, however, questioned his answer. See id at 43. Justice Breyer also pointed out that both the Due Process Clause and the Commerce Clause had acquired meanings different from what the language of those clauses might suggest. See id at 48.

[191] Dissenting in *INS v Chadha*, 462 US 919 (1983) (discussed above at text at notes 115–17), Justice White emphasized the long-standing practice of legislative vetoes but did not claim that such practice could override clear text. Instead, he argued that there was a "silence of the Constitution on the precise question." Id at 977 (White, J, dissenting). Specifically, White reasoned that the Presentment Clause applies to exercises by Congress of "original lawmaking authority," and that "[t]he power to exercise a legislative veto is not the power to write new law without bicameral approval or presidential consideration." Id at 979–80.

Recess Appointments Clause was ambiguous.[192] The majority thus seemed to embrace the proposition, emphasized by Justice Scalia, that clear text is controlling, regardless of other considerations.[193]

In that regard, the Justices in *Noel Canning* were reflecting the orthodox view in American constitutional interpretation. Similarly, in numerous prior decisions, the Supreme Court has endorsed the proposition that the modality of textual argumentation is distinct from the other modalities, and that nontextual modalities may appropriately be considered only to resolve ambiguities in the text.[194] Moreover, when dissenting opinions invoke that proposition, the majority does not contest it; instead, the majority typically argues that the text is unclear, inapplicable, or not a comprehensive provision.[195] The proposition that clear text is controlling has rhetorical power exactly because of the widely shared understanding that it is effectively an incontestable principle of American constitutional interpretation.

Of particular relevance to this article, that shared understanding means that the constitutional text has rhetorical primacy over claims based on historical practice. In addition, as Michael Dorf has observed, the constitutional text tends to have the effect of crowding out freestanding claims based upon practice even when those claims do not contradict the text.[196] As a result, practice-based claims generally must be connected in some fashion to the text. That is not, however, an inevitable effect of having a legal text. Under international law, for example, custom is a freestanding source of law that operates alongside written treaties, and it can operate even in opposition to

---

[192] See 134 S Ct at 2561 ("The constitutional text is thus ambiguous."); id at 2568 ("The question is whether the Clause is ambiguous."); id at 2577 ("We believe that the Clause's text, standing alone, is ambiguous.").

[193] See, for example, id at 2617 (Scalia, J, concurring in the judgment) ("What the majority needs to sustain its judgment is an ambiguous text and a clear historical practice.").

[194] See, for example, *Reid v Covert*, 354 US 1, 8 n 7 (1957) (plurality opinion) ("This Court has constantly reiterated that the language of the Constitution where clear and unambiguous must be given its plain evident meaning.").

[195] Compare, for example, *Seminole Tribe of Florida v Florida*, 517 US 44, 116 n 13 (1996) (Souter, J, dissenting) ("[P]lain text is the Man of Steel in a confrontation with 'background principle[s]' and 'postulates which limit and control . . . .'") (citations omitted), with id at 69 ("The dissent's lengthy analysis of the text of the Eleventh Amendment is directed at a straw man . . . .").

[196] See Michael C. Dorf, *How the Written Constitution Crowds Out the Extraconstitutional Rule of Recognition*, in Matthew D. Adler and Kenneth Einer Himma, eds, *The Rule of Recognition and the U.S. Constitution* 69 (Oxford, 2009).

that written law.[197] Custom does not work that way in U.S. constitutional law. On the contrary, while "judges sometimes admit that constitutional interpretation is sensitive to historical evolution and that history adds a 'gloss' on the text," those same judges "never admit to deriving the authority for the decision from outside the constitutional text."[198] Consistent with that phenomenon, the majority in *Noel Canning* claimed only that historical practice was "an important interpretive factor."[199]

B. CONSTRUCTED CONSTRAINT

We have argued elsewhere that the orthodox view of the role of the constitutional text is correct as far as it goes, but that it does not go far enough.[200] When the constitutional text is perceived to be clear, applicable, and comprehensive, it acts as a meaningful constraint on constitutional interpretation by limiting and shaping argumentation and thereby affecting the available courses of conduct that will be considered constitutional. The perceived clarity or ambiguity of the text, however, is often partially constructed by "extratextual" considerations. More precisely, the perceived clarity or ambiguity of the text is not only a product of typical "plain meaning" considerations such as dictionary definitions and linguistic conventions, but also can be affected by the other modalities of constitutional argumentation, which are commonly thought to come into play only in resolving ambiguities in the meaning of the text.[201] In other words, perceived

---

[197] See, for example, *Restatement (Third) of the Foreign Relations Law of the United States* § 102 n 4 (1987) ("Provisions in international agreements are superseded by principles of customary international law that develop subsequently, where the parties to the agreement so intend.").

[198] Andrzej Rapaczynski, *The Ninth Amendment and the Unwritten Constitution: The Problems of Constitutional Interpretation*, 64 Chi Kent L Rev 177, 192 (1988).

[199] 134 S Ct at 2560.

[200] See Bradley and Siegel, 64 Duke L J (cited in note 11).

[201] When referring to "ambiguity" in this part, we do so in the loose way that the Supreme Court often does—that is, as a reference both to situations in which the applicability of the text to particular circumstances is unclear (what legal philosophers would term "vagueness") and to situations in which the text could mean more than one specific thing (what legal philosophers would term "ambiguity"). See, for example, Lawrence B. Solum, *The Interpretation-Construction Distinction*, 27 Const Comm 95, 97–98 (2010). While the distinction between vagueness and ambiguity is important in some contexts, the distinction is not material for our account of constructed constraint.

textual clarity is not just some linguistic fact of the matter that exists apart from the overall process of constitutional interpretation.

Our theory of constructed constraint resurrects certain insights from the Critical Legal Studies (CLS) movement in the 1980s, without accepting the claim of some CLS scholars in constitutional law that there are no limits on the extent to which textual clarity is subject to extratextual construction.[202] Under our account, the clarity and ambiguity of the constitutional text is partially constructed, but in any given situation there are limits on the extent to which construction is available, including limits on the degree to which interpreters can persuasively identify textual work-arounds in the face of constraining text. For example, under ordinary circumstances, almost no one would be persuaded by a "purposive" construction of the various clauses in the Constitution imposing age qualifications for federal offices—such as a claim that someone under the age of thirty-five lawfully could be elected president as long as he or she had a certain level of maturity, or a claim that the age requirement is actually higher than thirty-five because, with increasing longevity, people tend to mature more slowly today. Similarly, even though before ratification of the Twenty-Second Amendment presidents sometimes contemplated violating an unwritten norm against running for a third term (and Franklin Roosevelt did so), after the amendment no one seriously contemplates that possibility.[203]

In many other instances, however, perceptions about textual clarity or ambiguity have been subject to construction. For example, there is a consensus that the First Amendment applies to the entire federal government, not just to Congress, notwithstanding the express and distinctive textual limitation of the amendment's strictures to Congress.[204] For a variety of purposive, structural, consequentialist, and ethos considerations, as well as extensive judicial precedent, almost all interpreters of the First Amendment read the text more broadly

---

[202] For a discussion, see Bradley and Siegel, 64 Duke L J (cited in note 11).

[203] See, for example, Frederick Schauer, *Easy Cases*, 58 S Cal L Rev 399, 414 (1985) ("The parties concerned know, without litigating and without consulting lawyers, that Ronald Reagan cannot run for a third term . . . ."). But see Mark V. Tushnet, *A Note on the Revival of Textualism in Constitutional Theory*, 58 S Cal L Rev 683, 687 (1985) (hypothesizing a situation in which this prohibition might be disregarded). Hypothesizing an unlikely scenario in which the text would be disregarded does not show that the text is unconstraining. Rather, it shows only that the text is not infinitely constraining.

[204] See US Const, Amend I ("Congress shall make no law . . . .").

than would be suggested by traditional "plain meaning" considerations. In fact, so powerful is this construction that interpreters
typically do not even *see* the first word of the First Amendment.[205]

The construction of textual ambiguity also is evident in the U.S.
Supreme Court's state sovereign immunity jurisprudence. In resisting the proposition that the expanse and limits of the states' sovereign
immunity from private lawsuits is covered by the text of the Eleventh
Amendment, the Court has not simply ignored the text, as some of its
critics have suggested. Rather, for purposive, structural, and consequentialist reasons, the Court has understood the amendment as a
noncomprehensive provision—that is, as not covering all that there
is to be said about the extent of the states' immunity from suit. As
the Court has explained, it has "understood the Eleventh Amendment to stand not so much for what it says, but for the presupposi-
tion . . . which it confirms."[206] On that view, the amendment was a
targeted response to a mistaken Supreme Court decision, not a comprehensive statement of the extent of the states' immunity from suit.
It is noteworthy that even the dissenters in those sovereign immunity decisions have not pushed for a literal approach to the Eleventh
Amendment—that is, one that would disallow even federal question
suits against states by citizens of another state while allowing such
suits if brought by citizens of the state.[207] Instead, for structural and
purposive reasons, the dissenting Justices have contended that the
amendment should be interpreted as "simply repeal[ing] the Citizen-
State Diversity Clauses of Article III for all cases in which the State
appears as a defendant."[208]

Noel Canning, too, exemplifies the construction of textual ambiguity. While the majority insisted that the relevant text was ambiguous, it did not appear simply to invoke the other modalities of
constitutional interpretation to clarify ambiguous text. Instead, the
majority's decision to regard the text as ambiguous seems itself to

---

[205] See Bradley and Siegel, 64 Duke L J (cited note 11).

[206] *Blatchford v Native Village of Notak*, 501 US 775, 779 (1991).

[207] The Eleventh Amendment provides that the federal judicial power "shall not be con-
strued to extend to *any suit* in law or equity, commenced or prosecuted against one of the
United States by Citizens of another State, or by Citizens or Subjects of any Foreign State."
US Const, Amend XI (emphasis added).

[208] See, for example, *Seminole Tribe of Florida v Florida*, 517 US 44, 109–10 (1996) (Souter, J,
dissenting); *Atascadero State Hospital v Scanlon*, 473 US 234, 289 (1985) (Brennan, J, dissenting).

have been affected by its understanding of the purpose of the Recess Appointments Clause, historical practice, and the consequences of an alternative interpretation. Or, to put it differently, those extratextual considerations seemed to have motivated a search for ambiguity. That is most evident in the majority's treatment of the phrase "vacancies that happen" during a recess.

The majority plausibly concluded that the linguistic meaning of the words "the Recess" was ambiguous because those words could mean either the single break between yearly sessions of the Senate or any substantial break in Senate business. As a linguistic matter, the phrase "the Recess," like the phrase "the person in the street,"[209] can be understood to reference one phenomenon or multiple phenomena.[210] By contrast, the Court's finding of ambiguity for the phrase "vacancies that may happen" suggests substantial extratextual construction. In that part of its analysis, the Court articulated a thin understanding of ambiguity, allowing ready invocation of extratextual considerations. Critically for present purposes, that thin understanding seems itself to have been prompted in part by the extratextual considerations.

As the Court conceded, "the most natural meaning" of the word "happen" as applied to the word "vacancy" is that the vacancy must occur during the recess.[211] The Court insisted, however, that this was "not the only *possible* way to use the word," because "happen" also may mean "exist."[212] The Court then reasoned that the purpose of the Recess Appointments Clause and historical practice supported the broader reading. Those extratextual considerations were pertinent, the Court stated, because there was "some linguistic ambiguity."[213]

---

[209] See, for example, Sunstein, 126 Harv L Rev F at 127 (cited in note 182) ("In ordinary language, a reference to 'the car,' or 'the ordinary American,' or 'the horse' need not suggest that there is only one!").

[210] In *Dred Scott v Sandford*, 60 US 394, 436 (1856), the Supreme Court controversially interpreted the phrase "the Territory" in Article IV, Section 3 of the Constitution to mean only territory held by the United States at the time of the Founding, and on that basis (among others) held that Congress could not prohibit slavery in American territories acquired after ratification of the Constitution.

[211] It could be argued, however, that the phrase "during the recess" in the clause modifies only "fill up" and not the word "happen." See Michael Herz, *Re-Diagramming the Recess Appointments Clause* (Jan 8, 2014), Balkinization, at http://balkin.blogspot.com/2014/01/re-diagramming-recess-appointments.html.

[212] 134 S Ct at 2567 (emphasis added).

[213] Id at 2573.

Importantly, however, the only reason for the majority to have sought out a *possible* reading—but not the most natural reading—were the extratextual considerations. In other words, if the Court's understanding of the practice and the purpose of the clause had not been contrary to the most natural meaning of the phrase, it seems unlikely that the Court would have characterized the text as ambiguous. But, as the Court emphasized, it was unprepared to "render illegitimate thousands of recess appointments reaching all the way back to the founding era."[214] Indeed, while the meaning of the word "happen" seems less ambiguous in context than the meaning of the phrase "the Recess," there was a substantially longer historical practice bearing on the term "happen" than there was regarding the phrase "the Recess." Accordingly, the thinness of the Court's understanding of ambiguity appears to have been inversely related to the duration of the historical practice.

Justice Scalia, by contrast, argued that the Recess Appointments Clause was clear, and that its clear meaning supported a substantially narrower recess appointments authority. Even in his opinion, it is possible to see the influence of extratextual considerations. In particular, throughout his opinion—and not merely in response to the majority's contrary arguments—Justice Scalia stressed what he believed to be the purpose of the clause: to operate as "a tool carefully designed to fill a narrow and specific need,"[215] while "preserv[ing] the Senate's role in the appointment process."[216] Given that understanding of the purpose of the text, Justice Scalia concluded, for example, that the clause clearly prohibited the use of recess appointments to avoid senatorial opposition to appointees, even though such use has been characteristic of practice since the 1920s. "The need [that the clause] was designed to fill no longer exists," he wrote, "and its only remaining use is the ignoble one of enabling the President to circumvent the Senate's role in the appointment process."[217] Ac-

---

[214] Id at 2577.

[215] Id at 2592 (Scalia, J, concurring in judgment).

[216] Id at 2597.

[217] Id at 2598. For another decision from the October 2013 Term in which the Court relied on extratextual considerations in determining that the text was unclear, this time in the context of statutory interpretation, see *Bond v United States*, 134 S Ct 2077, 2090 (2014) ("In this case, the ambiguity derives from the improbably broad reach of the key statutory definition given the term—'chemical weapon'—being defined; the deeply serious consequences of adopting such a boundless reading; and the lack of any apparent need to do so in light of the context from which the statute arose—a treaty about chemical warfare and terrorism.").

cordingly, both opinions in *Noel Canning* exemplify how perceptions of textual ambiguity or clarity can themselves be affected by extra-textual modalities.

C. IMPLICATIONS FOR "CONSTITUTIONAL CONSTRUCTION"

As discussed earlier, a number of theorists associated with the "new originalism" have distinguished between "constitutional interpreta-tion" and "constitutional construction." Under that approach, con-stitutional determinations that are closely linked to the text ("inter-pretation") are distinguished from those that supplement the text ("construction"). The approach is more receptive to historical prac-tice than earlier originalist accounts and is also more receptive than the Madisonian liquidation approach. Nevertheless, the phenome-non of constructed constraint described above presents difficulties for the distinction that this approach seeks to make.

Political scientist Keith Whittington—a prominent advocate of the distinction between interpretation and construction—explains that interpretation "takes the text as its touchstone," whereas con-struction does not "deal[] so explicitly and obsessively with the terms of the document itself."[218] Randy Barnett similarly makes clear that construction primarily occurs in situations in which the semantic meaning of the constitutional text is unclear, such that there is not enough information "contained in the text" to resolve an issue.[219] Law-rence Solum agrees that practitioners are in "the construction zone" when the constitutional text is "vague or irreducibly ambiguous."[220]

Jack Balkin, in setting out his theory of "framework originalism,"[221] likewise relies on the distinction between interpretation and con-struction. In Balkin's rendition, the constitutional text establishes the basic framework of governance upon which participants in consti-

---

[218] Whittington, *Constitutional Construction* at 9 (cited in note 129); see also Keith E. Whittington, *Constructing a New American Constitution*, 27 Const Comm 119, 119–20 (2010) ("Interpretive practice is supplemented through a process of constitutional construction. . . . Construction picks up where interpretation leaves off.").

[219] Randy E. Barnett, *Interpretation and Construction*, 34 Harv J L & Pub Pol 65, 67 (2011); see also Randy Barnett, *Restoring the Lost Constitution* ch 5 (Princeton, 2004).

[220] Solum, 82 Fordham L Rev at 458 (cited in note 136); see also Whittington, 27 Const Comm at 120–21 (cited in note 218) (defining "the realm of construction" as "when the Constitution as written cannot in good faith be said to provide a determinate answer to a given question").

[221] See generally Balkin, *Living Originalism* (cited in note 187).

tutional debates can build constitutional constructions. Balkin expressly distinguishes the "ascertainment of the meaning" of the text (which he calls "interpretation") from the activity of constitutional construction, which he says involves "arguments from history, structure, ethos, consequences, and precedent."[222] Constructions, as Balkin further explains, "exist to fill out and implement the text."[223]

The phenomenon of constructed constraint, however, unsettles the distinction that those theorists seek to draw between interpretation and construction. The considerations that are relevant to construction do not merely supplement the determination of the meaning of the text, and they do not come into play only when the text is unclear. Rather, they also affect the threshold assessment of whether the text is unclear. Construction, in other words, not only takes place on top of the textual framework, but also partially determines the framework itself. Thus, it is artificial to separate constitutional interpretation from (to use Solum's phrase) the "construction zone."

One attraction of the idea of "constitutional construction," as those theorists use the term, is that it makes originalism descriptively more accurate of existing practice. In particular, by acknowledging the phenomenon of constitutional construction, originalists have accepted the insight—emphasized by critics of originalism—that the Constitution sometimes enacts broad principles or standards rather than specific rules, and that in those situations the semantic meaning of the text does not—because it cannot—resolve concrete cases.[224] As noted earlier, that concession is too strong for some originalists. The theory of constructed constraint suggests, however, that originalists have conceded too little ground, not too much. Participants in constitutional interpretation characteristically feel bound by constitutional text that they deem clear, but their perception of its clarity is often not determined primarily—let alone exclusively—by its original semantic meaning.[225]

---

[222] Id at 4.

[223] Id at 54; see also Whittington, 27 Const Comm at 121 (cited in note 218) ("[C]onstitutional constructions are built within the boundaries, or to use Jack Balkin's phrase, within the framework, of the interpreted Constitution.").

[224] Colby, 99 Georgetown L J at 731 (cited in note 136).

[225] For ways in which the theory of constructed constraint complicates other efforts in recent constitutional theory to distinguish between the textual and nontextual aspects of American constitutionalism, see Bradley and Siegel, 64 Duke L J (cited in note 11).

Accordingly, it is difficult to limit the relevance of historical practice in constitutional interpretation to questions falling within the new originalist "construction zone." Historical practice itself may affect perceptions of whether one is in the construction zone. As a result, even constitutional construction, which is more receptive to historical practice than both traditional originalism and liquidation, does not go far enough because of its effort to strictly distinguish between textual meaning and construction.

Because historical gloss can both affect perceptions of textual clarity and shift over time, that approach to constitutional interpretation can in theory result in a reallocation of governmental authority and not just a resolution of ambiguity concerning such authority. That possibility is the premise of Justice Scalia's charge in *Noel Canning* that the majority was enabling executive aggrandizement by "adverse possession." Although his analogy to adverse possession highlights some reasons to be cautious before crediting historical practice, we explain in the next part why the analogy is largely misplaced.

V. CONSTITUTIONAL ADVERSE POSSESSION

In *Noel Canning*, Justice Scalia repeatedly accused the majority of applying an "adverse possession" approach to the separation of powers.[226] The majority, Justice Scalia complained, would allow presidents to expand their constitutional authority simply by acting in a certain way for a long period of time as long as Congress failed to contest the practice "with sufficient vigor."[227] In addition to his originalist objections, Justice Scalia raised two structural concerns. First, he argued that a practice-based approach to the separation of powers would unduly favor the expansion of executive authority given various differences between the structure of Congress and that of the executive branch. Second, he contended that such an approach would allow Congress and the executive branch to disregard constitutional limitations that are designed to protect the public. The majority denied the adverse possession characterization, but it did so without much explanation. It did note, however, that it was considering not only historical practice but also constitutional text and

---

[226] See 134 S Ct at 2592, 2605, 2614, 2617.

[227] Id at 2592.

purpose,[228] presumably to contest Justice Scalia's premise that the President was taking powers that originally belonged to Congress.

Justice Scalia is not the first to analogize the historical gloss approach to the adverse possession doctrine in property law.[229] The analogy does shed some light on what the historical gloss approach entails and what its justifications are. But the adverse possession analogy is in many ways problematic. While Justice Scalia's concerns should be taken seriously, they do not warrant a general disallowance of practice-based authority.

A. PROBLEMS WITH THE ADVERSE POSSESSION ANALOGY

Under the adverse possession doctrine in property law, someone who uses someone else's real property for a specified period of time can, under certain conditions, acquire valid ownership of the property.[230] Such a doctrine might seem strange, in that it potentially allows what could be considered a form of theft through a wrongful act of trespass as long as the trespass lasts long enough.[231] In analogizing the historical gloss approach to the adverse possession doctrine, critics are suggesting that it, too, allows unlawful behavior—usurpation of another branch's authority—to become a basis for the lawful acquisition of power.

Of course, adverse possession is a long-standing and well-accepted feature of property law, so it is not obvious why the analogy indicts the historical gloss approach. But in any event, there are several ways in which the analogy is not particularly apt.

1. *Uncertain allocations.* The original owner of a parcel of land is typically known, and it is clear when an alteration is being made to the owner's rights. The separation of powers, by contrast, is frequently

---

[228] See id at 2578. Scalia contended that the adverse possession label was a "characterization the majority resists but does not refute." Id at 2617.

[229] See, for example, John Hart Ely, *War and Responsibility* 10 (Princeton, 1993) (critically describing an "adverse possession" approach to presidential war powers based on presidential practice), and Jonathan Turley, *Constitutional Adverse Possession: Recess Appointments and the Role of Historical Practice in Constitutional Interpretation*, 2013 Wis L Rev 965, 971 ("It creates a type of constitutional adverse possession where the simple success of a president in usurping congressional territory is treated as proof of the validity of the underlying interpretation.").

[230] See generally Joseph William Singer, *Property* ch 4 (3d ed 2010).

[231] See Henry W. Ballantine, *Title by Adverse Possession*, 32 Harv L Rev 135, 135 (1918) ("Title by adverse possession sounds, at first blush, like title by theft or robbery, a primitive method of acquiring land without paying for it.").

marked by debate and uncertainty about the allocation of powers. That is particularly true of constitutional provisions relating to foreign affairs, which Edward Corwin famously described as "an invitation to struggle for the privilege of directing American foreign policy."[232] But it also characterizes a number of issues of domestic law as well, including, for example, the authority of the President to remove executive officials from office,[233] an "executive privilege" to withhold information from Congress or the courts,[234] and the "legislative privilege" (concerning, among other things, the internal powers of the two houses of Congress).[235]

Relying on historical practice to help resolve uncertainties about such allocations is different from allowing it to alter a clearly established allocation. To be sure, as discussed in Part III, the perceived clarity of the Constitution's allocations of governmental authority itself can be affected by historical practice, and that appears to have been the case in at least part of the majority opinion in *Noel Canning*. Nevertheless, it is still true that many separation of powers disputes do not implicate allocations thought to be clearly established at the Founding. Indeed, the Madisonian liquidation idea recognizes that possibility.

As noted above, the majority in *Noel Canning* resisted the idea that it was reallocating authority. Instead, the majority insisted that the relevant constitutional text was ambiguous regarding both intra-session appointments and preexisting vacancies. Moreover, while the majority placed particular emphasis on modern practice in its interpretation of the Recess Appointments Clause, it did not concede that the early practice clearly established or confirmed a contrary constitutional interpretation. Indeed, the majority pointed out that, as a practical matter, Justice Scalia's approach would reallocate authority, as it "would render illegitimate thousands of recess appointments reaching all the way back to the founding era."[236] That concern highlights the more general point that the application of originalism can require dramatic changes in the landscape of constitutional law,

---

[232] Edward S. Corwin, *The President: Office and Powers* 171 (NYU, 4th ed 1957).

[233] See, for example, Steven G. Calabresi and Christopher S. Yoo, *The Unitary Executive: Presidential Power from Washington to Bush* (Yale, 2008).

[234] See, for example, Archibald Cox, *Executive Privilege*, 122 U Pa L Rev 1383 (1974).

[235] See, for example, Josh Chafetz, *Democracy's Privileged Few* 10–19 (Yale, 2007).

[236] 134 S Ct at 2577.

even as it purports to resist the idea of constitutional change outside of the Article V amendment process.[237]

2. *Implications of acquiescence.* Another distinction between property law and the separation of powers concerns the implications of acquiescence. Under most accounts of historical gloss, there must be some acquiescence in the practice by the other political branch of government in order for the practice to be credited. Recall, for example, Frankfurter's reference to executive practices "long pursued to the knowledge of the Congress and never before questioned."[238] For adverse possession, by contrast, acquiescence actually can destroy the adverse possessor's claim, because the possession needs to be "hostile."[239] Given that difference between historical gloss and adverse possession, gloss is more analogous to the law governing a contractual course of dealing rather than property rights and therefore does not present the same concern about the acquisition of rights through "theft."[240] To be sure, acquiescence is a fraught concept in the separation of powers, especially when based on mere silence or inaction. As discussed below in Section C, however, the difficulties with that concept suggest caution about inferring acquiescence, not abandonment of the concept.

3. *Concurrent versus exclusive rights.* Another potential difficulty with the analogy concerns the results of adverse possession. When

---

[237] See, for example, Jack Balkin, *Is Noel Canning a Victory for the Living Constitution? Constitutional Interpretation in an Age of Political Polarization* (Sept 24, 2014) ("Scalia's argument in *Noel Canning* is radical, not in the sense of being left-wing, but radical in the sense of seeking to return to the root of things and argue them once again based on first principles."), online at http://balkin.blogspot.com/2014/09/is-noel-canning-victory-for-living.html.

[238] *Youngstown*, 343 US at 610–11 (Frankfurter, J, concurring). See also, for example, Michael J. Glennon, *The Use of Custom in Resolving Separation of Powers Disputes*, 64 BU L Rev 109, 134 (1984) (contending that in order for historical practice to be credited in discerning the separation of powers, the other branch must have been on notice of the practice and "must have acquiesced" in it); Peter J. Spiro, *War Powers and the Sirens of Formalism*, 68 NYU L Rev 1339, 1356 (1993) (reviewing Ely, *War and Responsibility* (cited in note 229) ("[T]he other branch must have accepted or acquiesced in the action.").

[239] See Singer, *Property* at 149 (cited in note 230) (noting that "all states require the adverse possessor to show that possession was not permissive").

[240] To the extent that historical gloss is premised only on the acquiescence of the affected branch, it is not thought to require an actual agreement or bargain between the branches. Compare Aziz Z. Huq, *The Negotiated Structural Constitution*, 114 Colum L Rev 1595 (2014) (considering how allocations of authority between governmental institutions that are the product of "interbranch bargains" should be treated). In *Noel Canning*, for example, the majority did not claim that Congress or the Senate had authorized the President to exercise a broad recess appointments authority. Rather, it claimed that the Senate had not taken "any formal action . . . to call into question" intrasession recess appointments and had not "countered th[e] practice" of filling preexisting vacancies. See 134 S Ct at 2564, 2573.

successful in property law, it results in a complete transfer of property rights, such that the original owner can now be excluded from using the property. While it is possible to imagine historical practice supporting a claim of exclusive congressional or executive authority, in many instances its invocation shows no more than concurrent authority. For example, in foreign affairs settings such as war powers, executive agreements, the termination of treaties, and the like, substantial historical practice supports unilateral presidential authority, but little practice establishes that Congress is disabled from restricting or regulating that authority. In other words, separation of powers custom does not yield many instances of a disallowance of congressional regulation—that is, situations in which the President would prevail under Justice Jackson's third category from *Youngstown*.[241] To the extent that custom-based presidential authority is considered nonexclusive, it is more analogous to some sort of license or easement than to adverse possession.[242]

Moreover, even when historical gloss does produce something like exclusive executive authority, Congress often will be able to regulate it indirectly. That appears to be true, for example, for recess appointments. As a result of the majority's decision in *Noel Canning*, presidents are permitted to make recess appointments during substantial intrasession as well as intersession recesses, and can do so for vacancies that predate the recess. In a sense, that authority resembles an exclusive property right. As the majority made clear, however, Congress or one of its houses can take various actions to restrict the exercise of that right. Options include not taking a substantial recess that would trigger the recess appointments authority, breaking up a long recess with pro forma sessions, and using the appropriations power to disallow payment of certain recess appointees, as it long did (and still does to some extent) under the Pay Act.

---

[241] See *Youngstown*, 343 US at 637 (Jackson, J, concurring) ("When the President takes measures incompatible with the expressed or implied will of Congress, his power is at its lowest ebb, for then he can rely only upon his own constitutional powers minus any constitutional powers of Congress over the matter").

[242] This is not to suggest that the President is entirely lacking in exclusive authority, and the pending *Zivotofsky* case may address the boundaries of such authority as it concerns the recognition of foreign governments. See *Zivotofsky v Secretary of State*, 725 F3d 197 (DC Cir 2103), cert granted, 134 S Ct 1873 (2014). Even there, however, the practice better supports presidential unilateralism relating to recognition than it does exclusive presidential authority. See, for example, Robert J. Reinstein, *Is the President's Recognition Power Exclusive?*, 86 Temple L Rev 1 (2013). But other modalities of constitutional interpretation, such as inferences from the constitutional structure and consequentialist considerations, may help to compensate for ambiguities in the practice.

B. JUSTIFICATIONS FOR CREDITING PRACTICE

Although the analogy between the adverse possession doctrine in property law and the separation of powers is problematic for the reasons discussed above, some of the justifications for allowing adverse possession have potential relevance to the separation of powers. Perhaps more importantly, there are additional justifications for deferring to historical practice in the separation of powers context that are specific to constitutional law.

1. *Reasons for allowing adverse possession.* There are a number of reasons why property law has long allowed acquisitions through long-standing use. Some of the reasons are historical and, as such, are specific to property law, but there are functional justifications as well. Some of the most commonly cited justifications include promoting clarity of title, encouraging the most productive use of the resource, protecting reasonable expectation interests, and incentivizing the monitoring and policing of boundaries.[243] It is instructive to consider how those justifications might map onto a practice-based approach to the separation of powers.

a) Clarity of title. By vesting title in a possessor of land after a prescribed period of time, the adverse possession doctrine can help to clarify title by eliminating potential disputes. At first glance, that justification seems to have little relevance to the historical gloss method of interpretation, given the lack of any specified period in which separation of powers custom becomes a legal entitlement. Moreover, a custom of exercising particular powers is likely to be more amorphous than a custom of using land. Indeed, it is an almost inevitable feature of custom-based claims that there will be disputes about the scope of what the practice covers.[244]

Nevertheless, there might be instances in which crediting long-standing practice is the best way of achieving clarity in the distribu-

---

[243] See Singer, *Property* at 155–62 (cited in note 230).

[244] See, for example, Martin S. Flaherty, *Post-Originalism*, 68 U Chi L Rev 1089, 1105 (2001) (reviewing David P. Currie, *The Constitution in Congress: The Jeffersonians*, 1801–29 (Chicago, 2000)) ("As a theoretical matter, custom has its own problems. Not least among these are the questions of what counts as the relevant custom, at what level of generality, and for how long."). See also Michael D. Ramsey, *The Limits of Custom in Constitutional and International Law*, 50 San Diego L Rev 867 (2013) (attempting to distinguish between applications of custom that do not involve contested value judgments and those that do); Frederick Schauer, *Pitfalls in the Interpretation of Customary Law*, in Amanda Perreau-Saussine and James Bernard Murphy, eds, *The Nature of Customary Law* 27 (Cambridge, 2007) (noting that custom always can be described at differing levels of generality).

tion of constitutional authority. For example, sometimes the constitutional text is unclear or silent about a particular issue of authority, in which case the practice may offer the most concrete decisional material. To take one example, the text describes how treaties are to be made by the United States but says nothing about how they are to be terminated. Allowing long-standing practice to resolve the issue might provide more clarity than having the issue continually subject to (potentially new) arguments about the implications of text or original understandings.[245] Similarly, for war powers, once it is conceded that the President has some (but not unlimited) constitutional power to direct the use of military force without congressional authorization beyond repelling attacks, it may be difficult to discern the boundary of that power without at least some consideration of past practice.[246]

b) Encouraging productive use. Another potential justification for allowing the acquisition of property rights through adverse possession is that it will encourage productive use of the property. Again, the fit with separation of powers is not immediately obvious. Nevertheless, it might be argued that, when one branch assumes authority that potentially falls within the prerogatives of the other branch, and continues to exercise that authority for a long period of time without substantial objection, it is likely that, as between the two branches, the actor exercising the authority is the best positioned to use it.[247]

---

[245] Modern practice supports a unilateral presidential authority to terminate treaties, although that does not appear to have been the general understanding in the nineteenth century. See Curtis A. Bradley, *Treaty Termination and Historical Gloss*, 92 Tex L Rev 773, 800–01 (2014).

[246] See Spiro, 68 NYU L Rev at 1355 (cited in note 238) ("Ultimately, war powers law does not lend itself to refined parchment solutions. It is rather the 'court of history,' an accretion of interaction among the branches, that gives rise to basic norms governing the branches' behavior in the area."); Jane C. Stromseth, *Understanding Constitutional War Powers Today: Why Methodology Matters*, 106 Yale L J 845, 876 (1996) (reviewing Louis Fisher, *Presidential War Power* (Kansas, 1995)) ("[W]here the constitutional text is genuinely ambiguous or silent, as it is regarding issues such [as] the President's power as Commander in Chief to deploy forces abroad for foreign policy purposes in peacetime or the precise scope of the President's authority to 'repel sudden attacks,' longstanding and consistent historical practice can shed light on how we should understand the President's constitutional power today.").

[247] See Huq, 114 Colum L Rev at 1646–56 (cited in note 240) (arguing, on efficiency and other grounds, against a categorical prohibition on bargains between government institutions about the exercise of authority); Sunstein, 105 Mich L Rev at 401 (cited in note 120) ("If Congress and President Bush have settled on certain accommodations, there is reason to believe that those accommodations make institutional sense.").

Originalists understandably will object that, for better or worse, the Constitution settled the question of allocations of authority. One problem with the originalist position, however, is that the Founders' functional assessments do not take account of genuinely monumental changes in the nature of governance and international relations. Consider, for example, the rise of the administrative state. Even if the widespread delegation by Congress of what amounts to lawmaking authority to administrative agencies seems to offend original understandings of the separation of powers, the Founders could not have anticipated the nature of the modern national economy or the widely expected role of government in that economy. Another example is the rise of congressional-executive agreements in the twentieth century. Even if the Founders thought that all international agreements needed to be approved by two-thirds of the Senate, they entertained that thought at a time when the United States was expected to maintain only a handful of bilateral treaty relationships. The functional assessment is potentially very different in a post–United Nations era in which the United States has an interest in maintaining thousands of treaty relationships, including on many topics that overlap with the traditional regulatory authority of Congress (and not merely the Senate).[248]

This is not to suggest that the judiciary always will be able to make those functional assessments. The point, rather, is that the judiciary may reasonably conclude for some separation of powers issues that it cannot do a better job of making those assessments than can the political branches. That is what the Court in *Noel Canning* seemed to suggest when it noted that "[w]e have not previously interpreted the [Recess Appointments] Clause, and, when doing so for the first time in more than 200 years, we must hesitate to upset the compromises and working arrangements that the elected branches of Government themselves have reached."[249] Moreover, to reiterate an earlier point, if judicial precedent can compromise original understandings (as

---

[248] See, for example, Bruce Ackerman and David Golove, *Is NAFTA Constitutional?*, 108 Harv L Rev 799, 805 (1995), and Oona A. Hathaway, *Treaties' End: The Past, Present, and Future of International Lawmaking in the United States*, 117 Yale L J 1236 (2008). This does not mean, however, that historical practice necessarily supports complete interchangeability between treaties and executive agreements. See, for example, Peter J. Spiro, *Treaties, Executive Agreements, and Constitutional Method*, 79 Tex L Rev 961 (2001).

[249] 134 S Ct at 2560.

even many originalists allow), historical practices of the political branches—especially those practices that respond to monumental changes in the world—should be able to do the same.

c) Reliance interests. For the use of land, one reason for giving weight to long-standing use is that someone may have invested time and resources based on the belief that she would continue to reap the benefits of the investment. The majority in *Noel Canning* seemed to be concerned that, in the separation of powers context, historical practice can similarly generate institutional reliance interests. It noted, for example, that it was "reluctant to upset this traditional practice where doing so would seriously shrink the authority that Presidents have believed existed and have exercised for so long."[250] By contrast, in holding that Senate breaks of less then ten days are presumptively too short to trigger the President's recess appointments authority, the majority said that it did not perceive any presidential reliance on a recess appointments power for breaks of fewer than ten days.[251] For his part, Scalia denied that the historical practices in question had "created any justifiable expectations that could be disappointed by enforcing the Constitution's original meaning,"[252] but he did not elaborate.

In general, reliance does not appear to be an especially strong argument for crediting historical practice in the area of separation of powers. After all, a branch of government that has been exercising a particular type of authority presumably could simply cease exercising the authority going forward. Of course, there might be *third-party* reliance interests created by governmental actions taken in the past,[253] such as the NLRB decisions that had been made by recess appointees, but there are legal doctrines (such as the de facto officer doctrine) that might safeguard such interests.[254] And while it seems unlikely

---

[250] Id at 2573.

[251] See id at 2566.

[252] Id at 2617.

[253] See, for example, *United States v Midwest Oil Co.*, 236 US 459, 472–73 (1915) (noting that "officers, law-makers and citizens naturally adjust themselves to any long-continued action of the Executive Department—on the presumption that unauthorized acts would not have been allowed to be so often repeated as to crystallize into a regular practice").

[254] See David H. Carpenter and Todd Garvey, *Practical Implications of Noel Canning on the NLRB and CFPB* (Cong Res Serv, Apr 1, 2013), at http://www.cfpbmonitor.com/files/2013/04/Practical-Implications.pdf.

that such doctrines always would prevent externalities, it is also possible that such externalities might themselves reduce the likelihood that courts would deem an issue justiciable.[255]

Nevertheless, there may be instances in which a long-standing exercise of authority is embedded in what in essence is an interbranch bargain, pursuant to which the branch exercising authority has ceded another type of authority. If a court invalidated only one-half of such a bargain, it might unsettle reliance interests. A possible example is the Senate's practice of attaching reservations to its advice and consent to treaties. That practice was novel, both domestically and internationally, when the Senate first initiated the practice in connection with the Jay Treaty in 1795.[256] Importantly, the Senate developed that practice in response to the President's effort to avoid Senate involvement in the treaty negotiation process, notwithstanding the Constitution's assignment to the Senate of "advice and consent" authority, and it is one reason the Senate acquiesced in having that dual role reduced primarily to one of "consent." Invalidating the reservations authority at this late date might place the Senate in the difficult institutional and political position of having to recover a role in the treaty process that it has not effectively exercised since the early days of the nation.

d) Policing boundaries. The doctrine of adverse possession is also said to give owners of property an incentive to monitor and police the boundaries of the property. In some ways, that justification might seem to have the best fit with separation of powers, but in fact it highlights one of Justice Scalia's concerns. James Madison wrote in *Federalist No. 51* that the separation of powers would be self-enforcing by "giving to those who administer each department the necessary constitutional means and personal motives to resist encroachments of the others."[257] Under such a scheme, Madison posited, "[t]he interest of the man must be connected with the consti-

---

[255] See, for example, *Made in the USA Foundation v United States*, 242 F3d 1300, 1318 (11th Cir 2001) (holding that the government's decision to conclude the NAFTA trade agreement as a "congressional-executive agreement" rather than as an Article II treaty presented a political question, in part because holding this process unconstitutional "would potentially undermine every other major international commercial agreement made over the past half-century").

[256] See Curtis A. Bradley, *International Law in the U.S. Legal System* 35–36 (Oxford, 2013).

[257] Federalist 51 (Madison) at 321–22, in *The Federalist Papers* (cited in note 14).

tutional rights of the place," and "[a]mbition must be made to counteract ambition."[258] The possibility of losing a prerogative through inaction should heighten the incentive.

The problem with that justification, as a number of scholars have discussed, is that congressional-executive relations do not work in a Madisonian fashion, at least in the modern era.[259] In particular, because of collective action difficulties, veto-gates, the focus of legislators on reelection, a strong identification of individual members with partisan interests, and a strong disidentification of members with the institution given its unpopularity, Congress as a body does not consistently seek to protect its institutional prerogatives. (One of the many signs of this phenomenon is that Congress lacks an institutional counterpart to the Office of Legal Counsel.) Of course, Congress frequently does resist the policy initiatives of the executive branch, especially during times of divided government, and it has a variety of tools for doing so. But such resistance overlaps only imperfectly with institutional policing.[260]

2. *Additional reasons for crediting practice.* In sum, the justifications for allowing adverse possession in property law are not a close fit with the context of separation of powers disputes, although some of those justifications have partial relevance in that context. Importantly, however, there are additional justifications for crediting historical practice that are more specific to the constitutional law of separation of powers and that are therefore not captured, at least not fully, by the analogy to property law.

a) Respect for the coordinate branches. One justification for courts to defer to historic governmental practices relates to the "counter-

---

[258] Id at 322. We take no position here on whether or to what extent those statements in *Federalist No. 51* reflected Madison's actual views. Compare Samuel Kernell, *"The True Principles of Republican Government": Reassessing James Madison's Political Science*, in Samuel Kernell, ed, *James Madison: The Theory and Practice of Republican Government* 92, 93 (Stanford, 2003) (arguing that *Federalist No. 51* "does not represent Madison's sincere theoretical views of the Constitution").

[259] See, for example, Bradley and Morrison, 126 Harv L Rev at 438–47 (cited in note 95); Daryl J. Levinson, *Parchment and Politics: The Positive Puzzle of Constitutional Commitment*, 124 Harv L Rev 657, 671 (2011); Eric A. Posner and Adrian Vermeule, *The Credible Executive*, 74 U Chi L Rev 865, 884 (2007).

[260] Thus, the majority in *Noel Canning* was too casual in suggesting that "the Senate, like the President, has institutional 'resources,' including political resources, 'available to protect and assert its interests.'" 134 S Ct at 2569, quoting *Goldwater v Carter*, 444 US 996, 1004 (1979). See Bradley and Morrison, 126 Harv L Rev at 446 (cited in note 95).

majoritarian" nature of constitutional judicial review.[261] Although the concerns animating the countermajoritarian difficulty can be overstated, those concerns are particularly strong when both political branches share a view that is different from the judiciary's and have held that view for a long time. Judicial deference to the long-standing practices of the political branches can reduce those concerns. That is true regardless of whether one holds a "judicial supremacist" or a "departmentalist" view of constitutional interpretation. That is because the issue is not whether the Supreme Court should be understood as having the last word on constitutional issues, but rather how much respect it should give to the considered views of other constitutional actors when it decides those issues.[262] This justification for giving weight to the practices of the political branches is most applicable when there is evidence that those branches understand the practice in constitutional terms.

b) *Limits on judicial authority and capacity.* Deference to historical practice also can reflect limitations on judicial authority and capacity. Part of the idea here is that if the judiciary is too assertive in disturbing institutional practices, it risks having its judgments ignored by the political branches. It is in part for this reason that courts will be reluctant, for example, to decide the constitutionality of a war. But even assuming that the political branches will adhere to judicial decisions policing the relationship between legislative and executive power, not all aspects of that relationship are reducible to justiciable cases and controversies appropriate for judicial resolution. For instance, courts will not always have a sense of whether a given practice by one political branch truly intrudes upon the prerogatives or powers of the other, or what the ripple effects will be if the judiciary changes the status quo ante in a fundamental way. Moreover, the judicial tools for remedying such intrusions may be rather blunt and

---

[261] On the "countermajoritarian difficulty," see generally Alexander M. Bickel, *The Least Dangerous Branch: The Supreme Court at the Bar of Politics* 16–23 (1962). For a recent critique of this purported difficulty, see generally Barry Friedman, *The Will of the People* (Farrar, Strauss and Giroux, 2009).

[262] Compare *City of Boerne v Flores*, 521 US 507, 535–36 (1997) ("Our national experience teaches that the Constitution is preserved best when each part of the government respects both the Constitution and the proper actions and determinations of the other branches."). For a judicial supremacist, deference to long-standing historical practice is unlike deference to a statute that responds to an unpopular judicial decision. Notably, Justice Kennedy wrote the "judicial supremacist" opinion of the Court in *Boerne* and yet also joined the majority in *Noel Canning*.

imprecise. If Justice Scalia's view had prevailed in *Noel Canning*, for example, it likely would have resulted in the end of the President's recess appointments power as a practical matter, given the relatively short length of modern intersession recesses.

c) Constitutional updating. Another reason to credit historic governmental practice in separation of powers disputes is that the U.S. Constitution is very old and difficult to amend, and so is subject to serious "dead hand" objections. Crediting historic practice in the area of separation of powers allows the Constitution to evolve in response to the changing needs of the government. To reconcile that feature with the rhetorical appeal of originalism and textualism, historical practice is frequently described as an "interpretive gloss" rather than as a freestanding claim of constitutional meaning. At least in theory, that gloss is available only where the textual assignments of authority are unclear or incomplete, although, as discussed above, it seems likely that there is a feedback loop whereby perceptions of clarity and coverage are themselves affected by practice.

3. *Role of judicial review.* The last point—about constitutional updating—implicates an inherent tension between the benefits of customary evolution and centralized judicial review. Given the authority that federal courts possess in our constitutional system today, practice is likely to coordinate around judicial decisions. As a result, a judicial decision crediting practice has the potential to freeze the practice in place. That possibility might counsel courts to pursue an approach that Cass Sunstein has called "judicial minimalism" when they engage with customary practice, particularly where it appears that the practice is still in flux.[263] In some instances, it might even suggest judicial abstention altogether, through the political question doctrine or other mechanisms.

For example, in the Jerusalem passport case that has now returned to the Supreme Court, *Zivotofsky v Secretary of State*,[264] the Court, having previously rejected the applicability of the political question doctrine,[265] is confronted with a choice between two potentially

---

[263] See Sunstein, 105 Mich L Rev (cited in note 120). One can approve of minimalism in this context without approving of it as a general approach to constitutional adjudication. For a general critique, see Neil S. Siegel, *A Theory in Search of a Court, and Itself: Judicial Minimalism at the Supreme Court Bar*, 103 Mich L Rev 1951 (2005).

[264] 725 F3d 197 (DC Cir 2103), cert granted, 134 S Ct 1873 (2014).

[265] See note 91.

problematic options: endorsing executive disregard of a statute, or allowing congressional intrusion in sensitive Middle East diplomacy in a manner that is contrary to long-standing executive branch positions held by presidents of both parties. In a case like that one, some uncertainty about the distribution of authority may be optimal. In other words, unlike in property law, clarity of title may not always be the desired aim in the area of separation of powers.

Furthermore, if one is concerned about the growth of executive power, one should not assume that more robust judicial review will be a corrective, because it is possible, if not probable, that courts will end up legitimating many exercises of executive authority.[266] For example, interpreters who regard the justiciability of *Zivotofsky* as a close question may be inclined to favor resolving a similarly close question on the merits in such a way as to preserve the state of affairs that would have prevailed in the absence of judicial intervention.[267] In *Zivotofsky*, that would mean holding in favor of the President's position.

This does not mean, however, that either abstention or minimalism is always the best course. For example, the majority opinion in *Noel Canning* was closer to maximalism than to minimalism. It decided all three of the questions before it, even though the case could have been resolved on the narrowest ground, which concerned the minimum length of a recess and the effect of the pro forma sessions.

On balance, we think the majority's decision to resolve all three issues made sense. First, the historical practice concerning both intrasession appointments and prevacancy appointments was well established before the D.C. Circuit's decision in the case, and further customary evolution was unlikely. Second, the decision of the D.C.

---

[266] Compare Eric A. Posner and Adrian Vermeule, *Inside or Outside the System?*, 80 U Chi L Rev 1743, 1752 (2013) ("[A]rguments for 'Madisonian' judging go wrong by assuming that judges stand outside the Madisonian system.").

[267] We are not suggesting that the Court should decide the merits of a case incorrectly in order to take proper account of justiciability concerns. We are instead suggesting that, in cases presenting close questions both of justiciability and on the merits, justiciability concerns may have a role to play in tipping the balance one way or the other even after the Court decides to reach the merits. Compare Bradley and Morrison, 126 Harv L Rev at 430 (cited in note 95) (suggesting that the political question doctrine and the historical gloss method of interpretation can be viewed as simply reflecting different degrees of deference to political branch practice); Richard H. Fallon, Jr., *Judicially Manageable Standards and Constitutional Meaning*, 119 Harv L Rev 1274, 1306 (2006) ("Viewed along a spectrum, a determination of nonjusticiability due to the absence of judicially manageable standards is simply the limiting case of a decision to underenforce constitutional norms.").

Circuit was itself maximalist, and it would have been left in place had the Supreme Court ruled narrowly. Third, because appointments to bodies like the NLRB implicate the legitimacy of administrative decision making, with a multitude of consequences for third parties, there were strong reasons for not leaving the questions unsettled in the face of the new uncertainty.[268] Fourth, other cases already were pending in the lower courts that implicated the broader questions,[269] so a minimalist approach would not have had much effect in terms of clearing space for a nonjudicial resolution. Finally, as noted above, the decision in *Noel Canning* leaves the Senate with several options for resisting broad exercises of the recess appointments power, so the effect of the decision on the relative balance of authority between the branches may be modest.

C. EXECUTIVE AGGRANDIZEMENT AND INDIVIDUAL LIBERTY

Despite those potential justifications for crediting historical practice in the area of separation of powers, Justice Scalia's two objections are serious ones. First, he expressed concern that a practice-based approach to the separation of powers would unduly favor the expansion of executive authority. "In any controversy between the political branches over a separation-of-powers question," Justice Scalia noted, "staking out a position and defending it over time is far easier for the Executive Branch than for the Legislative Branch."[270] Crediting practice, he therefore argued, will allow the President to continue accreting power vis-à-vis Congress over time.

That concern has force, and one of us has emphasized it elsewhere.[271] Nevertheless, it suggests caution in crediting historical practice, not a rejection of it. One way to reduce the concern would be to calibrate the test for historical gloss in a way that would take account of the institutional realities of the congressional-executive relationship. For example, given the diminished incentive of members of Congress to challenge the President if he or she is of the same party, more weight should be given to acquiescence in practice

---

[268] Compare Siegel, 103 Mich L Rev at 2007 (cited in note 263) (emphasizing that judicial minimalism may compromise the guidance function of the rule of law).

[269] See 134 S Ct at 2558.

[270] Id at 2605, citing Bradley and Morrison, 126 Harv L Rev at 439–47 (cited in note 95).

[271] See Bradley and Morrison, 126 Harv L Rev at 438–47 (cited in note 95).

by the opposing party as well as nonacquiescence by the same party.[272] In addition, to take account of Congress's greater collective action difficulties as compared with the executive branch, mere congressional inaction or silence rarely should be considered sufficient to constitute legally significant acceptance of a practice. Relatedly, evidence of congressional nonacquiescence should extend beyond the enactment of opposing statutes and should include various forms of congressional "soft law," such as committee reports and nonbinding resolutions.[273] And, in those instances in which Congress actually has managed to enact legislation restricting executive authority without constitutional objection from the President, arguments for contrary executive authority based on practice should be viewed with skepticism.[274] At the same time, when Congress has actively regulated in an area, what it chooses *not* to regulate potentially can be evidence of acquiescence, because in those instances Congress by assumption has overcome at least some of its collective action difficulties.

Given the greater ability and incentives of the executive branch to defend its institutional prerogatives, the test for executive acquiescence in assertions of authority by Congress should be less stringent. Thus, for example, long-standing executive inaction in the face of congressional assertions of authority should receive significant weight in discerning congressional authority. This point serves as a reminder that, although historical gloss is frequently invoked to justify claims of executive authority (and that is how Frankfurter described it), there is nothing inherent in the historical gloss approach to the separation of powers that would preclude Congress from gaining authority through custom. Indeed, as a general matter (putting aside for a moment conflicts with the President), Congress almost certainly has gained authority in that way. For example, a key reason that the vast majority of Justices and commentators reject a

---

[272] See id at 454.

[273] For discussions of congressional soft law, see Josh Chafetz, *Congress's Constitution*, 160 U Pa L Rev 716 (2012), and Jacob E. Gersen and Eric A. Posner, *Soft Law: Lessons from Congressional Practice*, 61 Stan L Rev 573 (2008). The majority in *Noel Canning* may have given a nudge to the consideration of soft law in noting that "neither the Senate considered as a body *nor its committees*, despite opportunities to express opposition to the practice of intra-session recess appointments, has done so." 134 S Ct at 2563 (emphasis added).

[274] For example, the existence of the 1978 Foreign Intelligence Surveillance Act, which limited and regulated electronic surveillance, should have made the Bush administration's practice-based arguments in support of a broader surveillance power difficult to sustain. See Bradley and Morrison, 126 Harv L Rev at 449 (cited in note 95).

narrow approach to Congress's enumerated powers is that Congress long has exercised broad powers to tax, spend, and regulate. Another reason, of course, is judicial precedent affirming the broader authority, including the *McCulloch* decision discussed in Part II. But it is easy to forget that deferring to such precedent itself can allow a form of "adverse possession," albeit by one group of Supreme Court Justices vis-à-vis a later group.

In *Noel Canning*, the majority's decision to credit the historical practice of broad presidential exercise of the recess appointments power is defensible even in light of the cautionary approach suggested above. That practice is long-standing and has been relied upon by presidents of both major political parties, during times of both unified and divided government. Moreover, allowing such presidential authority does not disable either Congress or the Senate from taking actions to resist exercises of that authority. Regarding the specific practice of intrasession recess appointments, Congress has done nothing, either as a body or even through committee action, to resist the exercise of presidential authority, even when Congress otherwise has regulated in the area. As for appointments to fill preexisting vacancies, even if one concludes that the 1863 Pay Act signified Congress's nonacquiescence, it seems reasonable to credit the 1940 amendments to the act as signifying a change of position, especially after the Comptroller General already had observed in 1927 that presidential authority to make those appointments was settled.

Scalia's second objection was that third-party interests are at stake in the distribution of institutional authority. In particular, Scalia emphasized that the purpose of distributing governmental authority is not to provide particular entitlements to the branches per se, but rather to protect liberty by diffusing power. Again, that is a legitimate concern, but it paints too broadly.

As an initial matter, protecting liberty may be a central justification for the Constitution's checks and balances, but that is only one aspect of the separation of powers. Another aspect is the distribution of authority in a manner that enables effective governance.[275] In addition, liberty is a deeply contested concept, and effective governance may itself be essential for the promotion of a positive conception of

---

[275] See *Youngstown*, 343 US at 635 (Jackson, J, concurring) ("While the Constitution diffuses power the better to secure liberty, it also contemplates that practice will integrate the dispersed powers into a workable government.").

liberty. Moreover, even under a purely negative conception of liberty, effective governance may be essential for liberty in the long term—for example, by safeguarding against external threats. Consistent with these points, the majority in *Noel Canning* quoted Alexander Hamilton from the first *Federalist Paper* for the proposition that the "vigour of government is essential to the protection of liberty."[276]

In any event, not all separation of powers issues have a direct connection to liberty. The connection between liberty interests and the recess appointments issues in *Noel Canning*, for example, is abstract and attenuated. Similarly, for other governmental practices that have been heavily informed by practice—such as the practice of having Congress rather than a supermajority of the Senate approve many international agreements—there is no obvious tension with individual liberty. Of course, some separation of powers issues *are* directly connected to negative liberty. An obvious example would be the separation of the power over criminal lawmaking from the powers over criminal law enforcement and interpretation. This is one reason why there was so much concern about the Bush administration's use of military commissions prior to the enactment of the Military Commissions Act.[277] Importantly, as illustrated by the Supreme Court's disallowance of these commissions in *Hamdan v Rumsfeld*, it is precisely where individual liberty interests are most implicated that judicial review is most likely to occur, which in turn leaves less space for the accretion of constitutional custom.[278]

VI. Conclusion

The significance of *Noel Canning* extends well beyond its resolution of important questions about the scope of the President's recess appointments power. The decision stands as one of the Supreme Court's most significant endorsements of the relevance of

---

[276] 134 S Ct at 2577.

[277] See, for example, Harold Hongju Koh, *The Case Against Military Commissions*, 96 Am J Intl L 337, 339 (2002) ("Fundamentally, [Bush's] Military Order undermines the constitutional principle of separation of powers."); *Hamdan v Rumsfeld*, 548 US 557, 638 (2006) (Kennedy, J, concurring in part) ("Trial by military commission raises separation-of-powers concerns of the highest order."). Another separation of powers concern relating to the commissions is that they bypass the regular federal courts, and that concern was not eliminated by Congress's authorization of the commissions in 2006.

[278] See also *Boumediene v Bush*, 553 US 723, 765 (2008) ("[T]he writ of habeas corpus is itself an indispensable mechanism for monitoring the separation of powers.").

"historical gloss" to the interpretation of the separation of powers. More generally, *Noel Canning* exemplifies how the constitutional text, perceptions about clarity or ambiguity, and "extratextual" considerations such as historical practice operate interactively rather than as separate elements of interpretation. The decision also provides a useful entry point into critically analyzing the concept of constitutional liquidation, which the majority in *Noel Canning* seemed to conflate with historical gloss but which seems more consistent with the approach to historical practice reflected in Justice Scalia's concurrence in the judgment. Finally, the decision illustrates that the historical gloss approach, when applied cautiously and with sensitivity to the potential concerns that Justice Scalia and others have raised, is not vulnerable to the charge of licensing executive aggrandizement by "adverse possession."

WILLIAM P. MARSHALL

BAD STATUTES MAKE BAD LAW:
BURWELL v HOBBY LOBBY

Employment Division v Smith[1] was a monumental decision. The case overturned an iconic holding of the Warren Court which held that laws that incidentally burden a believer's religious exercise must be supported by a "compelling state interest."[2] In so doing, *Smith* effectively reduced the role of the Free Exercise Clause in protecting religious exercise to one of only marginal significance.[3] After *Smith*, the Free Exercise Clause would no longer be interpreted to grant reli-

---

William P. Marshall is Kenan Professor of Law, University of North Carolina.

AUTHOR'S NOTE: I am deeply grateful to Ira Lupu, Reva Siegel, Douglas NeJaime, Dana Remus, Nelson Tebbe, and Tom Forgue for their comments on an earlier draft of this article. Thanks also to Claire O'Brien and Tyson Leonhardt for their outstanding research assistance.

[1] 494 US 872 (1990).

[2] See *Sherbert v Verner*, 374 US 398, 403 (1963), quoting *National Association for the Advancement of Colored People v Button*, 371 US 415, 438 (1963). See also *Sherbert*, 374 US at 406–09 (discussing the compelling interest standard). The compelling interest test requires that the state cannot burden free exercise absent a compelling state interest. As will be discussed below, the Court did not consistently apply the compelling interest standard with any rigor even prior to the *Smith* decision.

[3] *Smith* does hold that the Free Exercise Clause protects against the government singling out religion or religious believers for disfavored treatment. *Smith*, 494 US at 877 ("The government may not . . . impose special disabilities on the basis of religious views or religious status.") (citations omitted). See also *Church of the Lukumi Babalu Aye, Inc. v City of Hialeah*, 508 US 520, 533 (1993) ("Although a law targeting religious beliefs as such is never permissible . . . if the object of a law is to infringe upon or restrict practices because of their religious motivation, the law is not neutral, see [*Smith*] and it is invalid unless it is justified by a compelling interest and is narrowly tailored to advance that interest.") (citations omitted).

---

gious objectors constitutionally compelled exemptions from valid and neutral laws of general applicability.[4]

The response to *Smith* was equally dramatic.[5] The decision was denounced from nearly all directions[6] as not being sufficiently protective of religious freedom[7] and it was harshly condemned by prominent commentators for its reasoning and methodology.[8] Moreover, unlike many objections to Supreme Court decisions, the protests against *Smith* quickly turned into action,[9] as a broad coalition encompassing groups as diverse as the ACLU and the National Association of Evangelicals came together to seek legislative reform.[10] In 1993, three years after *Smith* was decided, the Congress over-

---

[4] *Smith*, 494 US at 879, quoting *United States v Lee*, 455 US 252, 263 n 3 (1982) (Stevens, J, concurring in judgment). See also *Smith*, 494 US at 886 n 3 ("[G]enerally applicable, religion-neutral laws that have the effect of burdening a particular religious practice need not be justified by a compelling governmental interest.").

[5] Nelson Tebbe, *Smith in Theory and Practice*, 32 Cardozo L Rev 2055, 2056–57 (2011) (noting that *Smith* "caused a kerfuffle at the time it was delivered" and continued to evoke tension twenty years after it was issued).

[6] I should note that I was one of the writers who contemporaneously defended the *Smith* decision. See William P. Marshall, *In Defense of Smith and Free Exercise Revisionism*, 58 U Chi L Rev 308 (1991).

[7] Linda Greenhouse, *Court Is Urged to Rehear Case on Ritual Drugs*, NY Times at A16 (May 11, 1990), online at http://www.nytimes.com (search article title) (discussing a motion filed by a coalition of groups to reconsider *Smith* that included the American Jewish Congress, the National Council of Churches, the National Association of Evangelicals, the American Friends Service Committee, the General Conference of Seventh-day Adventists, the American Civil Liberties Union, People for the American Way, and the Rutherford Institute). The *Times* article quoted Oliver S. Thomas, general counsel of the Baptist Joint Committee on Public Affairs, as noting that all these diverse groups agree that the opinion was "disastrous for the free exercise of religion." Id.

[8] See, for example, Douglas Laycock, *The Remnants of Free Exercise*, 1990 Supreme Court Review 1, 33; Michael W. McConnell, *Free Exercise Revisionism and the Smith Decision*, 57 U Chi L Rev 1109, 1127 (1990); James Gordon, *Free Exercise on the Mountaintop*, 79 Cal L Rev 91 (1991).

[9] See Frederick Mark Gedicks, *Towards a Defensible Free Exercise Doctrine*, 68 Geo Wash L Rev 925, 925 (2000) ("Almost from the moment that the Supreme Court abandoned the religious exemption doctrine in *Employment Division v Smith*, its defenders have worked to bring it back.").

[10] Some Catholic groups, notably, did not join this coalition primarily because they were concerned that a new law might allow for religious exemptions from abortion restrictions if *Roe v Wade* were to be overturned. See Douglas Laycock, *Free Exercise and the Religious Freedom Restoration Act*, 62 Fordham L Rev 883, 896 (1994). See also Marty Lederman, *Hobby Lobby Part XVIII—The One (Potentially) Momentous Aspect of Hobby Lobby: Untethering RFRA from Free Exercise Doctrine* (Balkinization, July 6, 2014), online at http://balkin.blogspot.com/2014/07/hobby-lobby-part-xviii-one-potentially.html (noting that some members of Congress expressed reservations about RFRA because of the concern that the statute might allow exemptions from antiabortion requirements).

whelmingly passed the Religious Freedom Restoration Act (RFRA)[11] to undo the Court's decision and resurrect the compelling interest standard.[12]

Two decades later, RFRA sparked another moment of high drama.[13] Bringing together the highly charged elements of religion, reproductive rights, and the Patient Protection and Affordable Care Act (referred to in this article as the Affordable Care Act [ACA] or "Obamacare"),[14] the Court in *Burwell v Hobby Lobby*[15] held that RFRA entitled certain for-profit corporations to religious exemptions from portions of the so-called "contraceptive mandate"[16] or "contraceptive coverage requirement" regulations promulgated under the Affordable Care Act.[17] In contrast to *Smith*, this time the reaction to the Court's decision, though raucous,[18] was neither uniform nor focused on issues of religious freedom. Rather, the response to the Court's decision turned as much on competing views of the ACA and reproductive rights as it did on freedom of religion.[19]

In the long run, however, *Hobby Lobby*'s significance as a judicial precedent will rest less on its treatment of the politically controversial issues of contraception and the ACA than on its understanding

---

[11] Religious Freedom Restoration Act, Pub L No 103-141, 107 Stat 1488 (1993), codified at 42 USC §§ 2000bb et seq.

[12] 42 USC § 2000bb-1(b).

[13] This is not to say that the litigation surrounding RFRA was uneventful during those two decades. To the contrary. In 1997, the Court in *City of Boerne v Flores*, 521 US 507 (1997), issued a landmark federalism decision when it held that RFRA's application to the states exceeded Congress's power under Section 5 of the Fourteenth Amendment.

[14] Patient Protection and Affordable Care Act, Pub L No 111-148, 124 Stat 119 (2010), codified at various locations throughout Titles 26 and 42 of the United States Code.

[15] 134 S Ct 2751 (*Hobby Lobby*).

[16] The obligations are referred to as a "mandate" (and, frequently, the "contraceptive mandate") in Justice Alito's majority opinion and in Justice Kennedy's concurrence but as the "contraceptive coverage requirement" in Justice Ginsburg's dissent.

[17] Specifically, the plaintiffs challenged sought an exemption from the requirement to provide coverage for contraceptive methods that can operate after the fertilization of an egg. See notes 60–73 and accompanying text (discussing the process leading to the implementation of the contraceptive coverage requirements). See also *Hobby Lobby*, 134 S Ct at 2762–64.

[18] See, for example, Robin Abcarian, *At the Supreme Court, Baffling Decision Follows Awful Hobby Lobby Ruling*, LA Times (July 7, 2014), online at http://www.latimes.com/local/abcarian /la-me-ra-supreme-court-baffling-decision-20140707-column.html (describing the Hobby Lobby decision as "deeply offensive to women").

[19] For example, New York Times Editorial Board, *Limiting Rights: Imposing Religion on Workers*, online at http://www.nytimes.com/2014/07/01/opinion/the-supreme-court-imposing -religion-on-workers.html.

of RFRA's central subject—the rights of religious objectors to be exempt from neutral laws. The majority in *Hobby Lobby* interpreted RFRA broadly, ostensibly affording more protection to religious exercise under the statute than had previously been recognized under the Free Exercise Clause in the Court's pre-*Smith* regime.[20]

Yet there are serious questions as to how, or whether, the Court's reading of RFRA in *Hobby Lobby* can be maintained in future cases.[21] Indeed, there is significant question whether even a narrower interpretation of RFRA, such as the one offered by the dissenters in *Hobby Lobby*, which would only restore the pre-*Smith* case law, could realistically be maintained going forward. *Smith* was decided the way it was for a reason. As I discuss below, the pre-*Smith* decisions demonstrated that the application of a compelling interest test to religious exercise challenge raises serious problems of coherency and consistency. It also leads to a troubling form of relief—special exemptions from neutral laws for a limited class of beneficiaries—that is in tension with other constitutional principles and that opens the door to a disconcerting favoritism for those able to frame their objections to neutral laws in religious terms. Further, the compelling interest test raises serious constitutional issues because it requires courts to get into the dangerous businesses of defining religion, evaluating religious sincerity, and measuring religious burdens.[22] These concerns do not subside because the compelling interest test stems from a statute rather than a constitutional provision.

The Court's suggestion in *Hobby Lobby* that RFRA accords more protection to religious claimants than the Free Exercise Clause cases

---

[20] *Hobby Lobby*, 134 S Ct at 2772 (noting that "nothing in the text of RFRA as originally enacted suggested that the statutory phrase 'exercise of religion under the First Amendment' was meant to be tied to [the pre-*Smith*] interpretation of that Amendment. . . . It is simply not possible to read [RFRA and RLUIPA] as restricting the concept of the 'exercise of religion' to those practices specifically addressed in our pre-*Smith* decisions."). See also id at 2762–63 (noting that in "an obvious effort to effect a complete separation from First Amendment case law, Congress deleted the reference to the First Amendment); id at 2767 ("By enacting RFRA, Congress went far beyond what this Court has held is constitutionally required.").

[21] See Ira C. Lupu, *Hobby Lobby and the Dubious Enterprise of Religious Exemptions*, 38 Harv J L & Gender 35 (2015) (arguing that applying a compelling interest test to religious exercise is "highly likely to be unprincipled, ad hoc, inconsistent, subject to manipulation, and frequently biased for or against certain faiths."). In RLIUPA cases decided after *Hobby Lobby*, the Court continued to assert that it will apply the compelling interest test expansively in religious exercise cases. See *Holt v Hobbs*, 135 S Ct 853 (2015) (striking down a prison regulation limiting facial hair as applied to a religious objector).

[22] See *Hobby Lobby*, 134 S Ct at 2778 ("the federal courts have no business addressing . . . whether the religious belief asserted in a RFRA case is reasonable.").

in the pre-*Smith* era exacerbates these concerns while raising others. A robust application of RFRA invites challenges to federal regulatory measures based upon relatively thin religious claims and potentially encourages a conflation of religious, economic, and political assertions by RFRA claimants in a manner that could potentially harm both religion and politics. To the extent that *Hobby Lobby* faithfully interpreted RFRA, then, it sends a clear lesson. Much like hard cases, bad statutes make bad law.[23]

In this article, I demonstrate why RFRA and its interpretation by the Court in *Hobby Lobby* are problematic. Part I traces the enactment of RFRA and its history before the Court leading up to *Hobby Lobby*. Part II introduces *Hobby Lobby*. It sets forth the factual background to the litigation and identifies the key points of statutory interpretation at issue, including the core question of whether RFRA should be interpreted as restoring the pre-*Smith* free exercise jurisprudence or as providing even greater protection for religious exercise than the free exercise cases had allowed. Part III provides insight into that issue by describing the free exercise jurisprudence that led up to *Smith* and explaining why that jurisprudence proved unsuccessful. Part IV than returns to *Hobby Lobby* to assess the majority and dissenting opinions in light of this pre-*Smith* history. Part V examines what the Court's construction of RFRA portends for future cases. It argues that, at best, the Court's interpretation of RFRA will lead to a jumbled jurisprudence beset by the same problems that plagued the Court's pre-*Smith* free exercise decisions. At worst it may lead to results that are normatively problematic and constitutionally unsound. Part V suggests, however, that the blame for any problems with RFRA going forward may rest less with the Court's construction of the statute than with the Congress that passed it. Part VI offers a brief conclusion.

One point before proceeding. Much has already been written about *Hobby Lobby* and its place in the debates regarding reproductive

---

[23] See generally *Northern Securities Co. v United States*, 193 US 197, 400–401 (1904) ("Great cases like hard cases make bad law. For great cases are called great not by reason of their real importance in shaping the law of the future, but because of some accident of immediate overwhelming interest which appeals to the feelings and distorts the judgment. These immediate interests exercise a kind of hydraulic pressure which makes what previously was clear seem doubtful, and before which even well settled principles of law will bend.") (Holmes, J, dissenting); Ronald Dworkin, *Hard Cases*, 88 Harv L Rev 1057 (1975); Frederick Schauer, *Do Hard Cases Make Bad Law?*, 73 U Chi L Rev 883, 884 (2006).

rights and/or civil rights.[24] My intention in this article is to focus on the viability of *Hobby Lobby* as a precedent for applying RFRA generally and not on its application in those specific substantive areas.

I. Background

A. RFRA

The enactment of RFRA was greeted with much celebration. In his remarks at the ceremony signing the bill into law, President Bill Clinton stated that "[t]oday this event assumes a more majestic quality because of our ability together to affirm the historic role that people of faith have played in the history of this country and the constitutional protections those who profess and express their faith have always demanded and cherished."[25] Political leaders from both parties expressed similar sentiments,[26] as did many religious leaders. J. Brent Walker, general counsel of the Baptist Joint Committee on Public Affairs, for example, called the new law "the most significant piece of legislation dealing with our religious liberty in a generation."[27]

The exuberance surrounding RFRA's passage did not last for long. Four years later, the Court substantially limited the statute's reach when it held in *City of Boerne v Flores*[28] that its application to the states was unconstitutional on federalism grounds.[29] Again, as after *Smith*, the Court was subjected to widespread criticism, and

---

[24] See, for example, Paul Horwitz, *The Hobby Lobby Moment*, 128 Harv L Rev 154 (2014); Erin Morrow Hawley, *The Jurisdictional Question in Hobby Lobby*, 124 Yale L J Forum 63 (2014); Ben Adams and Cynthia Barmore, *Questioning Sincerity: The Role of the Courts after Hobby Lobby*, 67 Stan L Rev Online 59 (2014); Corey A. Ciocchetti, *Religious Freedom and Closely-Held Corporations: The Hobby Lobby Case and Its Ethical Implications*, 93 Or L Rev (forthcoming 2015), http://papers.ssrn.com/sol3/papers.cfm?abstract_id=2495506##.

[25] William J. Clinton, *Remarks on Signing the Religious Freedom Restoration Act of 1993, Nov. 16, 1993, 1993[2] Public Papers of the President: Administration of William J. Clinton* 2000 (1994).

[26] See Peter Steinfels, *Clinton Signs Law Protecting Religious Practices*, NY Times (Nov 17, 1993), online at http://www.nytimes.com/1993/11/17/us/clinton-signs-law-protecting-religious -practices.html (noting the positive reactions of a broad range of liberal, conservative, and religious groups, including the National Association of Evangelicals and the American Civil Liberties Union).

[27] Id.

[28] 521 US 507 (1997).

[29] See id at 519 (holding that applying RFRA to the states exceeds Congress's power under § 5 of the Fourteenth Amendment). The Court's decision was anticipated in Daniel O. Conkle, *The Religious Freedom Restoration Act: The Constitutional Significance of an Unconstitutional Statute*, 56 Mont L Rev 39, 50 (1995) ("Federalism . . . weighs against the constitutionality of RFRA.").

again the Court's action brought together a broad coalition of organizations seeking legislative reform to provide strong free exercise
protections against state action. This time, however, the coalition
fragmented.[30] Some groups remained committed to expansive free
exercise protections,[31] whereas others grew concerned that too stringent protection of religious liberty might conflict with civil rights
legislation in circumstances in which believers might raise free exercise objections to laws requiring nondiscriminatory treatment of
gays and unmarried couples.[32]

In the end, Congress responded to *Boerne* with the Religious
Land Use and Institutionalized Persons Act of 2000 (RLUIPA).[33]
RLUIPA, however, did not offer the across-the-board protection
from state action infringing religious exercise that RFRA provided.
Rather, as its name suggests, it protected religious exercise only in
two circumstances—land use regulation and prisoners' rights.[34]

RFRA, however, continued to provide across-the-board protection of religious exercise against federal power. The Clinton administration construed *Boerne* as invalidating RFRA only as it applied
to the states,[35] and that position was subsequently confirmed by the
Supreme Court.[36] Congress, meanwhile, made clear in RLUIPA that
RFRA applied only to the federal government,[37] and further defined
the meaning of religious exercise in RFRA to include "any exercise
of religion, whether or not compelled by, or central to, a system of
religious belief."[38]

---

[30] See James M. Oleske, Jr., *Obamacare, RFRA, and the Perils of Legislative History*, 67 Vand L
Rev en banc 77, 81 (2014) (describing the unsuccessful efforts to pass the proposed Religious
Liberty Protection Act after the *Boerne* decision and the breakdown of the RFRA coalition over
the issue of whether religious exemptions should be allowed from civil rights legislation).

[31] Id.

[32] Id.

[33] Religious Land Use and Institutionalized Persons Act of 2000, Pub L No 106-274, 114
Stat 804 (2000), substantially codified at 42 USC § 2000cc, et seq (RLUIPA).

[34] 42 USC §§ 2000cc, 2000cc-1.

[35] See David M. Ackerman, *The Religious Freedom Restoration Act: Its Rise, Fall, and Current
Status*, CRS Report for Congress, 5–6 (1998) (noting that the Clinton administration took the
position that RFRA was still valid with respect to the federal government, because application
to federal government was supported by the "necessary and proper" clause of Article I, § 8 of
the Constitution, as opposed to the Fourteenth Amendment).

[36] *Gonzales v O Centro Espirita Beneficente Uniao do Vegetal*, 546 US 418 (2006).

[37] RLUIPA, Pub L No 106-274, § 7(a)(1), (a)(2), (b), 114 Stat at 806, codified at 42 USC
§§ 2000bb-2(1), 2000bb-2(2), 2000bb-3(a).

[38] RLUIPA, Pub L No 106-274, § 7(a)(3), 114 Stat at 806, codified at 42 USC § 2000bb-2(4)
(referencing the definition of "religious exercise codified in 42 USC § 2000cc-5(7)).

B. GONZALES V O CENTRO ESPIRITA BENEFICENTE UNIAO DO VEGETAL

The first case to reach the Court under RFRA was *Gonzales v O Centro Espirita Beneficente Uniao do Vegetal*.[39] *Gonzales* involved an RFRA challenge, brought by a small Christian spiritualist sect, the O Centro Espirita Beneficente Uniao do Vegetal (UDV), to restrictions imposed by the Controlled Substances Act (CSA) on the importation and use of a hallucinogenic substance (DMT) contained in a plant from the Amazon region in South America.[40] The UDV maintained that it used this ingredient to make a sacramental tea, "hoasca," for receiving communion, and that the restriction on DMT therefore burdened its religious exercise.[41]

The government conceded the religiosity and the sincerity of UDV's claim,[42] but contended that the restriction was justified by compelling state interests.[43] First, it argued that DMT created certain health risks to users. Second, it argued that providing an exemption for the UDV would send the message that the drug was not dangerous.[44] Third, the government asserted a general interest in uniformity in the administration of drug laws and contended that to allow an exemption in this case would invite other suits for exemptions from the CSA for the use of DMT and other controlled substances.[45]

In a unanimous opinion, the Court held RFRA required the grant of an exemption.[46] The result was not surprising. RFRA had been precipitated, after all, by a decision (*Smith*) that rejected a virtually identical claim. As the Court noted, "the very reason Congress enacted RFRA was to respond to a decision denying a claimed right to sacramental use of a controlled substance."[47]

---

[39] *Gonzales v O Centro Espirita Beneficente Uniao do Vegetal*, 546 US 418, 424 n 1 (2006).

[40] Id at 423.

[41] Id at 425–26.

[42] Id at 423.

[43] Id at 430–38.

[44] Id at 432–34.

[45] Id at 434–37.

[46] Id at 422, 439 (Justice Alito did not participate).

[47] Id at 436–37. It is also true, however, as Professor Ira C. Lupu notes, that Congressional intent regarding the facts in *Smith* itself may not have been so clear. As Lupu notes, when RFRA was passed, "[a]lmost everyone in the enacting Congress was a fan of religious freedom; not a single one stood up and said that members of the Native American Church had a constitutional right to use peyote in their sacraments." Lupu, 38 Harv J L & Gender (cited in note 21).

Some aspects of the Court's analysis, however, were surprising, especially in light of the Court's often lukewarm record with respect to free exercise challenges pre-*Smith*. As Ira Lupu has observed, the *Gonzales* Court made two things clear about RFRA cases—the burden is on the government to justify its restrictions, and government claims that uniformity in administration is important generally would not carry the day.[48] Both of these judgments would pose serious obstacles to government efforts to defend general laws of neutral application against RFRA challenges.[49]

The Court's strong defense of the feasibility of applying the compelling interest test in RFRA cases was also surprising. As I discuss below, *Smith* was based in large part on the inherent difficulties of applying that test in the context of free exercise claims. Nevertheless, the Court in *Gonzales* stated that it "had 'no cause to believe' that the compelling interest test 'would not be applied in an appropriately balanced way' to specific claims for exemptions as they arose."[50] *Gonzales*, in other words, seemed to suggest that RFRA's compelling interest test should be vigorously applied.[51]

Other aspects of the case, however, suggested a different reading. First, the Court relied heavily on the fact that the use of peyote for religious purposes was exempt from the CSA, thereby providing a ready blueprint for distinguishing *Gonzales* in later cases that did not involve an existing parallel government-granted exemption benefiting other religious sects. Second, as noted above, the result in *Gonzales* seemed largely a foregone conclusion given that RFRA was enacted in response to a case with virtually identical facts: a small religious sect seeking an exemption from the CSA for the sacramental use of a hallucinogen that had a very limited (if any) market for recreational use.[52] Other RFRA claims would be unlikely to have

---

[48] See Lupu, 38 Harv J L & Gender at 63 (cited in note 21) (noting the Court's strong dismissal of the government's arguments in what he calls "*O Centro*'s double move to strengthen RFRA—rigorous proof demands on the government's arguments that exceptions threaten its compelling interests, and reliance on analogous statutory exemptions as evidence of weakness in those interests").

[49] Id.

[50] *Gonzales*, 546 US at 436, quoting *Cutter v Wilkinson*, 544 US 709, 722 (2005).

[51] Lupu, 38 Harv J L & Gender at 64 (cited in note 21) (contending that although the reasoning in *Gonzales* could have led to a more rigorous application of the compelling interest inquiry, it did not do so).

[52] Both peyote and DMT apparently have unpleasant side effects. See *Gonzales*, 546 US at 426.

this clear a pedigree. Third, the Court did not completely discount the potential weight of the uniformity interest. Rather it suggested that that interest might well prevail in other situations.[53] For these reasons, it was unclear how much direction *Gonzales* provided for other applications of RFRA.[54] That direction would have to await future cases—the next of which turned out to be *Hobby Lobby*.

II. Burwell v Hobby Lobby, Inc.

In 2010, a bitterly divided Congress passed the Patient Protection and Affordable Care Act (ACA).[55] Virtually from the moment that President Obama signed the ACA into law, its opponents began developing legal strategies and filing actions challenging the constitutionality of the Act.[56] One of those cases, *National Federation of Independent Business v Sebelius*,[57] resulted in one of the most important Supreme Court decisions on federal power in more than eighty years, replete with major pronouncements on the meaning of the Commerce Clause, the Necessary and Proper Clause, the Taxing Power, and the Spending Power.[58] The *Sebelius* decision did not, however, end the legal battles, and a number of challenges to specific provisions of the Act remained in play. *Burwell v Hobby Lobby Stores, Inc.* was one of those challenges.[59]

---

[53] *Gonzales*, 546 US at 436 ("We do not doubt that there may be instances in which a need for uniformity precludes the recognition of exceptions to generally applicable laws under RFRA.").

[54] Lupu, 38 Harv J L & Gender at 66 (cited in note 21) (noting the *Gonzales* decision did not appear to change the pattern in the lower courts in not strictly applying RFRA). See also Matthew Nicholson, Note, *Is O Centro a Sign of Hope for RFRA Claimants?*, 95 Va L Rev 1281 (2009) (suggesting that *Gonzales* has failed to provide clear direction for lower courts in their determination of future free exercise claims).

[55] Patient Protection and Affordable Care Act (ACA), Pub L No 111-148, 124 Stat 119 (2010).

[56] Associated Press, *States Sue Over Health Care*, Chi Trib (Mar 24, 2010). For a comprehensive timeline of the Republican effort to derail the ACA, see generally Igor Volsky, *Blow by Blow: A Comprehensive Timeline of the GOP's 4-Year Battle to Kill Obamacare*, ThinkProgress (Center for American Progress Action Fund, Mar 23, 2014), online at http://thinkprogress .org/health/2014/03/23/3417482/gop-opposition/.

[57] 132 S Ct 2566 (2012).

[58] Id at 2578, 2573, and 2579 (respectively).

[59] 134 S Ct 2751 (2014). The Court has also recently granted review on another challenge to the ACA. See *King v Burwell*, 2014 WL 38117533 (2014); Jess Bravin and Louise Radnofsky, *Supreme Court to Hear Case on Health-Care Law Subsidies*, Wall St J (Nov 8, 2014), online at http://online.wsj.com/articles/supreme-court-to-hear-case-on-health-law-subsidies -1415383458 (explaining that the Supreme Court will be reviewing whether the Affordable Care Act is improperly providing tax credits to those who buy insurance through federal, as opposed to state, exchanges).

A. BACKGROUND

The ACA requires that covered employers[60] offer employees "group health plans or group health insurance coverage" providing "minimum essential coverage."[61] "Minimal essential coverage" requires that the employer's health plan or insurance provide, at no added cost to the plan participant or beneficiary, certain types of preventative health services.[62] The no-additional-cost services required under the ACA include "preventive care and screenings"[63] for women's health.[64]

The ACA does not set forth the specific preventive care and screening services that must be covered. Instead, it authorizes the Health Resources and Services Administration (HRSA), a component of HHS, to make those determinations.[65] Pursuant to that authorization, the HRSA consulted the Institute of Medicine (IOM), a nonprofit group of volunteer advisers, to determine which preventive services to require.[66] After consulting with other experts,

---

[60] ACA §§ 4980H, 5000A(f)(2), 124 Stat at 253, 248–49 (2012). The ACA does not apply to employers who have less than 50 employees. ACA § 4980H(d)(2), 124 Stat at 254 (2012).

[61] ACA §§ 5000A(f)(2), 124 Stat at 248–49 (2012). Any covered employer that does not provide such coverage must pay a substantial price. ACA § 4980H(a)–(d), 124 Stat at 253–54 (2012). Specifically, if a covered employer provides group health insurance but its plan fails to comply with ACA's group health-plan requirements, the employer may be required to pay $100 per day for each affected "individual." 26 USC §§ 4980D(a)–(b) (2012). And, if the employer decides to stop providing health insurance altogether and at least one full-time employee enrolls in a health plan and qualifies for a subsidy on one of the government-run ACA exchanges, the employer must pay $2,000 per year for each of its full-time employees. ACA §§ 4980H(a), (c)(1), 124 Stat at 253 (2012).

[62] See ACA § 2713(a)(1)–(4), 124 Stat at 131 (2012), codified at 42 USC §§ 300gg-13(a)(1)–(3) (requiring group health plans to provide coverage, without cost sharing, for (1) certain "evidence-based items or services" recommended by the U.S. Preventive Services Task Force, (2) immunizations recommended by an advisory committee of the Centers for Disease Control and Prevention, and (3) "with respect to infants, children, and adolescents, evidence-informed preventive care and screenings provided for in the comprehensive guidelines supported by the Health Resources and Services Administration.").

[63] ACA § 2713(a), 124 Stat at 131 (2012), codified at 42 USC § 300gg-13(a)(4).

[64] As Justice Ginsburg points out in her *Hobby Lobby* dissent: "the Affordable Care Act (ACA), in its initial form, specified [only] three categories of preventive care that health plans must cover at no added cost to the plan participant or beneficiary . . . it left out preventive services that 'many women's health advocates and medical professionals believe are critically important.'" *Hobby Lobby*, 134 S Ct at 2788 (Ginsburg, J, dissenting) (quoting 155 Cong Rec 28841 (2009) (statement of Sen. Barbara Boxer)). Justice Ginsburg explains that, "[t]o correct this oversight, Senator Barbara Mikulski introduced the Women's Health Amendment, which added to the ACA's minimum coverage requirements a new category of preventive services specific to women's health." Id.

[65] ACA § 2713(a), 124 Stat at 131 (2012), codified at 42 USC § 300gg-13(a)(4).

[66] See Internal Revenue Service, Amendment to ACA Coverage of Preventive Health Services, 77 Fed Reg 8725, 8725–26 (2012).

the IOM recommended that preventive coverage should include the "full range of FDA-approved contraceptive methods."[67] Those FDA-approved methods included both contraceptives designed to prevent egg fertilization and four other methods—two forms of emergency contraception commonly called "morning after" pills and two types of intrauterine devices, which can operate after the fertilization of an egg.[68]

Based on the IOM recommendation, HRSA developed guidelines requiring nonexempt employers to provide "coverage, without cost sharing" for "[a]ll Food and Drug Administration [(FDA)] approved contraceptive methods, sterilization procedures, and patient education and counseling."[69] Pursuant to HRSA's guidelines, HHS, the Department of Labor, and the Department of Treasury then promulgated formal rules requiring group health plans to cover the contraceptive services recommended in the HRSA guidelines.[70] The rules allowed certain exceptions for religious employers[71] and certain religious nonprofits.[72] Employers (both religious and nonreligious) providing "grandfathered health plans"—those that existed prior to March 23, 2010—were also exempt from the requirements.[73]

The contraceptive requirements, and most especially the mandatory coverage of contraceptive methods that could operate after egg fertilization, triggered a number of RFRA and Free Exercise Clause challenges.[74] The Court granted certiorari in two of those

---

[67] *Hobby Lobby*, 134 S Ct at 2789. As the *Hobby Lobby* Court explained, "[a]lthough many of the required, FDA-approved methods of contraception work by preventing the fertilization of an egg, four of those methods . . . may have the effect of preventing an already fertilized egg from developing any further by inhibiting its attachment to the uterus." *Hobby Lobby*, 134 S Ct at 2762–63 (majority).

[68] Id at 2765 ("These methods were two forms of emergency contraception commonly called 'morning after' pills and two types of intrauterine devices."). See also HHS, Coverage of Certain Preventive Services Under the ACA, Final Rules, 78 Fed Reg 39870, 39888 (2013), commentary on 45 CFR § 147.130 (2012) ("FDA-approved contraceptive methods [include] Plan B, Ella, and IUDs."); FDA, *Birth Control: Medicines to Help You* (HHS, Aug 27, 2013), online at http://www.fda.gov/ForConsumers/ByAudience/ForWomen/FreePublications/ucm313215.htm.

[69] 77 Fed Reg at 8725 (internal quotation marks omitted).

[70] 45 CFR § 147.130(a)(1)(iv) (2013) (HHS); 29 CFR § 2590.715-2713(a)(1)(iv) (2013) (Labor); 26 CFR § 54.9815-2713(a)(1)(iv) (2013) (Treasury).

[71] 45 CFR § 147.131(a).

[72] See 45 CFR § 147.131(b); 78 Fed Reg at 39874.

[73] ACA § 1251, 124 Stat 161–62 (2012), codified at 42 USC § 18011.

[74] Matt Fair, *Notre Dame, Others Join Fight Over Birth Control Mandate*, Law360 (May 21, 2012), online at http://www.law360.com/articles/342412/notre-dame-others-join-fight-over

cases, *Conestoga Wood Specialties Corp. v Sebelius*[75] and *Hobby Lobby Stores, Inc. v Sebelius*,[76] which were then consolidated. The plaintiffs in the first case were Conestoga Wood Specialties, a woodworking business with 950 employees, and its owners, Norman and Elizabeth Hahn and their three sons. The Hahns are Mennonites who believe that "life begins at conception."[77] They maintained that for them to be compelled to provide health insurance covering the four FDA-approved contraceptives that may operate after fertilization would violate their religious beliefs, because "it is immoral and sinful for [Mennonites] to intentionally participate in, pay for, facilitate, or otherwise support these drugs."[78]

The plaintiffs in the second case were Hobby Lobby Stores, Inc., an arts-and-crafts chain with more than 500 stores that employs over 13,000 people; Mardel, a corporation affiliated with Hobby Lobby that operates thirty-five Christian bookstores and employs close to 400 people; and the corporations' owners, David and Barbara Green and their three children.[79] The Greens are Christians who, like the Hahns, believe that "life begins at conception and that it would violate their religion to facilitate access to contraceptive drugs or devices that [may] operate after [fertilization]."[80]

-birth-control-mandate (Katherine Rautenberg, ed) (discussing a "growing campaign [in the federal courts] to overturn the [ACA contraception] mandate").

[75] 724 F3d 377 (3d Cir 2013).

[76] 723 F3d 1114 (10th Cir 2013) (*Hobby Lobby 10th Cir*).

[77] *Conestoga Wood*, 724 F3d at 382 (quoting the Conestoga's board-adopted "Statement on the Sanctity of Human Life").

[78] *Hobby Lobby*, 134 S Ct at 2765 (quoting *Conestoga Wood*, 724 F3d at 382). In *Conestoga Wood*, a Pennsylvania district court denied the Hahns' request for a preliminary injunction to the ACA's contraceptive mandate. Id at 381–82. On appeal, the Third Circuit, concluding that "for-profit, secular corporations cannot engage in religious exercise" under RFRA or the First Amendment, affirmed the district court's decision. Id at 381.

[79] *Hobby Lobby 10th Cir*, 723 F3d at 1122.

[80] *Hobby Lobby*, 134 S Ct at 2755. The Greens were denied a preliminary injunction to the ACA's contraception provision by a district court in Oklahoma. See *Hobby Lobby 10th Cir*, 723 F3d at 1125. Like the Hahns, the Greens appealed the trial court's ruling to the U.S. Court of Appeals. Id. Unlike the Third Circuit's decision in *Conestoga Wood*, however, the Tenth Circuit, finding no persuasive reason to think that Congress meant "person" in RFRA to mean anything other than its default meaning in the Dictionary Act—which includes corporations regardless of their profit-making status, reversed the district court's denial of the Greens' preliminary injunction motion. Id at 1132. The court remanded the case with instructions that the lower court should address the remaining preliminary injunction factors. Id at 1147.

In a five-to-four decision, the Court ruled that the challengers were entitled to the relief they sought under RFRA. The Court did not reach the First Amendment issue.

B. THE KEY ISSUES INVOLVED

As identified in Justice Ginsburg's dissent, *Hobby Lobby* presented four major issues of statutory construction:[81] (1) are for-profit corporations "persons" who exercise religion under the statute?; (2) if so, does the contraceptive coverage requirement "substantially burden" their religious exercise?; (3) is the mandate "in furtherance of a compelling government interest?"; and (4) does the requirement represent the least restrictive means for furthering that interest? To this list might be added a fifth: (5) would RFRA's provisions apply when "followers of a particular sect enter into commercial activity as a matter of choice" or would its protections cease in those circumstances, as the Court had indicated in its pre-*Smith* free exercise decision in *United States v Lee*.[82]

Justice Alito's majority opinion, which was joined by Chief Justice Roberts and Justices Kennedy, Scalia, and Thomas, sided with the plaintiffs on four of those issues. Justice Alito held (1) that for-profit corporations are protected "persons" exercising religion under RFRA;[83] (2) that RFRA requires deference to the religious adherents in determining whether a challenged restriction is burdensome, and on that basis he deferred to the plaintiffs' assertions that being required to provide coverage for certain contraceptive methods infringed their religious exercise;[84] (3) that there was a less restrictive alternative because the government could directly pay for the coverage,[85] an option that he asserted paralleled an accommodation

---

[81] *Hobby Lobby*, 134 S Ct at 2793 (Ginsburg, J, dissenting). See also Lupu, 38 Harv J L & Gender at 41–42, 75 (cited in note 21).

[82] *United States v Lee*, 455 US 252, 261 (1982).

[83] *Hobby Lobby*, 134 S Ct at 2768 (majority), citing 1 USC § 1 ("Under the Dictionary Act, 'the wor[d] "person" . . . include[s] corporations, companies, associations, firms, partnerships, societies, and joint stock companies, as well as individuals.' . . . We see nothing in RFRA that suggests a congressional intent to depart from the Dictionary Act definition, and HHS makes little effort to argue otherwise.").

[84] *Hobby Lobby*, 134 S Ct at 2778–79.

[85] Id at 2780 (citations omitted) ("The most straightforward way [for HHS to satisfy its desired goal without imposing a substantial burden on the exercise of religion] would be for the Government to assume the cost of providing the four contraceptives at issue to any

already in place for religious nonprofits that objected to the contraceptive requirements;[86] and (4) that the statute applied to commercial activity and that *Lee* was distinguishable on the dual grounds
that it was a tax case[87] and that, in any event, RFRA should be interpreted to provide greater protection to religious freedom than
the Court's pre-*Smith* free exercise decisions, including *Lee*.[88] Justice
Alito did not decide whether the government's interest in protecting
women's health was compelling.[89] His ruling that the contraceptive
mandate was not the least-restrictive alternative for accomplishing
the government's goal made the disposition of that issue unnecessary.[90]

Justice Ginsburg's dissenting opinion, which was joined by Justices Breyer, Sotomayor, and Kagan, supported the government's
position on all of these issues.[91] Justice Ginsburg rejected Justice

---

women who are unable to obtain them under their health-insurance policies due to their
employers' religious objections. This would certainly be less restrictive of the plaintiffs' religious liberty, and HHS has not shown that this is not a viable alternative.").

[86] Id at 2782, citing and quoting 45 CFR §§ 147.131(a)–(c) (2013) ("Under [HHS's exist-
ing] accommodation [for nonprofit organizations with religious objections], the organization
can self certify that it opposes providing coverage for particular contraceptive services. If the
organization makes such a certification, the organization's insurance issuer or third-party
administrator must '[e]xpressly exclude contraceptive coverage from the group health insurance coverage provided in connection with the group health plan' and '[p]rovide separate
payments for any contraceptive services required to be covered' without imposing 'any cost-
sharing requirements . . . on the eligible organization, the group health plan, or plan participants or beneficiaries.'").

[87] Id at 2783–84 (asserting that the decision in *Lee*, which rejected a challenge to the application of the social security tax requirement, "turned primarily on the special problems
associated with a national system of taxation").

[88] Id at 2784 n 43 ("*Lee* was a free exercise, not a RFRA, case, and the statement to which
HHS points, if taken at face value, is squarely inconsistent with the plain meaning of RFRA.
Under RFRA, when followers of a particular religion choose to enter into commercial activity, the Government does not have a free hand in imposing obligations that substantially
burden their exercise of religion. Rather, the Government can impose such a burden only if
the strict RFRA test is met.").

[89] Id at 2780 (assuming without deciding that RFRA's compelling interest prong is met and
proceeding to consider whether the contraceptive mandate meets the "exceptionally demanding" least-restrictive-means standard). Professor Lupu persuasively suggests that Justice
Alito's sidestepping of this issue may have been the result of a compromise to secure Justice
Kennedy's fifth and deciding vote. Lupu, 38 Harv J L & Gender at 85 (cited in note 21) ("[As]
is evident from [his concurrence], . . . the price of Justice Kennedy's fifth vote for the Court's
opinion was non-adjudication of—not agreement upon—the question of compelling interest.").

[90] Justice Kennedy's concurrence, however, suggests "that a premise of the Court's opinion
is its assumption that the HHS regulation here at issue furthers a legitimate and compelling
interest in the health of female employees." Id at 2786 (Kennedy, J, concurring).

[91] See generally id at 2787–2806 (Ginsburg, J, dissenting).

Alito's assertion that RFRA requires complete deference to the religious adherent's characterization of her own burden.[92] She concluded that the plaintiffs' objection to providing coverage for certain types of contraceptives in this case was "too attenuated" to their religious belief that life begins at conception to trigger RFRA's protections.[93] She contended that the government interest in protecting women's health was compelling,[94] and that "let[ting] the government pay" was not an acceptable less restrictive alternative.[95] She suggested that *Lee*'s reasoning that free exercise protections cease when believers voluntarily enter into commercial activity should also be applied in RFRA cases, in part because it would protect against an employer's authority to impose its beliefs on its employees.[96] Finally, though joined only by Justice Sotomayor on the issue, Justice Ginsburg construed RFRA as inapplicable to for-profit corporations.[97]

Justice Kennedy offered a brief concurring opinion supporting the majority's conclusions that RFRA imposed a "stringent test" and that there was a less restrictive alternative available to the government.[98] His opinion emphasized, however, his assessment that

---

[92] Id at 2792, citing *Rasul v Myers*, 563 F3d 527, 535 (DC Cir 2009) (Brown concurring) (describing the majority's "conception of RFRA as a measure detached from this Court's decisions [as] one that sets a new course," and arguing instead that RFRA, even as altered by RLUIPA, does not "relieve courts of the obligation to inquire whether a government action substantially burdens a religious exercise").

[93] *Hobby Lobby*, 134 S Ct at 2798–99 (Ginsburg, J, dissenting) ("Congress, no doubt, meant the modifier 'substantially' to carry weight. In the original draft of RFRA, the word 'burden' appeared unmodified. The word 'substantially' was inserted pursuant to a clarifying amendment.").

[94] Id at 2799 ("[T]he Government has shown that the contraceptive coverage for which the ACA provides furthers compelling interests in public health and women's well being. Those interests are concrete, specific, and demonstrated by a wealth of empirical evidence.").

[95] Id at 2802, citing 78 Fed Reg at 39888 ("The ACA, however, requires coverage of preventive services through the existing employer-based system of health insurance 'so that [employees] face minimal logistical and administrative obstacles.' Impeding women's receipt of benefits 'by requiring them to take steps to learn about, and to sign up for, a new [government funded and administered] health benefit' was scarcely what Congress contemplated.").

[96] *Hobby Lobby*, 134 S Ct at 2804 (Ginsburg, J, dissenting).

[97] Id at 2794–97, 2805–06 (Ginsburg, J, dissenting), quoting *Spencer v World Vision, Inc.*, 633 F3d 723, 748 (Kleinfeld concurring) (9th Cir 2010) ("I would confine religious exemptions under [RFRA] to organizations formed 'for a religious purpose,' 'engage[d] primarily in carrying out that religious purpose,' and not 'engaged . . . substantially in the exchange of goods or services for money beyond nominal amounts.'").

[98] *Hobby Lobby*, 134 S Ct at 2785, 2786–87 (Kennedy, J, concurring).

the majority assumed that "the HHS regulation here at issue furthers a legitimate and compelling interest in the health of female employees."[99] Justices Breyer and Kagan, in turn, submitted a one-paragraph dissent indicating they joined Justice Ginsburg's opinion rejecting the plaintiffs' RFRA challenge, but that, in doing so, they did not reach the issue of whether RFRA applied to for-profit corporations.[100]

Running through both the majority and dissenting opinions was the larger question of what role the Court's pre-*Smith* free exercise jurisprudence should play in its construction of RFRA. Was RFRA designed to return the protection of religious exercise to its same status prior to *Smith*? If so, then the pre-*Smith* cases might provide guidance as to proper resolution of the statutory issues before the Court in *Hobby Lobby*. Or was RFRA intended to expand religious exercise rights beyond those recognized in the pre-*Smith* era? If the latter, then the pre-*Smith* cases would serve only as a floor for religious exercise protection under RFRA. Justice Alito's majority opinion stressed that RFRA should be interpreted broadly and should not be limited by the pre-*Smith* decisions.[101] Justice Ginsburg's dissent vehemently disagreed.[102]

It is therefore necessary to revisit the pre-*Smith* regime in order to evaluate Justice Alito's and Justice Ginsburg's competing views on whether RFRA should be interpreted to expand, or merely to restore, religious exercise rights. This inquiry may also reveal the futility inherent in either approach. It is to that project that we now turn.

---

[99] Id at 2786 (Kennedy, J, concurring).

[100] Id at 2806 (Breyer and Kagan, JJ, dissenting).

[101] *Hobby Lobby*, 134 S Ct at 2772 ("When Congress wants to link the meaning of a statutory provision to a body of this Court's case law, it knows how to do so."). Justice Alito's majority opinion advances three primary reasons in rejecting HHS's argument that Congress intended RFRA to codify the Court's pre-*Smith* free exercise case law: "First, nothing in the text of RFRA as originally enacted suggested that the statutory phrase 'exercise of religion under the First Amendment' was meant to be tied to this Court's pre-*Smith* interpretation of that Amendment. . . . Second, if the original text of RFRA was not clear enough on this point—and we think it was—the amendment of RFRA through RLUIPA surely dispels any doubt. . . . Third, the one pre-*Smith* case involving the free-exercise rights of a for-profit corporation suggests, if anything, that for-profit corporations possess such rights." Id, citing *Gallagher v Crown Kosher Super Market of Mass, Inc*, 366 US 617 (1961).

[102] Id at 2791 (Ginsburg, J, dissenting), citing *Gonzales*, 546 US at 424 ("In RFRA, Congress 'adopt[ed] a statutory rule comparable to the constitutional rule rejected in *Smith*.'").

III. Free Exercise and the Compelling Interest Test

A. REYNOLDS V UNITED STATES

The Court's free exercise jurisprudence dates back to its 1878 decision in *Reynolds v United States*.[103] In that case, George Reynolds, a Mormon, appealed his conviction for bigamy on the ground that the antipolygamy law under which he was convicted infringed his free exercise rights.[104] The Court denied the challenge without seriously considering whether the law infringed the defendant's religious beliefs.[105] Rather, the Court concluded that to exempt individuals from criminal prohibitions on account of their religious beliefs would introduce "a new element into criminal law. . . . [and would make] the professed doctrines of religious belief superior to the law of the land, and in effect . . . permit every citizen to become a law unto himself."[106] According to *Reynolds*, the Free Exercise Clause did not require constitutionally compelled exemptions from neutral laws, even if those laws limited the free exercise of one's religious beliefs.

B. SHERBERT V VERNER

Reynolds remained the governing precedent in free exercise law until 1963[107] when the Court changed course.[108] In *Sherbert v Ver-*

---

[103] 98 US 145 (1878).

[104] Id at 165.

[105] The *Reynolds* Court, however, did emphasize the strength underlying the state's interest in outlawing polygamy. Id at 168.

[106] Id at 166–67.

[107] The Court decided relatively few pure free exercise cases during this period, the most notable being *Jacobsen v United States*, 197 US 11 (1905) (upholding a compulsory vaccination requirement). The Court did, however, decide a number of cases involving religious expression in which both free exercise and free speech challenges were raised against the government's action. See, for example, *Cantwell v Connecticut*, 310 US 296 (1940) (invalidating on free exercise and speech grounds convictions of a Jehovah's Witness and his sons for distributing written material without a license and creating a public nuisance).

[108] The Court's move away from *Reynolds* may have been signaled earlier. In *Braunfield v Brown*, 366 US 599 (1961), the Court indicated that it might apply greater scrutiny to government regulations burdening religion than it had applied in *Reynolds*. Id at 607. The *Braunfield* Court held that a statute could be valid despite its indirect burden on religious observance only if the state could not accomplish its purpose by "means which do not impose such a burden." Id at 607. This language suggests that the Court was beginning to impose a least restrictive means test. The *Braunfield* Court, however, did *not* apply a compelling state interest test, and the fact that the Court rejected the free exercise claim before it (a challenge to a Sunday closing law) left unclear how stringent the Court's review would be in subsequent cases. Id.

ner,[109] Seventh Day Adventist Adell Sherbert claimed that her free exercise rights had been violated when she was denied employment benefits because her religious beliefs made her unavailable for work on Saturdays. The Court held that for the government to require her to work on Saturdays as a condition for the receipt of unemployment compensation interfered with the exercise of her religion and that she was entitled to an exemption from the Saturday work requirement because the state's interest in enforcing its requirement was not sufficiently weighty to overcome her First Amendment rights. *Sherbert* concluded that any government infringement on free exercise must be supported by a compelling state interest.[110]

The Supreme Court nominally adhered to *Sherbert*'s compelling interest test in evaluating free exercise claims for the next three decades. The results in the cases, however, did not reflect the Court's announced standard. In other areas of constitutional law, the application of the compelling interest test is extremely demanding and the government seldom prevails. In the free speech context, for example, the Court has held that the government interests in promoting political equality,[111] protecting animals from crush videos,[112] and defending the flag from burning and desecration[113] are not sufficiently compelling to outweigh an individual's right of free expression. Moreover, one would expect the compelling interest test to be even more rights-protective when applied in religious exercise cases, because in those cases, unlike in other areas of constitutional law, the government must demonstrate that it has a compelling interest in applying the law to a limited class of religious objectors, rather than to a much broader class of individuals.[114] The *Gonzales* case illustrates the point. Even if the government has a compelling interest in prohibiting the use of the hallucinogen DMT generally, it cannot prevail in a case like *Gonzales* unless it demonstrates that its interest is compelling even as applied to only the 130 members of the UDV sect.[115]

---

[109] *Sherbert v Verner*, 374 US 398 (1963).

[110] Id at 406–09.

[111] *Citizens United v Federal Election Commission*, 558 US 310 (2010).

[112] *United States v Stevens*, 559 US 460 (2010).

[113] *Texas v Johnson*, 491 US 397 (1989).

[114] See Lupu, 38 Harv J L & Gender at 71 (cited in note 21).

[115] *Gonzales v O Centro Espirita Beneficente Uniao do Vegetal*, 546 US 418 (2006).

Nevertheless, despite the usual stringency of the compelling interest test, the Court in the pre-*Smith* era vindicated free exercise claims seeking exemptions in only five cases.[116] Four of those decisions, including *Sherbert*, addressed whether a state could deny unemployment compensation benefits to applicants who were not available for work because of religious reasons.[117] In each of these cases, the Court ruled for the religious adherent on the ground that she could not be forced to choose between receiving government benefits and practicing her religion.[118]

The fifth case, *Wisconsin v Yoder*,[119] held that the Amish were entitled to a free exercise exemption from compulsory education requirements.[120] *Yoder* could be read as suggesting that the Court was giving real bite to the *Sherbert* compelling interest inquiry. Although educating children is among the state's most compelling concerns,[121] the Court found that interest insufficient to outweigh the Amish's free exercise claim.[122] Another interpretation of *Yoder*, however, is also plausible. The Court's analysis was so tied to its solicitude for the Amish way of life that the decision could reasonably be understood as confined to the unique circumstances of the case.[123]

---

[116] In one other case, *Jensen v Quaring*, 472 US 478 (1985), an equally divided Court affirmed, without issuing an opinion, a lower court decision holding that a Jehovah's Witness was entitled to a free exercise exemption from a law requiring that she have her picture on her driver's license.

[117] *Thomas v Review Board*, 450 US 707 (1981); *Hobbie v Unemployment Appeals Commission*, 480 US 136 (1987), and *Frazee v Illinois Department of Employment Security*, 489 US 829 (1989).

[118] *Sherbert*, 374 US at 410; *Thomas*, 450 US at 717–18; *Hobbie*, 480 US at 146; *Frazee*, 489 US at 432.

[119] 406 US 205 (1972).

[120] *Yoder*, 406 US at 236.

[121] *Brown v Board of Education*, 347 US 483 (1954).

[122] Adding to the ambiguity in *Yoder* is the fact that the free exercise interest raised by the Amish was so nebulous. The Amish apparently did not object to compulsory education per se; they only rejected it after a certain grade when the schooling might lead the children to reject the Amish way of life. See *Yoder*, 406 US at 211 (noting that the Amish objection to formal education beyond the eighth grade was rooted in religious concepts because the values taught in high school are "in marked variance with Amish values and the Amish way of life; they view secondary school education as an impermissible exposure of their children to a 'wordly' (*sic*) influence in conflict with their beliefs").

[123] See, for example, Nadine Strossen, *"Secular Humanism" and "Scientific Creationism," Proposed Standards for Reviewing Curricular Decisions Affecting Students' Religious Freedom*, 47 Ohio St L J 333, 388 (1986) ("The Supreme Court ruling in *Yoder* was firmly anchored to the special situation presented by the Amish faith.").

At the same time, during this period the Court rejected numerous free exercise claims even when the state's asserted interests did not appear to be particularly weighty.[124] It turned back a free exercise challenge to the minimum wage, overtime, and recordkeeping provisions of the Fair Labor Standards Act.[125] It disallowed all free exercise claims seeking exemptions from tax laws.[126] It refused to exempt believers from the draft because of their religious objections to "unjust wars," even though the government granted parallel exemptions to those who objected to "all wars" on religious grounds.[127] It denied a claimed exemption from the government's use of social security number registration requirements in food stamp and welfare programs.[128] It rejected free exercise claims in a series of cases involving prisons and the military on the ground that special deference to government authority is warranted in these contexts.[129] It held that the Free Exercise Clause did not protect the interests of Native Americans who sought to prevent the government from developing government-owned lands that were sacred to Native American religious heritage,[130] ruling that "the Free Exercise Clause cannot be understood to require the government to conduct its own internal

---

[124] See Ira C. Lupu, *The Trouble with Accommodation*, 60 Geo Wash L Rev 743, 756 (1992) (noting that the test may have been strict in theory, but not in fact); see McConnell, 57 U Chi L Rev at 1127 (cited in note 8).

[125] *Tony and Susan Alamo Foundation v Secretary of Labor*, 471 US 290 (1985) (rejecting a claim by a religious institution that it did not have to comply with the FLSA because the receipt of wages conflicted with its workers' religious beliefs).

[126] *Jimmy Swaggart Ministries v Board of Equalization of Cal.*, 493 US 378 (1990) (no free exercise right to exemption from state sales tax on religious organization's sale of religious literature); *Bob Jones University v United States*, 461 US 574 (1983) (denial of tax-exempt status to religiously affiliated university that discriminates on the basis of race does not violate Free Exercise Clause); *United States v Lee*, 455 US 252 (1982) (denying Amish exemption from social security tax).

[127] *Gillette v United States*, 401 US 437 (1971).

[128] *Bowen v Roy*, 476 US 693 (1986) (rejecting a free exercise claim against the government's use of a social security number in reference to their child because using a number in this manner violated their religious beliefs).

[129] *O'Lone v Estate of Shabazz*, 482 US 342, 345 (1987) (reasonableness standard applies to free exercise challenges to prison restrictions burdening religious exercise); *Goldman v Weinberger*, 475 US 503, 507 (1986) (reasonableness standard applies to free exercise challenges to military requirements burdening religious exercise).

[130] *Lyng v Northwest Indian Cemetery Protective Association*, 485 US 439 (1988). The special significance of *Lyng* to the development of free exercise jurisprudence is discussed in Ira C. Lupu, *Where Rights Begin: The Problem of Burdens on the Free Exercise of Religion*, 102 Harv L Rev 933, 945 (1989).

affairs in ways that comport with the religious beliefs of particular citizens."[131]

C. EMPLOYMENT DIVISION V SMITH

Against this background, the Court in 1990 decided *Employment Division v Smith*.[132] Galen Smith was a counselor at a private drug rehabilitation organization who was fired from his job because he ingested peyote for sacramental purposes at a ceremony of the Native American Church.[133] He applied for unemployment compensation but was denied benefits because he had been terminated for employee-related "misconduct."[134] He appealed, claiming that the denial of benefits violated his rights under the Free Exercise Clause.

Smith's claim was particularly sympathetic. There was no question that peyote ingestion is a central practice in Native American religion[135] and that Smith was deeply committed to his religious beliefs. Furthermore, the practice of peyote ingestion was long-standing in the Native American Church[136] and was critical to its adherents' sense of cultural as well as religious identity.[137] As in *Yoder*, there was

---

[131] *Lyng*, 485 US at 448, quoting *Bowen*, 476 US at 699.

[132] 494 US 872 (1990).

[133] Id at 874.

[134] Id.

[135] Id at 919 (Blackmun, J, dissenting), citing Brief of Amici Curiae Association on American Indian Affairs in Support of Respondents, *Smith*, Action No 88-1213, *5–6 (US, filed July 14, 1989) ("AAIA Brief") ("Respondents believe, and their sincerity has *never* been at issue, that the peyote plant embodies their deity, and eating it is an act of worship and communion. Without peyote, they could not enact the essential ritual of their religion."). See also *Employment Division, Department of Human Resources of Or v Smith*, 485 US 660, 667 n 11 (1988) ("*Smith I*") (citations omitted) ("Peyote . . . plays a central role in the ceremony and practice of the Native American Church[,] . . . [which] combines certain Christian teachings with the belief that peyote embodies the Holy Spirit and that those who partake of peyote enter into direct contact with God.").

[136] See Garrett Epps, *Peyote vs. the State: Religious Freedom on Trial* 52–56 (Oklahoma, 2009). In his book, Epps examines the Court's decisions in *Smith* through a lens of incredible cultural and personal depth, detailing the Native American Church's historical adherence to the Peyote religion. Id. Epps argues that the elements of modern-day peyote services, which include instances where "participants are offered the opportunity to eat peyote . . . sing ceremonial songs. . . . [and] sit motionless, watching the fire and meditating on the gifts of peyote," can be directly traced to the emergence, during the 1880s, of a specific peyote ceremony in present-day Oklahoma. Id at 54–55.

[137] Id (discussing the Native American Church's attempt to explain peyote to members of Congress and the Christian clergy as "their 'sacrament,' just as wine or grape juice was the sacrament for their white Christian brothers," and a coordinated effort among church leaders to "shield white society from the knowledge that peyotism was a distinctively Native spiritual

therefore a strong cultural component to the case—just as compulsory public education threatened the Amish way of life, proscribing the practice of peyote ingestion threatened the way of life of Native Americans who had long adhered to this practice as an essential part of their religious tradition.[138]

Twice the case went to the United States Supreme Court. The first time,[139] the Court remanded to the Oregon Supreme Court to determine whether Smith's use of peyote for sacramental purposes violated the state's criminal law.[140] After the Oregon Supreme Court ruled that peyote use was, indeed, criminally proscribed,[141] the Court granted certiorari a second time. In a remarkably broad ruling,[142] the Court, in an opinion by Justice Scalia, held that the compelling interest test does not apply to free exercise challenges to neutral laws of general applicability.[143] As a result, Smith was not entitled to an exemption because the prohibition against peyote ingestion stemmed from a neutral law that was not directed at his religious belief.[144]

One of the more notable aspects of *Smith* was its treatment of precedent. The Court explicitly reinvigorated *Reynolds*, quoting directly from that opinion's passage that warned that granting relief from valid laws on the basis of religious conviction would allow

---

tradition."). See also AAIA Brief at 5–6 (cited in note 135) ("To the members [of the Native American Church], peyote is consecrated with powers to heal body, mind and spirit. It is a teacher; it teaches the way to spiritual life through living in harmony and balance with the forces of the Creation. The rituals are an integral part of the life process. They embody a form of worship in which the sacrament Peyote is the means for communicating with the Great Spirit.").

[138] See *Smith*, 494 US at 920–21 (emphasis added), quoting HR Rep No 95-1308, at 2 (1978) ("Congress [has] recognized that certain substances, such as peyote, 'have religious significance because they are sacred, they have power, they heal, they are necessary to the exercise of the rites of the religion, they are *necessary to the cultural integrity of the tribe*, and, therefore, religious survival.'").

[139] *Employment Division, Department of Human Resources of Or v Smith*, 485 US 660 (1988).

[140] Id at 673.

[141] *Smith v Employment Division*, 307 Or 68, 73 (1988).

[142] As Michael McConnell noted at the time of the *Smith* decision, this question of whether the compelling interest standard should be overturned was not before the Court. McConnell, 57 U Chi L Rev at 1112–13 (cited in note 8). As he explains, "neither of the parties asked the Court to reconsider its free exercise doctrine. The State expressly conceded the compelling interest test in its brief and the parties did not discuss the doctrinal issue at oral argument." Id.

[143] *Smith*, 494 US at 879, citing *Lee*, 455 US at 263 n 3 (Stevens, J, concurring in the judgment) ("the right of free exercise does not relieve an individual of the obligation to comply with a 'valid and neutral law of general applicability'").

[144] Id at 890.

every individual to become a "law unto himself."[145] At the same time, and presumably without irony, the Court purported to reaffirm *Sherbert* and *Yoder*. Although rejecting the compelling interest test, the Court did not overrule any previous decision and did not concede that it was changing course. It described *Sherbert* and the other unemployment cases as standing only for the "proposition that where the State has in place a system of individual exemptions, it may not refuse to extend that system to cases of 'religious hardship' without 'compelling reason.'"[146] It explained *Yoder* as an example of a "hybrid" right that combined free exercise interests with another constitutionally protected interest—the right to decide how best to education one's children.[147] The Court's application of the compelling interest test in other cases was dismissed as inconsequential because in all of those cases the state prevailed.[148]

D. THE FAILURE OF THE COMPELLING INTEREST INQUIRY
   IN FREE EXERCISE CASES

   1. *The inability of courts to consistently apply the compelling interest inquiry in free exercise cases.* The decision in *Smith* to abandon the compelling interest test in free exercise cases was unexpected insofar as the continued viability of that standard was not before the Court.[149] But the Court's ruling on this issue was not unforeseeable. At the time *Smith* was decided, it was clear that the Court was not consistently committed to a strict application of the compelling interest inquiry in free exercise cases.[150] The Court had ruled against free exercise claimants in too many contexts for that ordinarily very stringent test to be taken as the actual governing standard.

   It would be a mistake to assume, however, that the Court's commitment to the compelling interest test had eroded in the thirty years *Sherbert* was in place. Rather, the test as applied in this setting was just as tame (or vibrant) at the end of the period as at the beginning. The first free exercise case after *Sherbert*, for example, rejected the

---

[145] Id at 879 (citing *Reynolds v United States*, 98 US 145 (1878)).

[146] Id.

[147] Id at 882.

[148] Id.

[149] See McConnell, 57 U Chi L Rev at 1112–13 (cited in note 8).

[150] See James E. Ryan, *Smith and the Religious Freedom Restoration Act: An Iconoclastic Assessment*, 78 Va L Rev 1407, 1414 (1992).

free exercise challenge. In *Gillette v United States*,[151] the Court held that the Free Exercise Clause did not require exemption from the draft for those who objected to unjust wars, even though the Selective Service Act granted exemption to those who opposed *all* wars.[152] A year after *Gillette*, the Court upheld the free exercise claim in *Yoder* and did so again in the next major free exercise exemption case,[153] *Thomas v Review Board*, decided in 1981. One year later, in 1982, however, the Court rejected a free exercise challenge to the payment of social security taxes by a member of the Amish community in *United States v Lee*.

The end of the *Sherbert* timeline reflects a similar pattern of inconsistency. The last free exercise case decided before *Smith* was *Jimmy Swaggart Ministries v Board of Equalization*,[154] a 1990 decision that rejected a free exercise challenge to a sales tax imposed on religious literature. The penultimate case, however, was *Frazee v Illinois Department of Employment Security*,[155] an unemployment insurance case in which the Court unanimously vindicated the claim that the believer could not be compelled to work on Sundays, notwithstanding the facts that his objection to Sunday work was not based on a tenet, belief, or teaching of an established religious body and that he was not a member of any church or sect.[156] He asserted only that, as a Christian, he believed working on Sundays was wrong.[157] The Court, in short, was consistently inconsistent throughout the pre-*Smith* period.

Significantly, the failure consistently to apply a rigorous compelling interest test to religious exercise was not limited to the Supreme Court. As James Ryan has documented, lower courts during the pre-*Smith* regime also applied the compelling interest test only weakly and without consistency.[158] Moreover, as Ira Lupu notes, this

---

[151] 401 US 437 (1971).

[152] Id at 438.

[153] Between *Yoder* and *Thomas*, the Court also decided *McDaniel v Paty*, 435 US 618 (1978), striking down, on free exercise grounds, a provision of the Tennessee Constitution disqualifying ministers from serving as legislators. *McDaniel* was not an exemption case.

[154] 493 US 378 (1990).

[155] 489 US 829 (1989).

[156] Id at 831.

[157] Id.

[158] Ryan, 78 Va L Rev at 1416–37 (cited in note 150) (noting that the lower courts' pre-*Smith* cases "reinforce the assertion that the compelling interest test, at best, offered the religious claimant unreliable protection"). Id at 1434.

same pattern has continued in the lower courts under RFRA.[159] Applying the compelling interest test in religious exercise cases with any consistent or predictable rigor, it turns out, has proved to be consistently evasive.[160]

Why is this so? The compelling interest test is nothing new in constitutional law; it did not arise in *Sherbert* and it did not end in *Smith*. The test has been applied to a range of constitutional issues including free speech,[161] equal protection,[162] due process,[163] and dormant commerce.[164] Only in the free exercise context has its application proved to be particularly troublesome.

2. *Why the compelling interest test failed in free exercise cases.*

a. **The lessons from *Smith*.** The Court's opinion in *Smith* offers some of the reasons why courts have found the compelling interest test especially problematic in free exercise cases. First, as Justice Scalia explained, the sought-after relief is different and awkward. When a government action fails to survive strict scrutiny in other areas of constitutional law, the remedy is typically invalidation of the challenged law. In the free exercise context, however, the remedy is to exempt certain persons or entities from laws with which all other persons must comply. Thus, as *Smith* notes, "[what the compelling interests test] produces in those other fields—equality of treatment, and an unrestricted flow of contending speech—are constitutional norms; what it would produce here—a private right to ignore generally applicable laws—is a constitutional anomaly."[165] In the free speech context, for example, the Court generally evaluates the constitutionality of the challenged law as it would apply to all speakers even if the state's interest in applying the law to the particular speaker is weak and the speaker's First Amendment interest in avoid-

---

[159] See, for example, Ira C. Lupu, *The Failure of RFRA*, 20 U Ark Little Rock L J 575, 592 (1998); Lupu, 38 Harv J L & Gender at 63–65 (cited in note 21).

[160] Both Ira Lupu and Christopher Lund document similar results in the application of state statutes (so-called mini-RFRAs) that sought to restore the application of the compelling interest test to religious exercise after *Smith*. See Lupu, 38 Harv J L & Gender at 67–71 (cited in note 21); Christopher C. Lund, *Religious Liberty after Gonzales: A Look at State RFRAs*, 55 SD L Rev 466 (2010).

[161] *R.A.V. v St. Paul*, 505 US 377 (1992).

[162] *Adarand Constructors, Inc. v Pena*, 515 US 200, 227 (1975).

[163] *Carey v Population Services, International*, 431 US 678, 686 (1977).

[164] *Hughes v Oklahoma*, 441 US 322, 337 (1979).

[165] *Smith*, 494 US at 886.

ing the restriction is particularly strong.[166] In Free Exercise cases, in contrast, the Court is charged with forming an individualized assessment of both the government's and the religious claimant's interests as applied in the specific case—a task that literally invites highly subjective and arbitrary distinctions.

Second, as *Smith* also notes, free exercise is a particularly problematic area in which to apply the compelling interest test because the types of actions that can be said to be elements of religious exercise are virtually limitless. Other constitutional rights are not so boundless. In speech clause jurisprudence, for example, the Court has stated that an individual's actions do not become protected First Amendment expression merely because the person "intends thereby to an express an idea."[167]

That same action, however, does become religious exercise if the actor believes it to be. How a person dresses,[168] what he eats,[169] how he wears his hair,[170] what drugs he takes—all can be deemed matters of religious exercise.[171] The days a person chooses to work,[172] to whom she rents,[173] whom she employs,[174] what she reads or what she wants her children not to read[175]—all can be of religious significance. Even being required to file for a religious exemption from a law can be said to violate one's religious precepts.[176]

---

[166] See Geoffrey R. Stone and William P. Marshall, *Brown v Socialist Workers: Inequality as a Command of the First Amendment*, 1983 Supreme Court Review 583, 392–99. Accordingly the Court has seldom granted speakers exemptions from neutral laws and has done so only in three instances: *Brown v Socialist Workers*, 459 US 87 (1982); *Bates v City of Little Rock*, 361 US 516 (1960); *NAACP v Alabama*, 357 US 449 (1958).

[167] *United States v O'Brien*, 391 US 367, 376 (1968).

[168] *Goldman v Weinberger*, 475 US 503, 507 (1986).

[169] See generally *Baranowski v Hart*, 486 F3d 112, 122, 126 (5th Cir 2007) (religious obligation to eat only Kosher meals); *Koger v Bryan*, 523 F3d 789, 801 (7th Cir 2008) (religious requirement to eat only vegetarian meals); *DeHart v Horn*, 227 F3d 47 (3d Cir 2000) (religious requirement to have soy milk with every meal).

[170] See *Holt v Hobbs*, 135 S Ct 853 (2015) (addressing whether RLUIPA protects the right of a prisoner to grow a half-inch beard in accordance with his religious beliefs).

[171] *Gonzales*, 546 US at 418.

[172] *Sherbert*, 374 US at 410.

[173] *Swanner v Anchorage Equal Rights Commission*, 874 P2d 274 (Alaska 1994).

[174] See, for example, *Hosanna-Tabor Evangelical Lutheran Church and School v EEOC*, 132 S Ct 694 (2012); *Ohio Civil Rights Commission v Dayton Christian Schools*, 477 US 619 (1986).

[175] *Mozert v Hawkins County Board of Education*, 827 F2d 1058 (6th Cir 1987).

[176] See *Little Sisters of the Poor Home for the Aged v Sebelius*, 2013 WL 6839900 (D Colo 2013), injunction pending appeal granted, 134 S Ct 1022 (2014) (addressing the plaintiffs'

The problem with applying a compelling interest test on behalf of a right of such limitless dimension is that it means that virtually every law can precipitate a free exercise challenge. As Justice Scalia states: "because we are a cosmopolitan nation made up of people of almost every conceivable religious preference, and precisely because we value and protect that religious divergence, we cannot afford the luxury of deeming *presumptively invalid*, as applied to the religious objector, every regulation of conduct that does not protect an interest of the highest order. The [compelling interest test] would open the prospect of constitutionally required religious exemptions from civic obligations of almost every conceivable kind."[177]

Third, as *Smith* notes, merely inquiring into the merits of free exercise claims raises delicate constitutional issues by placing courts in the "unacceptable 'business of evaluating the relative merits of differing religious claims.'"[178] It does so, moreover, by forcing the courts to become involved in three separate problematic inquiries: (1) Is the presented claim actually "religious"? (2) Is the claimant's religious exercise "burdened" by the challenged government regulation? (3) Is the claimant sincere in her free exercise assertion?[179] All of these inquiries are highly problematic.[180]

The religiosity issue inserts courts into the business of defining religion—a problem laden with Establishment Clause overtones.[181] Should a court, after all, have the power or ability to tell a purported believer that her system of beliefs does not constitute a "religion"? Is

---

claim that completing and submitting the self-certification form in order to gain an exemption from the contraceptive coverage mandate would violate their rights under RFRA because completing the form could be construed as authorizing provision of contraception to Little Sisters employees). See also *Wheaton College v Burwell*, 134 S Ct 2806 (2014) (addressing plaintiffs' claim that using the Affordable Care Act self-certification form violates its religious exercise rights because using the form would make "itself morally complicit in the government's [contraception] scheme to which it objects and would change its relationship to its insurance carrier because it would cause the insurance plan administrator to begin to cover contraception services for College employees").

[177] *Smith*, 494 US at 888 (quotations and citations omitted). Alternatively, as Justice Scalia noted, the application of the compelling interest test in so many circumstances could lead to a watering down of the test itself. Id.

[178] Id at 887, citing *Lee*, 455 US at 263 n 2 (Stevens, J, concurring).

[179] The difficulties inherent in the judicial inquiry into these issues are closely examined in Lupu, 102 Harv L Rev at 953–60 (cited in note 130).

[180] For an excellent discussion contending that such inquiries should not be seen as problematic or threatening to religious freedom, see Michael A. Helfand, *Litigating Religion*, 93 BU L Rev 493 (2013).

[181] *Lee*, 455 US at 261–62 (Stevens, J, concurring).

it consistent with the Establishment Clause for a court to affirm or deny that a particular belief system is or is not a religion?

The burden question asks courts to evaluate how a believer interprets the demands of her faith. Yet, as *Smith* explains, granting courts the authority to decide this issue runs afoul of the "principle that courts must not presume to determine the place of a particular belief in a religion or the plausibility of a religious claim."[182] How is a court to decide how seriously the claimed infringement on a person's asserted religious beliefs actually burdens her faith? To what extent, for example, does an antidiscrimination law that prohibits a florist from refusing to provide flowers to a same-sex marriage "burden" the florist's religious belief that same-sex marriage is inconsistent with her religious beliefs? How is a court to evaluate the magnitude of the "burden"?

The sincerity inquiry poses two sets of issues. First, it creates the possibility that the government will need to use an inquisitor-like line of inquiry to demonstrate insincerity.[183] How else can the state refute the sincerity of a religious claim other than by uncovering alleged inconsistencies or contradictions in the claimant's religious convictions in order to impeach her assertions? Second, the sincerity inquiry inevitably subjects the legitimacy of the claimant's religious beliefs to judicial determination. Although the Court has held that fact finders cannot evaluate the validity of religious claims under the First Amendment,[184] it is doubtful that the sincerity question can actually be sequestered from the validity issue. As Justice Jackson contended in *United States v Ballard*, "I do not see how we can separate an issue as to what is believed from considerations as to what is believable."[185] In sum, the compelling interest test in this context would require judicial inquiries into matters that are potentially insoluble and that are themselves dangerous to First Amendment concerns.

b. The lessons from *Thomas*. *Smith* is not the only case demonstrating the difficulties of applying the compelling interest test in this context. An equally powerful illustration is *Thomas v Re-*

---

[182] Id at 887, citing, among others, *United States v Ballard*, 322 US 78, 85–87 (1944).

[183] See Lupu, 102 Harv L Rev at 954 (cited in note 130).

[184] *Ballard*, 322 US at 86–87.

[185] Id at 92 (Jackson, J, dissenting).

view Board,[186] a case where the free exercise claimant prevailed. Eddie Thomas, a Jehovah's Witness, worked in a roll foundry section of a steel fabrication factory. After his section was closed, he was transferred to a line producing gun turrets where he then learned that all of his employer's remaining divisions were engaged in one way or another in the production of armaments.[187] Thomas asked a coworker, who was also a Jehovah's Witness, whether their religion prohibited them from producing armaments. His coworker responded that it did not;[188] but Thomas nevertheless felt that he could not continue to work in the factory. After his request to be laid off was denied, he quit and sought unemployment compensation on the ground that he was unavailable for work because assisting in armaments production violated his religious principles.[189]

His claim was brought to an administrative hearing where Thomas struggled to articulate why he considered his working in the tank turret line in an armaments factory to be religiously objectionable. (He indicated that he believed, for example, that working in the same plant to make the raw materials used for the tank turrets would not be objectionable.[190]) The hearing officer concluded that Thomas had left work for religious reasons, and an Indiana appellate court found that he was therefore entitled to unemployment compensation under *Sherbert*.[191]

On appeal, the Indiana Supreme Court reversed, ruling that Thomas had left work for personal reasons.[192] It further asserted that granting benefits to a person who "voluntarily quits work for personal reasons and personal beliefs which can somehow be described as religious," while denying benefits to other employees

---

[186] 450 US 707 (1981). I have also made this point in another writing, William P. Marshall, *Smith, Ballard, and the Religious Inquiry Exception to the Criminal Law*, 44 Texas Tech L Rev 239 (2011).

[187] *Thomas*, 450 US at 709–10.

[188] Thomas also apparently reached out to other members of the congregation to determine whether the Jehovah's Witnesses religion prohibited working in armaments factories, but the record was silent as to whether he was eventually advised. *Thomas v Review Board of the Indiana Employment Securities Division*, 391 NE2d 1127, 1129 (Ind 1979).

[189] Id at 1128

[190] Id at 1131–32, quoting Thomas's testimony before an administrative hearing officer.

[191] Id.

[192] Id at 1133–34.

who quit work for nonreligious personal beliefs, would violate the Establishment Clause.[193]

The United States Supreme Court reversed. The Court first rejected the Indiana Supreme Court's premise that granting relief only to persons asserting religious beliefs was constitutionally problematic. As the Court stated, "[o]nly beliefs rooted in religion are protected by the Free Exercise Clause, which, by its terms, gives special protection to the exercise of religion."[194] It then admonished the Indiana Supreme Court for not deferring to Thomas's characterization of his own beliefs, stating: "Courts should not undertake to dissect religious beliefs because the believer admits that he is 'struggling' with his position or because his beliefs are not articulated with the clarity and precision that a more sophisticated person might employ."[195] Finally, the Court indicated that it was of no import that other Jehovah's Witnesses did not share Thomas's beliefs, because "the guarantee of free exercise is not limited to beliefs which are shared by all of the members of a religious sect" and because "it is not within the judicial function and judicial competence to inquire whether the petitioner or his fellow worker more correctly perceived the commands of their common faith."[196]

The Court's position on all of these issues is certainly defensible. The Free Exercise Clause refers only to religion,[197] so it follows that its protections should be limited to those who assert religious beliefs.[198] Moreover, merely because a person is "struggling" to identify and articulate the nature of his beliefs does not mean that his

---

[193] Id.

[194] *Thomas*, 450 US at 713.

[195] Id at 715–16.

[196] Id.

[197] See US Const, Amend I ("Congress shall make no law respecting an establishment of religion, or prohibiting the free exercise thereof").

[198] As I have argued elsewhere, the conclusion that the Free Exercise Clause applies only to religion does not mean that it authorizes constitutionally compelled exemptions from neutral laws. See William P. Marshall, *The Case Against the Constitutionally Compelled Free Exercise Exemption*, 40 Case W Res L Rev 357 (1989–90). For a historical analysis of the exemption issue, see Michael W. McConnell, *The Origins and Historical Understanding of Free Exercise of Religion*, 103 Harv L Rev 1409 (1990) (contending that the historical evidence supports exemptions); Philip Hamburger, *A Constitutional Right of Religious Exemptions: An Historical Perspective*, 60 Geo Wash L Rev 915 (1992) (concluding that the historical evidence does not support exemptions.).

beliefs are not religious.[199] And the fact that a belief may not comport with a religion's formal tenets does not mean that the belief is not religious; it means only that religion is often deeply individualistic.[200]

The implications of these positions for the workability of the compelling interest standard, however, are substantial. First, they demonstrate the inequality (if not the unconstitutionality) of favoring one form of belief over another. Thomas was entitled to an exemption because he claimed that his objection had a religious basis, whereas another person would be denied an exemption if his beliefs were premised upon a deeply held moral conviction.[201] This distinction may make sense in light of the text of the Free Exercise Clause, but it is problematic if the purpose of the clause is to protect deeply held conscientious principles.[202] In fact, two decades earlier, when the Court faced a similar issue in interpreting the conscientious objector provisions of the Selective Service Act (SSA), it avoided this very problem by interpreting the statutory definition of religion to include nontheistic beliefs.[203]

Second, the Court's conclusion that even those whose religious beliefs are largely inchoate can demand a religious exemption potentially overly expands the class that may gain free exercise protection to those whose beliefs may not actually be religiously based. After all, even sincere believers may not be sure of the foundations of their conscientious principles. Most people, I suspect, believe that it is wrong to cheat, but how many of us can explain whether this belief derives from our religious precepts, philosophical views, political principles, moral values, or fear of punishment? The holding

---

[199] *Thomas*, 450 US at 713.

[200] In fact, concluding that highly individualist religious beliefs would not merit constitutional protection would raise its own concerns because it would effectively privilege some types of religious beliefs over others. The Establishment Clause, however, generally prohibits such distinctions. See generally *Larson v Valente*, 450 US 904 (1981) (the Establishment Clause prohibits sect preferences). But see *United States v Gillette*, 401 US 437 (1971) (upholding the provision of the Selective Service Act providing conscientious status to conscientious objectors whose religious beliefs oppose all wars but not to objectors whose beliefs oppose only unjust wars).

[201] See Marshall, 58 U Chi L Rev at 319–23 (cited in note 6).

[202] Micah J. Schwartzman, *What If Religion Is Not Special?*, 79 U Chi L Rev 1351 (2012); Christopher L. Eisgruber and Lawrence G. Sager, *The Vulnerability of Conscience: The Constitutional Basis for Protecting Religious Conduct*, 61 U Chi L Rev 1245, 1291–97 (1994); Brien L. Leiter, *Why Tolerate Religion* (2013).

[203] *United States v Seeger*, 380 US 163, 165–66, 174–83 (1965); *Welsh v United States*, 398 US 333, 342–43 (1970) (plurality opinion); id at 354–56 (Harlan, J, concurring in judgment).

in *Thomas*, however, encourages those demanding exemptions to err on the side of claiming religious bases for their beliefs, whether or not they are actually grounded in religious faith.

Third, and most importantly, allowing an individual to self-identify the nature and scope of her religious claim eliminates one of the threshold elements that a claimant must establish in order to raise a free exercise challenge, that is, that her claim is religiously based. To be sure, eliminating this inquiry avoids some of the difficulties associated with the courts having to determine the bona fides of religious assertions.[204] But it raises equally weighty concerns of its own. Because almost any action can be cast as religiously motivated,[205] the jurisprudential effect of taking this element out of the free exercise calculus is likely to be considerable. If the government cannot contest the religiosity of the claimant's assertion, it is left with either contesting whether the claimed religious belief is burdened[206] or disputing its sincerity, an inquiry that we have already shown to be especially problematic.[207] Failing that, the government's only recourse is to demonstrate that it has a compelling interest in imposing the burden and that it has no less restrictive alternative to achieve its goals, both immensely difficult tasks.

This means that the resulting jurisprudence becomes one in which (1) free exercise claims are easily raised, (2) not easily opposed, and (3) sustainable in an almost limitless number of circumstances to the detriment of otherwise valid government policies and programs. It also means that the resulting legal landscape would likely be one in which government laws are pockmarked by constitutionally compelled religious exemptions, causing harm to both legitimate regulatory interests and, as Justice Scalia observed in *Smith*, threatening the rule of law by allowing individuals to become "laws unto themselves."[208] All of this would occur, moreover, without the courts

---

[204] See notes 178–85 and accompanying text.

[205] See, for example, *State v Hodges*, 695 SW2d 171 (Tenn 1985), in which the free exercise claimant asserted that his religious beliefs required him to dress like a chicken when going to court.

[206] The *Thomas* case is ambiguous as to whether it also calls for judicial deference to the claimant's self-characterization of "burden." Justice Alito reads *Thomas* to do so, *Hobby Lobby*, 134 S Ct at 2778–79; but *Thomas* can also be read as merely assuming that the claimant's religious objection to working on armaments was necessarily burdened by his being required to work on armaments.

[207] See notes 183–85 and accompanying text.

[208] *Smith*, 494 US at 879.

having any effective way of weeding out fraudulent, meritless, or exploitative religious exercise claims.

It is thus not surprising that immediately after *Thomas* the Court began to introduce new threshold obstacles to maintaining free exercise challenges. In *Lee*, decided one year after *Thomas*, the Court indicated that it would not recognize free exercise claims that arise when "followers of a particular sect enter into commercial activity as a matter of choice."[209] Later, in *Bowen v Roy*[210] and *Lyng v Northwest Indian Cemetery Protective Association*,[211] the Court ruled that Free Exercise Clause claims could not succeed when the claimant challenged the manner in which the government conducts its own internal affairs.[212] And in *O'Lone v Estate of Shabazz*[213] and *Goldman v Weinberger*,[214] the Court, post-*Thomas*, held that free exercise challenges to prison and military restrictions would be adjudged under only a reasonableness standard.[215]

IV. INTERPRETING RFRA

As noted previously, both the *Hobby Lobby* majority and dissent framed the central issue in the case as whether RFRA should be interpreted to provide greater protection to religious exercise than that accorded by the pre-*Smith* Court under the First Amendment, or whether it should merely "restore" the law to its pre-*Smith* status.[216] With an understanding of the pre-*Smith* jurisprudence behind us, we can now return to this question.

---

[209] *Lee*, 455 US at 261.

[210] 476 US 693 (1986).

[211] 485 US 439 (1988).

[212] Id at 448. It may also not be surprising that after *Thomas*, at least one Justice began to explicitly express serious reservations about the viability of the compelling interest test. Writing in *Lee*, only one year after *Thomas*, Justice Stevens wrote: "According to the Court, the religious duty must prevail unless the Government shows that enforcement of the civic duty 'is essential to accomplish an overriding governmental interest.' . . . That formulation of the constitutional standard suggests that the Government always bears a heavy burden of justifying the application of neutral general laws to individual conscientious objectors. In my opinion, it is the objector who must shoulder the burden of demonstrating that there is a unique reason for allowing him a special exemption from a valid law of general applicability."). Id at 263 n 2 (1982) (Stevens, J, concurring in judgment) (citation omitted). Significantly, Justice Stevens later joined the *Smith* majority.

[213] 482 US 342, 345 (1987).

[214] 475 US 503, 507 (1986).

[215] *O'Lone*, 482 US at 345; *Goldman*, 475 US at 507.

[216] See notes 101–02 and accompanying text.

A. TO RESTORE OR EXPAND?

1. *Justice Alito and the argument for expansion.* Justice Alito's central contention was that RFRA should be interpreted as expanding the protection of religious exercise beyond that afforded in the Court's pre-*Smith* decisions.[217] His position is certainly plausible. Why would one want to "restore" a jurisprudence that had enforced the compelling interest test only in a confused and erratic manner?[218] Justice Alito's position, however, also has several weaknesses. First, and most obviously, it ignores the name of the Act itself—the Religious Freedom *Restoration* Act. Restore does not mean expand.[219]

Second, and more importantly, Justice Alito's approach does not persuasively address the argument that by using the same terms in RFRA that the Court had used in its pre-*Smith* decisions—"compelling state interest," "burden," "lesser restrictive alternative"— Congress clearly indicated its intention to reinstate rather than to alter the pre-*Smith* regime.[220] Justice Alito's primary response to this point was to argue that Congress demonstrated its intent to separate RFRA from the pre-*Smith* line of cases when it later amended RFRA in its enactment of RLUIPA.[221] This argument, however, is misplaced. RLUIPA's amendment provided that an RFRA claimant, in order to prevail, does not have to show that government action burdens a religious exercise that is central to her belief system.[222] That is, the amendment addressed only the breadth of religious exercise protected under RFRA, not the degree of protection to be afforded to that exercise.[223] Indeed, to the extent that Justice Alito

---

[217] *Hobby Lobby*, 134 S Ct at 2772 (majority).

[218] See notes 150–59 and accompanying text.

[219] The purpose section of RFRA also emphasizes restoration. See RFRA, 42 USC 2000bb (b)(1):

(b) Purposes
    The purposes of this chapter are—
    (1) to restore the compelling interest test as set forth in *Sherbert v. Verner*, 374 U.S. 398 (1963) and *Wisconsin v. Yoder*, 406 U.S. 205 (1972) and to guarantee its application in all cases where free exercise of religion is substantially burdened.

[220] Lupu, 38 Harv J L & Gender at 76–77 (cited in note 21).

[221] *Hobby Lobby*, 134 S Ct at 2761–62, 2771–73.

[222] 42 USC § 2000cc-5(7) ("The term 'religious exercise' includes any exercise of religion, whether or not compelled by, or central to, a system of religious belief.").

[223] *Hobby Lobby*, 134 S Ct at 2791–92 (Ginsburg, J, dissenting)) ("RLUIPA's alteration clarifies that courts should not question the centrality of a particular religious exercise. But the amendment in no way suggests that Congress meant to expand the class of entities qual-

bases his claim on the RLIUPA amendment that the compelling interest test has a different meaning in RFRA than it had in the free exercise cases, he actually weakens his argument because his point suggests, by negative implication, that other operative terms in RFRA, such as compelling interest, were *not* altered from their pre-*Smith* judicial understanding.[224]

Third, Justice Alito's interpretation runs directly into the Court's explanation in *Smith* of why the compelling interest test did not work in the free exercise context.[225] If even a weak application of the compelling interest test creates serious issues of administrability, then a strong application of the standard will only exacerbate those concerns. Justice Alito, however, did not engage the *Smith* analysis other than to assert, in conclusory fashion, that his decision in *Hobby Lobby* will not compromise government enforcement of such matters as immunization requirements,[226] civil rights protections,[227] and tax laws.[228]

To be sure, Justice Alito has some precedential support for the proposition that the concerns raised about the compelling interest test in *Smith* are not insurmountable. The Court in both *Gonzales* and *Cutter v Wilkinson* indicated that the compelling interest test can be a workable standard when applied to religious exercise.[229] Justice Alito could also cite the Congressional finding in RFRA that "the compelling interest test as set forth in prior Federal court

---

ified to mount religious accommodation claims, nor does it relieve courts of the obligation to inquire whether a government action substantially burdens a religious exercise.").

[224] His argument is also weakened in that RFRA requires that the claimant's religious exercise be substantially burdened while the free exercise inquiry required only that her beliefs be burdened.

[225] See notes 165–85 and accompanying text.

[226] *Hobby Lobby*, 134 S Ct at 2783 ("Other coverage requirements, such as immunizations, may be supported by different interests (for example, the need to combat the spread of infectious diseases) and may involve different arguments about the least restrictive means of providing them.").

[227] Id ("Our decision today provides no such shield [against racial antidiscrimination laws and civil rights laws]. The Government has a compelling interest in providing an equal opportunity to participate in the workforce without regard to race, and prohibitions on racial discrimination are precisely tailored to achieve that critical goal.").

[228] Id at 2784 ("Recognizing a religious accommodation under RFRA for particular coverage requirements . . . does not threaten the viability of ACA's comprehensive scheme in the way that recognizing religious objections to particular expenditures from general tax revenues would.").

[229] See, respectively, *Gonzales*, 546 US at 436, and *Cutter v Wilkinson*, 544 US 709, 723–26 (2005).

rulings is a workable test for striking sensible balances between religious liberty and competing prior governmental interests"[230] (although Congress's affirmation of the pre-*Smith* doctrine in this finding actually *undercuts* Justice Alito's argument that RFRA's protections
should go beyond what those rulings allowed[231]). But as we have seen,
courts had unsuccessfully grappled with the application of the compelling interest test in the religious exercise context for more than fifty
years, suggesting that *Cutter* and *Gonzales* (and the Congress) may have
been too unrealistic in their assertions.[232] Justice Alito's reliance on
those decisions therefore would appear to be misplaced.

2. *Justice Ginsburg and the argument for restoration.* In her dissenting opinion, Justice Ginsburg maintained that RFRA should
be interpreted to *restore* religious exercise protections to the pre-
Smith doctrine.[233] She is supported in this position by the name of
the Act and by some of the Congressional findings.[234] But her contention also suffers from infirmities. First, as we have seen, free exercise case law prior to *Smith* was incoherent. It is hard to believe
that anyone who understood it would want it restored. Most of the
pre-*Smith* legal commentary on the free exercise jurisprudence was
highly critical of the Court's inconsistent approach and strongly advocated for more rigorous protection.[235] Some commentators came
to the issue from the other side, and called for the complete abandonment of free exercise protection in the face of neutral laws of
general application.[236] Nobody, as far as I am aware, endorsed the
pre-*Smith* status quo. The implication of Justice Ginsburg's thesis is

---

[230] 42 USC § 2000bb(a)(5).

[231] See notes 150–59 and accompanying text.

[232] See notes 71–75 and accompanying text. See also Lupu, 38 Harv J L & Gender at __
(cited in note 21), quoting Oliver Wendell Holmes's aphorism that "[t]he life of the law has
not been logic; it has been experience."). See Oliver Wendell Holmes, Jr., *The Common Law*
(Little, Brown, 1881).

[233] *Hobby Lobby*, 134 S Ct at 2791 (Ginsburg, J, dissenting).

[234] RFRA's Congressional Findings and Declaration of Purposes states, "the compelling
interest test as set forth in prior Federal court rulings is a workable test for striking sensible
balances between religious liberty and competing prior governmental interests." 42 USC
§ 2000bb(a)(5).

[235] See generally, Stephen Pepper, *Taking the Free Exercise Clause Seriously*, 1986 BYU L
Rev 299; Michael W. McConnell, *Accommodation of Religion*, 1985 Supreme Court Review 1,
1–10; Michael W. McConnell, *Accommodation of Religion: An Update and a Response to the
Critics*, 60 Geo Wash L Rev 685, 698–708 (1992).

[236] Marshall, 40 Case W Res L Rev at 357 (cited in note 198).

that Congress intended to restore a universally discredited jurisprudence.

Second, Justice Ginsburg's restoration argument becomes even more problematic in light of the *Smith* Court's characterization of the earlier free exercise cases. Justice Scalia's opinion for the Court in *Smith* contended that the decision did not overrule prior case law.[237] After noting that the compelling interest test had never been used to require a free exercise exemption from a neutral law, Justice Scalia distinguished the cases in which religious claimants prevailed as being either an instance of a hybrid right[238] (*Yoder*) or a situation in which the government already had in place a system of individualized, nonreligious exemptions (the unemployment compensation cases).[239] Notably, Justice Scalia did not suggest that these decisions were wrong. Rather, he embraced them as consistent with his *Smith* opinion.[240] Accordingly, if one accepts Justice Ginsburg's conclusion that RFRA was designed only to re-create the pre-*Smith* jurisprudence, it would mean that RFRA did not change anything. The pre-*Smith* decisions had already survived *Smith*.[241]

Third, if *Smith* was correct in its assessment of the preexisting case law, then Justice Ginsburg's restoration argument is undercut by the section of RFRA that explicitly provides that government "shall not substantially burden a person's exercise of religion even if the burden results from a rule of general applicability."[242] Applying a compelling interest test to neutral laws is an expansion of

---

[237] See note 146 and accompanying text.

[238] *Smith*, 494 US at 881 ("The only decisions in which we have held that the First Amendment bars application of a neutral, generally applicable law to religiously motivated action have involved not the Free Exercise Clause alone, but the Free Exercise Clause in conjunction with other constitutional protections.") (collecting cases).

[239] Id at 884, quoting *Bowen v Roy*, 476 US 693, 708 (1986) ("[W]here the State has in place a system of individual exemptions, it may not refuse to extend that system to cases of 'religious hardship' without compelling reason.").

[240] Id at 882 ("Respondents urge us to hold, quite simply, that when otherwise prohibitable conduct is accompanied by religious convictions, not only the convictions but the conduct itself must be free from governmental regulation. We have never held that, and decline to do so now.").

[241] Indeed, for that reason RFRA's first clause, which announces the statute's stated purpose, arguably makes little sense. The provision states that its purpose is "to restore the compelling interest test as set forth in *Sherbert v. Verner and Wisconsin v. Yoder*, and to guarantee its application in all cases where free exercise of religion is substantially burdened." 42 USC § 2000bb(b)(1). However, at least with respect to *Sherbert* and *Verner*, there was nothing to restore.

[242] 42 USC at § 2000bb-1(a).

pre-*Smith* law, at least according to *Smith*. According to *Smith*, the Court had *never* applied a compelling interest standard in cases involving neutral laws, even though it had claimed to have done so.[243]

Of course, one could respond to these points by contending (with some merit) that Justice Scalia's opinion in *Smith* was disingenuous[244] and that RFRA should be interpreted as restoring the *actual* pre-*Smith* jurisprudence, and not *Smith*'s re-creation of it. But what exactly would that jurisprudence be? The problem is that while the pre-*Smith* cases can be described as offering only a lukewarm protection for religious exercise, that description does not provide insight into how the Court approached each specific case. Sometimes the Court strongly protected the free exercise interest, sometimes it did not. In *Yoder*, the Court demanded an exceptionally strong interest from the state and found that even the government interest in educating children was not sufficiently compelling.[245] In *United States v Lee*,[246] it held that the government interest in imposing social security taxes on Amish employers was sufficient.[247] In *Thomas* and in *Frazee*, the Court deferred to the claimant's self-characterization of his claim that his religious beliefs were infringed by the challenged restriction.[248] In *Yoder* and in *Tony and Susan Alamo Foundation v Secretary of Labor*,[249] the Court inquired into that issue itself.[250] The pre-*Smith* case law, in short, was a moving target that did not even move in the same direction. The results in the cases were as haphazard at the end of *Sherbert*'s tenure as at the beginning.[251]

---

[243] *Smith*, 494 US at 883 ("Although we have sometimes purported to apply the *Sherbert* test in contexts other than that, we have always found the test satisfied.").

[244] I have made this point elsewhere. See Marshall, 58 U Chi L Rev at 309 (cited in note 6) ("[*Smith*'s] use of precedent borders on fiction.").

[245] *Yoder*, 406 US at 221.

[246] 455 US 252 (1982).

[247] Id at 258–59 ("Moreover, a comprehensive national social security system providing for voluntary participation would be almost a contradiction in terms and difficult, if not impossible, to administer. Thus, the Government's interest in assuring mandatory and continuous participation in and contribution to the social security system is very high.").

[248] See, respectively, *Thomas*, 450 US at 714, 715–16; *Frazee*, 489 US at 832–35.

[249] 471 US 290 (1985).

[250] See, respectively, *Yoder*, 406 US at 215–19; *Tony and Susan Alamo Foundation*, 471 US at 303–05.

[251] See notes 151–57 and accompanying text.

This then leads to a fourth objection. Justice Ginsburg does not explain why she accepts some of the pre-*Smith* decisions for guidance while rejecting others. Why should the Court accept *Lee's* premise that protections for religious exercise should not apply to commercial activity while rejecting the indication in *Braunfield v Brown*[252] and *Tony and Susan Alamo Foundation* that it does? Why reject *Thomas's* suggestion that the Court should not inquire into threshold issues such as burden but accept the notion in *Yoder* and *Tony and Susan Alamo Foundation* that it should?

Finally, Justice Ginsburg's assertion that Congress intended to restore the pre-*Smith* case law also raises serious administrability concerns. The application of the compelling interest test pre-*Smith* did not produce a coherent jurisprudence. Restoring that case law, while perhaps not adding to the difficulties faced by the Court pre-*Smith*, would not fix the problem. Justice Ginsburg's approach would simply take the law of religious exercise back to a broken system.[253]

3. *Summary*. Both the *Hobby Lobby* majority and dissent presented plausible arguments about whether RFRA should be interpreted to expand or to merely restore the protections for religious exercise that existed in the constitutional case law pre-*Smith*. Both interpretations, however, ignored the problems endemic in applying the compelling interest test that the pre-*Smith* regime so effectively illustrated. Justice Ginsburg's opinion called for the reinstitution of a broken system. Justice Alito's determination to expand religious exercise protection would make a bad system even worse. It is to that point that I now turn.

B. FOR-PROFIT CORPORATIONS, SELF-ASSESSED BURDENS, COMMERCIAL
   ACTIVITY, AND MAKING A BAD SYSTEM WORSE

Justice Alito's decision to construe RFRA as providing more expansive protection for religious exercise than was guaranteed in the Court's pre-*Smith* free exercise jurisprudence is reflected in his resolution of at least three of the five statutory construction issues

---

[252] 366 US 599 (1961).

[253] That of course does not mean her decision is "wrong" if restoring an incoherent and broken system is what Congress intended. Nor is Justice Alito's decision "wrong" if Congress intended to craft a statute that would exacerbate the problems that existed in the free exercise jurisprudence pre-*Smith*. In either case, the responsibility rests with Congress.

before the Court in *Hobby Lobby*[254]—specifically, his conclusions that
RFRA applies to for-profit corporations, that RFRA plaintiffs can
self-assess whether their religious beliefs have been "burdened" by
the government action, and that RFRA's protections apply even
when the adherent is voluntarily engaged in commercial activity.[255]
As we shall see, Justice Alito's conclusions on these three issues may
be defensible as matters of statutory construction, but they exacerbate the problems with the compelling interest test that the Court
was unable to overcome in its pre-*Smith* free exercise jurisprudence.

The first issue—whether for-profit corporations are entitled to
raise religious exercise claims—had never been directly addressed
in the pre-*Smith* cases[256] and was an issue of first impression.[257]
Relying primarily on the Dictionary Act, Justice Alito concluded
that RFRA provides for-profit corporations with such a right.[258]

---

[254] See notes 81–82 and accompanying text (outlining the five statutory construction issues
at issue in *Hobby Lobby*).

[255] Justice Alito's opinion, it may be remembered, did not reach the compelling interest
question. *Hobby Lobby*, 134 S Ct at 2780. His resolution of the "least restrictive alternative"
issue by pointing to the fact that the government already had in place a parallel accommodation for religious nonprofits, in turn, may be so idiosyncratic to the specific provisions of
the ACA so as to not provide much direction for future cases. This is not to say that Justice
Alito's opinion on lesser restrictive alternatives could not be interpreted to afford expansive
protection to religious exercise under RFRA. The rationale that religious-based exemptions
were already in place and existed specifically for the purpose of accommodating religious
objections to contraception coverage does offer a narrow ground for his opinion. But if this
approach were interpreted more broadly, it could also lead to the government rarely prevailing because, assuming other legal requirements are met, the government could almost
always provide some sort of religious-based exemption from a legal mandate.

[256] See Robert K. Vischer, *Do For-Profit Businesses Have Free Exercise Rights?*, 21 J Contemp
Legal Issues 369, 375–85 (2013) (surveying "constitutional law, corporate theory, and the
emerging theology of the corporation" to better understand the recurrent debate over corporate claims of free exercise). See also James D. Nelson, *Conscience Incorporated*, 2013 Mich
St L Rev 1565, 1566–67 (2013). In *Gallagher v Crown Kosher Super Market of Mass, Inc.*, 366
US 617 (1961), the Court reviewed (and rejected) a free exercise challenge brought by a for-
profit corporation but did not directly engage the question of whether for-profit corporate
status alone would disqualify a claimant for free exercise protections.

[257] One might have thought that the logical starting point for determining whether corporations should be deemed to have First Amendment rights would be *Citizens United v
Federal Elections Commission*, 558 US 310 (2010), but that case was not truly on point. In
concluding that corporations have speech rights, the *Citizens United* court relied in large part
on the principle that there is First Amendment value in speech entering the marketplace of
ideas regardless of its source because of the interest of the listener in being exposed to the
speaker's views. Id at 342. Religious exercise does not raise a parallel consideration.

[258] *Hobby Lobby*, 134 S Ct at 2768–73. The vote on this issue was 5–2. Justices Breyer and
Kagan did not join Justice Ginsburg's dissent on this issue. See id, 134 S Ct at 2806 (Breyer
and Kagan, JJ, dissenting) ("We agree with Justice Ginsburg that the plaintiffs' challenge to
the contraceptive coverage requirement fails on the merits. We need not and do not decide
whether either for-profit corporations or their owners may bring claims under [RFRA].").

This conclusion has been the subject of considerable criticism.[259] As Justice Ginsburg argued, the "exercise of religion is character-istic of natural persons, not artificial legal entities."[260] Moreover, the corporate form is specifically designed to distance owners and their personal obligations from the incorporated entity. Infusing the corporation with the religious beliefs of its owners therefore seems inconsistent with the corporate purpose.[261]

Nonetheless, the argument that for-profit corporations are "per-sons" under RFRA is not implausible. For example, nonprofit reli-gious corporations, such as churches, have long been recognized as having free exercise rights.[262] Accordingly, any suggestion that cor-porate status automatically eliminates a claimant from RFRA eligi-bility is a nonstarter, and the defendants in *Hobby Lobby* conceded the point.[263] Moreover, some of the Court's pre-*Smith* free exercise decisions had acknowledged that for-profit entities could claim free exercise protection. In *Braunfeld v Brown*,[264] for example, the Court

---

[259] See, for example, Thomas E. Rutledge, *A Corporation Has No Soul—The Business Entity Law Response to the PPACA Contraception Mandate*, 5 Wm & Mary Bus L Rev 1 (2014); James Nelson, *Conscience Incorporated*, 2013 Mich St L Rev 1565, 1586–1610. A summary of the law concerning the division between a corporate entity as a separate legal entity on one hand and its shareholders, directors, and officers on the other, the reasons for the division, and the potential problems with breaching that divide was presented to the Court in Amicus Curiae Brief of Corporate and Criminal Law Professors in Support of Petitioners, *Burwell v Hobby Lobby*, No 13-354 & No 13-356 (S Ct, filed Jan 28, 2014).

[260] *Hobby Lobby*, 134 S Ct at 2794 (Ginsburg, J, dissenting), quoting *Trustees of Dartmouth College v Woodward*, 17 US (4 Wheat) 518, 636 (1819) ("[A] corporation is 'an artificial being, invisible, intangible, and existing only in contemplation of law.'"); and *Citizens United v Federal Election Commission*, 558 US 310, 466 (2010) (Stevens, J, concurring in part and dissenting in part) ("Corporations, 'have no consciences, no beliefs, no feelings, no thoughts, no desires.'"). See also Nelson, 2013 Mich St L Rev at 1565, 1566–67 (cited in note 259) (arguing RFRA should not be interpreted to protect for-profit corporations).

[261] As the Sixth Circuit reasoned in another contraceptive mandate case:

> [b]y incorporating his business, [the owner] voluntarily forfeited his rights to bring individual actions for alleged corporate injuries in exchange for the liability and financial protections otherwise afforded him by utilization of the corporate form. Adoption of [the owner's] argument that he should not be liable individually for corporate debts and wrongs, but still should be allowed to challenge, as an indi-vidual, duties and restrictions placed upon the corporation would undermine com-pletely the principles upon which our nation's corporate laws and structures are based. *Eden Foods, Inc. v Sebelius*, 733 F3d 626, 632 (6th Cir 2013), cert granted, judgment vacated sub nom *Eden Foods, Inc. v Burwell*, 134 S Ct 2902 (2014).

[262] *Hobby Lobby*, 134 S Ct at 2768–69 (collecting cases) ("We have entertained RFRA and free-exercise claims brought by nonprofit corporations.").

[263] Id at 2769.

[264] 366 US 599 (1961).

took seriously a sole proprietor's free exercise claim that he was unfairly burdened in running his commercial enterprise by a Sunday closing law because his beliefs required that he could also not work on Saturdays. The Court did not see the fact that he was engaged in commerce as relevant to the outcome.[265]

This being so, the government's argument in *Hobby Lobby* had to be that an entity that had *either* corporate status *or* a profit motive could be a "person" exercising religion under RFRA, but that an entity that was *both* corporate and for profit could not. That leads not only to a contorted meaning of the word "person," but also to a more fundamental problem. The question raised in *Hobby Lobby* was not whether it made the best policy sense, as a matter of constitutional law or even corporate law, to assume that for-profit corporations can engage in religious exercise, but what the word "person" meant in the relevant provision. To resolve that question, resort to the Dictionary Act was not unreasonable, particularly given the concession that nonprofit corporations meet the statutory definition.[266] What Justice Alito did not address, however, was the potential effect that his decision regarding for-profit corporations might have in conjunction with his other rulings with respect to the ability of a claimant to maintain, and of the government to respond to, an RFRA action. I shall return to this point shortly.

Justice Alito did look to the pre-*Smith* case law in resolving the second issue—the meaning of "substantial burden" under RFRA.[267]

---

[265] Id at 601–02.

[266] As the Court noted, the Dictionary Act, 1 USC § 1, lists corporations as persons for the purpose of interpreting Acts of Congress without differentiating between for-profit corporations and not-for-profit corporations. *Hobby Lobby*, 134 S Ct at 2768–69. The Court's application of the Dictionary Act can be seen as a straightforward application of a fundamental rule of construction to interpret a law as written using the plain and ordinary meaning of the statutory words. See, for example, *Sebelius v Cloer*, 133 S Ct 1886, 1896 (2013) ("when [a] statute's language is plain, the sole function of the courts—at least where the disposition required by the text is not absurd—is to enforce it according to its terms," quoting *Hartford Underwriters Insurance Co. v Union Planters Bank, NA*, 530 US 1, 6 (2000) (internal quotation marks omitted)); *Negonsott v Samuels*, 507 US 99, 104 (1993) ("'Our task is to give effect to the will of Congress, and where its will has been expressed in reasonably plain terms, that language must ordinarily be regarded as conclusive,'" quoting *Griffin v Oceanic Contractors, Inc.*, 458 US 564, 570 (1982) (internal quotation marks omitted)).

At the same time, there is one weakness in Justice Alito's Dictionary Act argument. The Act itself requires resort to its provisions *"unless the context indicates otherwise."* 1 USC § 1.

[267] As Ira Lupu and Robert Tuttle have noted, the question of burden under RFRA comprises two parts, the secular costs imposed on the adherent by her noncompliance with the challenged law and the religious costs imposed by her compliance. Ira C. Lupu and Robert W. Tuttle, *Secular Government, Religious People* 198–99 (Eerdmans, 2014). In *Hobby Lobby*

Specifically, he invoked *Thomas v Review Board*,[268] in which the Court had deferred to a claimant's assertion that participation in the production of armaments violated his religious beliefs. On this authority, Justice Alito reasoned that the Court should similarly defer to the *Hobby Lobby* plaintiffs' assertions that providing insurance for objectionable contraception burdened their religious beliefs.[269] Otherwise, courts would have to enter into the precarious business of judging the *religious* merits of a claimant's assertion that her beliefs were burdened by the government's action.[270]

In fact, though, reliance on the claimant's self-assessment of burden does not follow as neatly from pre-*Smith* decisions as Justice Alito suggests. To begin with, in cases decided both before and after *Thomas*, the Court did not reflexively defer to a claimant's assertion of burden. In *Yoder*, for example, the Court independently determined whether the Amish's beliefs were burdened by compulsory school requirements,[271] and in *Tony and Susan Alamo Foundation* the Court independently assessed whether the Foundation's religious beliefs were burdened by minimum wage requirements.[272] Moreover, although *Thomas* addressed the question whether it would be inappropriate for a court to question the *religiosity* of a particular belief, it did not address the question whether courts could independently assess the *burden* imposed upon that belief by the government's action.[273] Finally, *Thomas* asked only whether the government

---

there was no question with respect to the secular costs—the financial penalties that the ACA levies for noncompliance were significant. The more difficult question was whether the religious costs incurred by the plaintiffs were similarly substantial.

[268] *Hobby Lobby*, 134 S Ct at 2778, citing *Thomas*, 450 US at 715.

[269] Id at 2779.

[270] Id at 2778 ("Arrogating the authority to provide a binding national answer to this religious and philosophical question, HHS and the principal dissent in effect tell the plaintiffs that their beliefs are flawed. For good reason, we have repeatedly refused to take such a step."); id at 2779 ("in these cases, the Hahns and Greens and their companies sincerely believe that providing the insurance coverage demanded by the HHS regulations lies on the forbidden side of the line, and it is not for us to say that their religious beliefs are mistaken or insubstantial. Instead, our 'narrow function' . . . in this context is to determine whether the line drawn reflects 'an honest conviction,'" quoting *Thomas*, 450 US at 716).

[271] *Yoder*, 406 US at 222–25, 235–36.

[272] *Tony and Susan Alamo Foundation*, 471 US at 303–05.

[273] See *Thomas*, 450 US at 714 ("the resolution of that question [of what is a religious belief or practice] is not to turn upon a judicial perception of the particular belief or practice in question; religious beliefs need not be acceptable, logical, consistent or comprehensible to others in order to merit First Amendment protection").

action "unduly burdens" religious exercise.[274] RFRA, on the other hand, demands a showing of "substantial burden,"[275] suggesting that RFRA might well require a judicial assessment of the extent of the burden, even if that inquiry had not been called for in the Court's pre-*Smith* free exercise cases.[276]

On the other hand, Justice Alito's assertion that courts are not competent to adjudge questions of burden is a powerful one. How is a court to ascertain which religious claims are too attenuated to an individual's belief structure without imposing its own sense of religious priorities and values on the believer? In *Hobby Lobby*, for example, one could reasonably assert, as did Justice Ginsburg, that providing contraceptive coverage to employees who might or might not use that coverage to access contraception methods that might or might not take effect after an egg is fertilized was "too attenuated" from the plaintiffs' beliefs that life begins at conception to trigger RFRA's protections.[277] But "too attenuated" to whom? Even seemingly objectively attenuated claims can be of central concern to a believer. For some adherents, it might be more adverse to their religious beliefs to be complicit in some action than to be forced to take an action contrary to their beliefs.[278] Consider a religion that both maintains that life begins at conception and prohibits working on the Sabbath. To an adherent of that religion, it may be more injurious to her conscience to be required to provide insurance coverage to her employees for contraception than for her to be com-

---

[274] Id at 717 ("'[a] regulation neutral on its face may, in its application, nonetheless offend the constitutional requirement for governmental neutrality if it unduly burdens the free exercise of religion,'" quoting *Yoder*, 406 US at 220). See also *Thomas*, 450 US at 717–18 ("Where the state conditions receipt of an important benefit upon conduct proscribed by a religious faith, or where it denies such a benefit because of conduct mandated by religious belief, thereby putting substantial pressure on an adherent to modify his behavior and to violate his beliefs, a burden upon religion exists. While the compulsion may be indirect, the infringement upon free exercise is nonetheless substantial.").

[275] 42 USC § 2000bb-1.

[276] Interestingly, although *Sherbert*, *Yoder*, and *Thomas* do not use the language of "substantial burden," that term is used in by the Court in *Smith* when articulating the *Sherbert* test. *Smith*, 494 US at 883 ("Under the *Sherbert* test, governmental actions that substantially burden a religious practice must be justified by a compelling governmental interest"). See also *Hernandez v Commissioner*, 490 US 680, 699 (1989).

[277] *Hobby Lobby*, 134 S Ct at 2799 (Ginsburg, J, dissenting).

[278] For an excellent analysis arguing that courts should be reluctant to recognize RFRA claims based upon an adherent's assertion that it would violate her religious beliefs to be complicit in the actions of another, see Douglas NeJaime and Reva B. Siegel, *Conscience Wars: Complicity-Based Conscience Claims in Religion and Politics*, 124 Yale L J (forthcoming 2015).

pelled to work on the Sabbath. Whether the government has imposed a "burden," in short, depends entirely on the faith of the believer. There is no rational way for a court independently to make that assessment. Thus, Justice Alito's decision to construe RFRA in a way that avoids the need for courts to inquire into burden is at least arguably defensible, as was the decision in *Thomas* not to have courts independently examine religiosity. What again lay unexamined, however, was the cumulative effect that this holding might have on a claimant's ability to maintain, and the government's ability to respond to, an RFRA challenge.

The third issue on which Justice Alito offered an expansive interpretation of RFRA's protections involved the question whether RFRA should protect individuals or entities that voluntarily engage in commercial activity. In *United States v Lee*, the Court turned back a free exercise challenge brought by an Amish sole proprietor who claimed that compelled participation in the social security program, including the payment of social security taxes, would violate his religious belief that caring for the elderly was the responsibility of the individual and not the government.[279] In so ruling, the Court stated that "[w]hen followers of a particular sect enter into commercial activity as a matter of choice, the limits they accept on their own conduct as a matter of conscience and faith are not to be superimposed on the statutory schemes which are binding on others in that activity."[280]

Justice Alito rejected the commercial activity argument for two reasons. First, he summarily distinguished *Lee* as a tax case.[281] Second, restating his fundamental position that RFRA should be interpreted to provide greater protection to religious freedom than that provided in the pre-*Smith* free exercise decisions, he asserted that a commercial activity exception was "squarely inconsistent with the plain meaning of RFRA."[282] He might have added a third rationale. In other pre-*Smith* cases, the Court had considered free exercise challenges based upon a religious adherent's voluntary participation in commercial activity.[283] In *Tony and Susan Alamo Foun-*

---

[279] *Lee*, 455 US at 255, 257.

[280] Id at 261.

[281] *Hobby Lobby*, 134 S Ct at 2783–84.

[282] Id at 2784 n 43.

[283] *Braunfield v Brown*, 366 US 599, 601–02 (1961); *Tony and Susan Alamo Foundation*, 471 US at 292.

dation, for example, the Court considered a free exercise challenge brought by a nonprofit religious foundation engaged in a wide range of commercial enterprises such as hog farms, service stations, and restaurants.[284]

What Justice Alito did not address, however, was the argument that a categorical exclusion of commercial activity from RFRA coverage might allow the courts to escape some of the concerns raised after *Thomas* (and exacerbated by *Hobby Lobby*'s ruling on burden) concerning the inability of the government to defeat a religious exercise challenge at the threshold level. As discussed previously, eliminating the ability of the government to question religiosity led to the likelihood that important government interests would be compromised, even if those interests might not be "compelling." It also raised the concern that fraudulent or otherwise nonmeritorious religious claims might too readily be asserted and then easily prevail— a concern that seems particularly problematic when such exemptions are sought from regulations affecting commercial activity.[285]

Thus, as we saw earlier, after *Thomas* the Court began to create new categorical obstacles to free exercise challenges when it held in *Lyng* that the Free Exercise Clause did not apply when the burden on religious exercise was caused by the government's conduct of its own internal affairs[286] and in *Goldman* and *O'Lone* when it indicated it would not apply the compelling interest test in free exercise cases arising in military and prison contexts. The commercial activity exception in *Lee* could be explained as a similar effort. To be sure, the Court never explicitly announced that it was engaging in this strategy and, indeed, it may not have been consciously doing so. But in considering these cases, at least some Justices must have recognized that applying a compelling interest test to all free exercise assertions without an effective filtering mechanism created the risk of unleashing an unboundable constitutional right. Indeed, the recognition of these difficulties is precisely what led to the decision in *Smith*.

The enactment of RFRA, of course, re-created the same possibility. Accordingly, one might have expected the Court to proceed cautiously before giving the statute an expansive interpretation. Justice Alito's opinion in *Hobby Lobby*, however, did the opposite. By

---

[284] *Tony and Susan Alamo Foundation*, 471 US at 292.

[285] See notes 206–08 and accompanying text.

[286] *Lyng*, 485 US at 439.

eliminating the threshold inquiry into burden (as well as religiosity), and by denying threshold exclusions for commercial activity and for for-profit corporations, he effectively removed some of the more powerful brakes that might otherwise have slowed down the RFRA express.[287]

In the following sections, I address two specific areas—commerce and politics—in which the application of RFRA, as construed by the Court in *Hobby Lobby*, may well lead to deeply troublesome results.

V. RFRA—POST HOBBY LOBBY

A. RFRA AND COMMERCE

Hobby Lobby's holdings that RFRA protects for-profit corporations[288] and entities engaged in commercial activity have economic, as well as religious exercise, implications. After *Hobby Lobby*, for-profit corporations and other entities engaged in commercial activity will have an incentive to bring RFRA claims, because exemptions from regulatory measures can provide them with a significant competitive edge in the market. The *Tony and Susan Alamo Foundation* case, in which the claimant sought a free exercise exemption from the minimum wage requirements of the Fair Labor Standards Act (FLSA), provides a good example.[289] If the Court had granted the foundation an exemption, it would have enjoyed lower labor costs than its competitors. Indeed, because compliance with almost any law costs money,[290] most exemptions from regulatory requirements will allow the excepted corporation to benefit vis-à-vis its competitors. This makes almost any regulatory measure affecting commercial activity an attractive target for an RFRA challenge.

For-profit corporations and other commercial entities will also have incentives to file RFRA challenges for another reason—*Hobby*

---

[287] To be sure, as will be discussed subsequently, categorical exclusions can raise their own sets of issues. See notes 335–36 and accompanying text.

[288] The holding that for-profit corporations are eligible for RFRA's protections is also likely to raise difficult issues in the law of corporate governance as courts will necessarily struggle with determining whether or when a particular corporation is espousing a religious view. Who will be deemed to represent the corporations for this purpose? What, if any, are the rights of the minority shareholders (or directors and officers) in the corporation who do not share the representative's religious views?

[289] *Tony and Susan Alamo Foundation v Secretary of Labor*, 471 US 290, 292 (1985).

[290] The exception being *Hobby Lobby* itself, as there was no indication in the case that the plaintiffs would receive economic benefits if excluded from the contraceptive mandate.

Lobby substantially increases the likelihood that they will prevail. *Hobby Lobby*'s holding that courts must defer to the claimant's characterization of the burden, combined with its rejection of the categorical exclusions from RFRA of for-profit corporations and commercial activities, means that the government will no longer be able to defeat RFRA claims at their threshold. In every case, the government will have to demonstrate both a compelling interest and the unavailability of a less restrictive means. This will not be easy. Although the strict scrutiny required by the compelling interest standard may not mean "fatal in fact," as Gerald Gunther once asserted,[291] it is nevertheless a demanding standard.[292] Moreover, as noted previously, the standard will be particularly difficult to satisfy in religious exercise cases because the government must show that its interests are compelling as applied to a limited class of religious objectors rather than to the general population.[293] Thus, to again reference the *Tony and Susan Alamo Foundation* case, although the government's interest in preventing wage deflation through minimum wage requirements might be compelling when applied to employers generally, that interest might not be seriously undermined if an exemption from its strictures is granted only to those raising religious objections, such as the Tony and Susan Alamo Foundation.[294]

To be sure, five Justices in *Hobby Lobby* indicated that they would find the government interest in protecting women's health to be sufficiently weighty, suggesting that RFRA's compelling in-

---

[291] Gerald Gunther, *Foreword: In Search of Evolving Doctrine on a Changing Court: A Model for a Newer Equal Protection*, 86 Harv L Rev 1, 8 (1972). See also Adam Winkler, *Fatal in Theory and Strict in Fact: An Empirical Analysis of Strict Scrutiny in the Federal Courts*, 59 Vand L Rev 793, 795–96, 822 (2006).

[292] See notes 111–13 and accompanying text (listing free speech cases in which strong state interests were found insufficiently compelling to outweigh the right of expression).

[293] *Hobby Lobby*, 134 S Ct at 2779 (RFRA "requires the Government to demonstrate that the compelling interest test is satisfied through application of the challenged law to the person—the particular claimant whose sincere exercise of religion is being substantially burdened. This requires us to look beyond broadly formulated interests and to scrutinize the asserted harm of granting specific exemptions to particular religious claimants—in other words, to look to the marginal interest in enforcing the contraceptive mandate in these cases.") (citations and internal quotations omitted).

[294] *Tony and Susan Alamo Foundation v Secretary of Labor*, 471 US 290 (1985). The Court in this case upheld the minimum wage requirement from the free exercise challenge under the tepid version of the compelling interest test utilized by the Court pre-*Smith*. Presumably, however, a more vigorous application of the test such as that proposed by Justice Alito could lead to a different result.

terest requirement might not be insurmountable.[295] Yet one can imagine many regulatory measures that would not meet this standard unless, as Justice Scalia warned in *Smith*, the compelling interest standard becomes so "watered down" that it "would subvert its rigor in the other fields where it is applied."[296]

The risk that *Hobby Lobby* invites flimsy but readily sustainable RFRA claims by entities engaged in commercial activity then should be apparent. A financial incentive combined with a high likelihood of success is a dangerous mix. But the issue extends beyond the culling of insincere or fraudulent claims. In many cases the availability of an RFRA exemption will lead to questionable filings by believers who are sincere, or at least think they are sincere, when they characterize their objections to regulatory measures as religiously based. The *Thomas* case is again illustrative. Was Thomas's objection to working in an armaments factory actually religious, or was he motivated, consciously or unconsciously, to portray his belief as theistically based? Possibly even he did not know. But one thing he did know was that articulating his belief as political or moral would defeat his desire not to work in the armaments factory while still collecting unemployment compensation. By characterizing his belief as religious, he was able to gain an exemption.

A similar lesson may be found in the *Eden Foods* case.[297] In that litigation, a for-profit corporation brought a claim against the contraceptive mandate similar to that in *Hobby Lobby*.[298] In a series of out-of-court statements, the company's CEO, Michael Potter, made clear that much of his objection to the contraceptive mandate was based upon his dislike of government regulation generally. When asked why he was bringing suit, Potter answered: "Because I don't care if the federal government is telling me to buy

---

[295] See *Hobby Lobby*, 134 S Ct at 2785–86 (Kennedy, J, concurring) (noting that the government had made the case that providing contraception health care insurance served a compelling governmental interest); id at 2788–90, 2799–02 (Ginsburg, J, dissenting, joined by Justices Breyer, Sotomayor, and Kagan, JJ) (making the case that the contraception health insurance requirement serves a compelling governmental interest).

[296] 494 US at 888.

[297] *Eden Foods, Inc. v Sebelius*, 733 F3d 626 (6th Cir 2013), cert granted, judgment vacated sub nom *Eden Foods, Inc. v Burwell*, 134 S Ct 2902 (2014).

[298] Id at 627 (setting forth the plaintiff's contention that offering contraceptive services to their employees would substantially burden their religious beliefs).

my employees Jack Daniel's or birth control. What gives them the right to tell me that I have to do that? That's my issue, that's what I object to, and that's the beginning and end of the story."[299]

At the same time, Potter, who is a Catholic, also claimed "that any action which either before, at the moment of, or after sexual intercourse, is specifically intended to prevent procreation, whether as an end or means—including abortifacients and contraception—is wrong,"[300] thus suggesting that there was also a religious basis for his objection to the contraceptive mandate. So how is a court to know whether Potter's objection to providing insurance coverage for contraception offends his religious principles or only his antiregulatory convictions? As with Eddie Thomas, it may be that Michael Potter himself does not know the answer. What *Hobby Lobby* teaches, however, is that when entrepreneurs like Michael Potter seek to decipher the nature of their own beliefs, they are best served by characterizing them as religious.

The ability of for-profit corporations and other entities engaged in commercial activity to seek RFRA exemptions, then, should be troubling. As Justice Scalia stated in *Smith*: "we cannot afford the luxury of deeming *presumptively invalid*, as applied to the religious objector, every regulation of conduct that does not protect an interest of the highest order."[301] That concern is even further enhanced when the claim for exemption yields substantial economic rewards.

This result should also be troubling from a religious perspective. A system that encourages persons to frame their objections to neutral laws in religious terms in order to gain economic benefit can corrupt the purity and integrity of religious beliefs, a concern that is also central to anti-Establishment principles.[302] It also brings the

---

[299] See Irin Carmon, *Eden Foods Doubles Down in Birth Control Flap* (Salon, Apr 15, 2013), online at http://www.salon.com/2013/04/15/eden_foods_ceo_digs_himself_deeper_in_birth_control_outrage/.

[300] See http://www.forbes.com/sites/clareoconnor/2014/07/14/whole-foods-shoppers-can-vote-with-their-dollars-on-pro-life-eden-foods/.

[301] *Smith*, 494 US at 888 (emphasis in original).

[302] Andrew Koppelman, *Corruption of Religion and the Establishment Clause*, 50 Wm & Mary L Rev 1831, 1831 (2009). See also Mark DeWolfe Howe, *The Garden and the Wilderness* 6 (Chicago, 1965) (discussing the anticorruption rationale as the basis of Roger Williams's commitment to separationism).

sanctity of religious belief into question when claims of religious hardship are seen as ploys for commercial gain. These are, to say the least, deeply disconcerting consequences.

B. RFRA AND POLITICS

As noted at the outset of this article, the Affordable Care Act triggered intense and sustained political opposition. Even before its enactment, opponents began developing legal strategies to try to undo the legislation. Following enactment, they pursued these strategies, which included not only the broad challenge to the individual mandate rejected in *National Federation of Independent Business v Sebelius*,[303] but also targeted attacks on particular provisions in order to undo the legislation in "bits and pieces," as one leading proponent of this strategy suggested.[304] The attack on the contraceptive mandate in *Hobby Lobby* fit comfortably within this strategy.

This background does not impugn the sincerity of the *Hobby Lobby* plaintiffs. But it does demonstrate an important fact: RFRA can, and does, have the potential to cause significant political effects. This political impact can take a variety of forms. First, as the anti-ACA strategy suggests, RFRA claims can be used for immediate political effect such as weakening the political viability of a challenged provision. A judicial determination that a law offends religious principle sends a negative message about that law, particularly when the determination is that the law transgresses the beliefs of a mainstream religion. The law's opponents can then reasonably assert the following position: "not only is the legislation bad, it violates the consciences of people of faith." In this way, a successful RFRA challenge can add considerable valiance to the political narrative attacking the legislation.

Second, even beyond short-term political gain, RFRA claims can have long-term effects on the social and cultural landscape in which political decisions are made. Religion, as I have stated elsewhere, is not insular.[305] It is a powerful force that competes with other forms of beliefs in the political, social, and cultural battles for

---

[303] 567 US 1 (2012).

[304] See http://talkingpointsmemo.com/livewire/halbig-obamacare-2010-bastard-has-to-be-killed (quoting Competitive Enterprise Institute CEO Michael Greve).

[305] Marshall, 58 U Chi L Rev at 321 (cited in note 6).

hearts and minds.[306] An adherent's claim that the use of certain contraception methods is wrong, or that working in an armaments plant
is sinful, for example, are politically laden messages that can affect
the views of others.[307] Exempting those beliefs from regulatory strictures therefore empowers them in relation to competing nonreligious assertions.[308] Indeed, sometimes the use of an exemption in
order to assist a religion in winning a battle of hearts and minds may
be explicit. The free exercise claim in *Yoder*, for example, was based
primarily on the desire of the Amish to protect their children from
more worldly influences that might challenge their worldviews.[309]
Similarly, the pre-*Smith* free exercise claim brought in *Mozert v
Hawkins County Board of Education*,[310] which sought to exempt public
school students from being required to read books that their parents
found to be religiously objectionable, was an effort to insulate the
children from competing ideas.[311]

Third, a favorable RFRA ruling provides its own political rewards in the form of judicial vindication for the asserted religious
claim.[312] A decision granting religious objectors an exemption to an
antidiscrimination law, for example, bestows credibility and legitimacy upon the substance of that religious belief. It literally confers
judicial imprimatur upon the discrimination claim.[313]

Finally, RFRA claims can further what Joey Fishkin terms the
"politics of recognition." In commenting on *Hobby Lobby*, he argues
that the case was actually about:

> recognizing conservative religious claims that (a) contraceptives are dif-
> ferent from other forms of health care . . . , (b) religious people's "con-
> science" deserves great deference and priority in the public sphere, cer-
> tainly a higher symbolic priority than women's health, and (c) perhaps
> most specifically on point, that religion is not something people do on
> their own time, in their own churches, but rather, is a way that apparently

---

[306] Id at 321–22.

[307] Id at 322.

[308] Id.

[309] *Yoder*, 406 US at 210–12, 218.

[310] 827 F2d 1058 (6th Cir 1987).

[311] Id at 1067 ("The parents in the present case want their children to [be] . . . excused from
exposure to some ideas they find offensive.").

[312] Marshall, 58 U Chi L Rev at 322, 323 (cited in note 6).

[313] See *Engel v Vitale*, 370 US 421, 429 (1962) (noting the Framers' concern with religious
groups competing for the government's stamp of approval).

even large for-profit businesses may conduct their affairs—and if they choose to do so, society must find ways to accommodate their "full participation in the economic life of the Nation." None of these—neither (a), (b), nor (c)—is really a legal claim. These are political claims. But this is high politics, not low politics. These are claims about how our nation is constituted and the place of religion in it.[314]

As with its potential commercial effects, the fact that RFRA provides substantial political benefits should be troubling. First, as with the commercial cases, it shows how RFRA can invite weak but potentially sustainable actions for purposes other than protecting religious freedom. Indeed, one reading of the *Eden Foods* case is that it represents exactly this type of behavior—a plaintiff mounting an RFRA claim for political purposes. Second, it reinforces other concerns illustrated by *Eden Foods*, such as the difficulty in distinguishing between religious and nonreligious objections to challenged laws and the incentives for claimants to frame those objections in religious terms no matter what their foundations. Third, recognizing RFRA's political implications demonstrates how RFRA exemptions, in effect, act as political subsidies that distort the political marketplace[315] and run counter to the principle of the equality of ideas that pervades Speech Clause jurisprudence.[316] Why should a religiously-based objection to a neutral law be granted exemption when a parallel secular-based objection would not? Fourth, RFRA's political implications illustrate the potential magnitude of the stakes in the exemption debate. The prize in prevailing in an RFRA claim is not just an exemption for the adherent; it is, as Fishkin argues, sending a powerful message that religion trumps secular values.[317]

---

[314] Joey Fishkin, *Hobby Lobby and the Politics of Religion* (June 30, 2014), Balkinization http://balkin.blogspot.com/2014/06/hobby-lobby-and-politics-of-recognition.html (quoting *Hobby Lobby*, 134 S Ct at 2783).

[315] Marshall, 58 U Chi L Rev at 322 (cited in note 6).

[316] Kenneth L. Karst, *Equality as a Central Principle in the First Amendment*, 43 U Chi L Rev 20, 25 (1975).

[317] Fishkin, *Hobby Lobby and the Politics of Religion* (cited in note 314). Of course, one could argue that recognizing and fostering religion's political primacy is exactly what RFRA was designed to do. And undoubtedly many supporters of RFRA had (and still have) that purpose in mind. But at the time of *Smith*, the leading arguments in favor of exempting religion from neutral laws were based upon the principle that religion needed to be accommodated—not that it needed to be treated as the preeminent liberty. Accordingly, leading scholars defended the right of religious exercise to be protected from neutral laws on the basis that its primary beneficiaries would be minority religious groups like the Amish (*Yoder*), Seventh Day Ad-

C. CONSTRAINING RFRA

If the free exercise cases are any guide, the energetic protection of religious exercise that *Hobby Lobby* portends will face considerable jurisprudential resistance. The concerns with the administrability of the compelling interest test, along with the disconcerting advantaging of religion in the commercial and political spheres, strongly militate against a sustained vigorous enforcement of the statute. Indeed, Justice Alito may have recognized this reality when he indicated that the decision should not be read to suggest that religious objectors will have a right to gain exemptions from tax, immunization, and civil rights laws under the statute.[318] The remainder of this section discusses some of the possible responses the Court may have to the overreach of RFRA.

1. *Constitutional limitations.* The most direct way in which the Court could constrain RFRA would be to impose constitutional limitations on some of its applications. An attack on the constitutionality of the statute as a whole, however, would likely fail. In *Cutter v Wilkinson*,[319] the Court ruled that RLIUPA did not violate the Establishment Clause because it benefited only religious believers,[320] even though some previous cases had suggested that an unyielding exemption in favor only of religion might be constitutionally suspect.[321] There seems little reason to think that the Court would treat RLIUPA and RFRA differently in this respect. And, as discussed above, *Thomas* seems to foreclose the claim that RFRA is unconstitutional because it affords greater protection to religious than secular conscience.[322] To be sure, *Thomas* could be distinguished on the ground that it construed a constitutional pro-

---

ventists (*Sherbert*), and idiosyncratic believers such as Eddie Thomas (*Thomas*)—groups or individuals who might not otherwise be able to protect themselves in the political process. McConnell, 57 U Chi L Rev at 1129–36 (cited in note 8); Pepper, 1986 BYU L Rev at 314 (cited in note 235); Douglas Laycock, *Formal, Substantive, and Disaggregated Neutrality Toward Religion*, 39 DePaul L Rev 993, 1015–16 (1990). It was not defended on grounds that religion generally needed an additional back-up resource available if it somehow was unable to initially succeed politically.

[318] *Hobby Lobby*, 134 S Ct at 2783–84.

[319] 544 US 709 (2005).

[320] Id at 720.

[321] *Estate of Thornton v Caldor*, 472 US 703 (1985); *Texas Monthly v Bullock*, 489 US 1 (1989).

[322] *Thomas*, 450 US at 713 (holding that the Free Exercise Clause protects only religious and not comparable philosophical or moral beliefs).

vision rather than a statute, but the case does suggest that the line between religious and nonreligious conscience is one that has a constitutional basis.[323]

A more fruitful line of attack might argue that, in certain circumstances, accommodating an entity's religious belief runs afoul of the Establishment Clause if the exemption imposes burdens on third parties.[324] This issue was raised in the *Hobby Lobby* litigation on the ground that exempting the employers would burden female employees by causing them to lose contraceptive coverage.[325] The Court deflected this concern, in part, by suggesting that the third parties (the female employees) could still receive coverage from the government.[326] But one can imagine instances in which such an alternative might not be available and in which the Establishment Clause's protection against accommodating religious beliefs to the detriment of third parties might be implicated. Exempting an employer from the minimum wage requirements of the FLSA, for example, could burden its employees in a manner that might trigger Establishment Clause concerns.[327]

---

[323] Some leading scholars, however, have offered powerful arguments contending that religious and secular conscience cannot be justifiably distinguished. See Schwartzman, 79 U Chi L Rev at 1351 (cited in note 202); Leiter, *Why Tolerate Religion* (cited in note 202); Christopher L. Eisgruber and Lawrence G. Sager, *Religious Freedom and the Constitution* (2010).

[324] *Estate of Thornton*, 472 US at 709–10 (noting that the challenged statute granting employees the absolute right to not work on the Sabbath of their choice compels employers and other employees to subordinate their interests to the religious demands of the employee and that "[t]his unyielding weighting in favor of Sabbath observers over all other interests contravenes a fundamental principle of the Religion Clauses," namely, that "'[t]he First Amendment gives no one the right to insist that in pursuit of their own interests others must conform their conduct to his own religious necessities,'" quoting Learned Hand in *Otten v Baltimore & Ohio Rail Co.*, 205 F2d 58, 61 (2d Cir 1953)); Frederick Gedicks and Rebecca Van Tassel, *RFRA Exemptions from the Contraception Mandate: An Unconstitutional Accommodation of Religion*, 40 Harv CR-CL L Rev 343, 356–71 (2014). Kara Loewentheil, *When Free Exercise Is a Burden: Protecting Third Parties in Religious Accommodation Law*, 62 Drake L Rev 434, 439–44 (2014).

[325] *Hobby Lobby*, 134 S Ct at 2791 (Ginsburg, J, dissenting).

[326] Id at 2781–82.

[327] The Court could also entertain the notion of effect on third parties more broadly and suggest that it applies every time exempting an adherent harms her commercial or political competitors. That construction, however, would suggest that *Hobby Lobby* was truly a narrow opinion in that it marks one of the few instances where an exemption from a commercial regulation would not provide the benefited entity with a competitive advantage. Few other commercial exemptions will likely have this little effect. Further, exemptions will more than likely affect third parties in almost every case. Exempting Adell Sherbert and Eddie Thomas from unemployment insurance requirements, for example, meant that others had to work in their stead.

The free speech guarantee might also provide a check against some RFRA applications, if the restriction from which an exemption is sought affects freedom of expression. This is because granting an exemption from a neutral law solely for religious speech would violate the principle of content neutrality.[328] To use one example, some religions assert that it is part of their religious obligations to proselytize, including soliciting funds and distributing religious literature, in areas not otherwise available to other speakers.[329] Exempting religious organizations from laws that regulate those activities, while continuing to apply those laws to secular organizations, would then create a result that would be impermissibly content-based.[330] Thus, when faced with such a case in *Heffron v International Society for Krishna Consciousness*,[331] the Court rejected the claim that the Free Exercise Clause should exempt a religious organization from restrictions on expression when the Free Speech Clause would not.[332] RFRA should be interpreted in the same way.

2. *Doctrinal solutions.* The Court could also respond to some of the difficulties created by a too-vigorous application of RFRA by following some of the doctrinal paths *Hobby Lobby* left open. For example, any claim put forth by a for-profit entity that would allow it to gain an economic advantage over its competitors should face judicial resistance because of the obvious unfairness to competitors and because of the likelihood that it would encourage strategic claims to exploit RFRA's protections. Accordingly, one option might be to construe RFRA as not requiring exemptions for religious enterprises when the exempted business would be competitively advantaged by the exemption, or more simply to disallow

---

[328] See *Rosenberger v Rector and Visitors of the University of Virginia*, 515 US 819 (1995) (prohibiting a state university from making content-based distinctions between religious and nonreligious speech); *Widmar v Vincent*, 454 US 263 (1981) (same). See also Geoffrey R. Stone, *Restrictions of Speech Because of Its Content: The Peculiar Case of Subject Matter Restrictions*, 46 U Chi L Rev 83 (1978).

[329] That assertion was advanced by the International Society for Krishna Consciousness in *Heffron v International Society for Krishna Consciousness*, 452 US 640, 645 (1981).

[330] See *Texas Monthly, Inc. v Bullock*, 489 US 1 (1989) (holding unconstitutional on Establishment Clause grounds a provision that exempted religious but not nonreligious publications from a sales tax).

[331] 452 US 640 (1981).

[332] Id at 652–53. See also *Prince v Massachusetts*, 321 US 158, 164 (1944) (holding that the First Amendment does not provide greater protection for "freedom of conscience" [religion] than "freedom of mind [speech]").

RFRA claims generally when their benefits would clearly invite strategic behavior.[333]

The problem with this solution, of course, is that it is precisely what the Court in *Hobby Lobby* rejected in concluding that other categorical exclusions from RFRA eligibility were inconsistent with the compelling interest inquiry.[334] And, in one sense, this conclusion is arguably correct. If the goal of RFRA is to protect religious exercise from the perspective of the believer,[335] categorical exclusions might be unwarranted. After all, it may be more important *from an adherent's religious perspective* to gain exemption from a law regulating economic activity than from a law affecting other aspects of her religious practices. One can be equally devout, or even more so, in adhering to religious beliefs that happen to bring financial or other benefits than to those that entail sacrifice.

Moreover, categorically holding that the government has a compelling interest when the granting of an exemption would provide the excepted individual or entity with a competitive advantage is arguably inconsistent with the case-by-case adjudication that the compelling interest standard purportedly demands.[336] The government, after all, does not have a greater interest per se in laws where exemptions might provide an economic advantage than in laws that do not. The state's interest in proscribing controlled substances, for example, may be far greater than its interest in the reporting and record-keeping provisions of a regulatory program. Of course, the Court could solve the problem by adopting a relatively weak interpretation of "compelling" interests under RFRA, a possibility that *Hobby Lobby* left open.[337] Similarly, it could confine *Hobby Lobby*'s holding to situations in which the government in fact has a less re-

---

[333] Such an approach would be consistent in result with the pre-*Smith* case law in that there was no case during that period where the Court vindicated a free exercise claim when to do so would have provided the claimant with an economic edge over its competitor. *Jimmy Swaggart Ministries v Board of Equalization of Cal.*, 493 US 378 (1990); *Tony and Susan Alamo Foundation v Secretary of Labor*, 471 US 290 (1985); *United States v Lee*, 455 US 252 (1982).

[334] The *Hobby Lobby* majority rejected two possible categorical exclusions from RFRA's protections: (1) for-profit corporations and (2) voluntarily undertaken commercial activities.

[335] *Hobby Lobby*, 134 S Ct at 2778–79.

[336] *Gonzales*, 546 US at 436.

[337] Notably, however, the Court may have elected not to pursue this tack in its most recent RLIUPA case, *Holt v Hobbs*, 135 S Ct 853 (2015). In *Hobbs* the Court unanimously upheld a prisoner's challenge to a regulation limiting facial hair. In so holding the Court emphasized that the state's interest had to be compelling as applied to the prisoner and not to the prison population generally. Id at 863.

strictive alternative available to achieve its goals, as was plausibly the case in *Hobby Lobby* itself.[338]

Finally, the Court could build upon the signs of retreat already evident in the *Hobby Lobby* holding. As noted previously, Justice Alito's opinion indicated that the case should not be construed as suggesting that religious objectors should subsequently be entitled under RFRA to exemptions from neutral laws imposing immunization requirements, civil rights protections, or tax laws.[339] But it is difficult to see how those results would necessarily follow if the Court truly adhered to an expansive interpretation of burden or the holding that RFRA does not permit categorical exclusions from eligibility. Accordingly, the Court might find itself reconsidering those positions.[340]

Any of these moves would considerably weaken a claimant's chance of success, and would thereby reduce some of the risks of encouraging strategic claims or bringing about outcomes that unfairly favor religiously based commercial or political activities over their secular equivalents. They would not, however, eliminate all of these concerns, and they would not extricate courts from the difficult task of having to assess the impact of regulatory laws on religious beliefs. More fundamentally, these doctrinal moves are hardly new. They were all employed by the Court, if only sporadically and inconsistently, in the pre-*Smith* free exercise cases. That effort was notably unsuccessful.

3. *Living with Hobby Lobby.* There is one other option. The Court could elect to soldier on and adhere to *Hobby Lobby*'s demand that RFRA's compelling interest test be applied rigorously.[341] If

---

[338] Another possible approach might be to construct remedies that could lessen RFRA's financial incentives. One such solution, for example, might require an employer that seeks an exemption from minimum wage laws to pay any wage differential to the government in the form of a tax rather than pay the higher wages directly to their employees. The problem with this approach, however, is that it would only address certain kinds of strategic behaviors—those aimed at financial rewards. It would not correct for those seeking to mount RFRA claims for political purposes. Further, the tax alternative would not address the claims of believers who might find the payment of that tax itself to be religiously objectionable—either because they believe that paying the tax would make them complicit in supporting a system that violates their religious precepts or because they believe that such a tax directly infringes upon their religious beliefs.

[339] *Hobby Lobby*, 134 S Ct at 2783–84.

[340] But see *Flood v Kuhn*, 407 US 258 (1972) (indicating the particularly strong role *stare decisis* plays in statutory construction).

[341] See *Holt v Hobbs*, 135 S Ct 853 (2015) (holding that RLIUPA's compelling interest test required strict application in the context of a religious prisoner seeking an exemption from a prison regulation limiting facial hair).

so, this means maintaining a jurisprudence that will lead to unequal treatment, will encourage plaintiffs to bring marginal claims, will undercut legitimate government interests, will apply to virtually every kind of regulatory measure imaginable (because of the limitless kinds of activities that can be couched in religious terms), and will demand that courts make inquiries into matters like religious sincerity that are virtually impossible to resolve. That is to say, adhering to *Hobby Lobby* will exacerbate the concerns inherent in a jurisprudence that the Court soundly rejected in *Smith* as both unworkable and normatively unsound.

VI. CONCLUSION

In an important article addressing the *Hobby Lobby* decision, Professor Ira Lupu noted that there is a significant question as to whether "judges [can] be reasonably consistent over time, and across widely different fact patterns, in applying concepts like substantial burden, compelling interest, and least restrictive alternative."[342] The courts' experience with the application of the compelling interest test to religious exercise proved him right. The free exercise cases decided under this standard were jumbled and the jurisprudence that emerged was largely incoherent. *Smith* was an effort to extricate the courts from this morass.

Congress, however, missed the point. In its rush to overturn the widely condemned decision in *Smith*, Congress passed RFRA, a statute that effectively asked the judiciary to reimmerse itself in the same troubled waters from which *Smith* had allowed it to escape. *Hobby Lobby* took Congress's direction seriously. Ignoring the reasons that led to the compelling interest test's original demise, it adopted an expansive interpretation of RFRA that, if anything, only worsens the problems that existed pre-*Smith*. Not only do many of the administrability problems associated with the application of a compelling interest test remain in place, but the decision increases the likelihood of problematic results. A statutory system that undermines legitimate government interests while fostering unequal treatment in the spheres of commerce and politics is not normatively sound. A statutory system that encourages individuals and en-

---

[342] See Lupu, 38 Harv J L & Gender at 77 (cited in note 21).

tities to frame their objections to regulatory measures in religious terms damages religion as much as it protects it.

Yet while *Hobby Lobby* exacerbates the concerns inherent in applying a compelling interest test to religious exercise, it did not create them. They are endemic in the test itself. For this reason, the true assessment of *Hobby Lobby* rests not with Justice Alito's majority opinion, nor with Justice Ginsburg's dissent, but with the Congress that passed RFRA in the first place. Bad statutes make bad law.

WILLIAM B. GOULD IV

ORGANIZED LABOR, THE SUPREME COURT, AND HARRIS v QUINN: DÉJÀ VU ALL OVER AGAIN?

The notion that economic and political concerns are separable is pre-Victorian.[1]

Harris v Quinn[2] presented this issue anew in 2014—it was the most recent chapter of litigation concerning "union security agreements" and their permissibility in the public sector—but by no means will it be the last. *Harris* relates to the constitutionality of such agreements, which compel membership or financial obligations on the part of union represented employees (frequently as a condition of employment) and endure throughout our economy in the private sector, as well as the more recently organized public portion of it.

William B. Gould IV is Charles A. Beardsley Professor of Law, emeritus, Stanford Law School; Chairman of the National Labor Relations Board (1994–98); Chairman of the California Agricultural Labor Relations Board (2014–).

AUTHOR'S NOTE: The author wishes to thank Jaryn Fields, Stanford Law School '15, for invaluable research assistance, as well as Jeremiah Collins, research assistant in 1974–76, now a distinguished counselor with the law firm of Bredhoff & Kaiser, PLLC for valuable insights obtained during a number of telephone discussions and e-mail exchanges with him. Mr. Collins's views are in no way associated or affiliated with this article. All errors and omissions are attributable to the author.

[1] *International Association of Machinists v Street*, 367 US 740, 814 (1961) (Frankfurter, J, dissenting).

[2] *Harris v Quinn*, 134 S Ct 2618 (2014).

The resolution of this and related issues inevitably affects, in some measure, the role of trade unions in American society.[3] It cannot be gainsaid that this involves the democratic process itself in a pluralistic society,[4] through which unions attempt to achieve their objectives through both the collective bargaining and political processes.[5]

For more than two centuries, the issue of so-called "union security agreements," which compel membership in a labor organization in some sense of the word, has been fought out in American labor-management relations and in the courts.[6] Complicating the contemporary relationship is that organized labor is in a period of retreat and decline.[7] Related to this issue is the question of appropriate

---

[3] In reviewing the constitutionality of legislation designed to limit or prohibit union security agreements in an earlier era, Justice Frankfurter had taken into account the rise of unions in rejecting the argument that "the compromise which this legislation embodies is no compromise at all because fatal to the survival of organized labor." *American Federation of Labor, Arizona State Federation of Labor v American Sash & Door Co.*, 335 US 538, 547 (1949) (Frankfurter, J, concurring). Said Justice Frankfurter:

> In the past fifty years the total number of employed, counting salaried workers and the self-employed but not farmers or farm laborers, has not quite trebled, while total union membership has increased more than thirty-three times; at the time of the open-shop drive following the First World War, the ratio of organized to unorganized non-agricultural workers was about one to nine, and now it is almost one to three. However necessitous may have been the circumstances of unionism in 1898 or even in 1923, its status in 1948 precludes constitutional condemnation of a legislative judgment, whatever we may think of it, that the need of this type of regulation outweighs its detriments.

Id at 547 (Frankfurter, J, concurring).

[4] *Citizens United v Federal Election Commission*, 130 S Ct 876 (2010) (overruling *Austin v Michigan Chamber of Commerce*, 494 US 652 (1990)) (holding that unions as well as corporations are protected under the First Amendment against campaign finance regulations). This controversial Supreme Court decision reversed the previously fashioned assumptions of both Congress and the Court that restraints could be placed upon labor organizations, employers, and corporations "on exactly the same basis." *United States v UAW-CIO*, 352 US 567, 579 (1957); *United States v CIO*, 335 US 106, 114–15 (1948). See generally Charlotte Garden, *Citizens, United and Citizens United: The Future of Labor Speech Rights*, 53 Wm & Mary L Rev 1 (2011).

[5] *Eastex Inc. v NLRB*, 437 US 556 (1978) (discussing the right of employees to engage in protected concerted activity through the distribution of literature aimed at legislation relating to working conditions). On the other hand, the distribution of political leaflets designed to promote the candidacy of candidates amongst employees and the support of outside political organizations do not constitute protected activity within the meaning of the act. See *Local 174, UAW v NLRB*, 645 F2d 1151 (DC Cir 1981); *NLRB v Motorola, Inc.*, 991 F2d 278 (5th Cir 1993).

[6] *Commonwealth v Hunt*, 45 Mass 111 (1842); *Plant v Woods*, 176 Mass 492 (1900) (Holmes, J, dissenting).

[7] For a discussion of the phenomenon of decline as it was first observed in the 1960s, see generally Solomon Barkin, *The Decline of the Labor Movement: And What Can Be Done About It*

union discipline authority imposed on workers who defy[8] various kinds of union rules and who are ostracized, for instance, over matters such as strike-breaking.[9]

Since the 1950s, first under the Railway Labor Act of 1926 (RLA)[10] and its regulation of both railroads and airlines, and then through constitutional litigation in the public sector,[11] the tension between the political process and collective bargaining has been addressed with a fair measure of frequency. Litigation under the National Labor Relations Act (NLRA) in most of the private sector, outside of the industries covered by the RLA, was soon to follow.[12] Justice Frankfurter's maxim that union political concerns were inevitably bound up with central union objectives to enhance employment conditions

---

(1961); A. H. Raskin, *The Big Squeeze on Labor Unions*, Atlantic Monthly 41 (Oct 1979); A. H. Raskin, *The Squeeze on the Unions*, Atlantic Monthly 55 (June 1961); Paul Jacobs, *The State of the Unions* (Atheneum, 1963). I wrote about the relationship of the law in William B. Gould, *Labour and the Law*, The Economist 153 (Oct 10, 1964). For a discussion of a continuation of this trend from the 1990s through the present, see William B. Gould IV, *Agenda for Reform: The Future of Employment Relationships and the Law* (MIT, 1993); Bruce Western and Jake Rosenfeld, *Workers of the World Divide: The Decline of Labor and the Future of the Middle Class*, 91 Foreign Affairs 88 (2012).

[8] See, for example, *NLRB v Allis-Chalmers Manufacturing Co.*, 388 US 175 (1967); *Scofield v NLRB* 394 US 423 (1969); William B. Gould IV, *Solidarity Forever—or Hardly Ever: Union Discipline, Taft-Hartley, and the Right of Union Members to Resign*, 66 Cornell L Rev 74 (1980); William B. Gould IV, *Some Limitations Upon Union Discipline Under the National Labor Relations Act: The Radiations of Allis-Chalmers*, 1970 Duke L J 1067 (1970).

[9] See *Commonwealth v Pullis* (the Philadelphia Cordwainer's case), Mayor's Court of Philadelphia (1806); J. Commons, ed, *A Documentary History of American Industrial Society* 294 (Cleveland, 1910) (Job Harrison testified, "If I did not join the body, no man would sit upon the seat where I worked . . . nor board or lodge in the same house, nor would they work at all for the same employer.").

[10] Railway Labor Act of 1926, Pub L No 69-257, 44 Stat 577 (as amended). See generally *Ellis v Brotherhood of Railway Employees*, 466 US 435 (1984); *Brotherhood of Railway & Steamship Clerks, Freight Handlers, Express & Station Employees v Allen*, 373 US 113 (1963); *Street*, 367 US at 740; *Railway Employees' Department v Hanson*, 351 US 225 (1956).

[11] Compare *Abood v Detroit Board of Education*, 431 US 209 (1977) (holding that nonmembers of a union can be assessed dues for germane purposes) with *Lehnert v Ferris Faculty Association*, 500 US 507 (1991) (holding that nonmembers of a union can be assessed a service fee for duties pertaining to its role as the "exclusive bargaining agent") and *Locke v Karass*, 555 US 207, 208 (2009) (holding that nonmembers may be charged for extralocal litigation which is local and reciprocal in nature, so long as it "ultimately inure[s] to the local union by virtue of its membership in the parent organization"). These cases were generally characterized as arising under so-called "fair share" agreements.

[12] See, for example, *Communications Workers of America v Beck*, 487 US 735 (1988). A veritable onslaught of executive orders have addressed notice-posting obligations for government contractors under *Beck*. Notification of Employee Rights Concerning Payment of Union Dues or Fees, 57 FR 12985 (1992); Revocation of Certain Executive Orders Concerning Federal Contracting, 58 FR 7045 (1993); Notification of Employee Rights Concerning Payment of Union Dues or Fees, 66 FR 11221 (2001); Notification of Employee Rights Under Federal Labor Laws, 74 FR 6107 (2009).

disappeared—perhaps, in part, because the Court came to assume that associational rights were impinged upon by restrictions upon the individual's right to financially support[13] one's own ideas[14]—and therefore dissenting employees could not be compelled to assist with so-called "nonemployment ideas" with which they disagreed.

Union security agreements in the private sector have been legislatively contentious at least since the Taft-Hartley amendments in 1947.[15] The amendments: (1) prohibited the "closed shop," compelling membership prior to employment,[16] (2) provided for the voluntary negotiation of a limited type of so-called "union shop" agreement, requiring membership or financial obligations as a condition of employment, and (3) and allowed the states to enact so-called "right-to-work" laws that prohibit such collective bargaining agreement clauses.[17] Almost half the states in the Union have enacted such laws,[18] and in the public sector, where the nomenclature is "fair share" agreements, a storm has been building by virtue of dual attacks upon both relatively successful public-sector unions in particular, and union security agreements generally (in both the public and private sector). One public-sector illustration of this trend is Wisconsin, which pioneered comprehensive collective bargaining legislation[19] and is now in the midst of debate about labor law reform, which

---

[13] See *Buckley v Valeo*, 424 US 1 (1976) (establishing the proposition that money is speech). *Buckley* was the precursor to *Citizens United*, 558 US 310 (2010), which created much mischief in both the campaign finance and labor law arenas.

[14] *Abood*, 431 US at 234–36. Of course, employees always have the right to refrain from any union activity by manifesting majority support in opposition to the union, and thus ridding themselves of union representation. See *J. I. Case Co. v NLRB*, 321 US 332 (1944); *Allentown Mack Sales & Service, Inc. v NLRB*, 522 US 359 (1998).

[15] Labor-Management Relations (Taft-Hartley) Act, Pub L No 80-101, 61 Stat 136 (1947) (codified as amended at 29 USC §§ 141–87).

[16] *Algoma Plywood v Wisconsin Board*, 336 US 301 (1949).

[17] See Benjamin Collins, *Right to Work Laws: Legislative Background and Empirical Research* (Congressional Research Service, Dec 6, 2012), online at http://fas.org/sgp/crs/misc/R42575 .pdf; Vincent G. Macaluso, *The NLRB "Opens the Union," Taft-Hartley Style*, 36 Cornell L Q 443 (1951); David H. Topol, *Union Shops, State Action, and the National Labor Relations Act*, 101 Yale L J 1135 (1992).

[18] Twenty-four states have enacted such legislation. See *Right to Work States* (National Right to Work Legal Defense Foundation, 2014), online at http://www.nrtw.org/rtws.htm. Kentucky, West Virginia, New Mexico, and Wisconsin are now considering such laws. See, for example, *Missouri House Passes Anti-Union Bill, Ignoring Threat of a Veto*, NY Times (Feb 13, 2015). Though Section 14(b) of the NLRA—one of the Taft-Hartley amendments—allows for the enactment of "state and territorial" laws, counties have now passed right-to-work ordinances. See Shaila Dewan, *Foes of Unions Try Their Luck in County Laws*, NY Times A1, A4 (Dec 19, 2014).

[19] See, for example, Arvid Anderson, *Labor Relations in the Public Service*, 1961 Wis L Rev 601 (1961).

threatens the very existence of public-sector unions in that state.[20] Even in California, where the labor movement enjoys more membership support than it possesses nationally,[21] there have been numerous statewide propositions attempting to circumscribe the role of unions in this area.[22]

I. THE EARLY UNION DUES—POLITICAL ACTIVITY CASES

As noted above, early cases exploring the legality of union dues were filed under the RLA, attacking the statutorily authorized so-called "union shop" agreements, which required membership as a

[20] The Walker administration has enacted much litigated legislation prohibiting a wide variety of union activity. See, for example, *Wisconsin Education Association Council v Walker*, 705 F3d 640 (7th Cir 2012); *Laborers Local 236, AFL-CIO v Walker*, 749 F3d 628 (7th Cir 2014); *Madison Teachers Inc. v Scott Walker*, 851 NW2d 337 (2014); Steven Greenhouse, *The Wisconsin Legacy*, NY Times (Feb 23, 2014). Apparently, Governor Walker has not encouraged passage of a Wisconsin right-to-work law—but so also did the governors of Indiana and Michigan adopt similar stances before their states fell into the right-to-work column. See Monica Davey, *Wisconsin Governor, Starting Second Term, Resists New Union Battle*, NY Times A12 (Jan 6, 2015). However, Governor Walker, like his Indiana and Michigan counterparts, has had a change of heart. See Michael Bologna, *Wisconsin Lawmakers Expected to Take Swift Action on Right-to-Work Legislation*, Bureau of National Affairs A13 (Feb 20, 2015); Monica Davey and Mitch Smith, *Walker Set to Deliver New Blow to Labor and Bolster Credentials*, NY Times A12 (Feb 26, 2015); Mitch Smith, *Word of Threat Cuts Short Hearing on Right-to-Work Measure in Wisconsin*, NY TImes A13 (Feb 25, 2015); *Wisconsin, Workers, and 2016*, NY Times (Feb 27, 2015).

[21] In 2013, the union membership rate—the percent of wage and salary workers who were members of unions—was 11.3 percent, the same as in 2012. During that period, the union membership rate in California was 17.2 percent and 16.4 percent in 2012 and 2013, respectively. See http://www.bls.gov/news.release/union2.t05.htm. Public employee unions have kept the American labor movement afloat through organizational activity. But see note 18 for a discussion of efforts to stifle union activity. But it is said that the "public has no appetite for a public-sector *intifada*. . . . Governments have no choice but to cut public-sector debt, which is ballooning across the rich world. Mighty private-sector unions were destroyed when they tried to take on elected governments in the 1980s. The same thing could happen to the survivors if they overplay their hands." *In Two Minds*, The Economist (June 3, 2010), online at http://www.economist.com/node/16271975. Meanwhile, the decline in private-sector unions has been addressed through debate about the Employee Free Choice Act of 2009. See William B. Gould IV, *Employee Free Choice Act: Bill No Cure-All for What Ails Labor*, San Jose Mercury News 11A (Mar 6, 2007); William B. Gould IV, *New Labor Law Reform Variations on an Old Theme: Is the Employee Free Choice Act the Answer?*, 70 La L Rev 1 (2009); William B. Gould IV, *The Employee Free Choice Act of 2009, Labor Law Reform, and What Can Be Done About the Broken System of Labor-Management Relations Law in the United States*, 43 USF L Rev 291 (2008). But as I and others have written, organized labor's decline is attributable to much more than the law itself. See *The Limits of Solidarity*, The Economist (Sept 21, 2006), online at http://www.economist.com/node/7951699.

[22] See, for example, Bob Egelko, *Prop. 32 Not Unions' Only Worry*, San Francisco Chronicle (Oct 23, 2012); Bob Egelko, *Romney Favors Restrictions on Union Dues*, San Francisco Chronicle (Nov 1, 2012). This series of attempts began in earnest in 1998. See William B. Gould IV, *Labored Relations: Law, Politics, and the NLRB—a Memoir* 386 (MIT, 2000) (discussing Proposition 226, characterizing it as "deeply flawed from both a policy and constitutional perspective").

condition of employment negotiated between unions and employers. Until Congress enacted amendments to the statute in 1951, the
practice on railways had been that of the "open shop"—where no
one could be compelled to become a member or pay dues exacted
by a labor organization. The year 1951 altered that, and constitutional litigation attacking negotiated union security clauses soon
followed. In the first of these cases, *Railway Employees' Department v
Hanson*,[23] the Court, speaking through Justice Douglas, said that
these agreements were made pursuant to the federal law, and by the
force of the Supremacy Clause[24] could not be invalidated.[25] Neither
the First Amendment nor the Fifth were violated, in the view of
the Court, when the obligation was the payment of "periodic dues,
initiation fees, and assessments" permitted by the statute.[26] Congress, said the Court, had a compelling interest in seeking to fashion
"[i]ndustrial peace along the arteries of commerce,"[27] and nothing
in the case spoke conclusively about the use to which dues were
being put. Thus, the Court was able to reserve the question of possible First Amendment violations in the event of attempts to secure
ideological conformity.[28]

A more important decision in which this issue was presented was
one authored by Justice Brennan, *International Association of Machinists v Street*.[29] In this case, the Court reiterated the point made
in *Hanson*,[30] that is, that the payment of dues and initiation fees as
a condition of employment was not unlawful or unconstitutional.
However, in *Street*, the majority staked out new ground and safe-
guarded the rights of dissidents when it said the following:

> A congressional concern over possible impingements on the interests
> of individual dissenters from union policies is . . . discernible. . . . We
> may assume that Congress was also fully conversant with the long his-

---

[23] *Hanson*, 351 US at 225.

[24] US Const, Art VI, § 2.

[25] *Hanson*, 351 US at 225.

[26] Id at 238.

[27] Id at 233.

[28] Id at 238.

[29] 367 US 740 (1961). Subsequently, the *Street* principle was reiterated in *Brotherhood of
Railway Clerks v Allen*, which said that "[t]he necessary predicate for such remedies [vis-à-vis
union expenditures over a proper objection] . . . is a division of the union's political expenditures from those germane to collective bargaining." *Allen*, 373 US at 113, 121.

[30] *Hanson*, 351 US at 225.

tory of intensive involvement of the railroad unions in political activities. But it does not follow that [the Act] places no restriction on the use of an employee's money, over his objection, to support political causes he opposes merely because Congress did not enact a comprehensive regulatory scheme governing expenditures.[31]

Expressing no view on the questions of whether "other union expenditures objected to by an employee and not made to meet the costs of negotiation and administration of collective agreements, or the adjustment and settlement of grievances and disputes,"[32] the Court held that, though dissent could never be presumed, dissidents could lawfully object to payments used for political causes with which they disagree. Thus began an unfolding drama, the tempo of which has begun to accelerate in this century.

Justice Frankfurter dissented in *Street*,[33] finding no legislative intent to preclude union expenditures on the political process.[34] He emphasized, properly, in my view, the deep involvement of the labor movement in the political process through its adoption of a "program of political action in furtherance of its industrial standards."[35] Justice Frankfurter noted that the dissidents had not been denied an ability to participate in the union so as to influence the collective position—nor were they precluded from speaking out in opposition to the union. Rejecting the argument that the union's role in the political process was unrelated to collective bargaining about employment conditions, the Frankfurter dissent noted that the pressure for legislation (e.g., legislation that established an eight-hour day for the railroad industry) "affords positive proof that labor may achieve its desired result through legislation after bargaining techniques fail."[36]

The extension of this controversy to the public sector, where constitutional objections articulated by dissenters could be made

---

[31] *Street*, 367 US at 766–67.

[32] Id at 769.

[33] Id at 797. Justice Frankfurter was joined by Justice Harlan. Justice Black registered a separate dissent.

[34] *Street*, 367 US at 800–802 (Frankfurter, J, dissenting). See generally Alan Hyde, *Economic Labor Law v Political Labor Relations: Dilemmas for Liberal Legalism* 60 U Tex L Rev 1 (1981); David B. Gaebler, *Union Political Activity or Collective Bargaining? First Amendment Limitations on the Uses of Union Shop Funds*, 14 UC Davis L Rev 591 (1981).

[35] *Street*, 367 US at 813 (Frankfurter, J, dissenting).

[36] Id at 814 (Frankfurter, J, dissenting).

more directly because of the involvement of government itself in the negotiated union security agreements, was accomplished in *Abood v Detroit Board of Education*.[37] In considering the expenditure of dues obtained through such union security agreements, the Court in *Abood* drew a line of demarcation between that which was "germane"[38] to collective bargaining and chargeable on the one hand, and those which were unrelated, including political activities, which were unconstitutionally imposed upon dissenters where they objected.[39] Again, the constitutional issue was directly presented because of the involvement of government.

A circle was closed when the Court, in *Communications Workers of America v Beck*,[40] held, albeit curiously under the so-called "duty of fair representation"[41] obligation to represent all within the bargaining unit fairly, that the same demarcation line would apply in cases involving the NLRA itself. Notwithstanding the dramatically different legislative history of the RLA and the NLRA—the former arising out of the open shop, where unions had had no union secu-

---

[37] *Abood*, 431 US at 209.

[38] Id at 235.

[39] Id at 235–36 ("We do not hold that a union cannot constitutionally spend funds for the expression of political views, on behalf of political candidates, or toward the advancement of other ideological causes not germane to its duties as collective-bargaining representative. Rather, the Constitution requires only that such expenditures be financed from charges, dues, or assessments paid by employees who do not object to advancing those ideas and who are not coerced into doing so against their will by the threat of loss of governmental employment."). The assumptions of campaign expenditure legislation regulating union involvement in politics have proceeded on the assumption that such monies would be obtained voluntarily. See, for example, *Pipefitters Local No. 562 v United States*, 407 US 385 (1972); *FEC v National Right to Work Committee*, 459 US 197 (1982).

[40] *Beck*, 487 US at 735. See generally Kenneth G. Dau-Schmidt, *Union Security Agreements Under the National Labor Relations Act: The Statute, the Constitution, and the Court's Opinion in Beck*, 27 Harv J Leg 51 (1990).

[41] See, for example, *Hines v Anchor Motor Freight, Inc.*, 424 US 554 (1976); *Vaca v Sipes*, 386 US 171 (1967); *Humphrey v Moore*, 375 US 335 (1964); *Ford Motor Co. v Huffman*, 345 US 330 (1953); *Railroad Trainmen v Howard*, 343 US 768 (1952); *Steele v Louisville and Nashville Railroad*, 323 US 192 (1944). I have expressed the view that the duty of fair representation is not the appropriate standard, given the fact that litigation before and since *Beck* involving employee rights has taken place under the rubric of the so-called "restraint and coercion" standard of § 8(b)(1)(A) under the NLRA. *California Saw & Knife Works*, 320 NLRB 224, 333 n 47 (Chairman Gould concurring), aff'd in *International Association of Machinists & Aerospace Workers v NLRB*, 133 F3d 1012 (7th Cir 1998). This standard, more ambitious in scope than the duty of fair representation standard, proved to be significant in the poorly reasoned Supreme Court's *Marquez* opinion. *Marquez v Screen Actors Guild, Inc.*, 525 US 33 (1998) (holding that there was no duty of representation obligation to specify workers' obligations in a collective bargaining agreement, in part because workers did not read them). But see *Monson Trucking Inc.*, 324 NLRB 933, 938 (1997) (Chairman Gould concurring) (referenced by Justice Kennedy in his *Marquez* concurrence, 525 US at 53, Kennedy, J, concurring).

rity agreements at all, and the latter involving Congress's attempt to regulate union power and abuses associated with such in the rest of the private sector—the Court held that the same standard applied. Said the Court in *Beck*: "however much union-security practices may have differed between the railway and NLRA-governed industries prior to 1951, it is abundantly clear that Congress itself understood its actions in 1947 and 1951 to have placed these respective industries on an equal footing insofar as compulsory unionism was concerned."[42] Though state action was more difficult to find under the NLRA,[43] the same freedom-of-association principles promoted by the First Amendment[44] seem to be in play.[45] Thus, the attempt to draw a line between representational activity, manifested through collective bargaining and the adjustment of grievances, and that which was not germane to it emerged in both the NLRA as well as the RLA—and *Beck* was to loom large in the NLRB's deliberations during the 1980s and 1990s.[46]

Finally, the Court in *Lehnert v Ferris Faculty Association*,[47] a public-sector case like *Abood*, attempted to define "chargeability" in greater detail—noting that the Railway Labor Act cases were "instructive" in delineating the "balance of the First Amendment" as well as *Abood*.[48] The majority in *Lehnert*, through Justice Blackmun, held that the union dues charges against nonmembers could not be sustained over objections where they involved: (1) lobbying or political activities

---

[42] *Beck*, 487 US at 756.

[43] Topol, 101 Yale L J at 1135 (cited in note 17).

[44] See *NAACP v Alabama*, 357 US 449 (1958).

[45] See, for example, Roger Hartley, *Constitutional Values and the Adjudication of Taft-Hartley Act, Dues Objector Cases* 41 Hastings L J 1 (1989); Clyde W. Summers, *Privatization of Personal Freedoms and Enrichment of Democracy: Some Lessons from Labor Law*, 1986 U Ill L Rev 689 (1986).

[46] Between 1988, when *Beck* was decided, and 1994, when I became Chairman of the NLRB, no case involving the application of the *Beck* standards to the NLRA was decided, notwithstanding the fact that a substantial number of unfair labor practice charges involving this issue were pending for at least six years. See, for example, Gould, *Labored Relations* at 73–74 (cited in note 22).

[47] *Lehnert*, 500 US at 507.

[48] In the interim, another vexatious issue had begun to emerge, that is, the precise procedures to be employed. See, for example, *Chicago Teachers Union, Local No. 1, AFT, AFL-CIO v Hudson*, 475 US 292, 310 (1986) ("the constitutional requirements for the Union's collection of agency fees include an adequate explanation of the basis for the fee, a reasonably prompt opportunity to challenge the amount of the fee before an impartial decisionmaker, and an escrow for the amounts reasonably in dispute while such challenges are pending."). The union bears the burden of establishing through the preponderance of the evidence that the agency fee is accurate.

for matters "outside the limited context of contract ratification or implementation,"[49] (2) general legislative efforts to obtain, in this case, public education in the state, (3) litigation unrelated to the bargaining unit, or (4) public relations efforts. But the opinion that appeared to be most influential at the time—and this continues through the present day in the *Harris* litigation which was to follow—was that of Justice Scalia.[50]

In essence, the Scalia view was that First Amendment jurisprudence recognized a "correlation between the rights and the duties of the union, on the one hand, and the nonunion members of the bargaining unit, on the other."[51] Justice Scalia's opinion in *Lehnert* was that a constitutionally "compelling state interest" standard was synonymous with the obligation imposed upon the union to fairly represent all within the bargaining unit—one which was "mandated by government decree."[52] Said Justice Scalia:

> I would make explicit what has been implicit in our cases since Street: A union cannot constitutionally charge nonmembers for any expenses except those incurred for the conduct of activities in which the union owes a duty of fair representation to the nonmembers being charged.[53]

This view was to loom large in *Harris*.

II. Recent Supreme Court Litigation

A. PRE-HARRIS V QUINN

Part of the Roberts Court's profound movement to the right, sometimes addressing matters even without the issues having been

---

[49] *Lehnert*, 500 US at 522. See also *Belhumeur v Labor Relations Commission* 732 NE2d 860, 870–71 (Mass 2000) ("the objective of the Statewide strike was to publicize the condition of public education funding, and the simultaneous resolve of educators, thereby raising the profile of the issue of public education funding. We conclude the expenses were not chargeable. . . . The purpose of the activity here [to secure funds for public education] is virtually identical; advocating for funding of public education in general is the type of political speech for which the union may not charge. With one exception, the union expenses related to the statewide strike were not chargeable."). For a discussion of comparable chargeability issues under the NLRA, see *Meijer Incorporated*, 329 NLRB 730, 735 (1997).

[50] *Lehnert*, 500 US at 550 (Scalia, J, concurring in part, dissenting in part). Justice Scalia was joined by Justices Souter and O'Connor, and Justice Kennedy joined in part.

[51] Id at 556.

[52] Id.

[53] Id at 558.

presented to them in briefs or arguments,[54] has been manifested in union security cases in connection with the so-called "fair share" arena (these cases involved attempts by unions to require public-sector employees to pay what they viewed to be their "fair share" of representational activity). The backdrop for all of this comes at a time when activist decisions by the Roberts Court usurp, in my view, the role of Congress itself. One such case from the 2013 Term, *Shelby County v Holder*,[55] invalidated portions of the Voting Rights Act of 1965.[56] At the same time, the Court has received praise from some corners for alleged recent illustrations of compromise and unanimity.[57] Whatever the accuracy of this assessment, most decidedly, this has not been the case in labor law.[58]

The first of the recent decisions involving union security issues is *Knox v Service Employees International Union, Local 100*,[59] where a 5–4 majority—reaching out for issues and arguments not even presented or briefed[60]—held that an agreement under which workers

---

[54] See, for example, *Knox v Service Employees International Union, Local 1000*, 132 S Ct 2277, 2296 (2012) (Sotomayor, J, concurring) ("I cannot agree with the majority's decision to address unnecessarily significant constitutional issues well outside the scope of the questions presented and briefing."). An excellent discussion of this general trend and the Court's ever rightward shift can be found in Marcia Coyle, *The Roberts Court: The Struggle for the Constitution* (Simon and Schuster, 2013).

[55] *Shelby County, Alabama v Holder*, 133 S Ct 2612 (2012).

[56] See William B. Gould IV, *The Supreme Court, Job Discrimination, Affirmative Action, Globalization and Class Actions: Justice Ginsburg's Term*, 36 U Hawaii L Rev 371, 375–79 (2014).

[57] See, for example, Jess Bravin, *Chief Justice's Balancing Act*, Wall St J A1 (July 2, 2014); Adam Liptak, *Supreme Court's Shift to Unanimity Veils Rifts*, NY Times A1, A17 (July 2, 2014).

[58] See, for example, *NLRB v Noel Canning, et al*, 134 S Ct 2550 (2014), on the constitutionality of recess appointments made by the President to the NLRB without the advice and consent of the Senate. But see *Mulhall v Unite Here Local 355*, 667 F3d 1211 (2012), cert granted as *Unite Here Local 355 v Mulhall*, 133 S Ct 2849 (2013), cert dismissed as improvidently granted, 134 S Ct 594. See also William B. Gould IV, *Argument Preview: Unite or Disunite—Another Roadblock to Union Organizing and Collective Bargaining?*, SCOTUSblog (Nov 1, 2013), online at http://www.scotusblog.com/2013/11/argument-preview-unite-or -disunite-another-roadblock-to-union-organizing-and-collective-bargaining/. Nonetheless, it must be noted that in the labor arena, this is not unprecedented and does not begin with the Roberts Court. See, for example, William B. Gould IV, *The Burger Court and Labor Law: The Beat Goes on—Marcato*, 24 San Diego L Rev 51 (1987); William B. Gould, *The Supreme Court's Labor and Employment Docket in the 1980 Term: Justice Brennan's Term*, 53 U Colo L Rev 1 (1981).

[59] 132 S Ct 2277 (2012). Justice Alito authored the majority opinion, where he was joined by Chief Justice Roberts and Justices Thomas, Scalia, and Kennedy. Justice Sotomayor wrote a concurring opinion, joined by Justice Ginsburg. Justice Breyer authored the dissent, in which Justice Kagan joined.

[60] Id at 2296 (Sotomayor, J, concurring).

provided compulsory union fees as a condition of employment was a "form of compelled speech and association"[61] which imposes a "significant impingement on First Amendment rights."[62] The Court, citing to an earlier opinion of Justice Scalia,[63] rejected the proposition that there was a balance to be struck between the rights of unions to finance their own expressive activities, on the one hand, and the rights of unions to collect fees from nonmembers on the other.[64] *Knox* held that a union, which sought to collect fees from both members and nonmembers through a special assessment to mount a political campaign, was required to give notice to nonmembers and allow them to opt out of it if they so chose. Said Justice Alito, writing for the majority: "This aggressive use of power by the SEIU to collect fees from nonmembers is indefensible."[65] Alito commented that if the state ballot proposition fostered by Governor Schwarzenegger had passed (a political campaign that the union opposed), it would have exempted nonmembers from "paying for the SEIU's extensive political projects unless they affirmatively consented. Thus, the effect of the SEIU procedure was to force many nonmembers to subsidize a political effort designed to restrict their own rights."[66] No balancing was required because, in the Court's view, only nonmembers who objected to the way in which their monies would be spent have constitutional rights at stake.[67] "Affirmative consent" of nonmembers was required, even though Supreme Court precedent had said that dissent was not to be presumed.

Knox did not involve a union security agreement itself, but rather a special assessment.[68] Nonetheless, the fact that "affirmative consent" was required and Justice Alito's comment that the Court's earlier uniform acceptance of a so-called "opt-out approach" which

---

[61] Id at 2282.

[62] *Knox*, 132 S Ct at 2282 (citing *Ellis*, 466 US at 455).

[63] *Davenport v Washington Education Association*, 551 US 177, 185 (2007) (holding that First Amendment principles are not violated when a state requires public-sector unions to obtain affirmative consent from a nonmember before spending that nonmember's agency-shop fees for election-related purposes).

[64] *Knox*, 132 S Ct 2277, 2291 (citing *Davenport* 551 US at 185). But the Court had earlier found a constitutional right for both members and nonmembers in a fair share union security agreement and had struck a balance between the competing interests of each. *Abood*, 431 US at 231–32.

[65] *Knox*, 132 S Ct at 2291.

[66] Id at 2292.

[67] Id at 2291.

[68] Id at 2285.

would require nonmembers or dissenters to affirmatively object to expenditure of union dues for purposes that are not germane to the collective bargaining process "appears to have come about more as a historical accident than through the careful application of First Amendment principles"[69] seemingly spelled out a substantial reconsideration of precedent. Thus, the Court's holding in *Knox* was ominously indicative of what was to come. Two years later, in *Harris v Quinn*, the Court took matters considerably further and now addressed a fair share, or union security, contract clause itself.

B. HARRIS V QUINN

Harris, a decision both narrow and yet potentially far-reaching, was handed down at the end of the 2014 Term with the Court divided 5–4, the exact same division that had been registered two years earlier in *Knox*.[70] Justice Alito, also the author of *Knox*, wrote the majority opinion in this case involving the state of Illinois's provision of home care services to individuals who would otherwise require institutionalization. The Illinois rehabilitation program allowed participants to hire a so-called "personal assistant" who "provides" home care services tailored to the employer's needs.[71] The statute in question provided that the customer act as the employer of the personal assistant,[72] an aspect of the legislation upon which a majority of the Court was to place great emphasis.[73] The state, with subsidies from the federal Medicaid program, paid the personal assistants' salaries.

The Illinois Public Labor Relations Act (IPLRA) authorized the labor relations scheme underlying *Harris*—it allowed employees, if they so wished, to join labor unions and to bargain collectively on terms and conditions of employment.[74] The statute authorized parties to enter into a so-called "fair share" agreement as part of their collective bargaining agreement with an exclusive representative through which employees who are "nonmembers" of an or-

---

[69] Id at 2290.

[70] Justice Alito wrote for the majority, joined by Justices Roberts, Scalia, Kennedy, and Thomas. Justice Kagan wrote a dissent, in which Justices Ginsburg, Breyer, and Sotomayor joined.

[71] *Harris*, 134 S Ct at 2623–24.

[72] Id at 2624.

[73] Id at 2636–38.

[74] 5 ILCS 315/6(a).

ganization "pay their proportionate share of the costs of the collective bargaining process, contract administration, and [pursuit of] matters affecting wages, hours and conditions of employment."[75]

After the Illinois Labor Relations Board's rejection of an SEIU petition to represent the personal assistants, Governor Rod Blagojevich[76] then—in the words of the Court—"circumvented" this decision through issuance of an executive order authorizing state recognition of a union representing personal assistants on an exclusive bargaining representative basis.[77] The Illinois legislation codified the executive order by amending the IPLRA, and in so doing, declared the personal assistants to be "public employees" of the state of Illinois, solely for the purpose of the IPLRA.[78]

The *Harris* litigation itself involved a putative class action on behalf of personal assistants employed in the personal rehabilitation program who sought an injunction against enforcement of the fair share clause.[79] They also prayed for a declaration that the IPLRA violates the First Amendment "insofar as it requires personal assistants to pay a fee to a union to which they do not wish to support."[80] Initially, it appeared that the First Amendment attack was aimed at not only the union security clause involved in this legislation, but also the very exclusive bargaining representative status itself, which *Abood* had deemed to be constitutional. But at the time of oral argument, these claims seemed to disappear.[81] The Court did not discuss them in the *Harris* opinion.

---

[75] Id. However, the Court mischaracterized the provision as mandating such "fair share" clauses rather than simply permitting them.

[76] Justice Alito expressed great interest in the involvement of Blagojevich, an Illinois governor who was convicted and subsequently sent to prison on corruption charges. See Transcript of Oral Argument at 52–53, *Harris v Quinn*, 134 S Ct 2618 (2014) (No 11-681). This is not the first time that Justice Alito has been so focused upon the political process which led to the legislation before him. His opinions reflect suspicion of corruption or venality. See, for example, *Ricci v Desefano*, 557 US 557, 598–604 (Alito, J, concurring) (discussing the impact of Reverend Boise Kimber on Mayor Destefano and New Haven politics).

[77] *Harris*, 134 S Ct at 2626.

[78] Id.

[79] Id.

[80] Id. The District Court dismissed on the authority of an earlier Supreme Court ruling in *Abood*, which had upheld fair share clauses as constitutional.

[81] Transcript of Oral Argument at 18–20, *Harris v Quinn*, 134 S Ct 2618 (2014) (No 11-681). (When asked whether the petitioners were challenging the idea of exclusive representation by a public-sector union, the attorney representing the petitioners replied: "It's not

The Supreme Court concluded[82] that, while the statutory per-
mission of unions to collect contractual fees from "nonmembers"
was designed to avoid nonmember "free riding" on the union's effort as exclusive bargaining representatives within an appropriate
unit, such "free rider" arguments are "generally insufficient to overcome First Amendment objections."[83] In the Court's view, *Abood*,
which had sanctioned such agreements for schoolteachers in Michigan, was a distinguishable case.[84] Writing for the majority, Justice
Alito argued that finding in favor of the State of Illinois would
provide for "a very significant expansion of *Abood*—so that it applies,
not just to full-fledged public employees, but also to others who are
deemed to be public employees solely for the purpose of unionization and the collection of an agency fee."[85]

The Court then proceeded to examine the jurisprudence of the
past decades in a rather derisive manner, similar to the tone struck by
Justice Alito in *Knox* itself. *Harris* proceeded to attack the Court's
First Amendment analysis in the first of the decisions, *Railway Employees' Department v Hanson*,[86] where Justice Alito characterized the
First Amendment analysis discussion in it as "thin."[87] But the principal focus of the majority in *Harris* was on *Abood* itself, inasmuch
as it was a public-sector case like *Harris*. Noting the fact that the
public employer response to union demands has a "blend of political ingredients" as acknowledged in *Abood*, Justice Alito was critical
of the fact that the earlier cases presented under the RLA have been
found to be "essentially controlling . . . despite these acknowledged
differences between private- and public-sector bargaining."[88] The
majority then concluded that the *Abood* analysis was "questionable on

---

directly challenged in this case, but it becomes relevant under the first *Knox* test, which asks
whether the mandatory association being supported by the compulsory fees is justified by a
compelling State interest.")

[82] The case reached the Supreme Court after being affirmed in part and remanded in part
by the Seventh Circuit in *Harris v Quinn*, 656 F3d 692 (7th Cir 2011). Previously, the
Northern District of Illinois dismissed the claims of the personal assistants in *Harris v Quinn*,
2010 WL 4736500 (ND Ill).

[83] *Harris*, 134 S Ct at 2627.

[84] Id.

[85] Id.

[86] 351 US 225 (1956).

[87] *Harris*, 134 S Ct at 2629. Along these lines, the Court also said that the First Amendment analysis in *Hanson* "deserved better treatment." Id at 2632.

[88] Id at 2632.

several grounds," some of which "have become more evident and troubling in the years since then."[89]

Justice Alito distinguished *Abood* from the earlier private-sector precedent by stating that Michigan had actually "imposed" the fair share fee in question rather than "authoriz[ing]" it,[90] noting that:

> *Abood* failed to appreciate the difference between the core union speech involuntarily subsidized by dissenting public-sector employees and the core union speech involuntarily funded by their counterparts in the private sector. In the public sector, core issues such as wages, pensions, and benefits are important political issues, but that is generally not so in the private sector. In the years since *Abood*, as state and local expenditures on employee wages and benefits have mushroomed, the importance of the difference between bargaining in the public and private sectors has been driven home.[91]

The *Harris* opinion said that *Abood* had "failed to appreciate the conceptual difficulty of a demarcation line in public-sector cases between union expenditures for collective bargaining purposes and those that are made to achieve political ends."[92] This point alluded to Justice Frankfurter's earlier view, expressed in private-sector cases, that it was "rather naïve" to view "economic and political concerns [as] . . . separable"[93]—a point made to support precisely the opposite conclusion in *Harris*, that is, to circumscribe union functions rather than to acknowledge, as Justice Frankfurter had, that unions historically were driven to accomplish their objectives through both collective bargaining and legislative avenues and that dues collected for these purposes did not unconstitutionally suppress speech, so long as dissidents could express their point of view in other arenas.

The Court then claimed that the line between the two in the public sector was "easier to see," inasmuch as in the public sector, "both collective bargaining and political advocacy and lobbying are directed at the government."[94] But this element of the Court's reasoning fails to take into account not only the substantial private-sector union involvement in the political process to which Justice

---

[89] Id.

[90] Id.

[91] Id.

[92] Id.

[93] Id at 2630 (citing *Street*, 367 US at 814 (Frankfurter, J, dissenting)).

[94] Id (citing *Street*, 367 US at 814).

Frankfurter had alluded, but also the fact that unions frequently act in concert with employers[95] in the private sector—the automobile industry is a good example in connection with the 2008 bailout—in approaching elected representatives.[96] Moreover, the focus in *Abood* was the associational right of employees,[97] not the impact upon the public sector and the public-sector enterprise.

Justice Alito then went on to state that *Abood* could not have foreseen the problems that would emerge in determining which portion of dues could be properly collected as "germane" to collective bargaining and the difficult problems that would "face . . . objecting nonmembers."[98] The Court also argued that a "critical pillar" of *Abood* rested on "unsupported empirical assumption[s],"[99] that is, that exclusive bargaining representative status in the public sector was dependent upon union security agreements, which, in the Court's view, was an "unwarranted" assumption.[100] Thus, the Court again noted that Illinois was seeking a "very substantial expansion of *Abood*" inasmuch as *Abood* involved "full-fledged public employees"[101] (i.e., personal assistants) which placed the state of Illinois's treatment of the personal assistants in question, in the view of the majority, in the private sector.

Personal assistants, in the view of the majority, were "almost entirely answerable to the customers and not to the state."[102] Moreover, these personal assistants were ineligible for a variety of benefits available to the state employees group for which Illinois did not as-

---

[95] In the public sector, this happens as well. The Supreme Court of California has held that expenditures of union dues undertaken in this context are permissible. See, for example, *Cumero v Public Employment Relations Board*, 49 Cal3d 575 (1989).

[96] See, for example, Micheline Maynard, *U.A.W. at Center of Dispute Over Bailout*, NY Times (Dec 8, 2008); Nick Bunkley, *Ahead of Auto Bailout Hearings, Union Ready to Make Concessions*, NY Times (Dec 3, 2008). The same was true in the earlier Chrysler bailout in 1979. See, for example, *First National Maintenance Corp. v NLRB*, 452 US 666, 682–83 (1981) ("If labor costs are an important factor in a failing operation and the decision to close, management will have an incentive to confer voluntarily with the union to seek concessions that may make continuing the business profitable." To reach this conclusion, the Court referenced the agreement reached in 1979 between the UAW and Chrysler.).

[97] See *Thomas v Collins*, 323 US 516 (1945); *NAACP v Alabama*, 357 US 449 (1958); *Shelton v Tucker*, 364 US 479 (1960); *Bates v City of Little Rock*, 361 US 516 (1960).

[98] *Harris*, 134 S Ct at 2633.

[99] Id at 2634.

[100] Id.

[101] Id.

[102] Id.

sume "responsibility for actions taken" during the course of their employment.[103] The majority's view was that, whereas in *Abood* the union possessed "the full scope of powers and duties generally available under American labor law,"[104] the Illinois statute had sharply circumscribed union powers and duties.[105] The fact that the wage was set by the state law, and the union's authority in the grievance processing was narrow—the customer having "virtually complete control over a personal assistant's work"[106]—also prompted the Court to refuse to extend *Abood* and its "questionable foundations" to a group of individuals who were "partial-public employees, quasi-public employees, or simply private employees."[107]

The majority then analyzed *Abood* as "not controlling," discussing the constitutionality of dues payment compelled under "generally applicable" First Amendment standards, relying upon some of its reasoning in *Knox* to do so.[108] Rejecting the contention that the speech in question was "commercial speech,"[109] the majority concluded that "no fine parsing of levels of First Amendment scrutiny is needed because the agency fee provision here cannot satisfy even the test used in *Knox*,"[110] that is, that the provision served a "compelling state interest" and cannot be achieved through means significantly less restrictive of associational freedom.[111] Before concluding that the agency fee played an unimportant role in maintaining labor peace within the meaning of *Abood* because personal assistants do not "work together"—ignoring the rise of telecommuting in both the public and private sector—as well as placing emphasis on the union's "very restricted role" to represent these employees under

---

[103] Id at 2635.

[104] Id at 2636.

[105] Id.

[106] Id at 2637.

[107] Id at 2638.

[108] Id at 2639.

[109] Id. Here, the majority looked to the Court's holdings in *United States v United Foods, Inc.*, 553 US 405, 409 (2001) and *Virginia Board of Pharmacy v Virginia Citizens Consumer Council, Inc.*, 425 US 748, 761–62 (1976) to determine what constitutes commercial speech.

[110] *Harris*, 134 S Ct at 2639.

[111] Id. A rather detailed discussion of these and other relevant constitutional standards is contained in Catherine Fisk and Erwin Chemerinsky, *Political Speech and Association Rights After Knox v SEIU, Local 1000*, 98 Cornell L Rev 1023 (2013). See also Benjamin I. Sachs, *Unions, Corporations, and Political Opt-Out Rights After Citizens United*, 112 Colum L Rev 800 (2012); Benjamin I. Sachs, *The Unbundled Union: Politics Without Collective Bargaining*, 123 Yale L J 100 (2013).

the Illinois law,[112] the Court broadly rejected the free rider argument
which had justified union security agreements by proclaiming: "A
union's status as exclusive bargaining agent and the right to collect
an agency fee from non-members are not inextricably linked."[113]
The arrangement in question was unconstitutional, said the Court,
because there had been no showing that the "cited benefits for
personal assistants could not have been achieved if the union had
been required to depend for funding on the dues paid by those
personal assistants who chose to join."[114]

Justice Alito then considered another argument made, that is,
that *Pickering v Board of Education*[115] provided "new justification"
for *Abood*, consideration not discussed or relied upon in the latter.
In *Pickering*, the Court had held that employee speech is unprotected if it is not expressed on a "matter of public concern."[116]
This holding was to subsequently shrink so as to eliminate constitutional protections for most public-sector employee speech involving the employment relationship itself. But in *Harris*, the Court
concluded that union contractual clauses requiring payment of dues
for nonmembers *were* public and thus subject to First Amendment
restrictions and standards in the workplace, simultaneously concluding that "a single public employee's pay [in the *Pickering* line
of cases] is usually not a matter of public concern" in contrast to the
"entire collective bargaining unit" involving the collective bargaining process in *Harris*, where such matters would have involved
substantial statewide budgeting decisions.[117] It was necessary for
the majority to make this kind of distinction because *Pickering* employee speech involved with previous grievances had a cost which
had involved state expenditures, inasmuch as they involved monetary judgments—and they had been previously regarded as constitutionally unprotected.[118] Inasmuch as agency fee agreements now

---

[112] *Harris*, 134 S Ct at 2640.

[113] Id.

[114] Id at 2641.

[115] *Pickering v Board of Education of Township High School District 205, Will County*, 391 US 563 (1968).

[116] *Harris*, 134 S Ct at 2642 (citing *Pickering*, 391 US at 568). But see *Developments in the Law—Public Employment*, 97 Harv L Rev 1611 (1984).

[117] *Harris*, 134 S Ct at 2642 n 28.

[118] See *Connick v Myers*, 416 US 138 (1983), *Garcetti v Ceballos*, 547 US 410 (2006), *Borough of Druyea v Guarnieri*, 131 S Ct 2488 (2011) as examples of employee grievances over First

impose a "heavy burden" on the rights of dissident objecting employees within the bargaining unit, the promotion of labor peace and the problems of free riders, previously acknowledged in *Abood*, could not sustain the constitutionality of such practices even under *Pickering*, in the view of the *Harris* majority.[119] Thus, while *Pickering* employee free speech in the workplace withered, the rights of dissident employees who protested their expenditure of dues now blossomed in *Harris*, and before that opinion in *Knox* as well.

Justice Kagan, in a blistering opinion both comprehensive and persuasive, dissented—and she was joined by Justices Ginsburg, Breyer, and Sotomayor.[120] Justice Kagan noted that the interest in a fair share agreement of the kind involved in Illinois was no less applicable to caregivers than for public employees generally. She pointed out that parties who had negotiated the Illinois agreement had acted in reliance upon the principles of *stare decisis* involved as a result of *Abood*. And though there was no departure from *stare decisis* in this case, notwithstanding the "potshots" at *Abood*,[121] she wrote: "The *Abood* rule is deeply entrenched, and is the foundation for not tens or hundreds, but thousands of contracts between unions and governments across the Nation. Our precedent about precedent, fairly understood and applied, makes it impossible for this Court to reverse that decision."[122]

The dissent was of the view that *Abood* resolved *Harris*, inasmuch as Illinois was truly a joint employer with the customer, sharing the authority with them, "each controlling significant aspects of the assistant's work."[123] Justice Kagan noted that the state-employed

---

Amendment protections for employee speech that, in the eyes of the Court, did not deserve constitutional protection.

[119] The Court also rejected the view that case law upholding the constitutionality of the integrated bar where an association of attorneys, in which membership and dues are required as a condition of practicing law, was inapplicable because licensed attorneys who are subject to ethics rules should be required to pay dues as part of this regulatory scheme. The same was true, said the Court, with regard to mandatory dues paid by students at state universities as administrative problems there would "likely be insuperable." *Harris*, 134 S Ct at 2643–44.

The *Harris* opinion is thus "a sui generis wedge" between the law of fair share agreements and public employee speech generally, "splashing doubt upon a key tool in the state's regulation of its own workforce." *The Supreme Court 2013 Leading Case: First Amendment, Harris v Quinn*, 128 Harv L Rev 211, 216 (2014).

[120] *Harris*, 134 S Ct at 2645 (Kagan, J, dissenting).

[121] Id (Kagan, J, dissenting).

[122] Id (Kagan, J, dissenting).

[123] Id at 2646 (Kagan, J, dissenting).

counselor developed a service plan relating to the customer, based upon state-established criteria, and that both the state and the customer played a role in determining whether the employee has demonstrated capabilities to the satisfaction of the counselor.[124] Dependent on the customer's guidance, the state of Illinois withheld payment from an assistant in the event of "credible allegations of consumer abuse, neglect, or financial exploitation."[125] The grievance procedure had been invoked by the SEIU, and an arbitration award had reversed the state's decision to disqualify an assistant from the program.[126] Illinois, noted Justice Kagan, had "sole authority" over terms and conditions of employment, those likely to be the subject of collective bargaining, and if the assistant was to receive an increase in pay, she directed her demands to the state, and not to the individual customer.[127]

The dissent emphasized the importance of state regulations regarding employment conditions so as to address both workplace shortages and high turnover, which "have long plagued in-home care programs" principally because of low wages and benefits."[128] Through the achievement or realization of these policies, said the dissent, the state was able to avoid the costs associated with institutionalization. Thus, the dissent noted that Illinois had acted as a "a veritable poster child for *Abood*" and not, as the majority contended, "some strange extension of that decision."[129] Said Justice Kagan: "It is not altogether easy to understand why the majority thinks what it thinks: Today's opinion takes the tack of throwing everything against the wall in the hope that something might stick."[130]

In a particularly telling passage, Justice Kagan noted the fact that the union was circumscribed in its right to engage in bargaining

---

[124] Id at 2647 (Kagan, J, dissenting).

[125] Id (Kagan, J, dissenting).

[126] Id n 2 (Kagan, J, dissenting).

[127] Id at 2647 (Kagan, J, dissenting).

[128] Id at 2648 (Kagan, J, dissenting). See also NY Times Editorial Board, *More Hurdles for Home Care Unions*, NY Times A30 (Oct 2, 2014) ("Providing home care services to the elderly and disabled is one of the nation's largest, fastest-growing, least-protected and lowest-paid professions, with typical wages of less than $9.50 an hour."). See generally NY Times Editorial Board, *Labor Rights for Home Care Workers*, NY Times A22 (Sept 27, 2014) (noting the "indefensible second-class status of home care workers").

[129] *Harris*, 134 S Ct at 2648 (Kagan, J, dissenting).

[130] Id (Kagan, J, dissenting).

with regard to pay rates set by the state mattered little. It was hardly different than state labor legislation as a general matter, noted Justice Kagan. Said the dissent:

> Most States limit the scope of permissible bargaining in the public sector—often ruling out of bounds similar, individualized decisions. . . . Here, the scope of collective bargaining—over wages and benefits, as well as basic duties and qualifications—more than suffices to implicate the state interests justifying *Abood*. Those are the matters, after all, most likely to concern employees generally and thus most likely to affect the nature and quality of the State's workforce. The idea that *Abood* applies only if a union can bargain with the State over every issue comes from nowhere and relates to nothing in that decision—and would revolutionize public labor law.[131]

The dissent also noted that the mandated legislative uniformity for caregivers was to be found only in the statute's substantive regulation of wages—not health benefits, which had been obtained through the collective bargaining process. Justice Kagan noted that the regulation of the subject matter in question—even if it covered virtually every item that may fall into the bargaining process—simply served "as suspenders to the duty of fair representation's belt: That Illinois has *two* ways to ensure that the results of collective bargaining redound to the benefit of all employees serves to compound, rather than mitigate, the union's free-rider problem."[132] From a policy perspective, as the dissent noted, the thrust of the majority's *Harris* opinion was to penalize disabled persons from participating in their own care, and to produce the applicability of *Abood* only where the system of the employment relationship was centralized.

Two final points in Justice Kagan's dissent are particularly compelling. The first, and most obvious, is *stare decisis*, that is, special justification is necessary to depart from this principle.[133] Here, as the dissent noted, not only was there not "so much as a whisper" which might constitute the basis for such a departure,[134] but also,

---

[131] Id at 2650 (Kagan, J, dissenting). In some measure, the same would apply to the private sector. See, for example, *Q-1 Motor Express, Inc.*, 323 NLRB 767, 769 (1997) (Chairman Gould concurring); *NLRB v American National Insurance*, 343 US 395 (1952).

[132] *Harris*, 134 S Ct at 2650 (Kagan, J, dissenting).

[133] See, for example, *Boys Market, Inc. v Retail Clerks Union*, 398 US 235 (1970); William B. Gould IV, *On Labor Injunctions, Unions, and the Judges: The Boys Market Case*, 1970 Supreme Court Review 215 (1970).

[134] Kagan thus reiterated a point that had been made emphatically by Justice Sotomayor— the lack of any briefing on the arguments that the Court precipitously addressed in *Knox*. See Transcript of Oral Argument at 17, *Harris v Quinn*, 134 S Ct 2618 (2014) (No 11-681).

on the other hand, the presence of an "enormous reliance interest" given that more than twenty states have authorized fair share provisions.[135] Finally, the dissent addressed an issue barely met in the majority opinion—that is, "that the government has wider constitutional latitude when it is acting as employer than as sovereign."[136]

III. The Meaning of Harris

Justice Alito had possessed the votes of four other Justices to produce an opinion which, as Justice Kagan noted for the dissenters, threw "everything against the wall in the hope that something might stick."[137] It is not entirely clear why the Alito opinion did not reach further than it did and sweep aside the *Abood* precedent entirely, given the obvious hostility of Alito to it. After all, the majority opinion in *Knox*, also authored by Justice Alito, had no hesitation to reach beyond issues presented or briefed to the Court in that case. The *Harris* opinion itself dismissed *Abood* as "an anomaly"[138] which rested on "questionable foundations."[139]

How much has *Harris* decided? One thing seems absolutely clear—that is, that Justice Alito's opinions in both *Harris* and *Knox* apply not only the First Amendment protection of free speech to dissident nonunion employees, but also a "compelling state interest" standard which, while thus far imprecise, is quite difficult to override. Moreover, the Court stated that "core issues" in the public sector are inevitably political, in contrast to the private sector—even though, as Justice Frankfurter noted in *Street*, the history of trade unions in the private sector is to obtain gains through the political process as well as at the bargaining table. Again, the freedom-of-association cases had never been concerned with the significance of governmental activity prior to *Harris*.

One puzzle about *Harris* is that it enlisted the support of Justice Scalia, who had said in *Lehnert* that compulsory financial support for unions followed logically from the exclusive bargaining representative principle and the duty of fair representation that

---

[135] *Harris*, 134 S Ct at 2652 (Kagan, J, dissenting).

[136] Id at 2653 (Kagan, J, dissenting).

[137] Id at 2648 (Kagan, J, dissenting).

[138] Id at 2627.

[139] Id at 2638.

is thrust upon all unions. How can, as Justice Scalia recognized, a union function as a bargaining representative when it provides services that cost money, for which free riders in the bargaining unit do not have an obligation to pay?[140] That is Justice Scalia's point in his *Lehnert* opinion. Yet, Justice Scalia's opinion is only cited twice in *Harris*: (1) for the proposition that Justice Blackmun's opinion for the majority in *Lehnert* is deficient, and (2) for the point that a "State may not force every person who benefits from [an advocacy] group's efforts to make payments to the group."[141]

It would seem that the Scalia opinion in *Lehnert* is inconsistent with the majority's observations (derided by Justice Kagan as "potshots" at *Abood*)—that "a critical pillar of the *Abood* Court's analysis rests on an unsupported empirical assumption, namely, that the principle of exclusive representation in the public sector is dependent on a union or agency shop."[142] And again, Justice Alito noted that a "union's status as exclusive bargaining agent and the right to collect an agency fee from nonmembers are not inextricably linked."[143] Yet insofar as Justice Scalia's opinion linked these two concepts—that is, exclusivity for the union as bargaining representative with the union's duty of fair representation—perhaps they remain linked, notwithstanding the *Harris* opinion. It may be that the Court has fudged this distinction, that is, a union's status as exclusive bargaining representative as opposed to its duty of fair representation as exclusive bargaining representative, in order to obtain Justice Scalia's vote. For surely, in Justice Scalia's view in *Lehnert*, there is a direct linkage where the union has an obligation to represent fairly, because of the problem with free riders who will obtain all of the benefits without paying for the services that the law requires the union to perform. The failure of *Harris* to place its explicit imprimatur on what Justice Scalia said in *Lehnert*, or to reject it altogether, means that this is the one critical issue which appears to be left open for future cases and

---

[140] Justice Alito said that the "the best argument that can be mounted in support of *Abood* is based on the fact that a union, in serving as the exclusive representative of all the employees in a bargaining unit, is required by law to engage in certain activities that benefit nonmembers and that the union would not undertake if it did not have a legal obligation to do so." *Harris*, 134 S Ct at 2637 n 18. This portion of the opinion, like others, goes on to distinguish that proposition from the facts of *Harris* itself.

[141] Id at 2638.

[142] Id at 2634.

[143] Id at 2640.

which will require Justice Scalia's vote in the present Court composition to keep the majority intact.

Yet the compelling state interest and strict scrutiny standard for
dissenting nonmembers, accepted in both *Harris* and *Knox*, make
this case a difficult one to sustain for the union even if it was charging dissidents for services owed by virtue of the duty of fair representation. In future litigation, the union will have to show that there
is a less burdensome way through which it can accomplish its objectives, a burden that seems inconsistent with the thrust of the
Scalia opinion. On the other hand, it is perhaps instructive that the
Alito opinion refers to Scalia's *Lehnert* dissent as "the" argument for
the agency shop, and at no point in the opinion is it explicitly criticized. This is the heart of the unresolved puzzle in *Harris*, which
makes the breadth of the opinion and its future applicability to the
public sector generally somewhat unclear.[144] The silence of the nor-
mally voluble Justice Scalia is both aberrant and enigmatic.

There is another aspect of *Harris* that is curious, though comparatively clear in its meaning as used in the *Harris* opinion. The
wellspring for modern jurisprudence relating to public-sector
employer-employee relations is the above noted *Pickering* decision,
discussed briefly by Justice Alito.[145] Over a quarter of a century ago,
in *Connick v Myers*,[146] the Court reiterated the proposition first pro-
pounded in *Pickering*, that is, that public employee speech was unprotected where the individual spoke "not as a citizen upon matters
of public concern, but instead as an employee upon matters only of
personal interest."[147]

---

[144] Compare Steven Greenhouse, *Ruling Against Union Fees Contains Damage to Labor*, A12
NY Times (July 1, 2014), with Cynthia Estlund and William E. Forbath, *The War on
Workers*, A21 NY Times (July 3, 2014).

[145] *Harris*, 134 S Ct at 2641–42.

[146] *Connick v Myers*, 416 US at 138 (1983). I have addressed *Connick* and some of the cases
discussed previously in *Elko County*, 131 LA 1593 (Arb 2013), but see *Alexander v Gardner-
Denver Company*, 415 US 36 (1974); 14 *Penn Plaza LLC v Pyett*, 556 US 247 (2009). See
generally William B. Gould IV, *A Half Century of the Steelworkers Trilogy: Fifty Years of Iro-
nies Squared*, in Paul D. Staudohar and Mark I. Lurie, eds, *Arbitration 2010: The Steelworkers
Trilogy at 50*, Proceedings of the Sixty-Third Annual Meeting, National Academy of Arbi-
trators, 35 (2011); Thomas Keenan, Note, *Circuit Court Interpretations of Garcetti v Ceballos and
the Developments of Public Employee Speech*, 87 Notre Dame L Rev 841 (2011); Helen Norton,
*Constraining Public Employee Speech: Government's Control of Its Workers' Speech to Protect Its Own
Expression*, 59 Duke L J 1 (2009); Elizabeth Dale, *Employee Speech & Management Rights: A
Counterintuitive Reading of Garcetti v Ceballos*, 29 Berkeley J Emp & Lab L 175 (2008); Comment, *Leading Cases, Constitutional Law: Public Employee Speech*, 120 Harv L Rev 273 (2006).

[147] *Connick*, 416 US at 147.

In *Connick*, a 5–4 majority, despite a strong dissent by Justice Brennan, expressed the view that a contrary conclusion, that is, one which would allow employee constitutional litigation about matters of "personal interest," would "constitutionalize the employee grievance," a matter of public concern within the meaning of *Pickering* in only the most limited sense.[148] In the opinion supporting the authority cited by Justice Kagan, the Court warned against the constitutionalization of employee grievances and stated that it would be a grave mistake to confuse such with "great principles of free expression."[149] Later, the Court had warned that constitutional rights in the workplace must be struck within the "realities of employment context."[150] The Court noted, as discussed in *Garcetti*, that government employers "need a significant degree of control over their employees' words" in order to "efficient[ly] provi[de] public services.[151]

Considerable debate has emerged about the significance of these cases.[152] Curiously, Justice Scalia, who joined the majority opinion in *Harris* without filing a separate opinion on the *Lehnert* issue, expressed much interest in this line of authority vis-à-vis the union security agreement presented during oral argument itself.[153] Yet here also, Justice Scalia, not speaking separately on any matter, was silent.

It was left to Justice Kagan's dissent to discuss the applicability of *Abood* to the public-concern principles articulated in Supreme Court jurisprudence of this century, manifested most prominently by *Garcetti*.[154] Justice Kagan noted that *Abood* had placed most speech about the employment relationship outside the public-concern arena,

---

[148] Id at 154.

[149] Id.

[150] *Harris*, 134 S Ct at 2653 (Kagan, J, dissenting) (citing *Engquist v Oregon Department of Agriculture*, 553 US 591, 600 (2008)).

[151] Id (Kagan, J, dissenting) (citing *Garcetti*, 547 US at 418).

[152] See, for example, *Garcia v Hartford Police Department*, 706 F3d 120 (2d Cir 2013); *Handy-Clay v City of Memphis*, 695 F3d 531 (6th Cir 2012); *Ross v Breslin*, 693 F3d 300, 305 (2d Cir 2012); *Fox v Traverse City Area Public Schools*, 605 F3d 345, 349 (6th Cir 2010); *Posey v Lake Pend Oreille School District No. 84*, 546 F3d 1121 (9th Cir 2008).

[153] Transcript of Oral Argument at 23, *Harris v Quinn*, 134 S Ct 2618 (2014) (No 11-681).

[154] Curiously, this Term, the Court moved back to a protection of public employee speech in *Lane v Franks*, 134 S Ct 2369 (2014). The case was later remanded to the Eleventh Circuit, where it vacated and remanded the decision to the district court on October 8, 2014. *Lane v Central Alabama Community College*, 12-16192, 2014 WL 5002100 (11th Cir, Oct 8, 2014).

articulated in *Connick*, *Garcetti*, and their progeny, inasmuch as it "pertains mostly to private concerns and implicates the government's interests as employer; thus, the government could compel fair-share fees for collective bargaining,"[155] given that First Amendment rights were not involved. Thus, as the dissent noted, under decided authority, speech related to politics would have no bearing upon the government's workforce restructuring interest. Here, upheld fees for such political activities would be unconstitutional under the public-concern authority.

Justice Kagan noted that an employee who speaks out "at various inopportune times and places"[156] for higher wages for himself and for coworkers which will drive up public spending cannot properly bring a First Amendment claim if the employer disciplines him. This would be a private issue notwithstanding its impact upon public spending. Said the dissent:

> In both cases . . . the employer is sanctioning employees for choosing either to say or not to say something respecting their terms and conditions of employment. Of course, in my hypothetical, the employer is stopping the employee from speaking, whereas in this or any other case involving union fees, the employer is forcing the employee to support such expression. But I am sure the majority would agree that that difference does not make a difference.[157]

IV. The Immediate Harris Aftermath

At least ten jurisdictions have enacted legislation providing for home care as an alternative to institutionalization with procedures allowing for collective bargaining in a manner similar to the Illinois statute declared unconstitutional in *Harris*.[158] As the Court itself noted in *Harris*, there are twenty jurisdictions with provisions for so-called "fair share union security agreements" which were at

---

[155] *Harris*, 134 S Ct at 2654 (Kagan, J, dissenting).

[156] Id at 2655 (Kagan, J, dissenting).

[157] Id at 2655–56 (Kagan, J, dissenting).

[158] See, for example, Mass Ann Laws ch 118G, §§ 28–33 (LexisNexis, 2007); Or Rev Stat §§ 410.600–410.614 (2005); Wash Rev Code Ann §§ 74.39A.220–74.39A.300 (West, 2002); Wis Exec Order No 172 (2006); Exec Order No 23 (2006); Iowa Exec Order No 45 (2006); Iowa Exec Order No 46 (2006); Conn Gen Stat § 17b-706a(e)(1); Md Code Ann, Health-Gen §§ 15-901 et seq; Vt Stat Ann tit 21, §§ 1631–44; Mo Rev Stat § 208.853; Pa Exec Order 2010-04 (Sept 14) (rescinded).

the heart of the litigation in the case.[159] These jurisdictions, at least with regard to the so-called "quasi public-private employee" category at issue in *Harris*, would appear to be vulnerable to constitutional attacks launched by dissenting and nonunion employees who object to their dues collection.

The next round of more consequential litigation will relate to public employees where the employment relationship is more firmly established than it was in *Harris*. At this point, it appears that the leading case in this category is *Friedrichs v California Teachers Association*, recently decided by the Court of Appeals for the Ninth Circuit.[160] Certainly, the disparaging commentary provided by Justice Alito in both *Knox* and in *Harris* about the viability of *Abood* would strongly suggest that the Court, at least as currently composed,[161] will hold that fair share agreements are inconsistent with the First Amendment's requirements, at least as they apply to the position of dissenting employees—notwithstanding the Court's earlier concerns regarding the constitutionalization of disputes between public employees and employers. Despite this logical inconsistency, it appears that the Court has devised one set of rules circumscribing employee rights when they are asserted against the state—as was the case in *Pickering* and *Garcetti*—and an entirely different approach when the interests of dissidents are asserted against unions which have negotiated union security clauses with employers in their collective bargaining agreement. Both *Knox* and *Harris* suggest a dual standard depending upon whether the union's or the employers' ox has been gored.

But in truth, the other public-sector shoe cannot drop until the Court clarifies the ambiguity of its opinion, which constitutes "potshots," as Justice Kagan would have it—regarding the question of whether Justice Alito's commentary on the status of exclusivity can be equated with the duty of fair representation obligation which springs from exclusivity. Again, that is the unresolved ambiguity in

---

[159] *Harris*, 134 S Ct at 2652 (Kagan, J, dissenting).

[160] *Rebecca Friedrichs, et al v California Teachers Association, et al*, No 13-57095 (9th Cir) (decided on the basis of *Abood*). Petition for writ of certiorari filed to the Supreme Court on Jan 26, 2015. Illinois, with a new conservative Republican governor, has seen executive branch initiatives predicated upon the view that *Harris* overruled *Abood*. See *A War on Workers in Illinois*, NY Times A20 (Feb 14, 2015); Monica Davey and Mitch Smith, *Illinois Governor Acts to Curb Power of Public Sector Unions*, NY Times A1 (Feb 10, 2015). See also Richard Pérez-Peña, *Governor of Illinois Takes Aim at Labor*, NY Times A13 (Feb 13, 2015).

[161] Again, this assumes that Justice Scalia's vote can be obtained.

Harris, and until it is resolved, one cannot speak with certainty about the applicability of the Scalia dissent in *Lehnert* to *Harris*.[162]

A. THE PRIVATE SECTOR

What does *Harris* mean for private-sector cases arising under both the RLA and the NLRA? Though the early RLA cases indicate some measure of constitutional protection on a state action theory,[163] similar to that employed in the judge-made promulgation of the duty of fair representation obligation,[164] the rationale of those cases was ultimately predicated upon statutory interpretation[165]—just as statutory interpretation dictated the manner in which similar NLRA disputes were resolved.

The lead case on the latter issue is *Communications Workers of America v Beck*,[166] where the Court held that the applicable standard was a "duty of fair representation"—that is, did the union violate its duty to represent employees within the unit fairly by its union security system and provision for dues objectors. This contrasts with the early union discipline cases like *NLRB v Allis Chalmers*,[167] addressing the relationship between a union's disciplinary authority and the scope of union security agreements resolving such issues under the "restraint and coercion" prohibition of Section 8(b)(1)(A).[168] Thus the standard which has evolved in the pri-

---

[162] The same was true of Justice Stewart's concurring opinion in *Fibreboard Paper Products Corporation v NLRB*, 379 US 203, 217 (1964). Later on, his approach became dominant. See, for example, *First National Maintenance Corporation v NLRB*, 452 US at 666; *Allied Chemical & Alkali Workers of America, Local Union No. 1 v Pittsburgh Plate Glass Company, Chemical Division*, 404 US 157 (1971).

[163] Compare *Marsh v Alabama*, 326 US 501 (1946) (where the Court used the First and Fourteenth Amendments to hold that a state trespassing law could not be used to prohibit the dissemination of religious material on closely held public property) with *Moose Lodge v Irvis*, 407 US 163 (1972) (in which the Court begins to take a much less expansive view of state action). The Court itself has referenced what it views as the appropriate state action standard in *Beck*, alluding to *United Steelworkers of America, AFL-CIO-CLC v Sadlowski*, 457 US 102, 121 n 16 (1982), and *United Steelworkers of America v Weber* 443 US 193, 200 (1979). See also Charles Black, *"State Action," Equal Protection, and California's Proposition 14*, 81 Harv L Rev 69, 100–103 (1967).

[164] *Steele v Louisville & Nashville Railroad Company*, 323 US 192 (1944).

[165] See *Hanson*, 351 US 225; *Street*, 367 US 740; *Allen*, 373 US 113.

[166] 487 US 735 (1988).

[167] 388 US 175 (1967). Justice Brennan authored the majority opinion. Justice White authored a concurrence. Justice Black authored the dissent, where he was joined by Justices Douglas, Harlan, and Stewart.

[168] *California Saw*, 320 NLRB at 333 n 47 (Chairman Gould concurring).

vate sector, duty of fair representation, thus far gives considerably more latitude to union action than will be the case with public-sector cases arising under the First Amendment—particularly that which has been circumscribed by the Court's reasoning in *Knox* and *Harris*.

At the end of 2014, it appears that *Harris* has produced little fall-out in the private sector.[169] Curiously, the major cases in the wake of the Supreme Court public-sector authority relate to the almost seventy-year-old Taft-Hartley amendments, which, as noted above, allow the states to prohibit certain forms of union security agreements as part of their right-to-work legislation. The constitutionality of Section 14(b) of the NLRA,[170] which allows states to retain jurisdiction where they enact right-to-work legislation prohibiting the compulsion of membership as a condition of employment, was first addressed by the Supreme Court in *Lincoln Federal Labor Union v Northwestern Company*.[171]

In *Lincoln Federal*, the Court considered the constitutionality of right-to-work legislation challenged on grounds of interference with the right to freedom of speech, assembly, and petition in the First and Fourteenth Amendments and the Equal Protection and Due Process Clauses of the Fourteenth Amendment. In that case, petitioners argued that the state legislation at issue "impair[ed] the obligation of contracts made prior to the [the statute's] enactment."[172] Justice Black, writing for the majority, examined the litigation and case authority which had declared numerous labor statutes unconstitutional beginning in 1908,[173] noting that the Court "at

---

[169] See, for example, *United Food & Commercial Workers International Union, Local 700 (Kroger Limited Partnership)*, 361 NLRB No 39 (2014). In this case, a 3–2 majority of the Board deemed applicable the same presumption articulated in favor of the opt-out requirement set forth pre-*Knox* and pre-*Harris*. Members Miscimarra and Johnson argued that the holdings in both *Knox* and *Harris* "support . . . [their] view that some greater and earlier notice to private sector employees under our Act is required. Otherwise, even under a duty of fair representation standard, judicial assessment of how our Act works, i.e., the rules of disclosure mandated by a federal agency, will inevitably be that it impermissibly abridges those freedoms." *Kroger Limited Partnership*, 361 NLRB No 39 at 13 (Members Miscimarra and Johnson concurring in part and dissenting in part).

[170] 29 USC § 164(b).

[171] *Lincoln Federal Labor Union v Northwestern Company*, 335 US 525 (1949).

[172] Id at 531.

[173] Id at 534–35 (citing *Adair v U.S.*, 208 US 161 (1908); *Coppage v State of Kansas*, 236 US 1 (1915)).

least as early as 1934 . . . has steadily rejected the due process philosophy" enunciated earlier. Said the Court:

> In doing so, it has consciously returned closer and closer to the earlier
> constitutional principle that states have power to legislate against what
> are found to be injurious practices in their internal commercial and
> business affairs so long as their laws do not run afoul of some specific
> federal constitutional prohibition or of some valid federal law.[174]

The Court's view was that the Due Process Clause could no longer
be broadly construed to place the legislative body in a "strait
jacket,"[175] and that the legislation afforded protection to both union
and nonunion members.[176] Practices which limited the ability of unions and employers to voluntarily agree to union security provisions
were not to be treated differently simply because they can be viewed
as more favorable to organized labor.

Attention was now to focus more particularly on the precise language of Section 14(b), beginning with the Court's 1963 rulings in *Retail Clerks Association v Schermerhorn*.[177] The Court noted
that agency shops, which require dues and initiation fees rather
than full membership, could be prohibited by the states under Section 14(b)—just as the Court had soon thereafter held that the
outer limit of union security agreements allowed under the NLRA
was the "financial core" of membership, that is, of the same payment of dues—as a "practical equivalent" of an agreement requiring
membership as a condition of employment.[178]

In oft-cited language, the majority in *Schermerhorn* wrote: "Whatever may be the status of less stringent union-security arrangements,
the agency shop is within §14(b). At least to that extent did Congress
intend §8(a)(3) and §14(b) to coincide."[179] What was different from
that which was considered in the discussions leading to the federal
statute's amendments, the union argued, was that the use of dues under the agreement in *Schermerhorn* governed by right-to-work state

---

[174] *Lincoln*, 335 US at 536.

[175] Id at 537.

[176] Id.

[177] *Retail Clerks Association v Schermerhorn*, 375 US 746 (1963).

[178] *NLRB v General Motors Corp.*, 373 US 734 (1963). At this point, it was thought that the
unfair labor practice prohibitions related to employment conditions only. See, for example,
Radio Officers v NLRB, 347 US 17 (1954).

[179] *Schermerhorn*, 373 US at 751–52.

legislation is forbidden "by the union for institutional purposes unrelated to its exclusive agency functions," in contrast to federal authority, where "the nonmember contributions are available to the
union without restriction."[180] The Court was not persuaded, and
concluded that inasmuch as the dues exacted from members and
nonmembers were identical in *Schermerhorn*, bookkeeping could simply shift union dues collected from union members to cover more so-
called "institutional matters" unrelated to collective bargaining and
contract administration, thus requiring nonmembers to assume a
more substantial financial burden as it relates to grievance adjustments and collective bargaining than was the case with members
themselves whose dues could be used for other purposes as well.

The question of whether a form of union security agreement or
service fee arrangement may impose smaller amounts of monies on
nonmembers has not been explicitly addressed by the Court since
Schermerhorn. In this century, the Board has successfully sought injunctive relief[181] against a state statute providing for a lesser form of
union security agreement, that is, a charge for the monies expended
in connection with grievance processing and arbitration on the
grounds that state interference is unconstitutionally preempted by
the act itself[182]—and the NLRB has held that such an agreement is
in restraint and coercion of the nonmember rights to refrain from
union activity protected by the employee right to refrain from union
activity contained in the Taft-Hartley amendments under the act.[183]
A fundamental problem here is that the union has an obligation
(underlined by Justice Scalia's opinion in *Lehnert*), as exclusive bargaining representative, to represent all workers in the appropriate
unit on the same basis—whether they are union or nonunion mem-

---

[180] Id at 752.

[181] The NLRB has no jurisdiction over public employers, but under *NLRB v Nash-Finch Co.*, the Board has been held to have authority to enjoin state laws that are inconsistent with federal law. *Nash-Finch*, 404 US 138 (1971).

[182] *NLRB v North Dakota*, 504 F Supp2d 750 (D ND 2007). I think that this decision would be correctly decided even if the Court ultimately concludes, as I do, that the Board's decisions in note 183 were wrongly decided. See *Lodge 76, International Association of Machinists v Wisconsin Employment Relations Commission*, 427 US 132 (1976); *Garmon v San Diego Building Trades*, 359 US 236 (1959). Preemption would still oust state jurisdiction.

[183] *Furniture Workers Division, Local 282 (the Davis Co.)*, 291 NLRB 182, 183 (1988); *Columbus Area Local American Postal Workers Union (U.S. Postal Serv.)*, 277 NLRB 541, 543 (1985); *Machinist, Local Union No. 697 (The H.O. Canfield Rubber Co.)*, 223 NLRB 832, 835 (1976).

bers. Nonmembers are "free riders"—a phenomenon which inevitably encourages employees to escape union membership and its obligations because it is cheaper to do so given the fact that all receive the same benefits—though the Court in *Harris* appeared to deride this assumption, albeit within the context of a union whose bargaining role was circumscribed.

In *Plumbers Local Union 141*,[184] a 1980 case involving a Mississippi state statute which banned payment of union "charges of any kind,"[185] the Board held that even though representation fees might be bargainable under §14(b) of the act, providing states with the authority to outlaw contractual schemes where nonunion dues were equal to union dues was an unlawful membership requirement which could be prohibited by the state under §14(b). On appeal, in *Plumbers Local Union 141 v NLRB*,[186] the Court of Appeals for the District of Columbia affirmed the Board and wrote: "Congress knew of the free rider problem; it knew of the state laws at issue here; it passed §14(b) anyway."[187] Lesser forms of union security agreements were to be viewed as consistent with the federal interest only if sanctioned through harmonization with state policy.[188] The court reasoned that a post-hiring union security agreement fell directly "within the ambit of §14(b)."[189]

Judge Mikva dissented. The dissent noted that in *Schermerhorn* the representation fee at issue was left unresolved inasmuch as equal payment for members and nonmembers made it possible for nonmembers to pay more of the bargaining costs thus impinging upon those right-to-work states which sought freedom for employees to avoid union compulsion, given the ability of the union to shift union member dues to institutional concerns. Judge Mikva also emphasized that Congress never specifically defined what it meant by "compulsory unionism" which was left to the states under §14(b).

---

[184] *International Union of the United Association of Journeymen and Apprentices of the Plumbing and Pipefitting Industry of the United States and Canada, Local Unions Nos. 141, 229, 681, and 706 and International Paper Company, Southern Kraft Division*, 252 NLRB 1299 (1980).

[185] Miss Const, § 198-A.

[186] *International Union of the United Association of Journeymen Local 141, et al v NLRB*, 675 F2d 1257 (DC Cir 1982).

[187] Id at 1261.

[188] Id at 1262 (quoting approvingly from Justice Stewart's dissenting opinion in *Oil, Chemical & Atomic Workers International Union v Mobil Oil Corp.*, 426 US 407, 417 (1976)).

[189] *Journeymen Local 141*, 675 F2d at 1262.

That provision's assumption of state jurisdiction relates to agreements which require "membership" as condition of employment. But "membership" representation fees, under Judge Mikva's view, fell outside state regulation. Said the dissent: "There is no suggestion whatsoever in the legislative history that a worker who pays a fee for services rendered by the union thereby becomes a 'member' of the union. In any other context, such a proposition would be facially absurd."[190] The individuals who pay the fee would not be:

> required to support the union, or fund its institutional, union-oriented activities. They would not sign membership cards or be carried on the union's rolls. They would not be required to embrace participation in union activities and maintain "good standing." They would not fill out applications, take oaths, or attend meetings. They would not be subject to union-imposed disciplinary measures enforceable in state courts. They would not have "fulfilled the requirements for membership in such organization."[191]

But there are at least two problems with the Mikva dissent, which has now been signed onto by Judge Diane Wood (in dissent) in the recent Seventh Circuit decision upholding the constitutionality of Indiana's right-to-work legislation.[192] The first is that, as union disciplinary cases involving union security clauses demonstrate, the demarcation line between membership and nonmembership is less than pristine. In *Allis-Chalmers*, the Court held that a union could impose fines upon workers who had assumed a member's full obligation and later crossed a picket line,[193] noting that this degree of involvement and obligations was voluntarily assumed since the statute only requires financial contributions as a condition of employment.[194] The fact is that workers (and employers, for that matter) infrequently understand the distinction between membership and nonmembership—that is why the Board itself has thrust upon the unions an obligation to explain in some form[195] the right

---

[190] Id at 1275 (Mikva dissenting).

[191] Id (Mikva dissenting). See *United Stanford Employees, Local 680 v NLRB*, 601 F2d 980, 981 (9th Cir 1979); *NLRB v Hershey Foods Corp.*, 513 F2d 1083, 1085 (9th Cir 1975).

[192] *Sweeney v Pence*, 767 F3d 654 (7th Cir 2014). The Supreme Court of Indiana has ruled to the same effect under state constitutional law. See *Zoeller v Sweeney*, 19 NE3d 749 (2014).

[193] *Allis-Chalmers*, 388 US at 196.

[194] See *General Motors*, 373 US at 742–44.

[195] Generally, this is imposed through union literature distributed to all employees within the bargaining unit. See *California Saw*, 320 NLRB at 224. But this is generally not imposed

to resign membership and the consequential right to object to expenditure of compulsory dues for political or other purposes not germane to the collective bargaining process.[196] Moreover, as the Court of Appeals for the Ninth Circuit has said, "there is no realistic difference from a legal standpoint between a union shop and an agency shop, although under a union shop the union may, if it wishes, place an employee who only pays dues on its 'membership' rolls."[197]

A second concern with Judge Mikva's opinion is that he cites *Abood* and its ideological activity exception to the fair share obligation as "analogous" to the issue under discussion[198] to which an employee could object—a proposition well accepted since the Railway Labor Act cases and *Abood*. Yet the Mikva opinion would really create three layers of union dues: (1) ideological and nongermane activity to which an employee could object, (2) everything that falls outside of that, which includes the ability to enhance the collective bargaining process outside of the bargaining table and the grievance and arbitration machinery involving the administration of a contract,[199] and (3) the union institutional interests which do not involve any activities in categories (1) or (2). In any event, this multi-layered approach may have difficulty in carrying the day, particularly given the concern of the *Harris* majority with the murkiness of the already-existing dividing line, albeit in the public sector,[200]

---

through the language of the collective bargaining agreement itself. See *Marquez*, 525 US 33. The theory expressed by the Court was that the duty of fair representation obligation to explain the collective bargaining agreement to the members was not owed, in part because workers infrequently read the agreements. However, the Court, within a few weeks, held that the language of the collective bargaining agreement was critical to the ability of individual workers to sue for antidiscrimination prohibitions and the like. See *Wright v Universal Maritime Service Corp.*, 525 US 70 (1998). The two nearly simultaneous decisions are squarely at odds with one another. In my judgment, *Marquez* was wrongly decided.

[196] *United Paperworkers International Union, AFL-CIO, CLC*, 320 NLRB 349 (1995). See also *Group Health, Inc.*, 323 NLRB 251 (1997); *Rochester Manufacturing Co.*, 323 NLRB 260 (1997).

[197] *United Food & Commercial Workers Union, Local 1036 v NLRB*, 307 F3d 760, 765 (9th Cir 2002) (citing *General Motors*, 373 US at 743–44).

[198] *Journeymen Local 141*, 675 F2d at 1279.

[199] See *Lehnert*, 500 US at 507.

[200] *Harris*, 134 S Ct at 2630. The Court in *Harris* relies upon Justice Frankfurter's opinion regarding the synthetic nature of an attempt to distinguish political from collective bargaining activities in *Street*, which is a private-sector case. Of course, Justice Alito drew the exact opposite conclusion from this reality. He would have found that the so-called First Amendment right of nonunion employees is in play in connection with the overwhelming

between that which is germane and nongermane to the collective bargaining process.

Nonetheless, as Judge Wood's dissent in *Sweeney* highlights, this issue may well come back to the Supreme Court. Judge Wood's opinion reads Section 14(b) narrowly, as did Judge Mikva in his earlier dissent, which Wood characterized as "prescient."[201] Both dissents dramatize the inequity and anti-union nature of not only the representation system which allows nonunion employees to free ride and get representation for nothing—as opposed to union members who must pay for it through their dues—but also, in the view of both judges, is beyond the scope of Section 14(b)'s prohibition on union security agreements at the state level. But given the broad expansive and vague nature of the membership construct, this argument seems tenuous.

As noted below, this issue involves questions of federal labor law—that is, whether a service charge rather than dues for nonunion members violates either the union's duty of fair representation under the act or the employees' right to refrain under prohibitions against "restraint and coercion" imposed upon unions under the Taft-Hartley amendments to the act. This is one of the more intriguing issues arising out of Judge Wood's dissent, an opinion which stresses the extent to which the union does not have recompense from anyone for the free rider problem. Clearly, it does not, though I am not sure whether this lack of recompense can be fully addressed through resolving the question of what constitutes a "taking" within the meaning of the Constitution as Judge Wood asserts.[202] But some of the arguments to the contrary seem to fail: first, that the union gets its recompense by virtue of its seat at the bargaining table, a point put forward by the Seventh Circuit majority. It does not, as Judge Wood correctly points out, even though she is incorrect in assuming that the seat at the bargaining table, which exists by virtue of federal labor laws, can only be obtained through a ballot box election.[203]

---

number of instances involving union activity at the bargaining table in the public sector as opposed to its private counterparts.

[201] *Sweeney*, 767 F3d 654 at 681 (Wood dissenting).

[202] Id at 674 (Wood dissenting) (referencing US Const, Amend V, which states in relevant part: "nor shall private property be taken for public use, without just compensation.").

[203] *Linden Lumber Division, Summer & Company v NLRB*, 419 US 301 (1974); *NLRB v Gissel Packing Company, Inc.*, 395 US 575 (1969) (holding that evidence of majority status manifested

B. SERVICE FEE ARRANGEMENTS

A "service fee" is an arrangement in which nonmembers assume costs for their representation. It is an attempt to skirt the shoals of that which is the equivalent of "membership as a condition of employment" prohibited by Section 14(b) or the federal statute itself.[204] Can this done in a manner which is compatible with federal labor law, and state prohibitions against union security agreements contained in right-to-work legislation enacted pursuant to Section 14 (b)? One argument in favor of a prohibition under Section 14(b) is that the states which have enacted right-to-work legislation are unsympathetic and hostile to the free rider problem, notwithstanding the fact that federal labor law, through the Taft-Hartley amendments, recognizes that free riders would undermine the exclusive bargaining agent principle.

What is "membership which may be prohibited"? *Schermerhorn* provides some guidelines through its holding that equality in fees would encourage membership inasmuch as union members would see more of their financial obligations diverted to institutional union financial obligations unrelated to the grievance handling and collective bargaining process, imposing a greater burden on nonmembers in the workplace. Uniformity of fees is thus swept within Section 14 (b)'s strictures as *Schermerhorn* states. What kinds of arrangements would pass muster?

It is possible that an arrangement which did not insist upon the dismissal of the offending nonunion worker for failure to meet his or her obligations, thus failing to make membership a condition of employment, might evade the state's role in Section 14(b) since that statutory provision speaks in terms of making membership a condition of employment. But the Board has held that a union can lawfully obtain employee monies under the act only pursuant to a union security agreement compelling membership as a condition of employment.[205] The Supreme Court of Nevada, under its public-

---

through union authorization cards, for instance, can compel an employer to recognize a union under some circumstances).

[204] Codified at 29 USC § 164[b]. See generally *General Motors*, 373 US at 734; *Schermerhorn*, 373 US at 746.

[205] *Professional Association of Golf Officials*, 317 NLRB 774, 778 (1995), but see *Electrical Workers IUE Local 444 (Paramax Systems)*, 311 NLRB 1031, 1033–36 (1993) (enforcement denied in *International Union of Electronic, Electric, Salaried, Machine & Furniture Workers, AFL-CIO v NLRB*, 41 F3d 1532 (DC Cir 1994)).

sector statute, has held that the imposition of a fee for nonunion employees for grievance processing was unlawful, holding that a contrary result would "lead to an inequitable result that we cannot condone, by essentially requiring union members to shoulder the burden of costs associated with nonunion members' individual grievance representation."[206] Yet this straightforward approach would not seem to satisfy federal labor law requirements, in light of *Schermerhorn* and the protection of the right to resign as part of the right to refrain.[207]

The leading Board decision on this issue is *International Association of Machinists and Aerospace Workers, Local Union No. 697, AFL-CIO (the H. O. Canfield Rubber Company of Virginia, Inc.)*,[208] where a majority, over Chairman Murphy's dissent, held that a union "by charging only nonmembers for grievance representation [as opposed to charging its members for dues], has discriminated against nonmembers."[209] The Board did not say why this was discriminatory, and, indeed, the Supreme Court of Nevada had held that the requirement of "reasonable costs associated with individual grievance representation"[210] did not "interfere with, restrain or coerce" employees under Nevada's state public-sector statute.[211]

It seems that the idea that any financial imposition upon nonunion members would constitute an unfair labor practice makes little sense as a general proposition. But the Board has continued to adhere to this proposition over the years.[212] In my judgment, however, the idea of a per se ban on fees for nonunion members as a condition of grievance processing seems wrong as a matter of law.

But what passes muster in light of *Schermerhorn*? The conundrum here is that union members subject to a union security clause have

---

[206] *Cone v Nevada Service Employees Union/SEIU Local 1107*, 998 P2d 1178, 1183 (2000).

[207] See *Pattern Makers*, 473 US 95 (1985). See also *NLRB v Boeing Co.*, 412 US 67 (1973).

[208] 223 NLRB at 832. See also *United Steel, Paper and Forestry, Rubber, Manufacturing, Energy, Allied Industrial and Service Workers International Union, Local 1192, AFL-CIO, CLC (Buckeye Florida Corporation, a Subsidiary of Buckeye Technologies, Inc. and Georgia Pacific, LLC)*, 12-CB-109694 (Mar 24, 2014).

[209] *The H.O. Canfield Rubber Company of Virginia, Inc.*, 223 NLRB at 835. The Board relied upon its holding in *Hughes Tool Company*, where a union had both a flat fee of $15 for grievance processing and $400 for arbitration. That Board was of the view that a disproportionate burden had been thrust upon the nonmembers. See *Hughes Tool Company*, 104 NLRB 318 (1953).

[210] *Cone*, 998 P2d 1178, 1182.

[211] Id.

[212] *American Postal Workers*, 277 NLRB 541 (1986); *Furniture Worker Local 282*, 291 NLRB 182 (1988).

already bought into a kind of insurance risk pool by providing dues for their own grievance processing, even though a substantial number of them may never invoke the process and utilize it. The ad-hoc utilization of grievance processing by nonunion members would be more expensive than union dues for this very reason. But it seems unlikely that the argument on behalf of the lawfulness of ad-hoc fees, which are so dramatically different in amount than union dues, would pass muster. Nonetheless, the idea that some union calculation of "proportion of regular dues payments that are used to fund representational activity"[213] would seem to be more compatible with the right to refrain policies built into the act.

The devil will always be in the details, but an approach along these lines seems to be the best one, insofar as it would protect both a union's ability to protect itself against excessive financial burden,[214] and at the same time protect the state's promotion of the free rider policy, given the fact that nonunion employees would not have to pay for the cost associated with the collective bargaining process itself, independent of grievance and arbitration matters. The difficulty for the Board and the courts lies in determination of the precise amount of any nonmember obligation. Notwithstanding the risk pool reality, a substantial fee assessment beyond the union dues amount would probably run afoul of the law.[215]

Something along these general lines seems best. In my view, the idea put forward by Professors Fisk and Sachs to the effect that the Board could devise a "members only" bargaining structure in right-to-work states,[216] so as to avoid the cost-burden problem, is a position at odds with that devised by the National Labor Relations Act.[217] Though the authors point out that the question of whether exclusive bargaining representative status is the sole representative

---

[213] Catherine Fisk and Benjamin Sachs, *Restoring Equity in Right to Work*, 4 UC Irvine L Rev 859, 879–880 (2014).

[214] See id at 873–75. This approach might be more persuasive than one that provided for four years worth of dues to pay for one single grievance taken to arbitration (on behalf of nonunion employee). See *American Postal Workers*, 277 NLRB 541, 543. See also *Hughes Tool Company*, 104 NLRB 318, where the charge was more than 100 times that imposed upon union members under their dues structure.

[215] See *Hughes Tool Company*, 104 NLRB 318.

[216] See Fisk and Sachs, 4 UC Irvine L Rev at 870–75 (cited in note 213).

[217] *Dick's Sporting Goods*, Advice Memorandum, Case 6-CA-34821 (June 22, 2006). But see Charles Morris, *The Blue Eagle at Work: Reclaiming Democratic Rights in the American Workplace* (ILR, 2004), which asserts that compulsory members-only bargaining is contemplated by the statute. Members-only bargaining is permissive under the act, but is generally viewed as noncompulsory.

structure mandated by the act[218] has never been squarely addressed by the Court, the fact of the matter is that numerous decisions decided by the high tribunal rest upon the idea of exclusivity.[219]

V. Conclusion

The 5–4 decision of the court in *Harris v Quinn* reflects the Court's activist approach to the area of labor law and employment cases, a theme sounded emphatically just a Term before.[220] Justice Alito could scarcely contain himself in *Harris*—indeed, he cannot wait to reverse more than a half century of the Court's labor law jurisprudence in the area of union security agreements, union dues, and the ongoing litigation regarding political expenditures. *Harris* is another step that reflects this trend. It casts a shadow over the ability of organized labor to rebound and to represent employees

---

[218] In dicta, Chief Justice Hughes appears to have suggested that the NLRA mandates recognition of negotiated agreements by a minority, where such agreements have not been superseded by an exclusive relationship. 305 US 197, 237 (1938). See also *Retail Clerks International Association v Lion Dry Goods Inc.*, 369 US 17, 29 (1961).

[219] See, for example, *International Ladies Garment Workers' Union v NLRB and Bernhard-Altmann Texas Corp.*, 366 US 731 (1961). *NLRB v Allis-Chalmers*, 388 US at 175; *Emporium Capwell v Western Addition Community Organization*, 420 US 50 (1975); *J. I. Case Co. v NLRB*, 321 US 332. See generally William B. Gould IV, *Black Power in the Unions: The Impact Upon Collective Bargaining Relationships*, 79 Yale L J 46 (1969); William B. Gould IV, *Status of Unauthorized and "Wildcat" Strikes Under the National Labor Relations Act*, 52 Cornell L Q 672 (1967). But Justice Rucker, concurring in *Zoeller*, seems to have taken this argument seriously:

> But the parties here vigorously dispute whether it is legally possible for a union to operate as something other than an exclusive representation union, and thus avoid the duty of fair representation and its concomitant costs. Here, the Union has not attempted to demonstrate that the Right to Work Law operates in such a way as to have actually eliminated or reduced its compensation from dues or "fair share" payments. Nor has the Union shown that upon expiration of a valid union security agreement, it was unable to operate in a manner that would allow the Union to charge all of its members for the services the Union provided them. In essence there may very well exist a set of facts and circumstances that if properly presented and proven could demonstrate that a union has actually been deprived of compensation for particular services by application of the Right to Work Law. And thus as to that union the statute would be unconstitutional as applied. However, this is not that case.

Zoeller, 19 NE3d at 755 (Rucker dissenting). Paradoxically, right to work opponents have seized upon this point to support the enactment of right to work legislation which includes "members only" agreements so that unions cannot claim that they are disadvantaged by free riders in an exclusive bargaining arrangement. See Thomas Cole, *A Primer on Right-to-Work Legislation*, Albuquerque Journal (Feb 16, 2015); Dan Boyd, *A Vote on a High-Profile Right-to-Work Bill Was Put Off*, Albuquerque Journal (Feb 19, 2015).

[220] See Gould, 36 U Hawaii L Rev at 371 (cited in note 56).

effectively in the current legal framework and "paints a landscape inhospitable to *Abood*."[221]

In the period immediately after Taft-Hartley, and its attempt to reshape a balance between labor and management,[222] the Court appeared to be above the fray,[223] and it was Justice Frankfurter in particular who noted how much the prospects for organized labor had changed in such a short period of time,[224] after an era in which the Court had cabined labor rights substantially.[225] It has done so again today. *Harris* takes us back to that history and imperils union participation in a more egalitarian democratic political process.[226]

The good news is that Justice Scalia (whose views—not directly addressed in *Harris*—looked so sensible in the union dues arena two decades earlier)[227] could still tip the delicate balance. The bad news is that Justice Scalia could tip the balance.

---

[221] *The Supreme Court 2013 Leading Case*, 128 Harv L Rev 211, 220 (cited in note 119).

[222] See William B. Gould IV, *Taft-Hartley Comes to Great Britain: Observations on the Industrial Relations Act of 1971*, 81 Yale L J 1421 (1972).

[223] See, for example, *Lincoln*, 335 US at 525.

[224] *AFL v American Sash & Door Co.*, 335 US 538, 547 (1949) (Frankfurter, J, concurring).

[225] See Gould, 24 San Diego L Rev at 51 (cited in note 58); *Lechmere Inc. v NLRB*, 502 US 527 (1992); *First National Maintenance*, 452 US at 666; *Pattern Makers*, 473 US at 95.

[226] See David Cooper and Lawrence Mishel, *The Erosion of Collective Bargaining Has Widened the Gap Between Productivity and Pay*, Economic Policy Institute (Jan 5, 2015); Lawrence Mishel and Will Kimball, *Unions' Decline and the Rise of the Top 10 Percent's Share of Income*, Economic Policy Institute (Feb 3, 2015).

[227] See *Lehnert*, 500 US at 550 (Scalia, J, concurring in part, dissenting in part).

JOSEPH FISHKIN AND
HEATHER K. GERKEN

THE PARTY'S OVER: McCUTCHEON, SHADOW PARTIES, AND THE FUTURE OF THE PARTY SYSTEM

Shaun McCutcheon, the Alabama lawyer who successfully challenged a key provision of the Federal Elections Campaign Act (FECA), seems an unlikely ally of supporters of campaign-finance reform. They share neither his politics nor his lack of irony. McCutcheon, after all, supports Republican candidates by writing them checks in the amount of $1,776. Moreover, supporters of campaign-finance reform hardly want to hasten the Supreme Court's dismantling of the FECA. Yet McCutcheon's suit was heralded by some as a remedy for what ails our politics.

To understand this strange turn of events, one must view *McCutcheon v Federal Election Commission*[1] against the deep shifts taking place in American politics. These are strange times for the two

Joseph Fishkin is Assistant Professor of Law, University of Texas School of Law. Heather K. Gerken is J. Skelly Wright Professor of Law, Yale Law School.

AUTHORS' NOTE: We are intensely grateful to those who read this in draft form, including Bob Bauer, Josh Chafetz, Guy Charles, James Fishkin, Michael Kang, Geof Stone, Sean Theriault, and Yale's Election Law Class 2014. Excellent research was provided by Hal Boyd, Rakim Brooks, Megan Browder, Daniel Herz-Roiphe, Chris Larson, Rebecca Lee, Noah Lindell, Jonathan Meltzer, Rosa Po, Daniel Randolph, Daniel Rauch, Noah Rosenblum, and Zayn Siddique, with special thanks owed to the patient and gracious Katherine Harris and Alex Holtzman.

[1] 134 S Ct 1434 (2014). See Part III.

dominant political parties. By some measures, the Democratic Party and the Republican Party are at the height of their power. Elected officials and the general public are more polarized than they have been in generations, and the polarization axis runs right between the parties' tents.[2] Party identity is very powerful, capable of shaping the behavior of both voters and legislators.

Other measures suggest that the parties are weak, perhaps dangerously so, and may even be losing their grip on politics. "Outside" groups—groups that are neither official party entities nor candidate campaigns—have taken over a startling array of core party functions. These groups do not just run campaign ads. They mobilize voters, test messages, organize donors, maintain comprehensive voter databases, employ long-term campaign workers, and make major strategic choices in individual campaigns and across multiple races.[3] State parties, once central to local and national campaigns, have become pale shadows of their former selves. The national parties are only somewhat stronger. Their bread-and-butter activities are increasingly being carried out by groups that exist outside the official party structure.

These two stories may seem contradictory, but keep in mind that the word *party* means something different in each one of them. The official party organizations and their various fundraising com-

---

[2] See Part I. To be sure, there is plenty of intraparty disagreement these days, especially on the Republican side. But *intra*party is the word. The "Tea Party" turned out not to be a party at all; it is simply a faction within the Republican Party. Actual third-party competitors to the two dominant parties are nowhere on the horizon, which strongly suggests that our party system is very stable.

[3] See, for example, Joe Arnold, *American Crossroads Spending Big in Kentucky*, Whas11 Political Blog (Whas11, Aug 27, 2010) (on file with authors); Edward-Isaac Dovere, *OFA Embraces Tea Party Blueprint for August Push* (Politico, July 23, 2010), online at http://www.politico.com/story/2013/07/ofa-embraces-tea-party-blueprint-for-august-push-94601.html; Derrick Harris, *Obama Seeks Data Scientists for Election Edge* (Gigaom, Sept 19, 2011), online at https://gigaom.com/2011/09/19/obama-seeks-data-scientists-for-election-edge; Nick Judd, *Obama's Targeted GOTV on Facebook Reached 5 Million Voters, Goff Says* (TechPresident, Nov 30, 2012), online at http://techpresident.com/news/23202/obamas-targeted-gotv-facebook-reached-5-million-voters-goff-says; Jeremy W. Peters, *Subtler Entry from Masters of Attack Ads* (NY Times, May 22, 2012), online at http://www.nytimes.com/2012/05/22/us/politics/new-cross roads-gps-ad-takes-a-soft-shot-at-obama.html; Ken Thomas, *A Permanent Campaign? President Obama Will Turn His Re-election Organization into a Group to Back His Agenda* (NY Daily News, Jan 18, 2013), online at http://www.nydailynews.com/news/politics/obama-wages-perma nent-campaign-article-1.1242364; Peter Wallsten and Tom Hamburger, *Conservative Groups Reaching New Levels of Sophistication in Mobilizing Voters* (Wash Post, Sept 20, 2012), online at http://www.washingtonpost.com/politics/decision2012/conservative-groups-reaching-new levels-of-sophistication-in-mobilizing-voters/2012/09/20/3c3cd8e8-026c-11e2-91e7-2962c 74e7738_story.html.

mittees—what we will call the "official" party—are weak in the sense that outside groups have taken over many of their functions. But for reasons we will discuss, it is more useful to conceptualize a "party" as a group of networked interests that take different forms at different times.[4] Viewed from this perspective, the outside groups are not lone wolves. They are deeply and durably aligned with one party or the other.[5] Indeed, the largest and most important "outside" groups are run by consummate party insiders. That's why we call these groups, taken together, *shadow parties*.[6]

The shadow parties have grown so muscular that we are even seeing what we term *shadow campaigns*. In the 2014 cycle, a majority of Senate races included a Super PAC spending unlimited funds on behalf of only one candidate.[7] In a recent special election in Florida, the campaigns of the two congressional candidates controlled less than one-third of the total money spent on the election.[8] Three-quarters of the money spent on behalf of a recent senatorial candidate in Mississippi was supplied by Super PACs.[9] Political observers now muse openly about the possibility of candidates with empty campaign coffers outsourcing all campaign activities to such shadow party groups.[10] The shadow parties and the official parties, then, are deeply intertwined and properly understood as part of what we call the "party writ large." And the parties writ large retain a commanding grip on American politics.

Nonetheless, the explosive growth of outside groups poses a fundamental challenge to settled understandings of the parties and explains why many campaign-finance supporters saw a silver lining to Shaun McCutcheon's suit. *McCutcheon* struck down the FECA's

---

[4] See Part II.B.

[5] For example, as of this writing in the 2014 cycle, nine out of the top ten Super PACs supported candidates of a single party. *Super PACs*, OpenSecrets.org (Center for Responsive Politics, Dec 9, 2014), online at https://www.opensecrets.org/pacs/superpacs.php.

[6] Heather K. Gerken, *Boden Lecture: The Real Problem with Citizens United: Campaign Finance, Dark Money, and Shadow Parties*, 97 Marq L Rev 903 (2014).

[7] Editorial Board, *The Custom-Made "Super-PAC,"* NY Times A20 (Aug 4, 2014).

[8] Michael Beckel, *Outside Groups Dwarf Candidate Spending in Florida Special Election: Less than One-third of Money Pumped into Race Controlled by Sink or Jolly*, Primary Source (Center for Public Integrity, Mar 6, 2014), online at http://www.publicintegrity.org/2014/03/06/14337/outside-groups-dwarf-candidate-spending-florida-special-election.

[9] Philip Bump, *Coming Soon: A Campaign Run Entirely by Super PACs*, Fix Blog (Wash Post, July 28, 2014), online at http://www.washingtonpost.com/blogs/the-fix/wp/2014/07/28/coming-soon-a-campaign-run-entirely-by-super-pacs/.

[10] See, for example, id.

aggregate limits, which capped how much hard money in toto one donor could give to candidates and party committees in a given year. The crude version of the "silver lining" argument suggests that *McCutcheon* will shore up the parties against outside spenders.[11] The more nuanced argument—and the emerging conventional wisdom in the field—is that *McCutcheon* will level the playing field between the official party leaders and the shadow parties by allowing donors to pour more money into the official party structure.[12] This shift in funding patterns, so the story goes, will strengthen the official party leadership and assure the official parties' long-term health.

Count us as skeptical. *McCutcheon* will surely allow some funds that would have flowed to outside groups to seep back into the official party structure. But for the reasons outlined in Part III, we expect this effect to be very modest.[13]

Moreover, the crude argument—pitting "outside" funders against "the parties" and mourning the weakness of the latter—fundamentally misdiagnoses the problem. Money has always influenced politics, and donors have always had a role to play in the party writ large. More importantly, the money has shifted toward groups that are outsiders in name only; these groups work hand in glove with the official party elites, and the parties writ large remain powerful. The real problem with the growth of shadow parties has less to do with the "strength" or "weakness" of the official parties relative to outside groups and more to do with who exercises power *within* the parties writ large. What we are witnessing is not outside spenders pulling power away from the parties but an intraparty battle for the heart and soul of the party writ large.

Although we see this battle as an intraparty fight, its likely outcome is one that "small-d" democrats ought to find disquieting. Parties are, of course, competitors in the democratic arena. But they are also democratic arenas unto themselves. For most of the twentieth century, a great deal of democratic contestation took place within the dominant political parties rather than between them. As democratic arenas, the parties have been important sites of pluralist competition, providing activists and interest groups many pathways for influencing politics.

---

[11] See Part II.

[12] See Part III.

[13] See Part III.

The shift toward shadow parties threatens to flatten the party structure and inhibit pluralist politics. Money isn't just shifting from one place to another within the party writ large; it is shifting from one type of institution to another, quite different type of institution. Both official parties and shadow parties are recognizably Democratic or Republican, but their structure is different. Compared to the official parties, the shadow parties are more hierarchical and less porous. Shadow parties are closed to most and controlled by few. They lack the many nodes of influence that have been used in the past by those who wish to influence party politics. We are especially concerned that the shift to the shadow parties will permanently squeeze out the party faithful—the activists and highly engaged citizens who serve as a bridge between everyday citizens and political elites—and largely eliminate their already-diminished role within the party writ large. The shift toward shadow parties thus raises important questions about the future of American politics. It also raises some fundamental normative questions about who *ought* to control political parties.

The article proceeds in four parts. Part I describes what was legally at stake in *McCutcheon*. Part II situates *McCutcheon* against the broader background of American party politics. Specifically, we examine what we believe to be two deeply intertwined phenomena: the weakness of the official parties and the strength of the parties writ large. Part III explains why *McCutcheon* is unlikely to have anything but a modest effect on current trends. Part IV explains why we should be less worried about the future of the official parties or their leadership and more concerned about the vibrant intraparty politics that the official parties once facilitated.

I. McCUTCHEON'S CHALLENGE

Midway into the 2012 election cycle, Shaun McCutcheon found himself in a bind. He had already donated a total of $33,088 to sixteen Republican candidates, but he wanted to donate to twelve others as well as to a handful of GOP committees.[14] The FECA, however, placed limits not just on the amount a single individual could contribute to a single candidate or party committee (the "base limits"),[15] but on the amount any individual donor could contribute

---

[14] *McCutcheon v Federal Election Commission*, 893 F Supp 2d 133, 136 (DDC 2012).

[15] 52 USC § 30116(a)(1); 11 CFR § 110.1–110.3.

in the aggregate (the "aggregate limits").[16] McCutcheon and the Republican National Committee (RNC) brought a First Amendment challenge to the aggregate limits. The three-judge district court rejected the claim, which eventually made its way to the Supreme Court.

Supporters of campaign-finance reform harbored little hope that the Supreme Court would uphold the aggregate limits. McCutcheon's suit was coming on the heels of a series of cases in which a five-Justice majority had systematically dismantled important parts of the FECA. *Citizens United* was, of course, the marquee case.[17] Nominally about corporate spending, the decision called into question any regulation not narrowly calibrated to address the narrowest forms of corruption, perhaps only quid-pro-quo corruption.[18] "Ingratiation and access," Justice Kennedy proclaimed, "are not corruption."[19] The ruling quickly led a lower court to lift other restrictions on independent spending and thereby gave birth to the Super PAC.[20]

In the wake of *Citizens United*'s ruling on corruption, the *McCutcheon* merits briefs all but wrote themselves. McCutcheon and the RNC insisted that the aggregate limits burdened the freedom of association and expression and could not be justified as a limit on quid-pro-quo corruption.[21] As long as McCutcheon stayed within the base contribution limits for each candidate and committee, they argued, there was no danger of corruption.

In response, the government downplayed the First Amendment interests and reminded the Court that *Buckley v Valeo* grants Con-

---

[16] The limits, for 2013–14, were up to $48,600 to federal candidates and up to $74,600 to other political committees including the national party committees. See 52 USC § 30116(a)(3); 11 CFR § 110.5.

[17] *Citizens United v Federal Election Commission*, 558 US 310 (2010).

[18] Id at 359.

[19] Id at 360.

[20] *Speechnow.org v Federal Election Commission*, 599 F3d 686 (DC Cir 2010). As Bob Bauer has pointed out, the blame for the "shadow parties" cannot be laid solely at the feet of *Citizens United*. Bob Bauer, *The Troubles of Political Parties and Misreadings of Citizens United, More Soft Money Hard Law* (June 2, 2014), online at http://www.moresoftmoneyhardlaw.com/2014/06 /troubles-political-parties-misreadings-citizens-united/. They are the product of long-standing trends in campaign finance that date back at least to the ban on soft money, perhaps even to *Buckley* itself. Id.

[21] Brief for Appellant Shaun McCutcheon, *McCutcheon v Federal Election Commission*, No 12-536 (US filed May 6, 2013) (available on Westlaw at 2013 WL 1927677); Brief on the Merits for Appellant Republican National Committee, *McCutcheon v Federal Election Commission*, No 12-536 (US filed May 6, 2013) (available on Westlaw at 2013 WL 1923314).

gress more leeway to regulate contribution limits, like those challenged by McCutcheon, than expenditure limits.[22] It also emphasized that the aggregate limits were intended to prevent circumvention of the base limits, an argument that had gotten considerable traction with the lower court.[23] Both the government and several amicus briefs—most notably one drafted by the Campaign Legal Center[24]—sketched out various scenarios in which a donor could circumvent the base limits by writing multiple checks to multiple PACs or by writing one large check to a Joint Fundraising Committee, which would then parcel out the funds among various committees and candidates. Advocates warned that a single donor could write a check for as much as $3.6 million dollars while still adhering to the base limits.

The oral argument was unusual in that real-world politics intruded on the Justices' consideration of the abstract First Amendment issue at hand. The circumvention problem proved to be the focal point of the argument, with the Justices playing out or resisting the hypotheticals put forward in the briefs.[25] Even more interestingly, the advocates and the Justices discussed the uneven playing field that now existed for the parties and outside funders and speculated that lifting the aggregate ban would prevent the parties from being, in the words of RNC lawyer Bobby Burchfield, "marginalized by outside forces."[26]

The Court ultimately sided with McCutcheon and the RNC. Chief Justice Roberts wrote a plurality opinion, which was joined by Justices Scalia, Alito, and Kennedy,[27] and Justice Breyer drafted a dissent joined by Justices Ginsburg, Sotomayor, and Kagan. Justice Thomas supplied the majority's fifth vote, suggesting in his concur-

---

[22] Brief for the Appellee, *McCutcheon v Federal Election Commission*, No 12-536 (US filed July 13, 2013) (available on Westlaw at 2013 WL 3773847).

[23] *McCutcheon*, 893 F Supp 2d at 139–40.

[24] Brief of the Campaign Legal Center, AARP, Asian Americans Advancing Justice, Asian American Legal Defense and Education Fund, Common Cause, Citizens for Responsibility and Ethics in Washington, the League of Women Voters of the United States, Progressives United, and Public Campaign as Amici Curiae in Support of Appellee, *McCutcheon v Federal Election Commission*, No 12-536 (US filed July 25, 2013) (available on Westlaw at 2013 WL 3894870).

[25] Transcript of Oral Argument, *McCutcheon v FEC*, 134 S Ct 1434 (2014) (No 12-536) (available on Westlaw at 2013 WL 5845702).

[26] Id at 20.

[27] *McCutcheon*, 134 S Ct at 1434.

rence that *Buckley*'s framework, which applies more searching scrutiny to limits on expenditures than limits on contributions, should be overturned so that all campaign-finance regulations would be subject to strict scrutiny.[28]

Roberts, however, found that there was no need to apply strict scrutiny to the contribution limits in this case because the aggregate cap failed even the less exacting test required by *Buckley*.[29] He dismissed most of the rationales offered by the government in short order. Roberts gave a little more attention to the argument that the aggregate limits were needed to avoid circumvention of the base limits, but ultimately concluded that, given the other protections in place, the aggregate limits were an unnecessary "prophylaxis-upon-prophylaxis."[30] Roberts closed his opinion by offering a ringing endorsement of *Citizens United*'s narrow conception of the corruption rationale. In response to the dissenters' worries that large donations would buy the "gratitude" of the parties, Roberts insisted that gratitude was not a form of corruption but merely reflects the shared interests and common beliefs that fuel party politics.[31]

McCutcheon dashed the hopes of those who had argued that the Court did not intend *Citizens United* to limit the definition of corruption to quid-pro-quo corruption. Chief Justice Roberts laid that claim to rest not just by quoting the relevant portions of *Citizens United* but also by doubling down. "Ingratiation and access . . . are not corruption," he wrote: "They embody a central feature of democracy—that constituents support candidates who share their beliefs and interests, and candidates who are elected can be expected to be responsive to those concerns."[32] Put differently, the influence that donors may gain over both parties and individual candidates is not corruption; it is democracy. Donors are key "constituents" to whom the parties and candidates ought to "be responsive."

The fact that the Court used such broad language to strike down contribution limits, once thought to be all but immune from challenge, sent a frisson through the reform community. Law professor Justin Levitt perfectly captured reformers' mood in the wake of *McCutcheon*: "Those who support limits see the Court right now

---

[28] Id at 1464 (Thomas, J, concurring).

[29] Id at 1437 (plurality).

[30] Id at 1444.

[31] Id at 1461.

[32] Id at 1441.

as the T. rex from 'Jurassic Park,'" with everyone asking "What's next? 'Just don't move. He can't see us if we don't move.'"[33]

What made *McCutcheon* unusual is that even as it felled yet another provision of the FECA, it earned begrudging praise from some supporters of campaign-finance reform, who argued that *Mc-Cutcheon* might help solve what they see as the core problem in American politics: weak parties. To understand why *McCutcheon* garnered praise from such unlikely circles, it is crucial to situate the case in the context of the massive changes that the party system has undergone in recent years.

II. The Parties—Both Weak and Strong

As we noted in the introduction, the parties have undergone substantial changes in recent years and now can be characterized as both weak and strong, depending on how one sees the "party." And how one sees the "party," in turn, determines whether or not *McCutcheon* has a silver lining from the point of view of campaign-finance reformers.

A. THE STRENGTH OF THE PARTIES WRIT LARGE

Party identity is quite powerful today. Federal officeholders now vote with their parties much more consistently than they did in prior decades.[34] The reason why is not hard to discern. The divide between the parties—in terms of both ideology and actual voting patterns—is the deepest it has been for a century.[35] Being

---

[33] Adam Liptak, *Ruling's Breadth Hints That More Campaign Finance Dominoes May Fall*, A14 NY Times (Apr 4, 2014).

[34] See, for example, Michael Barber and Nolan McCarty, *Causes and Consequences of Polarization*, in Jane Mansbridge and Cathie Jo Martin, eds, *Negotiating Agreement in Politics: Report of the Task Force on Negotiating Agreement in Politics* 19–21 (American Political Science Association, 2013) (describing a "steady and steep increase" in party-line voting and polarization since the 1970s).

[35] Keith T. Poole and Howard Rosenthal, *Ideology and Congress* 319 (Transaction, 2d ed 2007). Poole, Rosenthal, and several other scholars have recently expressed similar concerns. See Scott A. Frisch and Sean Q. Kelly, eds, *Politics to the Extreme: American Political Institutions in the Twenty-First Century* (Palgrave, 2013); Sean M. Theriault, *Party Polarization in Congress* (Cambridge, 2008); Keith Poole, Howard Rosenthal, and Chris Hare, *Polarization Is Real (and Asymmetric)*, The Monkey Cage (May 15, 2012), online at http://themonkeycage.org/2012/05/15/polarization-is-real-and-asymmetric/. For instance, the most moderate Republican is now considerably more conservative than the most moderate Democrat. Nolan McCarty, Keith T. Poole, and Howard Rosenthal, *Political Bubbles: Financial Crises and the Failure of American Democracy* 52 (Princeton, 2013). See also Richard Pildes, *Why the Center Does Not Hold: The Causes of Hyperpolarized Democracy in America*, 99 Cal L Rev 273 (2011).

a Democrat or a Republican really means something today. During the postwar era, liberal northeastern Republicans and conservative Southern Democrats stretched the fabric of each party's big tent. Now the tents are smaller, and there is far more space between them.

Voters, too, are more ideologically polarized. Like their representatives in Congress, voters have coherently sorted themselves by ideology, with nearly all liberals becoming Democrats and nearly all conservatives becoming Republicans.[36] With moderates in both parties rarer and with the Republican Party in particular moving dramatically to the right, the differences between Democrats and Republicans are clearer to voters than they have been for several generations.[37] Much has been made of the rise of "unaffiliated" voters, who officially refuse to call themselves Democrats or Republicans. But most of these voters are in fact strongly attached to one party or the other—they just don't say so when asked their party affiliation.[38]

The ideological polarization of the parties is not just the reason why the parties *look* strong; it is the reason why they *are* strong. While the parties are always fighting out internal disagreements,

---

[36] See generally Matthew Levendusky, *The Partisan Sort: How Liberals Became Democrats and Conservatives Became Republicans* (Chicago, 2009) (describing this phenomenon); Michael Dimock, et al, *Political Polarization in the American Public: How Increasing Ideological Uniformity and Partisan Antipathy Affect Politics, Compromise, and Everyday Life*, Pew Research Center Report (Pew Center, 2014), online at http://www.people-press.org/files/2014/06/6-12-2014-Political-Polarization-Release.pdf. Less engaged voters may not have become much more polarized during this time, but the more engaged and attentive voters are now much more closely aligned with their party on the issues than they have been before. See Alan I. Abramowitz, *The Disappearing Center: Engaged Citizens, Polarization, and American Democracy* (Yale, 2010). Even so, it appears that the polarization is greater among officeholders than it is among voters. See Joseph Bafumi and Michael C. Herron, *Leapfrog Representation and Extremism: A Study of American Voters and Their Members in Congress*, 104 Am Pol Sci Rev 519 (2010).

[37] These polarizing changes took place on both sides, but they were asymmetric in magnitude: by almost every measure, Republicans moved farther right than Democrats moved left. Thomas E. Mann and Norman J. Ornstein, *It's Even Worse Than It Looks: How the American Constitutional System Collided with the New Politics of Extremism* (Basic, 2012); Barber and McCarty, *Causes and Consequences of Polarization* at 21 (cited in note 34) (describing increased polarization as "far from symmetric" and "largely driven by changes in the positioning of the Republican Party").

[38] This is not a new point, but its salience only increases as the number of independent voters continues to rise. See, for example, Bruce E. Keith, et al, *The Myth of the Independent Voter* 4 (California, 1992) (explaining that the vast majority of nominally independent voters in fact lean strongly one way or the other—and vote that way). See also Dimock, et al, *Political Polarization* at 83–85 (cited in note 36) (explaining why it makes sense to classify many "independents" as "partisan leaners").

no major issues genuinely cut across party lines today (the way, for instance, that civil-rights issues did in the 1960s).[39] As a result, there is little room for intraparty cleavage and few footholds available to third parties.[40]

To get a full sense of the changes parties have undergone, it is useful to recall what party coalitions looked like thirty years ago in a less polarized environment. Democrats had to accommodate Southern conservatives. Republicans had to accommodate Northeastern liberals. At the national level, both parties had to pander to a noisy menagerie of constituencies and interest groups that made up their coalitions. These constituencies needed attention and rewards to shore up their enthusiastic participation—and they got them, in part because exit was often a real possibility. Even when exit was unlikely, these groups were important sources of campaign energy, manpower, and funding; it was critical to keep them enthusiastic. Add to that the vagaries of state and local variation in party membership, and the parties had to contend with plenty of internal disagreement.

We do not mean to offer a romantic view of the parties of yore. In many ways, they were far less democratic than today's parties. Even decisions as important as selecting presidential nominees were often made by party insiders in proverbial smoke-filled rooms. But even those smoke-filled rooms were arguably sites of coalition building and small-d democracy. A system that gave power to state and local party bosses was far from optimal,[41] but these power brokers did represent different geographic constituencies with different priorities, all seeking what they needed from the national parties.

The unruly menagerie of constituencies that constituted the parties of the past has been replaced by something different: large numbers of ideologically committed donors, candidates, officehold-

---

[39] Barber and McCarty, *Causes and Consequences of Polarization* at 22 (cited in note 34) (describing "the pronounced reduction in the dimensionality of political conflict" because "[m]any issues that were once distinct from the party-conflict dimension have been absorbed into it").

[40] Civil libertarians may be the one obvious issue-based constituency that remains up for grabs. In the post-9/11 era, this group has had reasons to be leery of whichever party is in the White House. But even civil libertarians show no signs of posing a third-party threat—far from it. Instead, this issue has only spawned candidates in party primaries, a fact that underscores the parties' strength.

[41] Compare with E. E. Schattschneider, *Party Government* 170–86 (Holt, Reinhart and Winston, 1942).

ers, and engaged voters. This shift is the natural result of polarization. The parties are far apart on policy issues, and their leaders and
members harbor a fair amount of animosity toward the other side.[42]
Intraparty disagreement persists, but the battle lines dividing the
parties are much sharper and starker than any internal cleavages.

It is worth dwelling for a moment on the critical role large donors play in today's coalitions. Ideological donors are as important
a part of the party writ large as the people they choose to oversee
how their money is spent—like Jim Messina, the campaign manager of the Obama 2012 campaign who now runs Organizing for
Action (OFA), or Karl Rove, the former Bush campaign strategist
who now runs the various Crossroads groups. To be sure, some
large donors today have their own issue agendas. Think of Tom
Steyer, who is emerging as a major donor on the Democratic side.
He wants Democrats to put more emphasis on the issue of climate
change,[43] and he has recently been described as one of the "billionaire oligarchs [who] are becoming their own political parties"
by the usually understated headline writers of the *New York Times*.[44]
But most major donors have a more straightforward agenda that
befits a polarized age: they want their side to win. They may have
strong views about which candidates ought to prevail in primaries,
and they surely have views about intraparty disagreements. But as
between the two parties, there is no question where they side. Because the parties as brands are so strong, and their identities are
so clear, it makes little sense to think of these donors as standing
outside the party looking in. They are standing *inside* the party as
we understand it.

B. THE WEAKNESS OF THE OFFICIAL PARTIES AND THE BURGEONING
   POWER OF THE SHADOW PARTIES

If the party writ large is now strong and relatively united, the
official party apparatus is weak. This is so because a "party" is not

---

[42] Dimock, et al, *Political Polarization* (cited in note 36).

[43] See Andrew Restuccia and Kenneth Vogel, *Tom Steyer Struggles to Find Big-Money Donors*
(Politico, July 16, 2014), online at http://www.politico.com/story/2014/07/tom-steyer-donor
-struggle-109016.html (discussing how even though Steyer has not managed to recruit many
outside donors other than himself for his NextGen Climate Action PAC, the scale of his
proposed spending has, as on supporter put it, "sent a wave through campaigns").

[44] Jim Rutenberg, *How Billionaire Oligarchs Are Becoming Their Own Political Parties*, NY
Times MM26 (Oct 19, 2014).

merely a formal structure. Instead, as the most sophisticated work on parties shows,[45] a party today is best understood as a loose coalition of diverse entities, some official and some not, organized around a popular national brand. The official party organization is part of it, but so too are independent entities—not just shadow parties, but groups likes the NRA, the teachers' unions, and the Heritage Foundation. Officeholders are also part of this coalition, as are donors and activists. All are part of the party writ large, and all may pull the party in different directions.

The official party leadership—particularly that of the Republican Party—has grown weaker in recent years. Party leaders are not the only ones setting the party's agenda, and they sometimes struggle to bring votes to the table when they need to cut a deal or strike a compromise.[46] The travails of Speaker Boehner illustrate the problem. His caucus will vote in lockstep with the NRA but not with him.

The rise of the shadow parties has deepened the problem for the official leadership on both sides of the aisle. The nominal party

---

[45] In legal academia, Dan Lowenstein and Michael Kang have been the leading scholars arguing for this view. See Michael S. Kang, *The Hydraulics and Politics of Party Regulation*, 91 Iowa L Rev 131 (2005); Daniel Hays Lowenstein, *Associational Rights of Major Political Parties: A Skeptical Inquiry*, 71 Tex L Rev 1741 (1993). A number of political scientists have made the case for a broader view of parties. See, for example, Kathleen Bawn, Martin Cohen, David Karol, Seth Masket, Hans Noel, and John Zaller, *A Theory of Political Parties: Groups, Policy Demands and Nominations in American Politics*, 10 Perspectives on Pol 571 (2012); Marty Cohen, David Karol, Hans Noel, and John Zaller, *The Party Decides: Presidential Nominations Before and After Reform* 15 (Chicago, 2008) (viewing parties "as larger coalitions that include not only top leaders but activists, fund-raisers, interest groups, campaign technicians, and others"); Gregory Koger, Seth Masket, and Hans Noel, *Partisan Webs: Information Exchange and Party Networks*, 39 British J Pol Sci 633 (2009); Richard M. Skinner, Seth Masket, and David Dulio, *527 Committees, Formal Parties, and Party Adaptation*, 11 Forum 137, 138 (2013); Richard M. Skinner, Seth E. Masket, and David A. Dulio, *527 Committees and the Political Party Network*, 40 Am Pol Res 60 (2012); Paul S. Herrnson and Justin H. Kirkland, *The Dollars and Cents of Party Campaign Networks* (conference paper, Conference on Political Networks in an Interdisciplinary World, 2013), online at http://www.polinetworks.org/uploads/papers/Dollars CentsOfPtyCampFinNtwkst.pdf. For a recent study on spending in state elections confirming this view, see Keith E. Hamm, Michael J. Malbin, Jaclyn J. Kettler, and Brendan Glavin, *Independent Spending in State Elections, 2006–2010: Vertically Networked Political Parties Were the Real Story, Not Business*, 12 Forum 305 (2014).

[46] See, for example, Gary W. Cox and Matthew D. McCubbins, *Legislative Leviathan: Party Government in the House* (California, 1993); Keith Krehbiel, *Pivotal Politics: A Theory of U.S. Lawmaking* 80–82 (Chicago, 1998); Barbara Sinclair, *Unorthodox Lawmaking: New Legislative Processes in the U.S. Congress* 82 (Praeger, 1977); Robert L. Peabody, *Party Leadership Change in the United States House of Representatives*, 61 Am Pol Sci Rev 675 (1967); Randall B. Ripley, *The Party Whip Organizations in the United States House of Representatives*, 58 Am Pol Sci Rev 561 (1964).

heads have never been the only ones who steer the ship, but now the shadow parties are taking over so many of the official parties' traditional functions—not only buying ads, but hiring campaign workers and running GOTV efforts—that they are gaining enormous influence over the party's message, the party's positions, and even the makeup of the party's coalition. Outside groups have always played some role in this process, to be sure. But now they are not just nibbling around the edges by buying ads for this or that race. They are controlling large amounts of political funds and carrying out core party activities on the ground.

Just as many of the functions of political parties have now been outsourced to shadow parties, an increasing number of individual candidate campaigns are ceding major functions to "outside" groups. To a layman's ears, it may seem paradoxical that a group whose sole purpose is to elect a particular candidate is not part of the "campaign." But as a legal matter, as long as there is no formal coordination between the candidate's campaign and the outside group, this type of *shadow campaign* is permissible. Shadow campaigns, in short, reproduce in miniature the story of shadow parties.

One way to show how important shadow parties and shadow campaigns have become is simply to follow the money, to borrow a phrase from *All the President's Men*.[47] Money is the oxygen of campaign politics, and it is plainly flowing toward the shadow parties, not the official ones. Super PACs did not exist in 2008, and 501(c)(4)s played a negligible role during that campaign. Both types of groups were major players in 2012,[48] and although they appear to have spent less in the 2014 midterm election year than they did in the 2012 presidential election year, it is clear that their influence is growing.[49] The flow of money is one of the main reasons some are worried about the hollowing out of the official parties.[50] Those worries are often tied up with larger debates about the breakdown of the political process as a whole. Some even worry that the

---

[47] *All the President's Men* (1976).

[48] Super PACs and 501(c)(4)s, standing alone, spent more than $860 million in 2012, according to FEC filings. *Outside Spending*, OpenSecrets.org (Center for Responsive Politics), online at https://www.opensecrets.org/outsidespending/fes_summ.php?cycle=2012.

[49] Super PACs and 501(c)(4)s reported spending $464 million through December 6, 2014. *Outside Spending*, OpenSecrets.org (Center for Responsive Politics), online at https://www.opensecrets.org/outsidespending/fes_summ.php?cycle=2014.

[50] See Part III.

parties are losing their ability to govern because the official parties are becoming so weak.[51]

It should now be clear why we resist the crude version of this story—as a fight between "outside" spenders and the parties.[52] These so-called outsiders are consummate party insiders. They have just directed their funds to different places and housed themselves in different institutions, which means that they relate to the official party leadership in a different manner than they once did. We have called the Super PACs and 501(c)(4)s on each side shadow parties precisely because we want to convey that they are tightly networked and closely aligned with the official party.

The law has had a fair amount to do with this change. Of course, that is nothing new. Indeed, what we are seeing today bears a strong resemblance to what happened in Wisconsin during the first half of the twentieth century. When Wisconsin imposed substantial limits on the ability of the parties to carry out core functions like electioneering and raising money, party elites did not stop pushing the parties' agenda. Instead, they abandoned the official party structure and joined private "statewide voluntary committees." These private associations provided the institutional sites for party leaders to do all the electioneering and fundraising they wished to do on the party's behalf.[53]

Super PACs and nonprofits are now playing the role of Wisconsin's voluntary committees. They receive large amounts of campaign money that cannot be given directly to candidates or to par-

---

[51] See id.

[52] See, for example, Matthew Cooper, *Justices Poised to Rule on Citizens United 2*, Newsweek (Mar 6, 2014), online at http://www.newsweek.com/justices-poised-rule-citizens-united-2 -231175 (noting that "some observers have argued that removing the limits would be good for democracy, allowing more money to go to parties and less to shadowy outside groups"); Napp Nazworth, *Analysis: Supreme Court's Campaign Finance Decision Is Not the End of Democracy*, Christian Post (Apr 3, 2014), online at http://www.christianpost.com/news/analysis -supreme-courts-campaign-finance-decision-is-not-the-end-of-democracy-117305/ ("Looking at the big picture, the overall impact of these laws and court decisions has been to give more power and influence to outside groups while diminishing the role of political parties.").

[53] The classic account is Frank J. Sorauf, *Extra-Legal Political Parties in Wisconsin*, 48 Am Pol Sci Rev 692 (1954) (describing the rise of private political organizations in Wisconsin during the twentieth century). See also Leon D. Epstein, *Politics in Wisconsin* 28–29 (Wisconsin, 1958); Steven E. Schier, *New Rules, New Games: National Party Guidelines and Democratic National Convention Delegate Selection in Iowa and Wisconsin, 1968–1976*, 10 Publius 101, 104–05 (1980) (same). For similar takes on this history, see Seth E. Masket, *No Middle Ground: How Informal Party Organizations Control Nominations and Polarize Legislatures* 44 (Michigan, 2011); Kang, 91 Iowa L Rev at 147 (cited in note 45).

ties because the base contribution limits still apply.[54] When Super PACs were unleashed after *Citizens United* and *Speechnow*, a close reader of the judicial opinions could be forgiven for assuming that these independent groups would be truly independent—funded by wealthy donors with agendas that might or might not dovetail with the parties' agendas. Instead, independent groups have found ways to work hand in glove with the candidates and parties they support.

In the 2012 presidential election, for instance, every serious candidate had a Super PAC wholly dedicated to electing that candidate and usually run by someone closely affiliated with the candidate. In 2014, an off-year election, there were at least ninety-four Super PACs supporting individual candidates.[55] While these groups and candidates carefully avoid legal "coordination," they manage to do a lot of what any sane observer would call "coordination."

Some of this "noncoordinated coordinating" is easily observed. Candidates and high-level campaign operatives often show up at Super PAC fundraisers, and they treat the Super PACs as arms of the campaign. Both the Super PAC donors and leadership are usually close to the candidates. In one memorable case during the 2014 cycle, a purportedly independent Super PAC working on behalf of a congressional candidate had only one donor—the candidate's mother.[56] In the Romney 2012 operation, companies working for both the campaign and the independent Super PAC shared an office in Alexandria, and the founder of one of the companies was married to a deputy campaign manager—who also ran a consulting firm out of the same office suite.[57] This was no reason to worry about coordination, though. All of the family members involved in these two examples insisted that they never shared information.

Much of this "noncoordinated coordinating" is more discreet but just as effective, as made clear by a new study by Dan Tokaji

[54] See 52 USC § 30116(a)(3); 78 Fed Reg 8532 (2013) (setting inflation-adjusted contribution limits for the 2013–14 cycle; an individual can give a federal candidate $2,600, the national party committee $32,400, and so on).

[55] *2014 Outside Spending, by Single-Candidate Super PAC*, OpenSecrets (Center for Responsive Politics, Oct 25, 2014), online at https://www.opensecrets.org/outsidespending/summ.php?chrt=V&type=C.

[56] Editorial Board, *Custom-Made "Super-PAC"* (cited in note 7).

[57] Mike McIntire and Michael Luo, *Fine Line Between "Super PACs" and Campaigns*, NY Times A1 (Feb 26, 2012).

and Renata Strause.[58] Networks facilitate the hidden cooperation between candidates and outside donors by allowing information to be passed indirectly. One of those interviewed for the Tokaji/Strause study said, "'you hear things'" even if no one from the campaign ever speaks directly to an outside group.[59] Other times, messages are deliberately passed by a "'friend of a friend of a friend,'" to quote another insider.[60]

Political operatives also use public tools—the mechanisms and strategies that we often bless as "transparent"—to send signals to outsider spenders. The campaign leadership serves as "conductor(s)" as they signal their messaging strategy in surprisingly public ways. Campaigns issue press releases that they know the media won't pick up, but outside groups will. Campaign operatives deliberately use journalists to send "smoke signals" to outsider funders. B-roll footage (high-resolution video clips) are embedded into the campaign website for outside groups to find. Donor lists are shared before they are disclosed to the Federal Election Commission in order to give supportive outside groups a leg up on fundraising. Official party committees sometimes share key information such as polling data with one another. One particularly cheeky effort involved publishing GOP polling data via Twitter in a format legible only to those in the know.[61] Such strategies enable candidate-specific Super PACs to coordinate without "coordinating," running what amount to shadow campaigns on behalf of the party or candidate.[62]

Not all Super PACs and 501(c)(4)s are closely tied to a single campaign.[63] Some support many candidates within the party and

---

[58] Daniel P. Tokaji and Renata E. B. Strause, *The New Soft Money: Outside Spending in Congressional Elections* (Moritz, 2014). This paragraph and the next are adapted from Heather K. Gerken, *The Political Thriller Published by the Moritz College of Law*, Election L Blog (June 18, 2014), online at http://electionlawblog.org/?p=62416.

[59] Tokaji and Strause, *New Soft Money* at 65 (cited in note 58).

[60] Id at 66–67.

[61] See Chris Moody, *How the GOP Used Twitter to Stretch Election Laws*, CNN (Nov 17, 2014), online at http://www.cnn.com/2014/11/17/politics/twitter-republicans-outside-groups/.

[62] The facts in this paragraph are all drawn from Tokaji and Strause, *New Soft Money* at 64–68 (cited in note 58), save the Twitter example discussed in note 61.

[63] The occasional Super PAC functions as a faction with a specific issue agenda. See, for example, NextGen Climate Action PAC (discussed in note 43). More often, Super PACs, nonprofits, and other shadow party groups are aligned with broad and influential factions

serve much like the parties' fundraising wings. The Senate Majority PAC served this role for the Democrats in 2014. Other shadow party groups, particularly issue-based or ideologically-fueled organizations, serve a different function: operating as a faction within a party. Tom Steyer, Michael Bloomberg, and the Koch brothers have all funded such organizations. They don't have much loyalty to official party insiders—they may even be prepared, in theory, to cross party lines. They are trying to seize more power over the party writ large, steering it in a different direction. These organizations also have plenty of strategies for communicating indirectly with candidates and elected officials. They score votes and publicly discuss the lists of candidates they are considering supporting or opposing, thereby making clear what candidates and elected officials must do in order to obtain or retain their support going forward. Such strategies—wholly permissible within the coordination rules—make it possible for shadow party groups unaffiliated with one specific candidate to wield significant influence over different parts of the party.

III. Why McCutcheon Won't Save the Parties

Given this backdrop, it is a mistake to think *McCutcheon* will save "the party," and we are skeptical even about the more nuanced claim that *McCutcheon* will shore up the official party leadership. As noted above, in the wake of the decision, many observers unsympathetic to the Court's shredding of campaign-finance regulations found at least "a little hope" in *McCutcheon*.[64] The crude version of the claim[65]—which was featured in the *McCutcheon* oral argument[66]—was that *McCutcheon* would level the playing field between the parties and outside influences. This is fundamentally mistaken, because the fight for power and funding is, at bottom, an intraparty fight.

The more nuanced argument was, as political scientist Ray La Raja wrote immediately following the decision, that the ruling will

within the core of the party, the way Karl Rove's Crossroads groups are associated with the so-called establishment wing of the Republican Party. See sources cited in note 3.

[64] See, for example, Nathaniel Persily, *Bringing Big Money Out of the Shadows*, NY Times (Apr 2, 2014), online at http://www.nytimes.com/2014/04/03/opinion/bringing-big-money-out-of-the-shadows.html.

[65] See Part II.B and sources cited in note 52.

[66] Transcript of Oral Argument, *McCutcheon v FEC* at 42–43 (cited in note 25).

help give "party leaders . . . more say in who runs for office."[67] Journalists like David Brooks wrote that the decision "enables party establishments to claw back some of the power that has flowed to donors and 'super PACs.'"[68] Law professor Rick Hasen observed, even more pointedly, that *McCutcheon* gives parties "more tools to control members scared of, or beholden to, Super PACs."[69] Many of these commentators speculated that *McCutcheon* would thereby reduce political polarization and further responsible government. As La Raja opined in an op-ed anticipating *McCutcheon*, "[a]nyone who dislikes the current stalemate in Washington should want party organizations to control campaign money rather than shadowy outside groups."[70] "Blowing up the aggregate limits," wrote Rick Hasen, "could help make our government somewhat more functional by strengthening party leaders in Congress and greasing the wheels toward compromise."[71] These arguments rest on the assumption that shadow parties are pushing the parties to extremes. If the same money flowed through the official parties, the argument goes, party leaders would be more likely to favor moderate positions and moderate candidates.[72]

---

[67] Ray LaRaja, *The McCutcheon Decision Could Be Good News After All*, Monkey Cage Blog (Wash Post, Apr 3, 2014), online at http://www.washingtonpost.com/blogs/monkey-cage/wp/2014/04/03/the-mccutcheon-decision-could-be-good-news-after-all/. For a fully developed analysis of this idea, one that doesn't rely on *McCutcheon* but does favor channeling more money to the parties in order to empower the party leadership and thereby encourage effective governance, see Richard H. Pildes, *Romanticizing Democracy, Political Fragmentation, and the Decline of American Government*, 124 Yale L J 804 (2014). See also Richard L. Hasen, *How "The Next Citizens United" Could Bring More Corruption—But Less Gridlock*, Wash Post (Feb 21, 2014), online at http://www.washingtonpost.com/opinions/how-the-next-citizens-united-could-bring-more-corruption–but-less-gridlock/2014/02/21/a190d1c6-95ab-11e3-afce-3e7c922ef31e_story.html (arguing that striking down the aggregate limits could have the "surprising positive side effect" of "strengthening party leaders in Congress and greasing the wheels toward compromise"); Persily, *Bringing Big Money Out* (cited in note 64) (arguing that *McCutcheon* will help "restore the balance between insiders (parties and candidates) and outsiders (corporations, unions, super PACs and other nonparty groups)").

[68] David Brooks, *Party All the Time*, NY Times A27 (Apr 4, 2014).

[69] Hasen, *More Corruption—But Less Gridlock* (cited in note 67).

[70] Ray La Raja, *The Supreme Court Might Strike Down Overall Contribution Limits, and That's Okay*, Monkey Cage Blog (Wash Post, Oct 9, 2013), online at http://www.washingtonpost.com/blogs/monkey-cage/wp/2013/10/09/the-supreme-court-might-strike-down-overall-contribution-limits-and-thats-okay/.

[71] Hasen, *More Corruption—But Less Gridlock* (cited in note 67).

[72] See, for example, La Raja, *The McCutcheon Decision* (cited in note 67) ("Unlike the factional extremist groups within each party, members of Congress don't have to worry about their own party organization attacking them for compromising on legislation.").

There is some truth to this. *McCutcheon* opens the sluices a little wider and lets large donors give more to the official parties and official campaigns. It seems clear that the official parties will receive some money that would otherwise have flowed to the shadow parties. The official parties can facilitate such donations by creating joint fundraising structures that allow donors to write one giant check to be divvied up among candidates, committees, and state parties, just as Justice Breyer noted in his dissent in *Mc-Cutcheon*.[73] As we write this, there is evidence that the Republicans, but not the Democrats, are already making a run at this strategy during the 2014 cycle.[74]

But there are good reasons to question how far this argument can go. We predict that powerful shadow party organizations like OFA and Crossroads will not shut their doors and tell their donors to give instead to the Democratic National Committee or the RNC. There are several reasons for this. The simplest is that the shadow parties offer donors something the official parties cannot. Even setting aside the fact that 501(c)(4)s can guarantee donors anonymity[75]—something neither Super PACs nor the official parties can provide—a shadow party group offers its donors a degree of control and responsiveness that the official parties and official campaigns cannot. The official parties serve several masters. Many groups and individuals contribute to official parties and campaigns and thus have some say over the parties' future direction. In the official party structure, large donors matter a lot, but they are not the only ones who matter. Shadow parties, in contrast, answer to their donors alone.

These facts, paired with the structure of the donor base, make it unlikely that *McCutcheon* will have a dramatic effect. To see why, we need to move away from simple dichotomies—the party elites versus ordinary members, donors versus voters—and instead visu-

---

[73] See *McCutcheon*, 134 S Ct at 1472–79 (Breyer, J, dissenting).

[74] See Byron Tau, *GOP Launches New Big Money Effort* (Politico, Aug 5, 2014), online at http://www.politico.com/story/2014/08/republicans-targeted-state-victory-fundraising-109724.html (describing the Targeted States Victory Committee, a 2014 Republican official-party joint fundraising effort that solicits single checks reaching "nearly $200,000" apiece, to be distributed to the national party and thirteen battleground state parties).

[75] See, for example, Paul S. Ryan, *Two Faulty Assumptions of Citizens United and How to Limit the Damage*, 44 U Toledo L Rev 585, 590 (2013).

alize several different strata of supporters within the party writ large (see fig. 1).

At the bottom of the pyramid are the ordinary voters who support the party on election day. Occupying the next level of the pyramid are the party faithful. They are a lot like ordinary voters, with one key difference: they invest their time and energies in campaigns by volunteering, knocking on doors, showing up at caucuses, voting in primaries, raising small amounts of money, and even working full time for campaigns.[76] Some work their way up the party food chain because they are so heavily involved in campaigns. Others interact regularly with the vast network of state and local party officials that become visible to us during the Iowa caucuses or the New Hampshire presidential primary but exist in every state. The party faithful are not party elites. No one will mistake them for Jim Messina or Karl Rove. Nonetheless, because of their work, the party faithful have a much better shot at influencing the party's direction than disconnected, individual voters.

Many of the party faithful are also small donors; some even help bundle small donations. This gives the party faithful an additional avenue of influence. But it is not one that requires them to worry about campaign-finance law. Campaign-finance limits will not get in the way of small donors. To the contrary, any contribution limit low enough to affect this group would be struck down.[77] Indeed, campaign-finance regulations can only benefit this group to the extent such regulations prevent their voices from being drowned out by folks higher in the pyramid.[78]

Our present campaign-finance regime affects only the next tier of the pyramid: large donors who might want to give even more than $2,600 (or $5,200) to a candidate or two in a single cycle, but cannot do so because of the contribution limits.[79] This group com-

---

[76] We don't mean to suggest here that the party faithful staff every aspect of the campaign's GOTV efforts. While presidential campaigns or inspiring Senate campaigns garner lots of volunteers, more quotidian campaigns must depend more on hired staff.

[77] *Randall v Sorrell*, 548 US 230 (2006) (striking down a contribution limit of $200–$400).

[78] The Court's deregulatory majority is often hostile to arguments about money "drowning out" other voices. But not always. See *Arizona Free Enterprise Club's Freedom Club PAC v Bennett*, 131 S Ct 2806, 2808, 2822 (2011) (Roberts, CJ) (finding that it is a "substantial burden" on a candidate's speech for the government to respond by subsidizing an opponent's message that will "counter that speech").

[79] 52 USC § 30116(a)(3); 78 Fed Reg 8532 (2013).

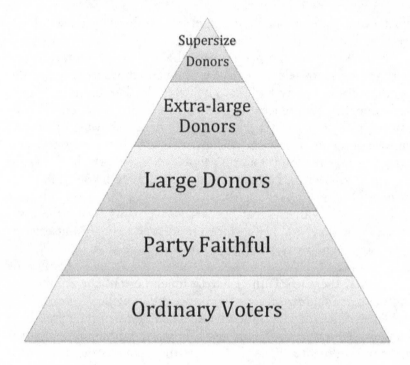

Figure 1. Supporters of a political party

prises a surprisingly large number of donors. But this group was unaffected by the aggregate limits struck down in *McCutcheon*.

McCutcheon affects the next higher tier, those we might call *extra-large donors*. These donors, like Shaun McCutcheon, want to give six-figure amounts in a single cycle to a collection of official party entities and individual campaigns. It is difficult to determine exactly how many donors exist in this tier, but in 2012 we know that 646 donors hit the maximum.[80] For this group, *McCutcheon* clearly makes a difference.

The real money in shadow parties today, however, comes from yet one tier higher: the *super donors* who spend tens of millions in a single election cycle. For these multimillionaires and billionaires— the Sheldon Adelsons and George Soroses—*McCutcheon* fades into

---

[80] See Bob Biersack, *McCutcheon's Multiplying Effect: Why an Overall Limit Matters*, OpenSecrets (Center for Responsive Politics, Sept 17, 2013), online at https://www.open secrets.org/news/2013/09/mccutcheons-multiplying-effect-why/.

the background once again. Even without aggregate limits, there is no way Adelson and his wife could have spent the $98 million they spent in the 2012 cycle[81] through official party entities. There are simply not enough candidates and state parties to absorb this amount while still complying with the contribution limits that remain in *McCutcheon*'s wake.

Spending on this order of magnitude necessarily involves the shadow parties, which offer significant benefits to donors in this tier. A shadow party group answers unambiguously to one and only one constituency: the donor who creates it. He retains the ultimate authority over both personnel and major strategic decisions. Donors in the tier below, like Shaun McCutcheon, cannot afford this kind of control and power. If someone like McCutcheon created his own shadow party group, it would have only a handful of employees, and it couldn't afford to pay for talent of the same caliber as a Karl Rove or a Jim Messina. But the highest tier of donors can afford these advantages and thus has little incentive to work within the official party where decisions get made by people who answer to constituencies other than the donor.[82]

Those who are betting on *McCutcheon* to strengthen the official parties, then, are betting on one of two things. Either they think far more McCutcheons exist than we do, or they think that—contrary to the arguments we outlined above—the super donors will allocate a large percentage of their spending to the official parties.

It is too early to know who is right; it always takes time for donation patterns to catch up with the law. But the early results do not support those who think *McCutcheon* will make a large difference. The Republican joint fundraising committees are now aiming to raise amounts that are only a little higher than the old aggregate limits, while the Democrats have not bothered to form such joint fundraising committees at all.[83] Over time, this is likely to change; the official parties will exploit every possible fundraising

---

[81] Theodoric Meyer, *How Much Did Sheldon Adelson Really Spend on Campaign 2012?*, ProPublica (Dec 20, 2012), online at http://www.propublica.org/article/how-much-did-sheldon-adelson-really-spend-on-campaign-2012.

[82] Mark Schmitt doesn't state these conclusions as strongly as we do, but he has clearly been thinking along the same lines. Mark Schmitt, *Guest Post: McCutcheon, the Parties, and What Comes Next*, Hewlett Foundation Blog (Apr 21, 2014), online at http://www.hewlett.org/blog/posts/guest-post-mccutcheon-parties-and-what-comes-next.

[83] See Tau, *GOP Launches New Big Money Effort* (cited in note 74).

opportunity. But we suspect that the parties' lackadaisical response to *McCutcheon* reflects an underlying reality: there just are not as many McCutcheons out there as some commentators have assumed. If so, the shadow parties and shadow campaigns will continue to grow in importance over the next election cycles, notwithstanding the elimination of the aggregate limits. What remains is to examine why this matters.

IV. INTRAPARTY PLURALISM AND THE ROLE OF THE PARTY FAITHFUL

A cynic might think that the rise of the shadow party does not matter at all to the structure of the party system. Money has always played an outsized role in American politics. Moreover, it has long shifted from one channel to another, taking different routes in response to changes in the regulatory scheme. Soft money was banned, and the money moved into "issue ads" and 527s.[84] Now it is flowing through Super PACs and nonprofits. As Sam Issacharoff and Pam Karlan memorably observed, there is a "hydraulics" to campaign finance, and money always finds its own level.[85] One might think that all we are witnessing now is the usual hydraulics of campaign finance, so it matters little whether the money flows through the official parties or the shadow parties.

Issacharoff and Karlan are right that closing off one outlet for money will send it down another, but it can matter which outlet the money travels down. Given the institutional differences between the official parties and the shadow parties, we think that the flow of money to the shadow parties is accelerating a deeper shift in the party system that was already underway.[86] Specifically, we think these new institutional arrangements are helping erase an underappreciated but important source of pluralism within the party system.

---

[84] These trends can be traced back to the 1990s, when previous rounds of deregulation created other ways for money to flow to the parties. Stephen Ansolabehere and James M. Snyder Jr., *Soft Money, Hard Money, Strong Parties*, 100 Colum L Rev 598, 605–06 (2000).

[85] Samuel Issacharoff and Pamela S. Karlan, *The Hydraulics of Campaign Finance Reform*, 77 Tex L Rev 1705 (1999).

[86] We take seriously the point made by Kate Andrias in a recent symposium that the party faithful's decline was occurring even before the rise of the shadow parties. Kate Andrias, *Hollowed-Out Democracy*, 89 NYU L Rev Online 48, 48–50 (2014). Nonetheless, we worry that the shadow parties are far more closed off to the party faithful than the official party, so the shift in money can only exacerbate this trend.

Returning to our pyramid, it is clear that people in every tier have views about the direction their party should take. These people may all be on the same team, but that does not mean they always agree. Who wins these disputes—who gets to steer the unwieldy and complex entity that we call the party writ large—will depend on which forms of influence have more weight. And that, in turn, depends on where the center of gravity lies within the party writ large.

In order to understand this point, it helps to begin with the normatively prior question: Who *ought* to steer the party? This is a surprisingly open question. Judges, of course, are loathe to offer any firm view on the topic. Political scientists tend to focus on what is, not on what ought to be. Their colleagues with a more normative bent—political theorists—have had surprisingly little to say on this particular subject, perhaps due to what Nancy Rosenblum has described as political theory's strange aversion to party politics.[87] As a result, the field lacks a well-developed sense of who should steer the party ship.[88] Or to put the question another way: Who are a party's real constituents?

The answer to this question depends on what parties are for. From one perspective, parties are valuable because they serve as *democratic arenas*. They give ordinary voters a way to participate in the political process at a crucial agenda-setting stage. Everyday citizens thus take part in a far deeper and richer form of democracy than they would if they showed up only at the very end of the process, when the general election is held and there is only one highly constrained choice to make. From this perspective, the answer to the question of who ought to steer the party is straightforward. It's the ordinary voters who support the party: the party-in-the-electorate, to use V. O. Key's famous formulation.[89] If parties are democratic arenas, then their voters are the real principals, and the party officials and the party-in-government are merely their agents.

---

[87] Nancy L. Rosenblum, *On the Side of the Angels* 1–6 (Princeton, 2008).

[88] This issue was of great interest to academics in the past, but their concern was largely about liberating the national party from the control of the state and local party bosses rather than democratizing the party full stop. See, for example, Schattschneider, *Party Government* at 170–86 (cited in note 41); American Political Science Association, *Toward a More Responsible Two-Party System: A Report of the Committee on Political Parties*, 44 Am Pol Sci Rev (Supp Sept 1950).

[89] V. O. Key, *Politics, Parties, and Pressure Groups* 181 (T. Y. Crowell, 4th ed 1958).

If the parties are democratic arenas, then we ought to structure them to encourage greater participation by voters in party governance. For instance, candidates should be chosen in high-turnout primaries rather than low-turnout caucuses. As for resolving intraparty disagreements, this conception of the party yields a straightforward answer: ideally, the party's voters ought to have an equal say over the party's direction. "One person, one vote" is often cast as equalizing voter influence over elections.[90] What we might call the *equality model* of party control extends this principle into the intraparty domain.

The equality model is very distant from our present political system. Any time a donor, a campaign volunteer, or even an officeholder has more say over the direction of the party writ large than a randomly chosen, disengaged voter, we have moved a step away from the equality model. To come anywhere close to this model, we would have to ban campaign contributions and fund campaigns publicly. Even leaving donations aside, it would seem mildly corrupting every time an enthusiastic volunteer donates a lot of time to a campaign and thereby acquires more influence than someone else.[91] Moreover, the equality model is hard to square with the reality that candidates and elected officials will inevitably play a substantial role in steering the party.

Even if the equality model cannot be fully realized, it might still function as a useful lodestar. We could structure the parties to minimize inequality of influence among party members. On this view, we should aim for parties that are as representative as possible of the views of all their members, broadly defined.

This model has some genuine appeal, but it misses something important. Parties are not simply democratic arenas. They are also critical players in the larger democratic arena. There are sellers as well as buyers in politics. When the general election rolls around,

---

[90] See *Reynolds v Sims*, 377 US 533, 555 (The one person, one vote rule is designed to prevent a "debasement or dilution of the weight of a citizen's vote."). But see Joseph Fishkin, *Weightless Votes*, 121 Yale L J 1888 (2012) (arguing that one person, one vote does not protect the influence of individual voters, but rather protects the equal influence of equally-sized numerical groups). Either way, the extension of the equality model to the internal governance of parties would mean that in any intraparty dispute, the majority of party members should rule.

[91] David Strauss makes this point in his seminal article on the equality roots of campaign finance. David Strauss, *Equality, Corruption, and Campaign Finance Reform*, 94 U Chi L Rev 1369 (1994).

ordinary voters need the parties to articulate clear alternatives so they can understand their choices.[92] From this perspective, parties are the means by which people with strong views band together and sell their views to the mass public.[93] For parties to perform this role, those with intense preferences and/or expertise ought to wield more influence over the party's direction than a randomly selected individual voter. Each party must function like a smart and nimble firm in a complex marketplace. It must be deliberative, yet decisive. It must know its own brand and customer base, and yet it must also respond to change and seek out new market niches even if it risks alienating another part of the base.

This analogy between the party and a firm is at the heart of a radically different model of the party from the equality model, an account we might call the *elite-driven model*.[94] In this model, parties are like firms, donors are like shareholders, and ordinary voters are like consumers choosing between the two parties' offerings. There is no equality of influence here. The normative roots of this ideal are not egalitarian. Instead they are bound up with the ideal of free association: people should be free to band together, build a party, and hawk their wares to the general public. On this model, parties must respond to ordinary voters, just as firms must respond to their customers. But large donors and party elites are the party's

---

[92] The idea that the parties need to present clear choices, and then act on them, so that voters can hold them accountable for the results, is the heart of the theory of "responsible party government." In 1950, an influential report by the American Political Science Association made the case for this view, *A Report of the Committee on Political Parties: Toward a More Responsible Two-Party System*, 44 Am Pol Sci Rev 1 (1950) ("An effective party system requires, first, that the parties are able to bring forth programs to which they commit themselves and, second, that the parties possess sufficient internal cohesion to carry out these programs."). See also Austin Ranney, *The Doctrine of Responsible Party Government: Its Origins and Present State* (Illinois, 1954). Some of the concerns about responsible party government from this era seem quaint today: we no longer worry that the national parties are too weak in comparison to their state and local branches.

[93] See *California Democratic Party v Jones*, 530 US 567, 574 (2000) (Scalia, J) (viewing the parties as vehicles that promote "the ability of citizens to band together in promoting among the electorate candidates who espouse their political views"). Justice Scalia is perhaps the Court's strongest advocate of this view of parties. He who wrote for the Court in this case, striking down a law requiring a "blanket" primary in which all voters—not merely those affiliated with the party—would in effect select the parties' nominees.

[94] The arguments of Rick Pildes and Sam Issacharoff are a good deal more subtle and complex than the extreme view we sketch here. But they should at least get a hat tip for pioneering efforts in our field to think of "politics as markets." Samuel Issacharoff and Richard H. Pildes, *Politics as Markets: Partisan Lockups of the Democratic Process*, 50 Stan L Rev 643 (1998).

real constituents. This market-based model obviously owes a great deal to a Schumpeterian conception of democracy, which casts democracy as a contest among elites for the assent of the people.[95]

Like the equality model, the elite-driven model captures something about the parties that is true . . . but partial. The elite-driven model might ring truer in a party system like Israel's, with its robust political market featuring low barriers to entry, many players, and regular shifts in public allegiances among the parties. In an extremely stable, highly polarized two-party system like our own, the shortcomings of the market analogy are more immediately apparent. In our system, neither liberals nor conservatives really have anywhere else to go to pursue their political aims. (They could in theory withhold their support or stay home, but that option borders on the self-defeating.) Without realistic exit options, they need voice.[96] They need and want a role in shaping the parties to which they are deeply and practically bound. And our system does, in fact, give them a variety of opportunities to exercise voice. The elite-driven model overlooks the fact that voters are not just customers of a political party; they constitute it.

The majority in *McCutcheon* firmly rejects the equality model without articulating any clear alternative. But the elite-driven model is closest to what the majority has in mind, as is made clear in the very first sentence of the opinion: "There is no right more basic in our democracy than the right to *participate* in electing our political leaders."[97] As retired Justice Stevens has pointed out, this sentence is an odd way to begin a case about aggregate contribution limits; it makes sense only if contributions are a form of participation.[98] Later on, the *McCutcheon* majority repeatedly refers to do-

---

[95] Joseph A. Schumpeter, *Capitalism, Socialism, and Democracy* (Harper, 1942).

[96] We draw here on the fundamental contribution of A. O. Hirschman, *Exit, Voice, and Loyalty* 70 (1970) (noting that an ideologically committed voter in stable two-party duopoly "cannot exit . . . but just because of that he, unlike the consumer or voter who can exit, will be maximally motivated to bring all sorts of potential influence into play so as to keep the firm or party from doing things highly obnoxious to him"). Hirschman goes on to note that this mechanism—the voice of those who have nowhere to go—has force in partisan politics in part because the parties know their success depends "on the enthusiasm which each of the parties can inspire among activist party workers and volunteers"—that is, the party faithful. Id at 72.

[97] *McCutcheon*, 572 US at 1440–41.

[98] Adam Liptak, *Justice Stevens Suggests Solution for "Giant Step in the Wrong Direction,"* NY Times A14 (Apr 22, 2014); John Paul Stevens, *Oops!* (Harold Leventhal Lecture, remarks

nors as "constituents," and says that responsiveness to these donor-constituents is "a central feature of our democracy . . . key to the very concept of self-governance through elected officials."[99]

This is a striking concept of "constituents," to put it mildly. On this view, many of the most important "constituents" of a state party or representative, for instance, are donors who live outside the state. That makes sense from the perspective of the elite-driven model. On that view, donors are like shareholders and thus properly the ones in charge. The individual voters—the people we ordinarily refer to as "constituents"—are the customers, not the firm.

Note how this contrasting view exposes a potential shortcoming of the equality model. In addition to failing to take into account the parties' roles as actors within a larger democratic arena, the equality model does not account for intensity of preferences. The elite-driven model of the party undergirding *McCutcheon* might seem better on this score. But it takes into account only intense preferences of a certain sort. There are many people whose commitments are sufficiently intense for them to put their time and energy into a campaign. But most of these people don't have hundreds of thousands of dollars lying around and thus aren't the sort of "constituents" that *McCutcheon* protects.

At this point in the argument, it should come as no surprise that we think that neither the equality model nor the elite-driven model fully captures the complex role the parties actually play or should play in our political system. Each of these models embodies only a half-truth, both empirically and normatively. Parties do act like firms when they sell their product in the democratic arena, just as the elite-driven model suggests. But they are also democratic arenas unto themselves, sites where individuals and groups engage in intraparty contestation that is itself an important form of political participation. That is why the equality model has real pull. With apologies to Schumpeter, American political parties are not

---

before the Administrative Law Section of the DC Bar, Sept 12, 2014), online at http://www
.supremecourt.gov/publicinfo/speeches/JPS%20Speech(DC)_09-12-2014.pdf (underscoring
the point and noting that McCutcheon—and any similar donor exceeding the aggregate
limits for candidate contributions—is certainly donating to candidates of whom she is not a
constituent in the more usual sense of the word). See also Yasmin Dawood, *Democracy Divided: Campaign Finance Regulation and the Right to Vote*, 89 NYU L Rev Online 17 (2014)
(outlining normative concerns raised by *McCutcheon*'s equation of voting and contributing).

[99] *McCutcheon*, 572 US at 1441.

solely elite institutions selling their brand to a passive public. They are also sites of democratic mobilization and engagement.

This engagement is an important, even essential, feature of our democratic order. It would be a thin sort of democracy indeed if the only moment when ordinary people engaged with politics were the general election, with the table already set and the menu already chosen. It is largely through activism *within* parties, be it primaries or campaigns or GOTV or small donations, that ordinary people exercise their most significant role in the political process.[100]

What the equality model misses is that this intraparty engagement and contestation takes place not just at the base of the party pyramid but at every level. Many people engage with the party only by voting in elections. While they may not be deeply connected to the party, each person gets a tiny say about its direction. The equality model captures this part of the story . . . and then stops. Meanwhile, the elite-driven model captures a different but just as partial story, one confined to the top of the pyramid. The party's elites do play an outsized role in steering the party. The elite-driven model explains and justifies their influence, but little else.

Neither of these models captures the full story of intraparty contestation. And both models have something of a blind spot for the role of the party faithful, who serve as a crucial bridge between the electorate and the elite. Both descriptively and normatively, these activists, volunteers, organizers, and small donors are "constituents" of the party in a deep sense: they constitute its active, committed membership and thus have a real stake in the party and its future. However, unlike the "constituents" protected by the *McCutcheon* decision, their form of influence does not involve large quantities of cash.

The party faithful play a distinctive role in our party system. They help parties function both as players in the democratic arena and as internally democratic arenas in their own right. The party faithful are the backbone of the party; they generate much of its energy and carry out much of its ground game.[101] They are every-

---

[100] For an overview and typology, see Sidney Verba and Norman Nie, *Participation in America: Political Democracy and Social Equality* (Chicago, 1972).

[101] Compare with Cohen, et al, *The Party Decides* at 29 (cited in note 45) (noting that the parties "are, and may long have been powered by large numbers of policy-oriented individuals").

day voters who have chosen to invest their energies in the parties. As a result, they have one foot in each world. They differ from ordinary voters in ways that help ensure the parties function coherently as players in the democratic arena. Their enthusiasm and strong ideological attachment pushes the party to offer a clear choice, not an echo.[102] They discipline the party and block elites from abandoning the core commitments of the people whose attachment to the party is strongest.[103] In this way, they make the party more accountable to its constituents. At the same time, however, in crucial ways the party faithful are more like ordinary voters than party elites. Their sheer numbers ensure that the party is more participatory and at least somewhat more broadly representative than the elite-driven model. With one foot in each world, they are uniquely positioned to convey some the concerns of ordinary voters to party leaders and campaign operatives. And they are more likely to be heard because they speak from inside the campaign, not outside of it.[104] Ultimately, the party faithful keep alive forms of democratic participation that have intrinsic value in a democratic society: They attend rallies, hold signs at conventions, show up at caucuses, hold fundraisers, and knock on doors, all of which makes for a more robust, active, and contested democratic sphere within and among the parties. Such forms of participation also have instrumental value, to the extent that they nudge the parties in the directions that the parties' active members desire.

Any account of who steers a political party must, as a descriptive matter, include some role for the party faithful. As a normative matter, any account of who *ought* to steer the party should give the party faithful a substantial role. As Kate Andrias and others have shown,[105] the status of the party faithful within the party has eroded considerably in recent decades, a trend that we believe ought

---

[102] We allude here to the title of Phyllis Schlafly's 1964 right-wing jeremiad against the moderate Republican establishment then in control of the national party. Phyllis Schlafly, *A Choice, Not an Echo* (Pere Marquette, 1964). Subsequent election outcomes suggest that Schlafly spoke for a substantial faction of the Republican party faithful.

[103] See Paul Allen Beck and Frank J. Sorauf, *Party Politics in America* 106 (Harper, 1992) (noting high-intensity volunteers' "interactions and relationships, the contributions they make to the organization, and the price they exact for their contributions").

[104] See id (noting that the "staff of national and state offices share many of the attributes of volunteers").

[105] Andrias, 89 NYU L Rev Online (cited in note 86).

to concern small-d democrats (and not only those who see intrinsic value in this form of political participation).

If parties were composed solely of the top and bottom of the pyramid—the elites and the electorate, with no role for the party faithful in between—much would be lost. If not for the higher level of engagement and deliberation among the party faithful, ordinary voters would be in even greater danger of manipulation by party elites, just as consumers are sometimes subject to manipulation by firms and their advertising. Strong ideological polarization gives elites too free a hand because ordinary voters are unlikely to exercise their exit option and switch to the other party, no matter what the elites do.[106] As a result, it is up to the party faithful to check the elites on behalf of a somewhat broader and more democratic constituency. In this way, the party faithful help solve a conundrum in politics.[107] Ordinary voters cannot directly monitor their representatives. So how does the principal control the agent? We often cast the political parties in this role because they enforce party discipline and punish defectors.[108] But *quis custodiet ipsos custodes*? Who will guard the guardians? Who will ensure that the parties do right by the voters?[109] One answer is the party faithful.

All this means we need a different model of the party, a hybrid approach that takes into account the party's multilayered role in our politics. The party speaks in part for its ordinary voters, in part for its elites, and in part for the party faithful who stand in between. We call this model the *pluralist model*. We use the term not to refer to multiparty democracy, but rather to evoke the competition and cajoling, the disagreeing and the deliberating, the buttonhol-

---

[106] The party faithful can, of course, stay home—a limited form of exit that remains open even when one's choice of party is extremely settled. In extreme cases, activists can refuse even to cast a ballot out of disappointment with their side's candidate, or can vote for a protest candidate. But like so much else, these limited forms of exit become less viable with the parties highly polarized. If even the disappointing candidate from your party is far better, from your perspective, than the candidate of the other party, then it begins to seem self-destructive to exercise these forms of exit.

[107] This discussion is adapted from Gerken, 97 Marq L Rev at 922 (cited in note 6). Thanks to Ana Muñoz for a comment in class that prompted at least one of us to think harder about the role of the party faithful.

[108] See, for example, John Aldrich, *Why Parties: The Origins and Transformation of American Politics* 1–26 (Chicago, 1995).

[109] For an overview of the literature and an astute take on the question, see Samuel Issacharoff and Daniel Ortiz, *Governing Through Intermediaries*, 85 Va L Rev 1627 (1999).

ing and bickering that takes place—and should continue to take place—within the party itself.

If you view the parties through a pluralist lens, it quickly becomes clear that one of the signal strengths of the modern political party is that it has many points of entry. The structure of modern American political parties is highly complex, in part because of the decentralized structure of American elections. Because of this decentralization, the official party leadership must answer to a variety of constituencies. Moreover, the official party leadership has reasons to listen not only to large donors and party elites, but also to the party faithful. Large donors bring with them large quantities of money, whose value is never underestimated in party circles. But the party faithful bring energy and time and attention—the people standing behind the candidates at rallies, the people who drive voters to the polls, the voters in low-turnout primaries and caucuses. Just as cold, hard cash matters to campaigns, so do warm bodies. When the party faithful enter into the campaign process, they become part of the diffuse network that helps steer the party. It is important to avoid romanticizing just how much influence the party faithful have today. In today's world of candidate-driven, television-based campaigning, party elites have primacy. But even so, the official party has multiple points of entry for the party faithful. This makes the party writ large more open than it would otherwise be.

The pluralist model suggests that every rung in the pyramid—the ordinary voters, the elites, and the party faithful in between—should have roles in steering the party. To make this argument more concrete, consider how the state of Texas chooses presidential nominees. In 2008, Texans endured much ridicule for their "Rube Goldberg-esque" system, which employs both a primary and a caucus to select delegates.[110] From the point of view of the pluralist model, however, the Texas approach makes some sense. The primary creates an opportunity for participation by the mass public. It is the most participatory and representative way to select a candidate. A caucus, by contrast, gives voice to the party's core constituents—the party faithful, the ones who know enough and

---

[110] Martin Frost, *Bigger—and More Confusing—in Texas* (Politico, Feb 18, 2008), online at http://www.politico.com/news/stories/0208/8576.html.

care enough to show up. These core constituents are likely to be more deliberative and less easily manipulated than the party-in-the-electorate. A well-functioning party should listen to both.

The party writ large is a complex, diffuse creature. This is why Bob Bauer rightly described the politician's job as "political trade-craft." Politicians, Bauer writes, are always "balancing political self-interest against representational responsibility, looking for a 'path' through the demands of conflicting constituencies, weighing short-term costs against longer-term gains and vice versa."[111] The official parties, with their layered structure and multiple nodes of influence, are inevitably messy and unruly. They force politicians to balance many constituencies and concerns at once.

The shadow parties are different. There is a lot less to balance: the groups are structured so that they answer ultimately to their funders. That is why they provide such an efficient mechanism for funders to exercise influence. But that efficiency comes at a price— the loss of the multiple nodes of influence offered by the messier and more complex structure of the official party. Despite the changes of recent years, the official parties are still relatively open to, even welcoming of, the party faithful. The shadow parties are closed to them.

It's possible this could change. You might think that the role of everyday voters will be erased entirely as bytes on the Web become more important than boots on the ground. Even as Facebook and phone calls and electronic "touches" displace the door knocking of the past, however, regular people still have a role to play, as was made evident in the Obama campaign's impressive use of its army of young volunteers. Peer-to-peer GOTV methods turn out to be remarkably effective.

In light of this, one might predict a different sort of shift. As long as activists are needed for GOTV efforts, perhaps the shadow parties will discover they need the party faithful, just as the official parties do. On this view, a new equilibrium will emerge, with the party faithful influencing the shadow parties of the future just as they influence the official parties of today.[112] For instance, some shadow

---

[111] Bob Bauer, *Politicians: The Good, the Bad, and the Corrupt—and Their Different "Constituencies,"* More Soft Money Hard Law Blog (July 31, 2014), online at http://www.moresoftmoneyhardlaw.com/2014/07/politicians-good-bad-corrupt-different-constituencies/.

[112] Thanks to Guy Charles for pressing us on this point.

party groups have begun to recruit activists for get-out-the-vote efforts[113]—strong evidence that engaged party members will continue to play a role in campaigns and will not be displaced by television ads and other technologies.

As the shadow party system develops, these groups will certainly pay some attention to the views of these volunteers, lest they lose their allegiance to the cause. But there are limits on how far this can go. Even if the party faithful had meaningful exit options—and they don't[114]—the structural differences between the official parties and the shadow parties will have out. In the shadow parties, activists will be people to recruit, perhaps manipulate, and, if necessary, jettison. That's because they are not the shadow parties' real constituents. The internal structure of the shadow parties is not democratic; they do not serve as democratic arenas in the same way that the official parties do. Funders alone pay the piper and call the tune, and there are precious few points of entry for anyone who lacks a massive checking account. Thus, the complex interest balancing—the "political tradecraft"—that inevitably occurs in the official parties will always be attenuated in the shadow parties. Shadow party groups may recruit activist volunteers for instrumental reasons, but there is a low ceiling on the amount of influence such "shadow party faithful" could ever exert in a tug of war with the donors.

Our worry is that as more and more money flows from the official parties to the shadow parties, the center of gravity within the parties writ large will also shift decisively toward the shadow parties. Party elites will always have to practice "political tradecraft," but there will be fewer constituencies to balance when they do. Candidates will look mostly to the shadow parties, and the party faithful will be hived off into the increasingly irrelevant official party (or given limited roles in shadow party groups that do not really represent them). If the official party has a role to play, it will be as a shell organization that is temporarily occupied by a candidate whose real campaign is being run by the shadow parties. The party faithful will still exist, and they will still participate in poli-

---

[113] Rutenberg, *Billionaire Oligarchs Are Becoming Their Own Political Parties* (cited in note 44) (suggesting that Americans for Prosperity has a "volunteer base [that] now numbers in the tens of thousands").

[114] For the reasons discussed in note 106.

tics, but they will be farther away from the decision makers who really matter. As a result, they will play less and less of a role in shaping the direction of the party with each election cycle. The system as a whole will continue to drift away from the pluralist model and toward the elite-driven model. The party faithful's already reduced role will become even more anemic.

That would be unfortunate, because we think the pluralist model has much to recommend it. It accounts for the multilayered role of the party in our system and captures much of what is valuable about parties. After all, parties are not, as Edmund Burke once posited, simply associations of like-minded individuals united by their policy program (what today we would call an ideology).[115] While this ancient account seems more salient as our politics becomes ever more polarized, it still misses the plethora of players in this game: the party leaders and elites, their major funders and backers, the officeholders who shape the policy program, and the activists who drive the ground game. At the same time, parties are also not mere coalitions of elected officials seeking to build and maintain power by appealing to the mass public. John Aldrich's influential model of political parties has that starting point—he puts politicians and office-seekers in the driver's seat, conceptualizing the party as fundamentally "the ambitious politicians' creation."[116] That is part of what parties are, to be sure, but only part.

Newer models of the political party conceptualize it as a looser coalition, with activists, donors, and interest groups playing various roles, but with party elites in the driver's seat.[117] Over the decades, some accounts have put more emphasis on the role of local parties in constituting the national parties.[118] Others have emphasized the role of patronage machines.[119] Each of these models be-

---

[115] Edmund Burke, *Reflections on the Revolution in France* (J. Dodsley, 1790).

[116] John H. Aldrich, *Why Parties: A Second Look* 5 (Chicago, 2011). Some of Aldrich's precursors even imagine politicians without substantive policy preferences of their own seeking marketing niches to sell the voters what they want to buy. See, for example, Anthony Downs, *An Economic Theory of Democracy* (Harper, 1957).

[117] See, for example, Cohen, et al, *The Party Decides* (cited in note 45); Bawn, et al, 10 Perspectives on Pol (cited note 45).

[118] David Mayhew, *Placing Parties in American Politics: Organization, Electoral Settings, and Government Activity in the Twentieth Century* (Princeton, 1986).

[119] See, for example, Martin Shefter, *Political Parties and the State: The American Historical Experience* (Princeton, 1994).

gins the story in a different place, and each captures an important dimension of what the party is. But the very multiplicity of these models—the fact that it is possible to conceptualize political parties from such divergent starting points—strongly suggests that political parties are plural in character.[120] They are organizations, and they are networks. They are vehicles in pluralist competition, and they are sites of pluralist competition. They are arenas of political participation, and they are brands to which many ordinary people feel intense loyalty.

In the political order that is rapidly developing, the party brands are no longer the sole property of the official parties. Instead, they are up for grabs in each election cycle, as different entities attempt to capture the party writ large. As the center of gravity shifts from the official parties and campaigns to their shadow counterparts, the Democratic or Republican mantle is there to be claimed by anyone who can convince a partisan group of voters that she is the best product for the party brand. There is a sense in which this new order is very open and small-d democratic: you need not rise up through the party ranks or please a motley assortment of local bosses in order to become either party's standard-bearer. But in a different sense, the new order is hardly democratic at all. The increasing strength of the shadow parties makes it far easier to convert economic power to political power. This rapidly developing system is open and pluralistic—for those with lots of money to spend.

From the point of view of the party faithful, the system that is emerging is not pluralistic at all. The real problem with shadow parties and shadow campaigns is not that they will reliably tilt in one direction or another, be it extreme or moderate. The problem is that the emerging order will make our politics look more like the broadcast television business—a system of professional producers and passive consumers, rather than one that features widespread democratic engagement and pluralism. A system built

---

[120] It is by now a trope in the field that the parties are complex and exceedingly difficult to pin down precisely. Samuel J. Eldersveld, *Political Parties in American Society* 407 (Basic Books, 1982) ("[P]olitical parties are complex institutions and processes, and as such they are difficult to understand and evaluate."), quoted in Aldrich, *Why Parties* at 16 (cited in note 116); Charles Perrow, *Complex Organizations: A Critical Essay* 14 (Scott, Foresman, 1972) ("Party organizational analysis is . . . one of the oldest in parties' research and one of the most frustrating.").

on the shadow parties is one with starring roles for those at the top of the pyramid and those at the bottom: the top because someone needs to fund the shadow parties, and the bottom because politicians still need votes in the end. But the role of those who stand between—the party faithful—is much less clear. We may soon find ourselves living in a world in which the main "constituents" of any party are indeed the ones Chief Justice Roberts identified in *McCutcheon*: the donors at the top, competing to secure the assent of the voters at the bottom. That is an elite-driven, Schumpeterian world, not a pluralist one.

V. CONCLUSION

For the reasons we have discussed, *McCutcheon* is not much of a solution to what ails American politics. The decision will make parties and candidates marginally more responsive to extra-large donors like Shaun McCutcheon—an effect we expect to be modest because donors in that tier are not terribly numerous. *McCutcheon* does not introduce a sufficient shock to the system to change it, and its effects cannot override the fast-moving shift toward shadow parties and shadow campaigns.

That is unfortunate, because this larger shift ought to be a source of concern. What were once relatively porous, diffusely organized official parties are being displaced by hierarchical, closed shadow parties beholden almost entirely to donors. If you have faith in the party faithful, if you are a small-d democrat, if you worry about flattening the party structure and inhibiting pluralist politics, this is a depressing shift indeed. It means that the story of the shadow parties is much more complex than the simplistic tale everyone tells about wealthy elite gaining even more political power than they once had. This isn't only a story about the rich getting richer. It's also a story about the parties being hollowed out and thereby losing their ability to serve as robust democratic arenas. It's a story about the party faithful, already in decline, being left with a depressingly anemic role in American political life.

Let us close with a final cautionary note about future reform. Regulating the shadow parties is, of course, the most obvious strategy for strengthening the official party and thus shoring up the influence of the party faithful. However, unless and until the Supreme Court changes its views about the relationship between independence and corruption, that option is a constitutional non-starter.

It is possible that we could instead continue down the deregulatory path *McCutcheon* marks out. We think shadow parties are here to stay because of the important benefits they offer big donors. But the more we deregulate direct contributions to parties and candidates, the stronger the hand of the official parties will be. Complete deregulation—unlimited donations to candidates and parties, coupled with transparency—was once unthinkable. But now some see it as a potential cure to what ails our democracy.[121]

In this article, we identify an important cost associated with deregulation, one that has been utterly neglected by commentators and academics alike. This approach would save the parties only by remaking them in the image of the shadow parties. The official parties, as reconstituted under a deregulated regime, would look very different from the more pluralist model of the past. Like the shadow parties today, they would be beholden to few, not many. The regulations currently imposed on the official parties are a hodgepodge—a system that no one could possibly have intended given its many perverse effects. But you can say one thing for the existing system: it has ensured that the official party serves many masters. To be sure, in this system, money matters a lot. But other modes of influence remain.

Small-d democrats ought to worry about the ways in which this unusual solution to a partially deregulated regime—still more deregulation—risks further flattening what was once a complex and pluralistic system. In thinking about our alternatives, we should worry about cutting out the party faithful and creating a system that features big donors and a mass voting public but nobody in between.

That kind of politics may be well adapted to a political world that is still dominated by broadcast media. But we think such broadcast-based politics is a hollowed-out kind of politics, missing some of the energy and engagement that makes politics worthwhile. Instead of trying to strengthen "the parties"—which, for the reasons discussed in Part II, are actually quite strong—we ought

---

[121] See, for example, Ron Faucheux, *The Only Way to Fix Campaign-Finance Regulation Is to Destroy It*, The Atlantic (July 30, 2012), online at http://www.theatlantic.com/politics/archive/2012/07/the-only-way-to-fix-campaign-finance-regulation-is-to-destroy-it/260426/.

to focus on a different problem. The question is not how to make the parties stronger, nor is it how to equalize influence between outsiders and insiders. The question is how to preserve the pluralist remains of the party system and ensure a robust role for the party faithful in our strange new political world.

LESLIE KENDRICK

NONSENSE ON SIDEWALKS:
CONTENT DISCRIMINATION
IN McCULLEN v COAKLEY

What does it mean to say that the government may not "restrict expression because of its message, its ideas, its subject matter, or its content"?[1] Whatever it means, how would one determine when it has occurred? First Amendment law has wrestled with these questions for more than forty years, and if *McCullen v Coakley* is a reliable indicator, the debates have only become more fractious.[2]

The Massachusetts Reproductive Health Care Facilities Act prohibited knowingly standing on a "public way or sidewalk" within thirty-five feet of the entrances or driveways of facilities, other than hospitals, where abortions were performed.[3] The law exempted peo-

Leslie Kendrick is Albert Clark Tate, Jr., Professor of Law, University of Virginia School of Law.

AUTHOR'S NOTE: For their insightful comments, the author would like to thank Fred Schauer, Micah Schwartzman, and Geoffrey Stone.

[1] *Police Dep't of Chicago v Mosley*, 408 US 92, 95 (1972).

[2] *McCullen v Coakley*, 134 S Ct 2518 (2014).

[3] The law provided, "No person shall knowingly enter or remain on a public way or sidewalk adjacent to a reproductive health care facility within a radius of 35 feet of any portion of an entrance, exit or driveway of a reproductive health care facility or within the area within a rectangle created by extending the outside boundaries of any entrance, exit or driveway of a reproductive health care facility in straight lines to the point where such lines intersect the sideline of the street in front of such entrance, exit or driveway." Mass Gen Laws ch 266, § 120E½(b).

ple entering or leaving a facility; facility employees "acting within the scope of their employment"; municipal agents, such as police officers, firefighters, and so forth, in the scope of their duties; and people crossing the sidewalk solely to reach a destination.[4]

The question for the Supreme Court was whether this law impermissibly discriminated against antiabortion speakers or merely maintained public safety and preserved access to health-care facilities. In this regard, the Court inquired into the purpose behind the law. A subsidiary question was, if the law served the latter goals, did it do so without treading too heavily on the expressive opportunities of antiabortion speakers. In this regard, the Court inquired into the effects of the law. These inquiries, into purpose and effects, are aspects of the standard First Amendment jurisprudence of "content discrimination," a term that describes both the principle that targeting speech for its content is highly suspicious and the various doctrinal tools used to determine when that is happening. Ultimately, the Court, with the Chief Justice writing for a five-person majority, determined that the law had no discriminatory purpose,[5] but its burdensome effects on speakers were not justified.[6] In two concurrences in the judgment, Justice Scalia and Justice Alito also concluded that the law was unconstitutional but did so on the ground that it discriminated against antiabortion speech.[7]

In their several approaches to content discrimination, the Justices' opinions demonstrated that the question of *how* to approach the issue is somewhat of a chameleon: it is likely to match the contentiousness of the factual context that surrounds it. Given that the context in *McCullen* was abortion, matters became controversial indeed. At several points, both jurists and advocates viewed a single phenomenon in strikingly different terms, beginning with the facts, continuing through both the mechanics and the results of the purpose inquiry, and ending with the assessment of the law's effects. These conflicts demonstrate both the potential benefits of clear rules in the content discrimination context and their lurking futility.

---

[4] Id at § 120E½(b) (1)–(4).

[5] *McCullen v Coakley*, 134 S Ct at 2531.

[6] Id at 2537.

[7] See id at 2541 (Scalia, J, concurring in the judgment); id at 2549 (Alito, J, concurring in the judgment).

I. THE FACTS

On this much, there was agreement: *McCullen* concerned the thirty-five-foot buffer zones created around the entrances to abortion clinics by the 2007 Massachusetts law described above.[8] The 2007 Act replaced a 2000 Act imposing an eighteen-foot radius around the entrances and driveways of abortion clinics, within which one could not knowingly approach within six feet of an unconsenting person "for the purpose of passing a leaflet or handbill to, displaying a sign to, or engaging in oral protest, education, or counseling with such other person."[9] This "floating buffer zone" or "bubble zone" approach[10] (in which speakers had to maintain a six-foot bubble between themselves and unwilling listeners) derived from a similar Colorado statute upheld by the Supreme Court in *Hill v Colorado*.[11]

In 2007, the Massachusetts legislature heard testimony from the Commonwealth Attorney General, law enforcement officers, and clinic employees and volunteers that the 2000 Act was not working. There was testimony that the areas outside the clinics were too crowded to ensure orderly access. There was testimony that the crowds were too dense for law enforcement officials to witness potential infractions of the law and to judge when the six-foot bubble had been purposefully breached. There was testimony that these on-the-ground difficulties led to further difficulties in proving a violation in court.[12] The legislature responded by replacing the bubble zones with the thirty-five-foot buffer zones, which kept people off the public ways in the immediate vicinity of the entrances to abortion clinics. Both the 2000 and 2007 Acts had the same four exceptions for clinic visitors, employees, municipal agents, and people crossing the sidewalk to reach another destination.[13] They both also separately prohibited "knowing" attempts to obstruct, detain, hinder, impede, or block facility entrances.[14]

---

[8] Mass Gen Laws ch 266, § 120E½(b). For the law's text, see note 3.

[9] Id at § 120E½(e) (West, 2000).

[10] Brief of Respondents at 5, *McCullen v Coakley*, 134 S Ct 2518 (2014) (No 12-1168).

[11] *Hill v Colorado*, 530 US 703 (2000).

[12] See *McCullen*, 134 S Ct at 2525–26.

[13] Brief of Respondents at 5–6, *McCullen* (No 12-1168).

[14] Mass Gen Laws ch 266, § 120E½(e).

There, the agreement ended. In arguing that the 2007 Act was unconstitutional, the petitioners, self-styled "sidewalk counselors,"[15] emphasized their own advanced years and anodyne methods ("Eleanor McCullen, for example, is a 76-year-old grandmother who aims to stand on public sidewalks near abortion clinics in order to reach this unique audience, at a unique moment, in a compassionate and non-confrontational way.").[16] The Commonwealth respondents, defending the constitutionality of the Act, opened with a history of violence at Massachusetts abortion clinics, beginning with protests in the 1980s, through the murder of two employees at a clinic in 1994, to the testimony of disruption offered in advance of both the 2000 and 2007 laws.[17]

The challengers emphasized that the 2007 Act was adopted "despite a complete lack of evidence that, from 2000 to 2007, there had been a single conviction under the 2000 law."[18] The Commonwealth, highlighting testimony by law enforcement officials, argued that the law was routinely disregarded, but there were no convictions because the bubble zones were nearly impossible to police.[19]

The parties also disagreed on the relative merit of the 2000 and 2007 Acts, with both sides taking rather complex positions. The challengers suggested, on the one hand, that the 2007 Act was overly draconian and compared poorly with the 2000 bubble zone Act.[20] On the other hand, they also asked the Court to overrule *Hill v Colorado*, in effect seeking a determination that the 2000 Act was also unconstitutional.[21] The Commonwealth characterized the 2007 Act as at once "narrower" than the 2000 Act, in that it regulated conduct rather than communication,[22] and as a more expan-

---

[15] Brief of Petitioners at 9, *McCullen v Coakley*, 134 S Ct 2518 (2014) (No 12-1168).

[16] Id at 7. See also id at 10.

[17] Brief of Respondents at 1–12, *McCullen* (No 12-1168).

[18] Brief of Petitioners at 7, *McCullen* (No 12-1168).

[19] Brief of Respondents at 10–11, *McCullen* (No 12-1168) ("the consent requirement was unenforceable as a 'practical matter.' J.A. 67, 68, 70, 77, 79, 122–23. As a result, police made few arrests. J.A. 68, 69.").

[20] Brief of Petitioners at 6–7, *McCullen* (No 12-1168) ("The Act dispenses with any effort to target only unwanted physical approaches. Instead, it creates large painted zones on public sidewalks near abortion clinics in which traditionally protected speech—even consensual conversation or silent prayer—is forbidden.").

[21] Id at 54 ("Hill has proved to be badly reasoned, out of step with the Court's other First Amendment jurisprudence, and unworkable or destructive in practice.").

[22] Brief of Respondents at 57, *McCullen* (No 12-1168).

sive response after the 2000 Act allowed speakers to crowd entrances up to the clinic's property line.[23]

Most of all, the parties disagreed about what was going on on the sidewalks outside the clinics. The challengers enumerated their various peaceful activities, including prayer, distribution of literature, display of signs, and "offers to counsel clinic visitors."[24] They said they "[had] good reason to believe that some women entering these clinics would welcome their offers of information and help, and would ultimately find petitioners' assistance valuable in making a difficult decision."[25] Meanwhile, respondents painted a picture of the overall scene in front of the clinics:

> Protesters stood still in facility doorways to pass out leaflets, crowding the entrance. [ ] Sidewalk counselors massed in doors and driveways, attempting to approach patients until the very moment they entered facilities. [ ] And counter-protesters jockeyed for their own positions, occasionally pushing and shoving, within the same 18-foot space. [ ] Whether they intended to or not, protesters created a wall of sometimes agitated or angry people in front of facility entrances, effectively blocking them.[26]

They highlighted legislative testimony that, under the 2000 Act, the entrances were as crowded and frenetic as a "goalie's crease," that protestors "st[ood] up right in front of the door," and that "everybody is in everybody's face no matter what."[27]

The challengers emphasized the peaceful nature of their aims, such as "sidewalk counseling, advocacy of abortion alternatives, or peaceful expression of moral opposition to abortion."[28] The Commonwealth cited legislative testimony that some protestors seemed "desperate to prevent people from entering the clinic,"[29] that some would stick their heads or hands into open car windows,[30] that one clinic spent $300,000 a year on security,[31] and that women regularly turned back from clinics "out of fear."[32]

---

[23] Id at 48 ("Massachusetts has already experimented with preserving peaceful protest right up to facility doors, and the experiment was a failure. . . . [E]ven the peaceful protest permitted by the 2000 Act had the effect of blocking facilities.").

[24] Brief of Petitioners at 10–11, *McCullen* (No 12-1168).

[25] Id at 11.

[26] Brief of Respondents at 7, *McCullen* (No 12-1168) (citations to Joint Appendix omitted).

[27] Id at 7–8 (citing JA 69, 67, 69).

[28] Brief of Petitioners at 10, *McCullen* (No 12-1168).

[29] Brief of Respondents at 8, *McCullen* (No 12-1168) (citing JA 69, 67, 72).

[30] Id at 9 (citing JA 51).

[31] Id at 10 (citing JA 61).

[32] Id (citing JA 88–89); see also id at 9 (citing JA 41).

The challengers asserted that, "[a]s a practical matter, the [2007] Act primarily, if not exclusively, affects anti-abortion speakers."[33] Both the Commonwealth and United States as its amicus claimed that pro-choice advocates were as much part of the problem as anti-abortion advocates, if not more so,[34] and emphasized that the 2007 Act applied to both groups.[35]

In describing the impact of the 2007 Act, the challengers focused on the effects on their preferred activities, particularly distribution of literature and sidewalk counseling. They noted that "most people will not make an effort to accept proffered literature unless it can be placed near their hands."[36] They suggested that sidewalk counseling is "impossible" without "close personal contact and . . . confidential discussion."[37] They claimed that "[t]hese problems cannot be ameliorated by distributing leaflets or conversing at normal volumes outside the exclusion zones," for a number of reasons.[38] For one, beyond the thirty-five-foot buffer zone it is more difficult to distinguish clinic visitors from other pedestrians.[39] For another, if a clinic visitor is identified, it may be difficult to reach her before she enters the buffer zone.[40] Also, the buffer zone "forces any conversation that may be initiated outside the zone to stop at the boundary line."[41]

In describing the impact of the 2007 Act, the Commonwealth claimed that "the areas immediately around facility entrances finally function as they should."[42] Patients have access to the clinics, while "interested individuals can . . . effectively proffer their

---

[33] Brief of Petitioners at 8, *McCullen* (No 12-1168).

[34] Brief of United States at 5, *McCullen v Coakley*, 134 S Ct 2518 (2014) (No 12-1168) ("Pro-choice protestors could be 'particularly disruptive,' since they sometimes would 'push, shove, and step on other people's feet in order to get a good position'") (quoting JA 123); Brief of Respondents at 12, *McCullen* (No 12-1168).

[35] Brief of Respondents at 38, *McCullen* (No 12-1168) ("[I]f that same advocate—or for that matter, a pro-choice advocate—repeatedly walked back and forth across the buffer zone, with no obvious destination on the other side, that act would be prohibited.").

[36] Brief of Petitioners at 12, *McCullen* (No 12-1168).

[37] Id at 11. See also id at 15 ("[T]he Act's restrictions change the nature of [McCullen's] conversations, making them shorter and less effective because she is forced to speak hurriedly, sometimes speak louder, and stop walking at the painted exclusion line.").

[38] Id at 13.

[39] Id.

[40] Id.

[41] Id at 13–14.

[42] Brief of Respondents at 15–16, *McCullen* (No 12-1168).

messages outside facilities and within the sight, hearing and presence of their target audience."[43] The Commonwealth suggested that it was not necessary for the challengers to carry on conversations "as close as possible to facility doors and driveways": the challengers could have prolonged conservations with willing listeners beyond the buffer zones, and their claims "ignor[ed] the evidence that [they] do, in fact, engage in close, quiet conversations with patients before they enter facilities."[44]

In sum, before the 2007 Act, the areas outside the clinics were either a fearsome scrum of bodies and noise or a haven for intimate conversations between willing individuals. After the 2007 Act, the buffer zone was either a safe area that ensured patient access or a barren expanse that stamped out irreplaceable expressive opportunities. Meanwhile, the area beyond the buffer zones was either an ample space in which speakers could conduct their activities or a permanent frustration to those activities.

It is hardly unusual for parties to litigation to disagree on the facts. It is somewhat more unusual for parties before the Supreme Court to disagree so starkly and comprehensively on the basic factual background of their dispute. It is even more unusual for those factual disagreements to spill over so thoroughly into the legal questions at hand. On questions of how to define content discrimination, how to identify content discrimination, and how to evaluate nondiscriminatory laws, the disagreements that characterized the factual dispute, far from receding, grew to take on legal significance.

II. The Nonissue: Defining Content Discrimination

The primary point of legal disagreement between the parties was whether the 2007 Act engaged in "content-based discrimination," or, in shorthand, was "content-based." The basic idea behind content discrimination is that, within the scope of First Amendment protection,[45] it is usually wrong for the government to regu-

---

[43] Id at 16; see also id at 16–18 (offering details on expressive activity around the three clinics at which the challengers were active).

[44] Id at 54.

[45] The content discrimination principle applies to speech that is otherwise protected by the First Amendment. It defines when the government may regulate such speech and when it may not. Outside of the realm of First Amendment protection, innumerable laws regulate content, beginning with laws against criminal conspiracy and solicitation and continuing through particular regulatory areas such as securities law (e.g., insider trading) and antitrust. See, e.g.,

late speech because of what it says, and it is much less worrisome for the government to regulate speech—or to take actions that have incidental effects on speech—for other reasons.[46] Thus, a law that prohibits only sound trucks blaring pro-Republican messages is clearly unconstitutional. Meanwhile, a law that prohibits all sound trucks, simply because they are noisy, is almost certainly permissible, as is a general noise ordinance having an incidental effect on sound trucks.[47]

Under existing doctrine, a law is content-based if (1) on its face it regulates speech on the basis of its "content"[48] or (2) it is justified by reference to the "content" of the regulated speech.[49] Laws that are not content related either on their face or in their justification are content neutral. When content-based laws regulate citizen speech in the absence of an additional special relationship between citizen and government (such as an employment relationship, or a subsidy), the laws are subject to strict scrutiny, which they virtually always fail.[50] Content-neutral laws are subject to a much less demanding form of balancing.[51] At times, courts have referred to this standard as "intermediate scrutiny,"[52] but in practice

---

Frederick Schauer, *The Boundaries of the First Amendment: A Preliminary Exploration of Constitutional Salience*, 117 Harv L Rev 1765, 1769–71 (2004). My point here is not to argue about the proper scope of the First Amendment but to note that such arguments are distinct from arguments about the function of the content discrimination principle, whatever its scope.

[46] See, e.g., John Hart Ely, *Flag Desecration: A Case Study in the Roles of Categorization and Balancing in First Amendment Analysis*, 88 Harv L Rev 1482, 1498 (1975).

[47] See, e.g., *Kovacs v Cooper*, 336 US 77 (1949). See also *RAV v City of St. Paul*, 505 US 377, 385 (1992) ("[B]urning a flag in violation of an ordinance against outdoor fires could be punishable, whereas burning a flag in violation of an ordinance against dishonoring the flag is not.").

[48] See, e.g., *Turner Broad. Sys., Inc. v FCC*, 512 US 622, 642–43 (1994).

[49] *Ward v Rock Against Racism*, 491 US 781, 791 (1989); see also *Police Dep't of Chicago v Mosley*, 408 US 92, 96 (1972) ("Selective exclusions from a public forum may not be based on content alone, and may not be justified by reference to content alone.").

[50] Regulations that do not meet this definition—such as regulation of speech by the government, or regulations of speech by government employees, public school students, inmates, members of the military, beneficiaries of government subsidies such as arts funding, and speech undertaken on certain forms of government property—are subject to a wide variety of other standards. These various circumstances are not at issue in this case. See, e.g., Robert Post, *Subsidized Speech*, 106 Yale L J 151 (1996).

[51] The standard requires a law to be "narrowly tailored to serve a significant governmental interest" and that it leave open "ample alternative channels of communication." *Ward v Rock Against Racism*, 491 US 781, 791 (1989).

[52] See, e.g., *Turner Broad. Sys., Inc. v FCC*, 512 US 622, 642 (1994). With perhaps more accuracy, Laurence Tribe has referred to content-neutral scrutiny as "track two," as opposed to the strict scrutiny given to content-based laws on "track one." Laurence Tribe, *American Constitutional Law* § 12-2, at 792 (2d ed, 1988).

the Supreme Court's implementation of it has been extremely light and deferential.[53]

One debate about content discrimination concerns the definition of "content." The Supreme Court has said that the "government has no power to restrict expression because of its message, its ideas, its subject matter, or its content," but what exactly does this mean?[54] If it is wrong for the state to target particular viewpoints, is it also wrong for it to regulate on the basis of subject matter? If subject matter discrimination is wrong, is it also wrong for the government to target entire classes of messages, such as solicitation or counseling? What about particular forms of communicative activity, such as picketing or leafleting? If a particular form of speech regulation seems wrong, is it wrong in and of itself, or is it wrong for prophylactic reasons, because it is likely to conceal a different, substantively impermissible form of discrimination? These questions force reflection on the nature of the wrong that content discrimination doctrine is meant to address.[55]

Some cases place this definitional question in the foreground. *Hill v Colorado* was one.[56] In *Hill*, the Supreme Court upheld a Colorado "bubble zone" statute that became the template for the 2000 Massachusetts Act. The Colorado statute prohibited approaching within eight feet of an unwilling listener for purposes of "oral protest, education, or counseling" in a 100-foot radius of the entrance to a health-care facility.[57] The Supreme Court concluded that the law was content-neutral.[58] This decision was controversial in part because the law on its face singled out particular types of messages—oral protest, education, and counseling—for restriction.[59] The disfavored categories were not viewpoint based: the law restricted oral protest, education, and counseling from any view-

---

[53] See, e.g., Robert Post, *Recuperating First Amendment Doctrine*, 47 Stan L Rev 1249, 1256–57, 1261–62 (1995) (describing doctrine).

[54] *Police Dep't of Chicago v Mosley*, 408 US 92, 95 (1972).

[55] See, e.g., Elena Kagan, *Private Speech, Public Purpose: The Role of Government Motive in First Amendment Doctrine*, 63 U Chi L Rev 413, 431 (1996); Leslie Kendrick, *Content Discrimination Revisited*, 98 Va L Rev 231, 241–48 (2012); Frederick Schauer, *Categories and the First Amendment: A Play in Three Acts*, 34 Vand L Rev 265 (1981); Geoffrey R. Stone, *Content Regulation and the First Amendment*, 25 Wm & Mary L Rev 189 (1983); Geoffrey R. Stone, *Restrictions of Speech Because of Its Content: The Peculiar Case of Subject-Matter Restrictions*, 46 U Chi L Rev 81 (1978).

[56] 530 US 703 (2000).

[57] Id at 707.

[58] Id at 725.

[59] See id at 743 (Scalia, J, dissenting).

point. Nor were they subject-matter based: oral protest, education, and counseling on all subjects were prohibited. But clearly the law on its face singled out certain types of messages for restriction. Another point of controversy was that, even if message-based regulation might be neutral in some instances (say in the regulation of monetary solicitation[60]), in this case it seemed to some to conceal viewpoint discrimination against antiabortion speech.[61] Thus *Hill* raised both of the definitional questions identified above: which types of speech discrimination are wrongful in themselves, and which are suspicious because they may conceal other, wrongful forms of discrimination?

The parties in *McCullen* disagreed on whether their case raised similar questions. The challengers viewed *Hill* as potentially central to the disposition of the 2007 Act and urged the Court to overrule it.[62] A group of law professors filed an amicus brief in support of the challengers dedicated entirely to urging the Court to overrule *Hill*.[63] The amicus brief argued that the 2007 Act was "the progeny of *Hill*," because the Massachusetts legislature modeled the 2000 Act on the law in *Hill* and then proceeded to the 2007 Act when the 2000 Act proved ineffective.[64] The Commonwealth respondents, meanwhile, devoted a scant paragraph to arguing that *Hill* was irrelevant to the disposition of the case.[65]

The Court's majority opinion can only be said to have settled this disagreement insofar as its substantive analysis contained not a single reference to *Hill*. More broadly, the Court's analysis did not frame *McCullen* as a case involving the definition of content discrimination. Instead, the Court's analysis seemed to take for granted two things. First, unlike so many other aspects of the case, there was never any real debate over the type of discrimination allegedly involved and its wrongfulness under the law. The suspicion was that Massachusetts was targeting antiabortion messages and that it was

---

[60] See, e.g., *United States v Kokinda*, 497 US 720, 736 (1990) (treating a solicitation ban as content-neutral); *Heffron v Int'l Soc. for Krishna Consciousness, Inc.*, 452 US 640, 648 (1981) (same).

[61] See 530 US at 768 (Kennedy, J, dissenting).

[62] Petition for Writ of Certiorari at (i), *McCullen v Coakley*, 134 S Ct 2518 (2014) (No 12-1168); Brief of Petitioners at 53–57, *McCullen* (No 12-1168).

[63] Brief of Eugene Volokh, et al, in Support of Petitioners, *McCullen v Coakley*, 134 S Ct 2518 (2014) (No 12-1168).

[64] Id at 17–18.

[65] Brief of Respondents at 57–58, *McCullen* (No 12-1168).

doing so out of disagreement with, or animus toward, those mes-sages.[66] There is widespread consensus that, whatever else the con-tent discrimination principle means, it generally prohibits the state from penalizing a disfavored viewpoint.[67] Such viewpoint discrimi-nation, if it occurred, would be a serious problem under the First Amendment. Doctrinally speaking, it would warrant strict scrutiny and would surely fail.[68] Thus, the type of "content" discrimination at issue was clear to everyone.

Second, there was no other type of "content" discrimination to be scrutinized, either as a wrong in itself or as a pretext for view-point discrimination. The 2007 Act, on its face, regulated not mes-sages, or even communicative activities such as picketing, but physi-cal access. The law prohibited "knowingly enter[ing] or remain[ing] on a public way or sidewalk adjacent to a reproductive health care facility" within the thirty-five-foot buffer zone.[69] A person remain-ing in the buffer zone but undertaking no expressive activity would violate the law just as much as a protestor.[70] Whether the physical access rule itself concealed viewpoint discrimination is a separate question, but there was no other form of "content" discrimination whose wrongfulness—either inherently or as a proxy for viewpoint discrimination—had to be considered. The 2007 Act thus did not raise the question, so prominent in *Hill*, of what categories of speech regulation are inherently suspicious enough to be classified as content-based.

Justice Scalia, concurring in the judgment, sided with the chal-lengers and their amici about the relevance of *Hill* and criticized the majority for ignoring it.[71] He endorsed an argument that the Court in *Hill*, in addition to ignoring content discrimination on the face of the statute, also treated as content-neutral a plainly content-

---

[66] Id at 2530 (rehearsing petitioners' arguments for why law was viewpoint discriminatory).

[67] See, e.g., Marjorie Heins, *Viewpoint Discrimination*, 24 Hastings Const L Q 99, 115 (1996); Schauer, 34 Vand L Rev at 283–84 (cited in note 55); Paul B. Stephan III, *The First Amendment and Content Discrimination*, 68 Va L Rev 203, 233 (1982); Stone, 25 Wm & Mary L Rev at 233 (cited in note 55).

[68] *McCullen*, 134 S Ct at 2530.

[69] Mass Gen Laws ch 266, § 120E½(b).

[70] *McCullen v Coakley*, 134 S Ct 2518 at 2531 ("Indeed, petitioners can violate the Act merely by standing in a buffer zone, without displaying a sign or uttering a word.").

[71] Id at 2545 (Scalia, J, concurring in the judgment) ("[W]e granted a second question for review in this case (though one would not know that from the Court's opinion, which fails to mention it): whether *Hill* should be cut back or cast aside.").

based justification for the law: that it advanced a state interest in protecting listeners from unwanted messages.[72] Justice Scalia argued that the 2007 Act clearly involved the same interest.[73] He criticized the majority for "avoid[ing] that question by declaring the Act content neutral on other (entirely unpersuasive) grounds," namely, that the law was justified by interests in patient safety and access.[74] The majority, without mentioning *Hill*, rejected the claim that the 2007 Act had anything to do with shielding unwilling listeners. Instead it relied solely upon patient safety and access.[75] Although the majority expressed skepticism about shielding unwilling listeners as a neutral state interest, it stated clearly that such an interest was not in play in this case and thus was not grounds for invalidation.[76]

Thus, the debate over *Hill* fell by the wayside. Far from being central to the resolution of the case, *Hill* became notable mainly for the sheer level of disagreement it sparked. In disputing *Hill*'s relevance, the parties, and the Justices, suggested that they had fundamentally different understandings of the legal context surrounding *McCullen*—and of its rightful legal significance.

III. THE REAL ISSUE: IDENTIFYING CONTENT DISCRIMINATION

The real issue for both parties was whether the 2007 Act discriminated against antiabortion speech. This is a question of how to identify viewpoint discrimination, a form of "content" discrimination widely agreed to be wrongful. This question of *how* is yet another matter of contentious debate within content discrimination jurisprudence. More broadly, it is part of the larger questions of what legislative purpose is and whether and how courts ought to set about identifying it. However courts choose to police for viewpoint discrimination has ramifications for these larger questions.

As noted above, the standard test for content discrimination asks whether a law (1) targets particular content on its face or (2) is jus-

---

[72] Id.

[73] Id ("The provision at issue here was indisputably meant to serve the same interest in protecting citizens' supposed right to avoid speech that they would rather not hear.").

[74] Id.

[75] Id at 2531–32.

[76] Id.

tified by reference to the content of the regulated speech. The majority of the Court applied this test to conclude that the 2007 Act was content-neutral. On its face, it did not target a particular viewpoint, or indeed speech of any kind.[77] And the interests Massachusetts invoked to justify the law were patient access to health-care facilities and physical safety—interests that turn not on the content of protestors' speech, but on the physical situation in front of the clinics.[78]

One might consider this content discrimination framework highly artificial. Faced with deciding whether a legislature passed a particular law because of an unfavorable view of particular expression, the content discrimination framework turns to proxies. It asks about the face of the law, on the assumption that any law that on its face targets particular expression is driven by a likely invidious concern about what that expression is saying. It asks about the justifications of the law, typically as stated in the law itself and by the state in litigation, to give the state a chance to explain its view of the law's objects. Neither of these inquiries can expose the particular purposes behind a law's passage—or, to put it another way, neither can definitively reveal whether the law would have passed if the speech involved were completely different, or incomprehensible.[79] But the framework gives courts a way to approximate an answer.

Two questions we might ask about this framework are (1) are there other proxies we should employ, and (2) should we dispense with these proxies altogether and rely on less formalistic ways of identifying content discrimination? *McCullen* raised both issues, and the Court proved deeply divided about each of them.

A. IDENTIFYING CONTENT DISCRIMINATION: THE LIMITS OF RULES

Although the 2007 Act did not single out any form of communication on its face, it did make other sorts of distinctions. For one,

---

[77] Id.

[78] Id.

[79] See, e.g., Ely, 88 Harv L Rev at 1498 (cited in note 46) ("Had [the speaker's] audience been unable to read English, there would have been no occasion for the regulation."); Stone, 25 Wm & Mary L Rev at 232 (cited in note 55) ("[T]he critical motivational inquiry is not whether the governmental officials would have adopted the restriction even if they did not disfavor the restricted speech, but whether they would have adopted it even if it had been directed at speech that they themselves favored.").

the law only applied to "reproductive health care facilit[ies]," defined as facilities other than hospitals that performed abortions.[80]
For another, it exempted four categories of people, including "employees or agents of such facility acting within the scope of their
employment."[81] Should either of these distinctions be regarded as
evidence that this law discriminated against antiabortion speech?

As to the law's focus on reproductive health-care facilities, the
majority concluded that this place specificity did not render the law
content-based.[82] The other Justices, however, believed that this feature made the law content-based and flagrantly so. Justice Scalia,
joined by Justices Kennedy and Thomas, argued, "It blinks reality
to say, as the majority does, that a blanket prohibition on the use
of streets and sidewalks where speech on only one politically controversial topic is likely to occur—and where that speech can most
effectively be communicated—is not content based."[83] Not only did
these Justices argue that place specificity *should*, normatively speaking, render the law content-based, but they also argued that any
other conclusion departed from precedent. In Justice Scalia's view,
in finding the law content-neutral, the majority was "carr[ying] forward this Court's practice of giving abortion-rights advocates a pass
when it comes to suppressing the free-speech rights of their opponents."[84]

Descriptively speaking, however, past Supreme Court cases have
never treated place regulations as inherently suspicious. It is no
coincidence that another term for "content-neutral" regulations is
"time-place-manner" regulations: laws routinely regulate speech according to place without raising serious First Amendment scrutiny.[85] The Supreme Court has seen nothing suspicious about, for
example, regulating picketing only around schools,[86] or regulating

---

[80] Mass Gen Laws ch 266, § 120E½(a), (b).

[81] Id at § 120E½(b)(2).

[82] *McCullen v Coakley*, 134 S Ct 2518, 2532 (2014).

[83] Id at 2543 (Scalia, J, concurring in the judgment).

[84] Id at 2541 (Scalia, J, concurring in the judgment).

[85] See, e.g., *Clark v Cmty for Creative Non-Violence*, 468 US 288, 294 (1984).

[86] *Police Dep't of Chicago v Mosley*, 408 US 92, 95 (1972). The law in *Mosley* was struck down,
but this was because it exempted labor picketing, and this subject-matter exemption triggered
the Court's regular content discrimination principles. The Court nowhere suggested that the
limitation of the regulation to schools was suspicious.

signage only at residences,[87] or regulating solicitation only at a fair-ground[88] or around a post office.[89]

A number of such place regulations could easily be cast in a sinister light. Regulations on leafleting and solicitation at an airport clearly had a disparate impact on Hare Krishnas, but the Court never suggested that the place-specific nature of the regulations constituted evidence of discrimination against this group.[90] The Court did not consider a residential picketing ordinance inherently suspicious simply because antiabortion protestors were associated with the tactic.[91] More recently, Congress and more than forty states have passed laws against picketing within a certain radius of a funeral.[92] Lower courts have considered them content-neutral, despite the fact that the laws single out funerals, and a certain group, the Westboro Baptist Church, is infamous for picketing at funerals.[93] The Supreme Court grounds are protected by their own antidemonstration statute,[94] and though the Court in 1983 invalidated it with respect to the surrounding public sidewalk (not the grounds themselves), the Court has never suggested, then or since, that it finds it in the least suspicious for a statute to regulate expressive activity only around the Supreme Court.[95] To conclude that there was something inherently suspicious in the place regulation in *McCullen*,

---

[87] *City of Ladue v Gilleo*, 512 US 43, 45 (1994).

[88] *Heffron v Int'l Soc. for Krishna Consciousness, Inc.*, 452 US 640, 648 (1981).

[89] *United States v Kokinda*, 497 US 720, 736 (1990).

[90] *International Society for Krishna Consciousness, Inc. v Lee*, 505 US 672 (1992); *Lee v Int'l Soc. for Krishna Consciousness, Inc.*, 505 US 830 (1992). See also *Heffron v Int'l Soc. for Krishna Consciousness, Inc.*, 452 US 640, 648 (1981) (challenge to state fair regulations brought by Hare Krishnas).

[91] *Frisby v Schultz*, 487 US 474 (1988).

[92] See *Snyder v Phelps*, 131 S Ct 1207, 1218 (2011).

[93] See, e.g., *Phelps-Roper v Koster*, 713 F3d 942, 951 (8th Cir 2013); *Phelps-Roper v City of Manchester*, 697 F3d 678 (8th Cir 2012) (en banc); *Phelps-Roper v Strickland*, 539 F3d 356 (6th Cir 2008); see also *Snyder v Phelps*, 131 S Ct 1207, 1218 (2011) (suggesting that funeral-picketing statutes could be content-neutral).

[94] 40 USC § 13k ("It shall be unlawful to parade, stand, or move in processions or assemblages in the Supreme Court Building or grounds, or to display therein any flag, banner, or device designed or adapted to bring into public notice any party, organization, or movement.").

[95] *United States v Grace*, 461 US 171, 181 n 10 (1983). In ongoing litigation, a district court struck down the law as unreasonable and overbroad, but did not suggest it was suspicious simply by virtue of being place-specific. See *Hodge v Talkin*, 949 F Supp 2d 152, 155 (DDC 2013).

the majority would have had to explain how the 2007 Act differed from the many, many regulations whose place specificity has passed virtually without comment. Instead, the majority had no trouble concluding that the place regulation in this case was no more worrisome than those predecessors.[96]

A similar theme emerges from the treatment of the employee exemption. The majority concluded that "there is nothing inherently suspect about providing some kind of exemption to allow individuals who work at the clinics to enter or remain within the buffer zones."[97] The majority found it implausible that the Act was designed to give clinic employees a lopsided opportunity to express their views in the buffer zone when the "'scope of their employment' limitation . . . seems designed to protect against" that very thing.[98] As to testimony that employees were speaking their views outside the clinic, the majority concluded that, if such speech occurred inside the buffer zones, it was evidence of employees breaking the law, not evidence that the law itself was viewpoint discriminatory.[99]

The separate opinions, on the other hand, took the employee exemption as patent evidence of viewpoint discrimination. While the majority saw "nothing inherently suspect" in the exemption, Justice Scalia viewed it as, on its face, viewpoint discriminatory, tantamount to "[g]ranting waivers to favored speakers."[100] He argued that the limitation to "scope of employment" did not insulate the state from the charge of viewpoint discrimination, because expressing pro-abortion views could foreseeably be within the scope of clinic employees' employment.[101] Justice Alito, meanwhile, wrote an entire separate opinion arguing that the employee exemption alone was sufficient to render the Act viewpoint discriminatory: "Speech in favor of the clinic and its work by employees and agents is permitted; speech criticizing the clinic and its work is a crime. This is blatant viewpoint discrimination."[102] (All three opinions ig-

---

[96] *McCullen v Coakley*, 134 S Ct 2518, 2532 (2014).

[97] Id at 2533.

[98] Id.

[99] Id.

[100] Id at 2546 (Scalia, J, concurring in the judgment).

[101] Id at 2547 (Scalia, J, concurring in the judgment).

[102] Id at 2549 (Alito, J, concurring in the judgment).

nored guidance letters issued by the Massachusetts Attorney General's Office interpreting the Act's exemptions not to allow people, including clinic employees, to congregate or engage in "partisan speech" in the buffer zones.)[103]

In sum, the place limitation and employee exemption revealed deep disagreement over the rules of content discrimination—both over what those rules should be from a normative standpoint and what they are from a descriptive standpoint. This deep disagreement signals some limits to a formalistic, rules-based approach: no matter how automatic and unstinting the Court's approach to laws that facially single out speech on the basis of its viewpoint or subject matter, there will remain other types of distinctions, distinctions that are not themselves about content but might serve as proxies for content. Place limitations and employee exemptions are but two examples. Others include laws regulating certain forms of media but not others,[104] laws targeting forms of communication typically employed by those less wealthy and connected,[105] injunctions directed at certain individuals,[106] and laws distinguishing classes of speakers on some basis other than message.[107] The Supreme Court has never concluded that any of these classifications inherently render a law content-based. Instead, the Court has nearly always concluded that such laws are content-neutral.[108]

Exceptions are extremely rare. One involved a medium-specific regulation: the Court concluded that, given the history of press

---

[103] Brief of Respondents at 37–38, *McCullen* (No 12-1168).

[104] Compare *Minneapolis Star & Tribune Co. v Minnesota Comm'r of Revenue*, 460 US 575, 585 (1983) (treating differential taxation of newspapers as inherently content-based) with *Turner Broad. Sys., Inc. v FCC*, 512 US 622, 643 (1994) (treating differential regulation of cable operators as content-neutral); *Leathers v Medlock*, 499 US 439, 444 (1991) (same).

[105] See, e.g., *United States v Kokinda*, 497 US 720, 723 (1990) (prohibiting "[s]oliciting alms and contributions" on post office property).

[106] *Schenck v Pro Choice Network*, 519 US 357 (1997) (holding injunction of abortion protestors content-neutral but subjecting it to higher scrutiny than usual); *Madsen v Women's Health Center, Inc.*, 512 US 753 (1994) (same).

[107] Compare *Sorrell v IMS Health Inc.*, 131 S Ct 2653, 2663 (2011) (criticizing law for making "speaker-based restrictions"); *Citizens United v FEC*, 558 US 310, 340 (2010) (positing "the Government may commit a constitutional wrong when by law it identifies certain preferred speakers.") with *Leathers v Medlock*, 499 US 439, 444 (1991) ("Our cases have held that a tax that discriminates among speakers is constitutionally suspect only in certain circumstances.").

[108] For more discussion of the Supreme Court's treatment of these classifications, see Kendrick, 98 Va L Rev at 262–74 (cited in note 55).

censorship, a tax singling out newspapers was suspicious enough to be content-based.[109] Elsewhere, however, the Court has upheld medium-specific laws as content-neutral.[110] Another exception involved speaker discrimination in the abortion context: in two cases, the Court found injunctions against particular protestors to be content-neutral but nevertheless applied a novel, heightened level of scrutiny to ensure against invidious discrimination.[111] (This exception, it should be noted, far from "giving abortion-rights advocates a pass when it comes to suppressing the free-speech rights of their opponents," benefited abortion protestors.[112]) I am unaware of any cases in which the Supreme Court deemed a law content-based because of a place limitation. In sum, the Court has operated with a de facto presumption that classifications not explicitly related to content are inoffensive, while reserving the right to view rare cases in a more suspicious light.

From a normative perspective, this approach makes sense. Place-specific regulations offer an illustration. In explaining why the 2007 Act singles out abortion clinics, the majority essentially echoes Willie Sutton, who, when asked why he robbed banks, supposedly replied, "Because that's where the money is." Massachusetts targeted the space around abortion clinics because that is where the problem was: that is where people were congregating in a way that interfered with individuals' safety and access. It makes sense to regulate speech at a particular place when that is where the problem is. Indeed, the First Amendment places limits on governments' powers to regulate broadly in the name of fixing a focused problem. Certainly banning leafleting and demonstration on all public streets and sidewalks in a town—or throughout a state, in the case of the Massachusetts law—would be patently unconstitutional.[113] If place-specific regulations were inherently content-based, federal, state,

---

[109] *Minneapolis Star & Tribune Co. v Minnesota Comm'r of Revenue*, 460 US 575, 585 (1983) (treating differential taxation of newspapers as content-based). See also *Grosjean v Am. Press Co.*, 297 US 233, 250 (1936) (striking down a tax on certain newspapers, prior to the development of contemporary content discrimination doctrine).

[110] *Turner Broad. Sys., Inc. v FCC*, 512 US 622, 643 (1994) (treating differential regulation of cable operators as content-neutral); *Leathers v Medlock*, 499 US 439, 444 (1991) (treating differential taxation of cable operators as content-neutral).

[111] *Schenck v Pro Choice Network*, 519 US 357 (1997) (holding injunction of abortion protestors content-neutral but subjecting it to higher scrutiny than usual); *Madsen v Women's Health Center, Inc.*, 512 US 753 (1994) (same).

[112] *McCullen v Coakley*, 134 S Ct 2518, 2541 (2014) (Scalia, J, concurring in the judgment).

[113] See, e.g., *Board of Airport Commissioners of Los Angeles v Jews for Jesus*, 482 US 569 (1987) (striking down law banning all "First Amendment activity" in airport); *Schneider v State of*

and local government officials would find themselves in an impossible bind, unable to target specific problems at specific places while forbidden from regulating across the board. Thus a categorical rule against place regulations would flag as suspicious many laws merely attempting to address real problems in a reasonable way. To adopt such a rule would be to ignore this reality in favor of an ultimately artificial inquiry.

At the same time, however, a categorical rule in the opposite direction—holding that such classifications are *never* suspicious— would risk the same thing. Although "time-place-manner regulation" is synonymous with "content-neutral regulation," it is entirely possible that regulation according to place (or time or manner) may sometimes occur for invidious reasons. The concurring Justices in *McCullen* could also say that the 2007 Act singles out abortion clinics "because that's where the money is"—meaning, in their case, because that is the location of the speakers whom the Commonwealth wishes to oppress. There is a certain overlap that characterizes most place regulations that face First Amendment challenge: such laws target a place where a particular problem manifests, but they also disparately affect the speakers who frequent that place. The speakers feel that they are being targeted for their message; the state claims it is targeting the place for a non-message-related problem. This overlap means that, as a general matter, governments must be permitted to regulate according to place in order to have a reasonable opportunity of addressing real problems that have nothing to do with the message of particular speakers. At the same time, however, the Supreme Court may want to reserve the possibility that, in some instance or other, the speakers may be right about what is happening.

A rules-based approach, therefore, has its limits. The kind of automatic, categorical rules that the Court uses to treat all viewpoint and subject-matter classifications as content-based are inappropriate for the other types of classifications, such as the place and employee classifications of the 2007 Act. It is risky to claim that these classifications are *never* vehicles for content-related discrimination, but they are hardly regular and reliable proxies for it. The lack of an absolute rule means that courts will, to some degree, have to determine for themselves when laws are suspicious and when

---

New Jersey, 308 US 147 (1939) (striking down town-wide bans on leafleting, as well as permitting requirements for door-to-door solicitation). See also *Marsh v Alabama*, 326 US 501, 509 (1946) (striking similar town-wide ban in privately owned municipality).

they are not. Unsurprisingly, this alternative has its own problems, also prominently on display in *McCullen*.

B. IDENTIFYING CONTENT DISCRIMINATION: THE VIRTUES OF RULES

In the absence of a categorical rule, judges are left to use their intuitions to ferret out whether a particular law is suspicious. In *Mc-Cullen*, unfortunately, what the majority and the remaining Justices disagree about most is what is really going on in the 2007 Act. The majority views the law as a good-faith attempt to deal with a physical problem: too many people in too little space, in an environment that has had its share of assaults and even murders. The others view the law as an unnecessary, and therefore invidious, attempt to regulate the speech that occurs outside abortion clinics, the vast majority of which is harmless. The disagreements about the place limitation and employee exemption, though framed as arguments about doctrine and consistency across cases, may actually be symptoms of this deeper perceptual divide. The majority finds these classifications innocuous because it credits a portrayal of the situation in which they are reasonable. The others find them highly suspicious because their view of the situation forecloses any legitimate explanation for them. The majority says the law exists because that is where the problems are; the others believe it was passed because that is where the speakers are.

The same pattern emerges more starkly when the analysis turns from the law's face to its justifications. Recall that a law can be content-based either on its face or in its justifications, if those justifications relate to the "content" of the messages being regulated. The majority accepts the Commonwealth's assertions that the interests behind the law are in patient safety and access, as well as preserving unobstructed use of the sidewalks. Because these interests are unrelated to the messages expressed by protestors, they are content-neutral. Thus, in the majority's view, the 2007 Act is neutral both on its face and in its justifications.[114]

Justice Scalia simply rejects that the state's asserted interests are actually the interests behind the law:

> Really? Does a statute become "justified without reference to the content of the regulated speech" simply because the statute itself and those

---

[114] *McCullen v Coakley*, 134 S Ct 2518, 2531 (2014).

defending it in court *say* that it is? Every objective indication shows
that the provision's primary purpose is to restrict speech that opposes
abortion.[115]

The problem is that the objective indications primarily relied
upon by the Court to assess a law's justifications are (1) the justification, if any, offered in the statute itself and (2) the interests
asserted by the state in the course of litigation. It is difficult to
think of a single case of a facially neutral law where the Court
rejected the interests offered by the state as not the "real" justification.[116] The Court has routinely accepted justifications related
to traffic flow,[117] for example, even when the law on its face seemed
underinclusive with respect to that interest.[118]

At the very outset of its content discrimination jurisprudence,
in upholding the draft-card-burning law in *United States v O'Brien*,
the Court stated in no uncertain terms, "It is a familiar principle
of constitutional law that this Court will not strike down an otherwise constitutional statute on the basis of an alleged illicit legislative motive."[119] In particular, the Court rejected legislative history
as a sound basis on which to judge the object of legislation.[120] The
Court instead adopted a formalistic approach and accepted the
United States' claim that the law was justified by a neutral interest in
administrative efficiency.[121] In the years since, the Supreme Court
has continued to show the same deference to the justifications offered in First Amendment cases. Moreover, this approach squares
with the Court's general reluctance to impugn the government's asserted interests in a number of areas of constitutional law.[122]

---

[115] Id at 2544 (Scalia, J, concurring in the judgment).

[116] See Kendrick, 98 Va L Rev at 285–86 (cited in note 55) (concluding that the Court
routinely accepts the government's justifications for content-neutral laws).

[117] See, e.g., *International Society for Krishna Consciousness, Inc. v Lee*, 505 US 672 (1992); *Lee
v Int'l Soc. for Krishna Consciousness, Inc.*, 505 US 830 (1992); *United States v Kokinda*, 497 US
720, 733–35 (1990) (plurality opinion); *Heffron v Int'l Soc. for Krishna Consciousness, Inc.*, 452
US 640, 649–50 (1981).

[118] See, e.g., *Kokinda*, 497 US at 723 (banning "[s]oliciting alms and contributions" and
some other, but not all, forms of stationary communication).

[119] *United States v O'Brien*, 391 US 367, 383 (1968).

[120] Id at 384.

[121] Id at 377–78.

[122] See, e.g., *Wallace v Jaffree*, 472 US 38, 57 (1985) (invalidating school-prayer law where
"the State did not present evidence of *any* secular purpose"); *Vill. of Arlington Heights v
Metro. Hous. Dev. Corp.*, 429 US 252, 264–65 (1977) (setting out criteria for discriminatory

Some might argue that this approach has its limitations, ex-
emplified by *O'Brien* itself: sometimes the state's word should not
be good enough, and anyone who believes that the law in *O'Brien*
was passed for administrative efficiency does not excel at critical
legal thinking. Normatively speaking, the Court's deferential approach has the serious drawback of potentially permitting invidious discrimination. Because of this normative limitation, it might
also be the case that, descriptively speaking, there is some limit to
the Court's deference: hypothetically, there are some justifications
that, to the minds of at least five Justices, would beggar belief. A
flag-burning statute justified by an interest in fire safety, for example, might provoke due skepticism.[123] Certainly in the civil rights
era, majorities of the Court sometimes found ways to push back
against discriminatory practices, even if they did not name them as
such.[124]

Perhaps, then, the most charitable reading of Justice Scalia's
claim is that, if a limit exists to the Court's deference, this case
should trigger it. The accusations of doctrinal inconsistency seem
unfounded, with regard to both the place and employee exceptions
and the Court's acceptance of the state's justifications. There simply
is not a categorical rule that these features are *always* treated with
suspicion. But there remains the possibility that, in rare instances,
they should be. And perhaps this is one of those cases.

This possibility, however, raises all the problems of eschewing
rules. Judges are likely to have different intuitions about what is
"really going on" with any number of laws. In *McCullen*, it is precisely this point upon which the Justices cannot agree. Justice Scalia
asks if the Court would consider a law content-neutral that banned

---

purpose in Equal Protection context and concluding they were not met); *Hunter v Underwood*,
471 US 222, 233 (1985) (finding a discriminatory purpose in Equal Protection context); but
see Tribe, *American Constitutional Law* § 16–20, at 1509 (cited in note 52) ("What distinguishes *Underwood* . . . is that the facts of the case allowed the Court to find a racially motivated government actor without pointing the finger at anyone who was alive.").

[123] In *Minneapolis Star & Tribune Co. v Minnesota Comm'r of Revenue*, 460 US 575, 580
(1983), the Court claimed that its earlier decision to strike down a newspaper tax in *Grosjean v
American Press Co.*, 297 US 233 (1936), had been informed by the political context of the time.
This form of retrospective analysis, however, is easier than accusing government officials of
invidious discrimination in real time, and it is informative that the *Grosjean* Court itself
steered clear of such assertions.

[124] See, e.g., *New York Times Co. v Sullivan*, 376 US 254, 279 (1964); *Nat'l Ass'n for Advancement of Colored People v State of Alabama ex rel. Patterson*, 357 US 449, 460 (1958).

access to the streets and sidewalks "used annually to commemorate the 1965 Selma-to-Montgomery civil rights marches."[125] In *Hill v Colorado*, Justice Kennedy said,

> If, just a few decades ago, a State with a history of enforcing racial discrimination had enacted a statute like this one, regulating "oral protest, education, or counseling" within 100 feet of the entrance to any lunch counter, our predecessors would not have hesitated to hold it was content based or viewpoint based.[126]

Even if we accept this confident view of the Court's ability to perceive and check racial animus,[127] the fact remains that the Court's ability to police discrimination ad hoc operates entirely by the rule of five: whichever side gets five votes wins. In the civil rights era, to the extent that the Court intervened in racially tinged cases, it did so by virtue of the fact that a majority of Justices perceived a problem and agreed on a way to remedy it.[128] Thus far, five Justices have yet to agree with Justice Scalia about abortion protests. On the question of whether a particular case is so suspicious as to warrant an exception to the usual rules, the only way to answer is to consult intuitions and take a vote.

This prospect is a reminder that, while the rules of content discrimination may be artificial, sometimes absurdly so, they also have their virtues. Adopting a freewheeling approach, in which intuitions are not channeled into a framework but are imposed directly as law, could have serious ramifications for both the predictability and legitimacy of the Court's jurisprudence. There is something to be said for an approach that, rather than indulging subjective impulses, tries to contain them. When disagreements about a law run so deep, perhaps there are good reasons for approaching the law obliquely, and through predetermined avenues.

In reality, however, the problem in *McCullen* goes even deeper. The concurrences suggest not so much that the case is an exception to established methods but that the majority is ignoring established methods. The rules of content discrimination, far from

---

[125] *McCullen v Coakley*, 134 S Ct 2518, 2543 (2014) (Scalia, J, concurring in the judgment).

[126] *Hill v Colorado*, 530 US 703, 767 (Kennedy, J, dissenting).

[127] But see *Palmer v Thompson*, 403 US 217, 221 (1971) (rejecting Equal Protection claim where city closed public swimming pools rather than desegregate).

[128] See, e.g., *New York Times Co. v Sullivan*, 376 US 254, 279 (1964).

channeling the Justices' perceptions, themselves fall victim to those perceptions. If the rules themselves become infected by the disagreements they are trying to contain, then the entire inquiry collapses into subjectivity. This is what is at stake between the majority and the concurrences in *McCullen*. The most pernicious aspect of the debate is not about the 2007 Act at all, but rather about the fact that the majority believes it is playing by the rules, while the remaining Justices believe those rules are routinely broken in the abortion context. The members of the Court seem to view their own system as divergently as they view the scene on the sidewalks at the Massachusetts clinics.

It is difficult to know what, if anything, to prescribe. Perhaps more formal rules for content discrimination would help. But the more rules, the more artificial these inquiries become. Even if we are willing to accept some artificiality as the price for consistency, there is still the possibility that any new rules would simply become casualties of the substantive disagreements they were designed to contain. *McCullen* illustrates both the virtue of rules and their vulnerability.

IV. The Future Issue: Assessing Content-Neutral Laws

Although the majority managed to hold, consistently with precedent, that the 2007 Act was content-neutral, it then made a departure of its own, one whose ramifications have yet to be determined. After having concluded that the 2007 Act was content-neutral, it went on to invalidate it under the standard for content-neutral laws, which the Court has sometimes called "intermediate" scrutiny.[129] This standard has historically required that the law be "narrowly tailored to serve a significant governmental interest" and that it leave open "ample alternative channels of communication."[130] The Court has never rejected a proffered government interest as not "significant," and it has specified that "narrowly tailored" in this context need not be a least restrictive means and may be underinclusive in the way it advances an interest, though not substantially overinclusive.[131] The vast majority of laws subjected to

---

[129] *Turner Broad. Sys., Inc. v FCC*, 512 US 622, 642 (1994).

[130] *Ward v Rock Against Racism*, 491 US 781, 791 (1989); see *McCullen*, 134 S Ct at 2544.

[131] See, e.g., *Ward v Rock Against Racism*, 491 US 781, 798–99 (1989); *Members of the City Council v Taxpayers for Vincent*, 466 US 789 (1984).

this standard by the Supreme Court have passed, to the point that it has been likened to rational basis review.[132]

The majority in *McCullen* departed from this past practice and applied the tailoring requirement with a newfound stringency. The Court took quite seriously the challengers' assertions that the 2007 Act reduced their ability to reach patients for quiet conversations and to hand them literature.[133] The majority quoted extensively from the challengers' testimony on these matters and admonished that "[t]he Court of Appeals and respondents are wrong to downplay these burdens on petitioners' speech."[134] At the same time, the majority was skeptical of the Commonwealth's arguments that the law was important for advancing its interests. The Court listed a number of alternative approaches that other jurisdictions had taken and was unimpressed with the Commonwealth's imagined reply of, "We have tried other approaches, but they do not work."[135]

Although no members of the Court dissented from this tailoring analysis, one could imagine a dissent that accused the majority's tailoring analysis of inconsistency with the same vitriol that the concurrences reserved for its content-neutral analysis. Content-neutral scrutiny has historically been enormously deferential. This is why so few laws have failed it. Any hard look would have turned up questions about whether Congress really needed to ban draft-card burning for administrative reasons,[136] whether the postal service had to ban solicitation of alms and contributions on postal premises to preserve its patrons from "the potentially unpleasant situation created by solicitation,"[137] or whether the city of Los Angeles had to ban all written communication on all sidewalks, light posts, and myriad other public properties in order to advance its "substantial" government interest

---

[132] See Frederick Schauer, *Cuban Cigars, Cuban Books, and the Problem of Incidental Restrictions on Communications*, 26 Wm & Mary L Rev 779, 788 (1985). The exceptions are *City of Ladue v Gilleo*, 512 US 43 (1994) (striking down law for lack of ample alternative channels); *United States v Grace*, 461 US 171 (1983) (striking down law for insufficient nexus with asserted interests). Some cases decided before the content-neutral test was devised could also be explained in its terms. See, e.g., *Schneider v State of New Jersey*, 308 US 147 (1939) (striking down blanket bans on leafleting and door-to-door solicitation).

[133] *McCullen v Coakley*, 134 S Ct 2518, 2535–36.

[134] Id at 2536.

[135] Id at 2539.

[136] *United States v O'Brien*, 391 US 367, 383 (1968).

[137] *United States v Kokinda*, 497 US 720, 736 (1990) (plurality opinion).

in "esthetic values."[138] In past cases, the Court has shown great deference to the government's understanding of its own agenda; suddenly, it is anything but deferential.

While the government received less credit than usual, the speakers received more. All content-neutral laws affect speech opportunities. All the content-neutral laws previously upheld by the Supreme Court were challenged precisely because they interfered with a particular speaker or speakers' ability to communicate in their desired way. For O'Brien and many others, burning a draft card expressed their message in a way that nothing else could.[139] For advocates for the homeless, being unable to stage a sleep-in demonstration in Lafayette Park, across the street from the White House, removed an irreplaceable method of expressing their message.[140] For Hare Krishnas, being unable to solicit passersby at the airport or a state fair was a frustration to their expressive, indeed their religious, mission.[141] For countless speakers, being denied the ability to express themselves at a particular place or in a particular method fundamentally alters the power of what they are saying, the substance of what they are saying, or both.[142] If it is wrong to downplay these effects in one case, it is wrong to downplay them in others.

It remains to be seen whether *McCullen*'s new approach will take hold for all content-neutral laws or whether instead it will become an abortion-specific standard (which would then favor abortion protestors over other speakers). One has the suspicion that the five members of the Court's majority were not precisely of one mind about the case, but it is hard to know who, if anyone, had the advantage of whom—whether, for example, the price of a majority on content-neutrality was an opinion invalidating the law on tailoring grounds, or whether the liberal Justices, seeing the chance to raise the level of scrutiny to the benefit of many speakers besides abortion protestors, happily took it. Perhaps subsequent cases will

---

[138] *Members of the City Council v Taxpayers for Vincent*, 466 US 789, 805 (1984).

[139] *United States v O'Brien*, 391 US 367 (1968).

[140] *Clark v Cmty for Creative Non-Violence*, 468 US 288 (1984).

[141] *Int'l Society for Krishna Consciousness, Inc. v Lee*, 505 US 672 (1992); *Lee v Int'l Soc. for Krishna Consciousness, Inc.*, 505 US 830 (1992); *Heffron v Int'l Soc. for Krishna Consciousness, Inc.*, 452 US 640 (1981).

[142] See Susan H. Williams, *Content Discrimination and the First Amendment*, 139 U Pa L Rev 615, 707 (1991) (content-neutral laws have effects on communicative aspects of many speakers' speech).

give some indication. If the decision signals a new interest in the effects of content-neutral laws generally, this development would be, in some respects, praiseworthy.[143] These effects on speaking opportunities are real enough, and past jurisprudence has undoubtedly given them short shrift. But this is just to say that these effects have been a casualty of the Court's past preference for a rule—one in which the government's interests and choice of remedy are given heavy presumptive weight. Once again, there are costs to revoking this rule. One is the fact, noted above, that all content-neutral laws have effects on speech opportunities; indeed, all laws affect speech opportunities.[144] And such effects are difficult, if not impossible, to measure.[145] If the Court intends to make it its business to police laws for their speech effects, it has its work cut out for it.

A related drawback is the fact that, given their unquantifiability, any assessments of speech effects are bound to be approximate, intuitive, and ultimately subjective. They are likely to be fraught in the same way as the parties' debates about the facts, or the Justices' debates about content-neutrality. It will be extremely difficult to cabin these inquiries with rules, and in their rulelessness they will appear wholly subjective. In *McCullen*, five Justices thought the toll of the 2007 Act was too great. What this means for the myriad buffer zones that governments use in other contexts, from political conventions, to funerals, to the regulation of panhandling—or for content-neutral laws generally—is anyone's guess. One might worry that the Court would perceive the trade-offs differently when it comes to certain laws. The statute prohibiting demonstrations on the Supreme Court grounds essentially insulates the Court's building and members in their own buffer zone.[146] When eminent personages, such as Supreme Court Justices, make public appearances on campuses and elsewhere, demonstrators and gawkers are often kept far from their

---

[143] Leslie Kendrick, *Disclosure and Its Discontents*, 27 J L & Pol 575, 594–95 (2012) (on many views of the First Amendment, effects of regulations on speech should be cause for concern).

[144] Larry A. Alexander, *Trouble on Track Two: Incidental Regulations of Speech and Free Speech Theory*, 44 Hastings L J 921, 929 (1993) ("[A]ll laws affect what gets said, by whom, to whom, and with what effect.").

[145] Id at 932 (it is impossible to assess the value of speech that has not been expressed); Kendrick, 27 J L & Pol at 575, 593–94 (cited in note 143) (measuring speech effects of laws is extremely difficult).

[146] 40 USC § 13k.

path, whether through permanent so-called "free speech zones" or through specialized security measures.[147] It would be interesting to know how the Justices would balance access and safety in such contexts against speakers' interests in their preferred methods of speech.

V. CONCLUSION

The notion of content discrimination is ultimately about identifying suspicious governmental action. This task is complicated by the facts that (1) the "real" objects behind governmental regulation are, on many levels, unknowable, and (2) everyone is suspicious of different things. To meet these problems, content discrimination doctrine has developed a series of rule-like proxies that attempt to triangulate legislative purpose in a somewhat predictable way. *McCullen*, like some cases before it, subjects this framework to the stress test of the abortion context, and, unsurprisingly, it shows some strain. With regard to both content discrimination analysis and content-neutral scrutiny, the opinions in *McCullen* show some Justices ready to jettison rule-like frameworks and rely upon their own sense of what the Massachusetts legislature did, or what effects it had. In this, the case demonstrates both the need for rules and their potential futility in highly polarized contexts. In the end, the Court seems no more able than the litigants to rise above the level of the sidewalks and their confusing, cacophonous din.

---

[147] See, e.g., Teresa Watanabe, *Students Challenge Free-Speech Rules on College Campuses*, LA Times (July 4, 2014), http://www.latimes.com/local/lanow/la-me-ln-free-speech-20140701 -story.html.

PAUL HORWITZ

THE RELIGIOUS GEOGRAPHY OF TOWN
OF GREECE v GALLOWAY

> To attempt to come to terms with American religious history
> apart from its geographical dimensions . . . is to risk missing
> something crucially important.[1]

Americans are obsessed with history. That's especially true for American lawyers, constitutional lawyers not least among them. Of course there are practical reasons for this obsession, including the age of the Constitution itself. As long as some form of originalism remains important to judicial or scholarly interpretation of the Constitution, moreover, there are strategic reasons for any constitutional lawyer to take an interest in historical questions. But history alone is an insufficient interpretive guide. Among other things, in a word, we might consider geography.

This is certainly true for the study of American religion and religious freedom. Martin Marty, a leading figure in that field, has noted "American religionists' . . . obsession with time over space"—

Paul Horwitz is Gordon Rosen Professor, University of Alabama School of Law.

AUTHOR'S NOTE: Jared Searls provided fine research assistance and the University of Alabama School of Law offered generous financial support. I am grateful to the participants in talks given on this paper at Emory Law School and Washington University School of Law in St. Louis. I thank Marc DeGirolami, Chad Flanders, Rick Garnett, Mark Rosen, Richard Schragger, and Steven Smith for comments on a draft.

[1] Edwin Scott Gaustad and Philip L. Barlow, *New Historical Atlas of Religion in America* xxii (Oxford, 2001).

with a temporal, rather than a spatial, understanding of American religion and religious pluralism.[2] The fixation with history is equally apparent in judicial decisions and legal scholarship dealing with church-
state law. Many of the key decisions of the United States Supreme
Court dealing with the Religion Clauses center on grand historical
narratives, as much mythical as real,[3] that purport to dictate the shape
of the law in this area.[4] Fueled both by the cases and by their own needs
and interests, many scholars are equally focused on the lessons history
holds for Religion Clause adjudication.[5]

   While many judges and legal scholars continue to focus rather
single-mindedly on history, scholars of American religion itself have
long since shifted focus. A half-century ago, the American religious
historian Sidney Mead famously observed: "Americans have never
had time to spare. What they did have during all their formative
years was space—organic, pragmatic space—the space of action."[6] In
modern scholarly lingo, Mead called on religious scholarship to take
a spatial turn:

> The story of America is the story of uprooted emigrant and immigrant
> people, ever moving rapidly onward through space so vast that space came
> to take precedence over time in the formation of their most cherished ide-
> als, chief of which has been the ideal of freedom. But since the freedom of
> space did not appeal to all in the same way, there was created a strange
> mingling of attitudes toward the predominant conception of freedom . . . .
> The "story of religion in America" must be reinterpreted in this general
> context.[7]

   Since then, a substantial body of scholarship has emerged that
examines religion—including both the past and the present of American religion—in *spatial* as well as temporal terms. In the description of
a leading text, "the lens of geography is useful in considering interactions between religion and diverse realms of human activity as ex-

---

[2] Martin E. Marty, *Religion and Republic: The American Circumstance* 198 (Beacon, 1987).

[3] See, for example, Alfred H. Kelly, *Clio and the Court: An Illicit Love Affair*, 1965 Supreme Court Review 119, 137–42.

[4] See, for example, *Reynolds v United States*, 98 US 145 (1878); *Everson v Board of Education of Ewing Township*, 330 US 1 (1947).

[5] See, for example, Symposium, *The (Re)turn to History in Religion Clause Law and Schol-arship*, 81 Notre Dame L Rev 1697 (2006).

[6] Sidney E. Mead, *The Lively Experiment: The Shaping of Christianity in America* 5 (Harper and Row, 1963).

[7] Id at 15.

pressed in social space."[8] As an "integrative" discipline (like law), geography "provides an effective framework for analyzing the connection of religious belief to other spheres of thought and action at diverse scales."[9]

Legal scholarship has shown some interest in taking the spatial turn.[10] It has made scattered appearances in constitutional scholarship.[11] With a few valuable exceptions, however,[12] and despite the spatial turn in American religious scholarship itself, law and religion scholars have not yet taken full advantage of the insights that a geographical orientation might offer their subject.

The Supreme Court's decision in *Town of Greece v Galloway*[13] offers a good reason to change course. In *Galloway*, the Supreme Court did two things. First, all of the Justices agreed that the Court should reaffirm the decision in *Marsh v Chambers*,[14] which upheld the Nebraska legislature's practice of offering opening prayers. Second, by a 5–4 vote, the Court applied *Marsh* to uphold a similar practice, one that included openly sectarian prayers, before meetings of a town board.[15]

---

[8] Roger W. Stump, *The Geography of Religion: Faith, Place, and Space* 6 (Rowman & Littlefield, 2008). For another introduction to the geography of religion, see Chris C. Park, *Sacred Worlds: Introduction to Geography and Religion* (Routledge, 1994). Key early work in the field of geography of religion includes David E. Sopher, *Geography of Religions* (Prentice-Hall, 1967), and Yi-Fu Tuan, *Humanistic Geography*, 66 Annals Ass'n Amer Geographers 271 (1976).

[9] Stump, *The Geography of Religion* at 6 (cited in note 8).

[10] See, for example, Nicholas Blomley, David Delaney, and Richard T. Ford, eds, *The Legal Geographies Reader* (Blackwell, 2001); Irus Braverman, Nicholas Blomley, David Delaney, and Alexandre Kedar, eds, *The Expanding Spaces of Law: A Timely Legal Geography* (Stanford, 2014).

[11] See, for example, Joseph Blocher, *Selling State Borders*, 162 U Pa L Rev 241 (2014); Allan Erbsen, *Constitutional Spaces*, 95 Minn L Rev 1168 (2011); Timothy Zick, *Constitutional Displacement*, 86 Wash U L Rev 515 (2009); Timothy Zick, *Speech Out of Doors: Preserving First Amendment Liberties in Public Places* (Cambridge, 2008).

[12] See especially Richard C. Schragger, *The Relative Irrelevance of the Establishment Clause*, 89 Tex L Rev 583 (2011); Adam M. Samaha, *Endorsement Retires: From Religious Symbols to Anti-Sorting Principles*, 2005 Supreme Court Review 135; Richard C. Schragger, *The Role of the Local in the Doctrine and Discourse of Religious Liberty*, 117 Harv L Rev 1810 (2004); Mark D. Rosen, *The Radical Possibility of Limited Community-Based Interpretation of the Constitution*, 43 Wm & Mary L Rev 927 (2002); Mark D. Rosen, *Our Nonuniform Constitution: Geographical Variations of Constitutional Requirements in the Aid of Community*, 77 Tex L Rev 1129 (1999). Although I disagree with many of his substantive conclusions, I am particularly indebted to Richard Schragger's important article on localism and the Religion Clauses, which had a great influence on Part III.B of this article.

[13] 134 S Ct 1811 (2014).

[14] 463 US 783 (1983).

[15] See *Galloway*, 134 S Ct at 1819–25.

From a historical perspective, *Galloway* was not terribly interesting. It did not add much more detail than *Marsh* itself provided. From a doctrinal perspective, *Galloway* was interesting in two respects. First, it was interesting for what it did *not* do. It did not do away with any of the Establishment Clause tests governing the use of religious speech or symbols by government. In particular, it did not, as has long been anticipated, deliver the coup de grâce to the endorsement test for Establishment Clause violations.[16] Second, the Court indicated that it would give history greater weight in future Establishment Clause cases. The majority opinion, written by Justice Anthony Kennedy, made clear that "it is not necessary to define the precise boundary of the Establishment Clause where history shows that the specific practice is permitted."[17] This is an important development; but, notwithstanding the excitement that greeted it,[18] it is not clear how far-reaching it will be.

Galloway is, however, an excellent subject for geographically inflected analysis. The extension of *Marsh* from state legislatures to individual town boards is not an immense step doctrinally, but it certainly is spatially. As Justice Elena Kagan noted in the case's principal dissenting opinion, it involves a very different set of factual and practical considerations than does legislative prayer in the state legislatures.[19] And those differences, when viewed through the lens of religious geography, present a good occasion to think about a number of perennial problems in American church-state relations and the law of the Establishment Clause.

Part I of this article offers a summary, interspersed with analysis, of *Town of Greece v Galloway*. Part II focuses on one aspect of the majority opinion and the principal dissent: the differences—and, in some respects, the striking similarities—in their competing visions of American religious pluralism. Part III offers an introduction to some basic animating concepts of religious geography, and examines *Galloway* from two geographical perspectives: the role of *region* in

---

[16] See Samaha, 2005 Supreme Court Review at 137 (cited in note 12).

[17] *Galloway*, 134 S Ct at 1819.

[18] See Eric Rassbach, *Town of Greece v Galloway: The Establishment Clause and the Rediscovery of History*, 2014 Cato S Ct Rev 71, 71 (2013–14) (arguing that *Galloway*, with its "embrace" of history, "marks a major inflection point in the development of the law of the Establishment Clause").

[19] *Galloway*, 134 S Ct at 1846–47 (Kagan, J, dissenting) (comparing and contrasting the practices in the Nebraska state legislature and at town of Greece board meetings).

the study of American religious pluralism and its influence on the opinions in the case, and the failure of the majority to fully confront the role of the *local* in the life and law of the Establishment Clause.

I. Galloway: Five Opinions in Search of a Church-State Settlement

The town of Greece, in Monroe County, New York, dates back to 1822.[20] Once an agricultural community, today it is a "residential suburb" of the neighboring upstate city of Rochester, with a 2010 population of about 96,000.[21]

In 1999, John Auberger, the town supervisor, added opening prayers to the town's monthly board meetings. The move was inspired by Auberger's experience with prayers in the county legislature.[22] Auberger wrote that he found those prayers to be "a thoughtful practice," a "kind of humbling of ourselves, before making decisions that would ultimately impact our whole community."[23]

The town had no written prayer policy. Town officials said anyone could give the invocation, including non-Christians and atheists; but the town did not publicize the opportunity to deliver invocations.[24] Before 2007, the employees responsible for finding prayer-givers relied variously on a chamber of commerce directory of religious organizations, a list of those who had previously given the invocation, the list of religious groups in the local weekly newspaper, and some additional notes.[25] One employee testified that she believed she was only supposed to invite individuals and groups "located within the Town of Greece."[26]

A map produced during the litigation showed that most of the groups on the lists maintained by the town of Greece were located within its borders. It showed no Jewish synagogues, Mormon temples, or Baha'i groups within those borders. A Buddhist temple and a

---

[20] See The Town of Greece, *All About Greece*, online at http://greeceny.gov/aboutgreece.

[21] Id.

[22] See *Galloway*, 134 S Ct at 1816.

[23] John Auberger, *The Problem with Prayer in Greece, NY*, 7 Faith and Justice 14, 14 (2014), online at http://www.alliancedefendingfreedom.org/content/docs/FnJ/FnJ-7.1.pdf. *Faith and Justice* is a publication of the Alliance Defending Freedom, which represented the town of Greece in the legislative prayer litigation.

[24] See *Galloway v Town of Greece*, 732 F Supp 2d 195, 197–200 (WDNY 2010).

[25] Id at 197–200.

[26] Id at 200.

Jehovah's Witnesses church were located in Greece, but neither appeared on the town's lists.[27]

All the prayers given at town board meetings between 1999 and 2007 were Christian.[28] Many referred to Jesus Christ, or ended the prayer "in Jesus' name."[29] For the most part, however, the substance of the prayers was fairly standard for such civic occasions.[30] The town offered no guidance to the prayer-givers about the content of the invocations and did not review the prayers in advance.[31]

The plaintiffs, Susan Galloway and Linda Stephens, complained to the board about its invocation practices in the fall of 2007. Following those complaints, the town invited representatives of the Jewish and Baha'i faiths to offer the invocation, and a Wiccan priestess asked and was permitted to do so as well.[32] The plaintiffs nevertheless filed suit, alleging that the practice violated the Establishment Clause by "preferring Christians over other prayer givers and by sponsoring sectarian prayers."[33] They sought an order limiting invocations to "inclusive and ecumenical prayers."[34]

The district court upheld the practice. It found insufficient evidence that the town had "intentionally excluded non-Christians from giving prayers at Town Board meetings."[35] The overwhelmingly Christian nature of the invocations simply "reflect[ed] the fact that there are comparatively few non-Christian organizations in the Town."[36] The prayers were not required to be strictly nonsectarian, and did not improperly engage in religious proselytization.[37]

The Second Circuit reversed, in an opinion by Judge Guido Calabresi.[38] Reading the decision in *Marsh* in light of subsequent

---

[27] Id at 203.

[28] *Galloway*, 134 S Ct at 1816.

[29] *Galloway*, 732 F Supp 2d at 203.

[30] A large sample of invocations is provided in Joint Appendix, *Town of Greece v Galloway*, 2013 WL 3935056, *26a-143a (2013).

[31] *Galloway*, 134 S Ct at 1816.

[32] Id at 1817.

[33] Id.

[34] Id.

[35] *Galloway*, 732 F Supp 2d at 217.

[36] Id at 239.

[37] See id at 241–43.

[38] *Galloway v Town of Greece*, 681 F3d 20 (2d Cir 2012).

glosses placed on it, the court concluded that while "legislative prayer does not *necessarily* run afoul of the Establishment Clause,"[39] prayers that "invok[e] particular sectarian beliefs *may*, on the basis of those references alone, violate the Establishment Clause."[40] It applied a form of endorsement test, asking "whether the town's practice, viewed in its totality by an ordinary, reasonable observer, conveyed the view that the town favored or disfavored certain religious beliefs."[41]

A combination of factors doomed the practice. First, whatever its intent, the town's practice had not "*result*[*ed*] in a perspective that is substantially neutral amongst creeds."[42] In particular, its failure to look outside the town borders when searching for prayer-givers ignored the fact that the town's residents might belong to faiths "that are not represented by a place of worship within the town." Second, given the volume of sectarian prayers at the meetings, the town was obliged to warn the prayer-givers not to promote their own faith or disparage others.[43] Finally, the town had not adequately policed the format of the invocations; they often appeared to be given directly to the public on *behalf* of the board, with the expectation that the public would participate in them, rather than given *to* the board.[44]

The Supreme Court reversed, in an opinion by Justice Kennedy. There was no chance that the Court would overrule *Marsh v Chambers*.[45] The real question in the case was whether the Court would eliminate the endorsement test,[46] a version of which Judge Calabresi

---

[39] Id at 26.

[40] Id at 27 (emphasis added), discussing *County of Allegheny v ACLU Greater Pittsburgh Chapter*, 492 US 573 (1989).

[41] *Galloway*, 681 F3d at 29.

[42] Id at 31 (emphasis added); see also id at 32 ("We ascribe no religious animus to the town or its leaders. . . . But when one creed dominates others—regardless of a town's intentions—constitutional concerns come to the fore.").

[43] Id at 32.

[44] Id at 32–34.

[45] Strikingly, the Obama administration's brief in the Supreme Court sided with the town of Greece and did not urge reconsideration of *Marsh*. See Brief for the United States as Amicus Curiae Supporting Petitioner, *Town of Greece v Galloway*, 2013 WL 3990880 (2013); Nelson Tebbe and Micah Schwartzman, *The Puzzle of Town of Greece v Galloway*, SCOTUSblog, Sept. 24, 2013, online at http://www.scotusblog.com/2013/09/symposium-the-puzzle-of-town-of-greece-v-galloway/.

[46] See, for example, *Lynch v Donnelly*, 465 US 668, 687–95 (1984) (O'Connor, J, concurring); *County of Allegheny*, 492 US at 574; *Santa Fe Independent School District v Doe*, 530 US

had employed in his decision for the Second Circuit. Often criticized,[47] the test was widely predicted to be on its way out after the departure of its creator, Justice Sandra Day O'Connor.[48] That is not the Roberts Court's typical approach, however,[49] and it is not what it did here, although there is at least one significant doctrinal move in the majority opinion.

That move came in the Court's discussion of *Marsh v Chambers*. *Marsh* has long been treated as "carving out an exception" to standard Establishment Clause tests, which could be read as prohibiting legislative prayer.[50] Indeed, for those who dislike *Marsh*, thinking of it in those terms—as a narrow "historical easement" over the usual terms of Establishment Clause law—is a form of damage control, which helps limit *Marsh*'s application in other cases.[51]

Justice Kennedy rejected this account. Recourse to additional Establishment Clause doctrine was "unnecessary" in *Marsh*, he wrote, because "history supported the conclusion that legislative invocations are compatible with the Establishment Clause."[52] He continued:

290, 308 (2000); *McCreary County v ACLU*, 545 US 844, 860 (2005) (folding endorsement considerations into a variant of the test in *Lemon v Kurtman*, 403 US 602 (1971)).

[47] Classic critical treatments include Steven D. Smith, *Symbols, Perceptions, and Doctrinal Illusions: Establishment Neutrality and the "No Endorsement" Test*, 86 Mich L Rev 266 (1987), and Jesse H. Choper, *The Endorsement Test: Its Status and Desirability*, 18 J L & Pol 499 (2002). For defenses of the endorsement test, see, for example, William P. Marshall, *The Concept of Offensiveness in Establishment and Free Exercise Jurisprudence*, 66 Ind L J 351, 355 (1991); Alan Brownstein, *A Decent Respect for Religious Liberty and Religious Equality: Justice O'Connor's Interpretation of the Religion Clauses of the First Amendment*, 32 McGeorge L Rev 837 (2001).

[48] See, for example, Samaha, 2005 Supreme Court Review at 137 (cited in note 12); Erwin Chemerinsky, *The Future of Constitutional Law*, 34 Cap U L Rev 647, 665–66 (2006).

[49] For an interesting discussion, see Richard M. Re, *Narrowing Precedent in the Supreme Court*, 114 Colum L Rev 1861 (2014) (discussing the virtues of the Supreme Court "pruning but not abolishing" its precedents); see also id at 1863 n 2 (collecting examples of criticisms of the Roberts Court for what some have called "stealth overruling" of Supreme Court precedent); Barry Friedman, *The Wages of Stealth Overruling (with Particular Attention to Miranda v Arizona)*, 99 Georgetown L J 1 (2010).

[50] *Marsh*, 463 US at 796 (Brennan, J, dissenting). I have elsewhere described *Marsh* and similar cases as "historical easements" over the Establishment Clause. See Paul Horwitz, *The Agnostic Age: Law, Religion, and the Constitution* 233–34 (Oxford, 2011).

[51] Horwitz, *The Agnostic Age* at 233–34 (cited in note 50) (discussing legislative prayer and other practices, such as the use of the motto "In God We Trust" on coins or the phrase "one nation under God" in the Pledge of Allegiance, in those terms). See also *Marsh*, 463 US at 795 (Brennan, J, dissenting) (suggesting that the Court's "limited [historical] rationale should pose little threat to the overall fate of the Establishment Clause").

[52] *Galloway*, 134 S Ct at 1818.

> *Marsh* must not be understood as permitting a practice that would amount to a constitutional violation if not for its historical foundation. The case teaches instead that the Establishment Clause must be interpreted by reference to historical practices and understandings. . . . *Marsh* stands for the proposition that it is not necessary to define the precise boundary of the Establishment Clause where history shows that the specific practice is permitted. . . . The Court's inquiry, then, must be to determine whether the prayer practice in the town of Greece fits within the tradition long followed in Congress and the state legislatures.[53]

This is hardly the end of the Court's analysis. Indeed, the remainder of the opinion refers more often to current doctrine than to historical materials. It is unlikely that the Court will abandon its standard repertoire of Religion Clause tests. It is thus too early to say that *Galloway* "marks a major inflection point in the development of the law of the Establishment Clause."[54]

But it *is* surely true that the decision signals an important change in "the treatment of history in Establishment Clause cases."[55] Rather than treat *Marsh* as a historically based exception to the doctrinal rules that govern most Establishment Clause cases, it treats Establishment Clause *doctrine* as a supplement. That doctrine enters in only where history runs out. Any public religious practice that is well settled in American history should need no further doctrinal justification.[56]

The likely target of this passage is a narrow set of governmental practices: those that are generally associated with American civil religion. Those practices have been the source of recent political and ju-

---

[53] Id at 1819. The Court has made a similar move in some recent free speech cases. See *United States v Stevens*, 559 US 460, 471 (2010) (holding that the Court will not recognize new categories of so-called "low-value speech" unless the proposed category involves "historically unprotected" speech); see also *Brown v Entertainment Merchants Association*, 131 S Ct 2729, 2734 (2011) (to avoid the application of the rule of content neutrality, government must provide "persuasive evidence that a novel restriction on content is part of a long (if heretofore unrecognized) tradition of proscription"). One commentator has called this a "historical-categorical" approach to low-value speech doctrine. *Leading Cases*, 126 Harv L Rev 196, 202 (2012). See also Paul Horwitz, *The First Amendment's Epistemological Problem*, 87 Wash L Rev 445, 460–61 (2012) (discussing this phenomenon).

[54] Rassbach, 2014 Cato S Ct Rev at 71 (cited in note 18).

[55] Id at 89.

[56] See also *Galloway*, 134 S Ct at 1834 (Alito, J, concurring) ("[T]he Court of Appeals appeared to base its decision on one of the Establishment Clause 'tests' set out in the opinions of this Court, but if there is any inconsistency between any of those tests and the historical practice of legislative prayer, the inconsistency calls into question the validity of the test, not the historic practice.") (citation omitted).

risprudential controversy, such as the litigation over the recitation in public schools of the Pledge of Allegiance.

As the Court's abortive and unconvincing attempt to address that issue shows,[57] there is general agreement on the Court that "civil religion" practices should not be disturbed, either because they are actually constitutional or because striking them down would be too politically costly. But there has been little agreement on *how* to uphold them. The result, in the Pledge case at least, was a splintered set of opinions, with no consensus on anything besides the result.

This is the probable significance of the "historical-categorical" approach announced in *Galloway*. It provides a blueprint for rejecting at least some challenges to civil religion practices. That seems to be the import of a later passage in the opinion, in which Kennedy writes:

> The prayer opportunity in this case must be evaluated against the backdrop of historical practice. As a practice that has long endured, legislative prayer has become part of our heritage and tradition, similar to the Pledge of Allegiance, inaugural prayer, or the recitation of "God save the United States and this honorable Court" at the opening of this Court's sessions.[58]

In short, and despite Kennedy's insistence elsewhere in *Galloway* that the imposition of civil religion is forbidden by the Constitution,[59] the historical approach announced by *Galloway* provides a one-size-fits-all method that will allow the Court to easily reject future challenges to the standard practices of American civil religion, without repeating the difficulties that arose in the Pledge case. Never mind that this passage casually mixes together genuinely long-established practices, such as prayer at inaugural ceremonies, with far more recent practices, such as the insertion of religious language into the Pledge.[60] The Court appears to have settled on a way to uphold these practices on historical grounds.[61]

---

[57] See *Elk Grove Unified School Dist. v Newdow*, 542 US 1 (2004) (holding, on novel grounds, that the plaintiff's father lacked standing to challenge the state law requirement of a teacher-led Pledge of Allegiance on his own behalf and as his daughter's next friend).

[58] *Galloway*, 134 S Ct at 1825.

[59] See id at 1822.

[60] See, for example, Act of June 14, 1954, ch 297, 68 Stat 249 (adding the words "under God" to the Pledge of Allegiance); Steven B. Gey, *"Under God," the Pledge of Allegiance, and Other Constitutional Trivia*, 81 NC L Rev 1865, 1875–79 (2003) (noting the Cold War origins and purposes of the alteration of the Pledge).

[61] *Galloway*, 134 S Ct at 1819.

From here, the Court proceeded to reject the plaintiffs' two primary claims. First, the Court flatly rejected the plaintiffs' "insistence on nonsectarian or ecumenical prayer as a single, fixed standard" in legislative prayer cases.[62] Historically, this standard was inconsistent with a long practice of sectarian references in legislative prayers in Congress.[63] Doctrinally, the Court rejected as dictum a suggestion to the contrary in the Court's endorsement-oriented decision in the holiday display case, *County of Allegheny*.[64]

The Court rejected the plaintiffs' argument that the town board should have reviewed the invocations in advance or provided mandatory guidelines for their content. General Establishment Clause principles bar the government from weighing in on questions of religious truth[65] or involving itself deeply in religious matters and, thus, approving or disapproving particular religious messages.[66]

The opinion also described the nature and purpose of acceptable legislative prayer practices. Kennedy's language here was sweeping, prescriptive, and faintly pious, with echoes of the thin public religiosity of the Eisenhower era.[67] Legislative prayers are "meant to lend gravity to the occasion and reflect values long part of the Nation's heritage."[68] Proper legislative prayer "is solemn and respectful in tone [and] invites lawmakers to reflect upon shared ideals and common ends before they embark upon the fractious business of governing."[69] As long as such practices "provide particular means to

---

[62] Id at 1820.

[63] Id at 1821, 1823–24.

[64] Id at 1821–22, discussing *County of Allegheny*, 463 US at 603 (arguing that "[t]he legislative prayers involved in *Marsh* did not violate this principle [that government practices cannot demonstrate allegiance to a particular religious sect or creed] because the particular chaplain had removed all references to Christ.") (quotation marks and citation omitted).

[65] See generally Horwitz, *The Agnostic Age* (cited in note 50); Andrew Koppelman, *Defending American Religious Neutrality* (Harvard, 2013).

[66] *Galloway*, 134 S Ct at 1821–22, citing, among other cases, the Court's recent decision in *Hosanna-Tabor Evangelical Lutheran Church & School v EEOC*, 132 S Ct 694, 705–06 (2012).

[67] See Gary Scott Smith, *Faith and the Presidency: From George Washington to George W. Bush* 254 (Oxford, 2006) (quoting Eisenhower's famous statement, "Our form of government has no sense unless it is founded in a deeply felt religious faith[,] and I don't care what it is."). Mark Massa calls this an era in which religion in American public life entailed "high visibility and almost contentless theology." Mark S. Massa, *Catholics and American Culture: Fulton Sheen, Dorothy Day, and the Notre Dame Football Team* 130 (Crossroads, 1999) (emphasis omitted). For discussion, see Paul Horwitz, *Religion and American Politics: Three Views of the Cathedral*, 39 U Memphis L Rev 973, 978 (2009).

[68] *Galloway*, 134 S Ct at 1823.

[69] Id.

universal ends," it doesn't matter that individual prayers are "given in the name of Jesus, Allah, or Jehovah."[70]

The Court imposed *some* limits. A couple of the invocations given at town board meetings in Greece fell outside the acceptable range of civic piety directed at "universal ends." One "lamented that other towns did not have 'God-fearing' leaders."[71] Another, which was delivered after the plaintiffs had complained about Greece's practice, criticized the objectors as "a 'minority' who are 'ignorant of the history of this country.'"[72] Kennedy conceded that such prayers "strayed from the rationale set out in *Marsh*,"[73] but held that "*Marsh* . . . requires an inquiry into the prayer opportunity as a whole, rather than into the contents of a single prayer."[74] Viewed as a whole, the invocations in the town of Greece did not demonstrate "a pattern of prayers that over time denigrate, proselytize, or betray an impermissible government purpose."[75] But he warned:

> If the course and practice over time shows that the invocations denigrate nonbelievers or religious minorities, threaten damnation, or preach conversion, many present may consider the prayer to fall short of the desire to elevate the purpose of the occasion and to unite lawmakers in their common effort. That circumstance would present a different case than the one presently before the Court.[76]

This passage accomplishes three things. First, by demanding proof of a *pattern* of impermissible prayer practices, it raises the bar for plaintiffs challenging legislative prayers. Second, notwithstanding the opinion's stated preference for historical certainty over the kind of ambiguity and discretion that critics attributed to the endorsement test,[77] it gives a reviewing court a substantial amount of discretion.[78] Third, it allows the Court, in future cases, to step in and impose its particular vision of legislative prayers, and their unifying civic pur-

---

[70] Id.

[71] Id at 1824 (citation omitted).

[72] Id (citation omitted).

[73] Id.

[74] Id (citing *Marsh*, 463 US at 794–95).

[75] Id.

[76] Id at 1823.

[77] See, for example, Choper, 18 J L & Pol at 520 (cited in note 47).

[78] Not incidentally, it also makes a hash of Justice Kennedy's insistence that the Court stay out of the job of "supervisor[ ] and censor[ ] of religious speech." *Galloway*, 134 S Ct at 1822.

pose, against outliers.[79] Given that *Galloway* makes clear that legislative prayers are permitted not only in Congress and the fifty states but in a vast number of local bodies as well,[80] outliers there will surely be.

Alabama provides a hell of an example. The Alabama Public Service Commission is a statewide elected body that oversees rate-setting for various utilities. Its president, Twinkle Cavanaugh, invited a friend, a Baptist minister, to give an invocation at one meeting in which he first "poll[ed] those present to see who believed in God," and then directly addressed the Lord: "We've taken you out of our schools and out of our prayers. We have murdered your children. We've said it's okay to have same-sex marriage. We have sinned and ask once again that you forgive us for our sins."[81] Cavanaugh forcefully defended the prayer.[82]

It is safe to say that this kind of prayer is unlikely to be unusual, for Cavanaugh and at least some other elected officials and bodies. At least some local politicians will surely, from time to time, see invocations as an opportunity to practice a divisive form of local politics, not to ensure that "people of many faiths [are] united in a community of tolerance and devotion."[83] Although the requirement of

---

[79] See, for example, Richard H. Pildes, *Is the Supreme Court a "Majoritarian" Institution?*, 2010 Supreme Court Review 103 (agreeing with the general conclusion that the Court is often responsive to majoritarian views but warning against excesses in this scholarship); Adam Samaha, *Low Stakes and Constitutional Interpretation*, 13 U Pa J Const L 305, 309 (2010); Barry Friedman, *The Will of the People: How Public Opinion Has Influenced the Supreme Court and Shaped the Meaning of the Constitution* (Farrar, Straus, 2009); Michael J. Klarman, *From Jim Crow to Civil Rights: The Supreme Court and the Struggle for Racial Equality* 453 (Oxford, 2004); Robert A. Dahl, *Decision-Making in a Democracy: The Supreme Court as a National Policy-Maker*, 6 J Pub L 279 (1957).

[80] See, for example, Marie Wicks, *Prayer Is Prologue: The Impact of Town of Greece on the Constitutionality of Deliberative Public Body Prayer at the Start of School Board Meetings* (working paper 2014), online at http://papers.ssrn.com/sol3/papers.cfm?abstract_id=2547761.

[81] Hunter Stuart, *Alabama Government Agency Holds Prayer Against Abortion, Gay Marriage*, Huffington Post, July 25, 2013, online at http://www.huffingtonpost.com/2013/07/25/alabama-prayer-gay-marriage_n_3651756.html.

[82] Kristen Hwang, *Twinkle Cavanaugh Stands by Controversial Prayer at Public Service Commission Meeting*, AL.com, July 31, 2013, online at http://blog.al.com/breaking/2013/07/twinkle_cavanaugh_adresses_pra.html.

[83] *Galloway*, 134 S Ct at 1823. See also Paul Horwitz, *Learning from Bedrosian, Cavanaugh, and Town of Greece v Galloway*, PrawfsBlawg, May 7, 2014, online at http://prawfsblawg.blogs.com/prawfsblawg/2014/05/learning-from-bedrosian-cavanaugh-and-town-of-greece-v-galloway.html; Christopher C. Lund, *Legislative Prayer Goes Back to the Supreme Court*, Slate, Aug 15, 2013, online at http://www.slate.com/articles/news_and_politics/jurisprudence/2013/08/the_supreme_court_will_have_another_chance_to_decide_when_government_can.html (noting, among other examples, the case of a small California town that considered ban-

a *practice* of doing so makes it harder to win such claims, *Galloway* makes clear that at least some members of the Court would gladly intervene in such cases. Any apparent federalism or experimentalism in the *Galloway* opinion is skin deep.

The Court concluded its treatment of the "sectarian prayer" issue with another significant statement. It rejected the view of the Court of Appeals that the town of Greece had erred because its process of selecting prayer-givers, which "was limited by the town's practice of inviting clergy almost exclusively from within the town's borders," resulted in a massive "preponderance of Christian clergy" giving the invocations at board meetings.[84] Justice Kennedy wrote:

> The town made reasonable efforts to identify all of the congregations located within its borders . . . . That nearly all of the congregations in town turned out to be Christian does not reflect an aversion or bias on the part of town leaders against minority faiths. So long as the town maintains a policy of nondiscrimination, the Constitution does not require it to search beyond its borders for non-Christian prayer givers in an effort to achieve religious balancing.[85]

I return to this point below.[86]

The second major argument by the plaintiffs relied on Justice Kennedy's expansive version of the coercion test.[87] Speaking only for himself, Chief Justice Roberts, and Justice Alito, Justice Kennedy rejected the contention that Greece's practice "coerces participation by nonadherents."[88] He emphasized that the coercion test is "a fact-sensitive one." But, in keeping with the opinion's enhanced attention to history, he also stressed that "[t]he prayer opportunity in this case must be evaluated against the backdrop of historical practice," including its finding that "legislative prayer has become part of our heritage and tradition, part of our expressive idiom."[89]

---

ning denominational prayers; "[i]n response, a citizens' group purchased billboard space on nearby highways and threatened to display each council member's vote under one of two columns—"For Jesus" and "Against Jesus."); Christopher C. Lund, *Legislative Prayer and the Secret Costs of Religious Endorsements*, 94 Minn L Rev 972, 974–76, 1045–46 (2010).

[84] *Galloway*, 681 F3d at 31.

[85] *Galloway*, 134 S Ct at 1824.

[86] See Part III.B.

[87] See generally *Lee v Weisman*, 505 US 577 (1991).

[88] *Galloway*, 134 S Ct at 1824.

[89] Id at 1825.

Although the facts showed that the invocations were often "directed . . . squarely at the citizens" and invited their personal participation,[90] Kennedy asserted: "The principal audience for these invocations is not, indeed, the public but lawmakers themselves."[91] Absent a "pattern and practice of ceremonial, legislative prayer . . . to coerce or intimidate others," he refused to find coercion in the simple fact that some audience members were offended or felt "excluded or disrespected" by the prayer practice: "Offense . . . does not equate to coercion."[92] Unlike the graduation ceremony in *Lee v Weisman*, the audience here was composed mostly of adults; they were free to enter or leave at any time, or to skip the invocation entirely.[93]

Justice Alito, joined by Justice Scalia, filed a concurrence responding to Justice Kagan's dissent, which it accused of combining a "niggling" central complaint with sweeping rhetoric that could have broad effects.[94] Kagan's criticisms of Greece's prayer practice, Alito complained, would lead logically to the conclusion that "prayer is *never* permissible prior to meetings of local government legislative bodies."[95] By rejecting many common practices, he argued, the dissent would, at best, permit "perfunctory and hidden-away prayer" by legislative bodies, and at worst lead litigation-averse local gov-

---

[90] Id at 1848 (Kagan, J, dissenting).

[91] Id at 1825. Again signaling his potential willingness to act in other cases, he added, "The analysis would be different if *town board members* directed the public to participate in the prayers, singled out dissidents for opprobrium, or indicated that their decisions might be influenced by a person's acquiescence in the prayer opportunity." Id at 1826 (emphasis added). Presumably, given the careful use of language here, no constitutional violation would occur if a *prayer-giver* "directed the public to participate" or castigated "dissidents" in the audience. If this happened habitually, however, one assumes Justice Kennedy might act.

[92] Id at 1826.

[93] *Galloway*, 134 S Ct at 1827. Curiously, Justice Kennedy closed his discussion of the coercion argument with a flat contradiction of an earlier statement in the same section of the opinion. He had previously said legislative prayers were primarily intended not for the public but for the legislators, "who may find that a moment of prayer or quiet reflection sets the mind to a higher purpose and thereby eases the task of governing." Now, however, he described ceremonial prayers as having the "purpose and effect of acknowledg[ing] religious leaders and the institutions they represent"—like some kind of introduction of the special guests at a club banquet—not of excluding nonbelievers. See id at 1825, 1827. Not much turns on this inconsistency, but it reflects poorly on the coherence of the opinion.

[94] Id at 1829, 1831 (Alito, J, concurring).

[95] Id at 1831.

ernmental bodies to treat "local government [as] a religion-free zone."[96]

More directly than Kennedy, Alito also stressed the importance of the fact that local legislative bodies have more limited resources than Congress or state legislatures, and that their prayer practices will reflect this. The dissent complained that the town had done an inadequate job of seeking invocations by representatives of different faiths. For Alito, this boiled down to the view that "[t]he town's clerical employees did a bad job in compiling the list of potential guest chaplains."[97] But whatever failings the town's employees had manifested were "at worse careless, and . . . not done with discriminatory intent."[98] With greater care, the employee might have "realized that the town's Jewish residents attended synagogues on the Rochester side of the border" and added those temples to the invitation list.[99] The Court should not make a federal case out of the failure to do so.

Similarly, local clergy lack the experience of the pros in Congress or the state legislatures. If the prayer-givers here faced the public rather than the board or began their invocations with "Let us pray," Alito said, they were simply behaving in a way that is "commonplace and for many clergy, I suspect, almost reflexive."[100] Tellingly, he exclaimed, "If prayer is not allowed at meetings with those characteristics, local government legislative bodies, unlike their national and state counterparts, cannot begin their meetings with such a prayer" at all.[101] Alito argued that the Court should recognize the "informal, imprecise way" in which "small and medium-sized units of local government" work. Provided that it did not act with discriminatory intent, "then a unit of local government should not be held to have violated the First Amendment simply because its procedure for lining up guest chaplains does not comply in all respects with what might be termed a 'best practices' standard."[102] In short,

---

[96] Id at 1831, 1832.

[97] Id at 1830.

[98] Id at 1831 (Alito, J, concurring).

[99] Id.

[100] Id at 1832.

[101] Id.

[102] Id at 1831.

given the importance of legislative prayer, the Court should cut local officials some slack in their implementation of prayer policies.

Justice Thomas, joined in part by Justice Scalia, filed a concurrence to reiterate his position that "the Establishment Clause is 'best understood as a federalism provision'" that applies to Congress and allows individual state establishments of religion.[103] Even if the Establishment Clause were properly read as having been incorporated against the states, he argued, the result here should not change, because the conduct at issue bore "no resemblance to the coercive state establishments that existed at the founding."[104]

Justice Kagan, joined by Justices Ginsburg, Breyer, and Sotomayor, filed the principal dissent in the case.[105] Like the majority, her opinion reflects a particular vision of "the" American church-state settlement, and indeed of American political identity itself.[106] She announces it in an extended passage at the outset of the dissent:

> Our Constitution promises that [Americans] may worship in their own way, without fear of penalty or danger, and that in itself is a momentous offering. Yet our Constitution makes a commitment still more remarkable—that however those individuals worship, they will count as full and equal American citizens. A Christian, a Jew, a Muslim (and so forth)—each stands in the same relationship with her country, with her state and local communities, and with every level and body of government. So that when each person performs the duties or seeks the benefits of citizenship, she does so not as an adherent to one or another religion, but simply as an American.[107]

---

[103] Id at 1835 (Thomas, J, concurring in part and concurring in the judgment), quoting *Newdow*, 542 US at 50.

[104] *Galloway*, 134 S Ct at 1837 (Thomas, J, concurring in part and concurring in the judgment).

[105] Justice Breyer filed a short solo dissent as well to "emphasize several factors that I believe underlie the conclusion that, on the particular facts of this case, the town's prayer practice violated the Establishment Clause." Id at 1839 (Breyer, J, dissenting). For present purposes, the most significant factor pointed to in his opinion was the town's decision to "limit[ ] its list of clergy almost exclusively to representatives of houses of worship situated within Greece's town limits," despite the proximity of houses of worship, such as several Jewish temples, "just outside its borders, in the adjacent city of Rochester." Id at 1839, 1840. As a result, "although it is a community of several faiths, its prayer givers were almost exclusively persons of a single faith." Id at 1841.

[106] See Part II.

[107] *Galloway*, 134 S Ct at 1841 (Kagan, J, dissenting); see also id at 1851 ("In this country, when citizens go before the government, they go not as Christians or Muslims or Jews (or what have you), but just as Americans (or here, as Grecians)"), 1854 ("When the citizens of this country approach their government, they do so only as Americans, not as members of one faith or another").

Strikingly, Justice Kagan quickly disclaimed any interest in revisiting the Court's decision in *Marsh v Chambers*.[108] This represented a departure from her liberal predecessors on the Court, three of whom dissented in *Marsh*.[109] Justice Brennan, for example, argued in *Marsh* that legislative prayer by *any* state legislature violated the Establishment Clause and was "not saved either by its history or by any of the other considerations suggested in the Court's opinion."[110] In contrast, Justice Kagan asserted that *Marsh* lends to legislative prayer "a distinctive constitutional warrant by virtue of tradition," and declared that the Court was right to uphold Nebraska's practice.[111]

Nevertheless, Kagan argued, a town board meeting differs from state legislative proceedings. Individual members of the public can interact with board members, "often on highly individualized matters."[112] A different standard must perforce apply.[113] The board must "exercise special care to ensure that the prayers offered are inclusive—that they respect each and every member of the community as an equal citizen."[114] This, Greece's town board failed to do. Its prayers were directed at the public, not the board members, and those prayers were too "explicitly Christian."[115] These factors "remove this case from the protective ambit of *Marsh* and the history on which it relied."[116] It is allowed to have prayers, but it must "take especial care to ensure that the prayers . . . seek to include rather than serve to divide."[117]

In practical terms, this means that one of two things ought to have happened here. The town could have issued prayer-givers advance instructions to "speak in nonsectarian terms, common to diverse religious groups."[118] Or it could have allowed sectarian prayer, *if* it

---

[108] Id at 1841–42.

[109] See *Marsh*, 463 US at 795 (Brennan, J, dissenting) (joined by Justice Marshall), 822 (Stevens, J, dissenting).

[110] Id at 796 (Brennan, J, dissenting).

[111] *Galloway*, 134 S Ct at 1845 (Kagan, J, dissenting).

[112] Id.

[113] Id at 1849 (town board must meet its own set of "constitutional requirements").

[114] Id at 1845.

[115] Id at 1848.

[116] Id at 1849 (Kagan, J, dissenting).

[117] Id at 1850.

[118] Id at 1851.

took care to "invite[ ] clergy of many faiths to serve as chaplains."[119] This makes it sound as if Kagan is concerned only with *process*—as if a good-faith effort to invite speakers of different faiths to give the invocation would "transform[ ]" "even sectarian prayer" into something constitutional.[120] A footnote in her dissent, however, suggests that the town must also guarantee a fair *result* where sectarian prayers are involved.[121] In any event, Kagan argued, the town here fell short of *any* acceptable process or result. The majority, she charged in closing, failed to properly appreciate "the multiplicity of Americans' religious commitments, along with the challenge they can pose to the project— the distinctively American project—of creating one from the many, and governing all as united."[122]

II. KENNEDY, KAGAN, AND "THE" AMERICAN RULE OF RELIGIOUS PLURALISM

Kennedy and Kagan agreed that *Galloway* called for "fact-sensitive" analysis.[123] Moreover, there was little significant disagreement between them as to interpretive method. Both agreed that history and tradition were the primary interpretive tool here.[124] One might therefore conclude that the disagreement in *Galloway* was mostly fact driven. But there is more to it than that.

The true fundamental disagreement between them concerns the competing visions of American religious pluralism that animate their opinions. It is this disagreement that helps us properly understand *Galloway*. A consideration of that disagreement leads in turn to the broader questions of religious geography that are the focus of this

---

[119] Id.

[120] Id.

[121] Id at 1845 n 2 (Kagan, J, dissenting) ("[I]n this citizen-centered venue, government officials must take steps to *ensure*—as none of Greece's Board members ever did—that opening prayers are inclusive of different faiths, rather than always identified with a single religion."). See also id at 1851 (suggesting that, under conditions in which sectarian prayer is permitted, "one month a clergy member refers to Jesus, and the next to Allah or Jehovah," and so on).

[122] Id at 1853.

[123] Id at 1825; see also id at 1838 (Breyer, J, dissenting), 1851–52 (Kagan, J, dissenting).

[124] See, for example, id at 1845 (Kagan, J, dissenting) ("I agree with the majority that the issue here is 'whether the prayer practice in the Town of Greece fits within the tradition long followed in Congress and the state legislatures.'") (quoting *Galloway*, 134 S Ct at 1819).

article. Those larger questions also ultimately offer insights into two more opinions in this case, those of Justices Thomas and Alito.

It is worth stressing first what the majority opinion and the principal dissent have in *common*.[125] As distant as they are on many points of law and fact, they share a common denominator: both are monistic and nationalist in orientation. In other words, each opinion presents a single vision of American religious pluralism, one that is meant to apply uniformly across the United States.

For Justice Kennedy, the vision is one of active, public, but friendly *American* religiosity, an American religiosity that is in equal measure hallowed and hollowed by tradition. That it is public, and that it may be active—full-throated in tone, sectarian in content—is clear from his opinion. He treats legislative prayer with great approval, calling it a "benign acknowledgment of religion's role in society."[126] He insists on the value of allowing chaplains at official events "to express themselves in a religious idiom."[127] That idiom can be sectarian, not just "generic."[128] People are entitled to use public proceedings as an opportunity to "show respect for the divine in all aspects of their lives and being."[129]

Thus, prayer isn't just permissible: it is a positive good. But it is a particular kind of public good. It serves an essentially civic purpose. It is about unifying the nation, albeit through sectarian language, and hallowing the public affairs of a democratic republic. It "lends gravity to public business, reminds lawmakers to transcend petty differences in pursuit of a higher degree, and expresses a common aspiration to a just and peaceful society."[130] There may be an element of religion for religion's sake in these prayers. But in Kennedy's account, there is,

---

[125] Consider Perry Dane, *Prayer Is Serious Business: Reflections on Town of Greece*, Rutgers J L & Religion *28 (forthcoming), online at http://papers.ssrn.com/sol3/papers.cfm?abstract_id=2535931 ("Justice Kennedy's majority opinion and Justice Kagan's dissent are much more alike than either author seems to have supposed," in that neither "really treats prayer as serious business—serious theological business," and both "reduce civic prayer to essentially political declarations of identity").

[126] *Galloway*, 134 S Ct at 1819.

[127] Id at 1820.

[128] Id at 1820–21.

[129] Id at 1823.

[130] Id at 1818. See also id at 1823 (prayer at the beginning of a legislative session "is meant to lend gravity to the occasion and reflect values long part of the Nation's heritage, . . . [to] invite[ ] lawmakers to reflect upon shared ideals and common ends before they embark on the fractious business of governing").

centrally, a *civic* element as well. Thus, in describing congressional prayers, he writes, "[T]heir purpose is largely to accommodate the spiritual needs of lawmakers *and* connect them to a tradition dating to the time of the Founders."[131] Their goal is to "provide particular means to universal ends."[132] Those universal ends have to do with the *civic* virtues attendant upon governing, not with the personal *religious* goals of worship or salvation.

For Kennedy, legislative prayer is necessarily *civil* as well as civic. Prayer must be "solemn and respectful in tone," inviting reflection "upon *shared* ideals and *common ends*."[133] It aims to realize the principle of "e pluribus unum"—to show that "people of many faiths may be united in a community of tolerance and devotion."[134] Thus, notwithstanding Kennedy's assertion that neither legislators nor courts should scrutinize or impose conditions on the content of individual prayers, he emphasizes that there must be "an inquiry into the prayer opportunity as a whole," to ensure that the process of selecting and holding legislative prayers ensures reasonable equal access to the opportunity to pray.[135] And not the process alone: the *content* of the prayers is also open to scrutiny. A recurring practice of prayers, no matter how sincere and devout, that "denigrate nonbelievers or religious minorities, threaten damnation, [ ] preach conversion," or "betray an impermissible government purpose" may require judicial intervention.[136]

Perry Dane has written of Kennedy's description of permissible purposes for legislative prayer in *Galloway*: "Conspicuously missing in this list . . . is the most obvious purpose of genuine prayer—to pray."[137] This may be too harsh but is surely close to the mark. Although it disclaims any interest in having legislators or judges "act as supervisors and censors of religious speech,"[138] the Court in fact assigns itself this very role. It does so in the interest of serving what

---

[131] Id at 1826 (emphasis added).

[132] Id at 1823.

[133] Id (emphasis added).

[134] Id.

[135] Id at 1824; see also id at 1831 (Alito, J, concurring) ("I would view this case very differently if the omission of [the] synagogues were intentional.").

[136] Id at 1823, 1824.

[137] Dane, Rutgers J L & Religion at *18 (cited in note 125).

[138] *Galloway*, 134 S Ct at 1822.

Justice Kennedy thinks is the *right* kind of legislative prayer: prayer that respects religious differences but puts them to work to achieve "values that count as universal."[139] Sectarian references to God are acceptable only if God agrees to play nice and work well with others. If God has another message—that Democrats are sinners, that Republican policies stink in the nostrils of the Almighty, that some "divisions along religious lines"[140] are important and true and call upon us to bear witness to them—the Lord can deliver it somewhere else.

Compared to the vision of religious pluralism offered by the dissent, this may be a "thick" form of religious diversity, as Chad Flanders has suggested.[141] But *only* compared to the dissent. By normal standards, this is not "no holds barred" prayer.[142] To the contrary, it is a highly constrained and distinctively American sort of prayer, offered in "a kind of optimistic and voluntaryistic spirit."[143]

In contrast, Flanders is quite right to call the vision of American pluralism offered in Justice Kagan's dissent a "thin" version of religious diversity.[144] Like Kennedy's version of religious pluralism, hers serves a particular version of what she sees as a single American creed. Like Kennedy, Kagan sees this "distinctively American project" as one of "creating one from the many, and governing all as united."[145] Like Kennedy—and unlike the dissenters in *Marsh*—she does not believe that project requires the elimination of religion from legislative proceedings.[146]

Nevertheless, there are some differences in Kagan's conception of that American project, and many differences in how she would achieve it. The key message of her vision of American identity is

---

[139] Id at 1823.

[140] Id at 1819.

[141] Chad Flanders, *Religious Diversity, Thick and Thin*, SCOTUSblog, May 6, 2014, online at http://www.scotusblog.com/2014/05/symposium-religious-diversity-thick-and-thin/.

[142] Id.

[143] Marty, *Religion and Republic* at 245 (cited in note 2).

[144] Flanders, *Religious Diversity* (cited in note 141).

[145] *Galloway*, 134 S Ct at 1853 (Kagan, J, dissenting).

[146] Although, unlike Kennedy, Justice Kagan has little that is positive to say about the practice upheld in *Marsh*. She agrees, apparently, with the Court in *Marsh* that legislative prayer is "a tolerable acknowledgment of beliefs widely held among the people of this country." *Marsh*, 463 US at 792; see *Galloway*, 134 S Ct at 1845 (Kagan, J, dissenting). Beyond this, however, she has nothing else to say in justification of the practice, and mostly accepts it not for its own sake but because it "has a constitutional warrant by virtue of tradition." Id at 1844.

summed up by the telling phrase, *"only as Americans"*: "When the citizens of this country approach their government, they do so only as Americans, not as members of one faith or another."[147]

Of course there is something right about this. Kagan is speaking of the duties and benefits of citizenship as such, not all aspects of the citizen's life. Still, any language referring to citizens as being *"only"* Americans, especially in this context, calls to mind a decades-old complaint of religiously devout Americans: that they have been subjected to a set of public rules that require them to "bracket" their political selves from the "essential aspects of one's very self."[148] It calls to mind, too, the response that devoutly religious people give to this requirement: that this kind of bracketing, if it is possible at all, constitutes a kind of "annihilat[ion]" of key aspects of one's self.[149]

It is, no doubt, easy to be unfair to Justice Kagan's point here.[150] I stress again my assumption that Kagan means only that one's religion should not be a cause of good or bad treatment at the hands of government, *not* that one cannot or must not be publicly religious. Nevertheless there is something remarkably tone-deaf in her language. If this were a different case, involving a different aspect of one's identity, one might wonder what it means to speak to government as "only an American." One expects not to be treated differently by government because of one's gender, for example. But one need not therefore assume that it is possible to attain a state of pure

---

[147] *Galloway*, 134 S Ct at 1854 (Kagan, J, dissenting); see also id at 1841 ("[W]hen each person performs the duties or seeks the benefits of citizenship, she does so not as an adherent to one or another religion, but simply as an American."), 1845 (repeating the phrase "only as Americans").

[148] Michael J. Perry, *Morality, Politics, and Law: A Bicentennial Essay* 181 (Oxford, 1988); see also Sanford Levinson, *The Multicultures of Belief and Disbelief*, 92 Mich L Rev 1873, 1875–76 (1994) (book review) (finding similarities between Perry's complaint and those of one of the books under review, Stephen L. Carter, *The Culture of Disbelief: How American Law and Politics Trivialize Religious Devotion* (BasicBooks, 1993)).

[149] Perry, *Morality, Politics, and Law* at 181 (cited in note 148).

[150] Especially because, as Perry Dane points out, Kagan does state that individual responses to the invocations given at town meetings and other legislative proceedings "reveal[ ] a core aspect of identity—who that person is and how she faces the world." *Galloway*, 134 S Ct at 1853 (Kagan, J, dissenting); see Dane, *Prayer Is Serious Business*, Rutgers J L & Religion at *16 (cited in note 125) (commending Kagan for recognizing "that religious particulars matter and that religion can constitute a 'core aspect of identity'"). It is striking, nevertheless, that Kagan's recognition of this fact appears only in a discussion of the possibility of audience members' negative reactions to prayer, and nowhere else. It certainly does not seem to have shaken her conviction that one can talk meaningfully about a citizen being "only an American."

"American-ness" that involves not having a gender at all. Even for those devoutly religious Americans who oppose legislative prayer altogether, Kagan's language is bound to rankle, and to recall past battles over the seeming requirement that one bring an "unencumbered self" to one's civic activities.[151]

Kagan also differs from the majority in the rules she believes must govern legislative prayer if it is to be consistent with the "distinctively American project." Those rules are determinedly—and relentlessly—egalitarian.[152] They leave the town with one of two choices.[153] It may insist that *all* the invocations given are nonsectarian. Or, whatever the actual religious makeup of the audience, it may require a constant turnover of faiths among those giving the invocation. Only in those circumstances may government see fit to allow those giving the invocation to mention the name of their deity or deities, or to add any meaningful religious content to their remarks.[154] In short, it can either regulate religious speech, demanding that each speaker "tone down [his or her] particular faith,"[155] or it can ensure that both the process and the result of the legislative prayer process observe a kind of lockstep diversity.

Given the uncertainties inherent in the second option—what if the invitations don't yield a diverse range of speakers? What *is* a sufficiently diverse range of speakers? Will a court impose any additional restrictions on what those speakers say?—a government body

---

[151] Michael J. Sandel, *Democracy's Discontent: America in Search of a Public Philosophy* 66 (Belknap, 1996). See also Michael J. Sandel, *Political Liberalism*, 107 Harv L Rev 1765, 1774 (1994) (book review) ("Why should our political identities not express the moral and religious and communal convictions we affirm in our personal lives? Why insist on the separation between our identity as citizens and our identity as moral persons more broadly conceived?"), 1793–94 ("[D]emocratic politics cannot long abide a public life as abstract and decorous, as detached from moral purposes, as Supreme Court opinions are supposed to be. A politics that brackets morality and religion too completely soon generates its own disenchantment. . . . [Political liberalism's] vision of public reason is too spare to contain the moral energies of a vital democratic life.").

[152] See *Galloway*, 134 S Ct at 1852 (Kagan, J, dissenting) (calling the town board's approach to legislative prayer "determinedly—and relentlessly—noninclusive"). See also id at 1841 (describing the animating vision of her dissent as one of "religious equality"). The move on and off the Court from a focus on *liberty* as the lodestar of the Religion Clauses to a primary concern with *equality* is itself significant, although it is not the primary concern of this article. Consider Noah Feldman, *From Liberty to Equality: The Transformation of the Establishment Clause*, 90 Cal L Rev 673 (2002).

[153] Not, as she writes, "multiple ways." *Galloway*, 134 S Ct at 1851 (Kagan, J, dissenting).

[154] Id at 1850–51.

[155] Flanders, *Religious Diversity* (cited in note 141).

facing such a choice might well take option one, the insistence on nonsectarian prayer, in the interest of avoiding litigation. Thus, as a practical matter Kagan's approach might quickly reduce to a system of so-called "ceremonial deism" and little else.[156]

These are significant differences with the majority, to be sure. Ultimately, however, I find both opinions unsatisfying.[157] Although Kennedy and Kagan's opinions have been labeled as "thick" and "thin" versions of religious pluralism, respectively,[158] both seem rather thin. Neither writer offers an especially rich account of prayer, legislative or otherwise. Both rely on "armchair psychology."[159] For Kennedy, this leads to the placid assumption that religious minorities will welcome sectarian prayers at legislative sessions "as historically benign parts of our common expressive idiom."[160] For Kagan, the armchair psychology has less to do with her assumption that sectarian prayers may "exclude and divide,"[161] and more to do with her incuriosity about whether an insistence on nonsectarian prayer will have the same divisive effect on religiously devout Americans, and her confidence that it is possible for an individual to approach the government as "only an American."

Judges are not novelists. It is less important that they write rich, imaginative opinions than that they provide stable and workable resolutions of disputes.[162] But it is hardly clear that either opinion accomplishes *that* goal either. When will a prayer practice cross the line into an impermissible "course and practice" of denigration or proselytization?[163] What is the dividing line between sectarian and nonsectarian language?[164] When does a pattern of sectarian prayer by

---

[156] Id; see also, for example, Caroline Mala Corbin, *Ceremonial Deism and the Reasonable Religious Outsider*, 57 UCLA L Rev 1545, 1549 (2010) (defining ceremonial deism as involving governmental invocations of God that are of a long-standing nature and whose "religious impact is minimal and nonsectarian").

[157] For similar sentiments, see generally, for example, Dane, Rutgers J L & Religion (cited in note 125); Flanders, *Religious Diversity* (cited in note 141).

[158] See Flanders, *Religious Diversity* (cited in note 141).

[159] Dane, Rutgers J L & Religion at *17 (cited in note 125).

[160] Id.

[161] *Galloway*, 134 S Ct at 1851 (Kagan, J, dissenting). This is Dane's complaint. See Dane, Rutgers J L & Religion at *17 (cited in note 125).

[162] See, for example, Frederick Schauer, *Opinions as Rules*, 62 U Chi L Rev 1455, 1455–56 (1995).

[163] *Galloway*, 134 S Ct at 1823.

[164] Id at 1851 (Kagan, J, dissenting).

different faiths meet the requirement of being sufficiently "inclusive"?[165] The residue of uncertainty left behind by both opinions is something else they have in common.

The most important common point between the majority and the principal dissent, however, is that each opinion offers a single vision of American religious pluralism. Both insist that the circumstances of legislative prayer vary greatly and that any judicial resolution of such disputes is "fact-sensitive."[166] But neither seems to think that American religious pluralism *itself* is subject to any variation. The American religious historian Bret Carroll has written that "the religious meaning of the national space is as multiform and as much the stuff of public pluralistic wrangling as the religious culture within it, varying from individual to individual, group to group, locality to locality, and region to region."[167] Both Kennedy and Kagan simultaneously ignore and exemplify this point. Each attempts to declare definitively *the* meaning of American religious pluralism: *the* rules that govern it, *the* responses that citizens will have to different regimes, *the* "distinctively *American* project" that it represents.[168] In attempting to invest American religious pluralism with "a single authoritative meaning,"[169] neither stops to reflect that there may be no such meaning. It is little wonder that neither opinion feels true to life, or that neither seems likely to resolve the legislative prayer controversy. It is to this point—to the role of geography in church-state relations, and the diversity of American religious pluralism—that I now turn.

III. Law, Religion, and Geography in Galloway and Elsewhere

Eric Rassbach has written that *Galloway* marks the rise of a new principle in Religion Clause interpretation, in which "the historical background of the religion clauses serves to delineate their

---

[165] Id at 1845 n 2.

[166] Id at 1825; see also id at 1851–52 (Kagan, J, dissenting), id at 1838 (Breyer, J, dissenting).

[167] Bret E. Carroll, *Worlds in Space: American Religious Pluralism in Geographic Perspective*, 80 J Am Acad Religion 304, 341 (2012). I am grateful to Professor Sarah Barringer Gordon for first pointing me to this valuable article.

[168] *Galloway*, 134 S Ct at 1853 (Kagan, J, dissenting).

[169] Carroll, 80 J Am Acad Religion at 335 (cited in note 167).

scope today."[170] If so, *Galloway*'s emphasis on religious history calls to mind a warning delivered long before the American Revolution: "For as Geography without History seemeth a carkase without motion[,] so History without Geography wandereth as a Vagrant without a certaine habitation."[171] *Galloway* purports to give a historical account of legislative prayer and its relation to American church-state law. What is missing from that account, however, is a sense of American religious pluralism as a *spatial* phenomenon, not just a temporal one. Without that spatial sense, the opinions in this case are rendered incomplete and unpersuasive.

Religious studies scholars have long recognized the value of exploring the "complex relationships between religion and the geographical motifs of space and place."[172] "Geographical perspectives, focusing on the concepts of space and place," says a leading text on religion and geography, "are crucial in understanding essential aspects of religion as an expression of human culture."[173] A burgeoning literature has "provid[ed] substantial insights into humanity's diverse religious traditions and their relationships with the geographical contexts within which they have developed."[174]

Religious historians also recognize the importance of geography. Writing fifty years ago, Sidney Mead argued that those who seek to understand the "lively experiment" in religious liberty in the United States must focus on space, not just time. Compared to the centuries of development in European history, Mead wrote, "[t]here really was not much time in America for the traditionally antagonistic religious groups to learn to live together in peace."[175] What they *did* have was space—"practically unlimited geographical and social space," space "so vast that space came to take precedence over time in the formation of their most precious ideals," including religious liberty.[176] Just as different spatial circumstances suggested

---

[170] Rassbach, 2014 Cato S Ct Rev at 74 (cited in note 18) (discussing *Hosanna-Tabor*, 132 S Ct 694).

[171] Captain John Smith, *General Historie of the Bermudas* (1624), quoted in Edwin S. Gaustad, *The Geography of American Religion*, 30 J Bible & Religion 38, 38 (1962) (citing Goldwin Smith, *The Heritage of Man* 464 (Charles Scribner's Sons, 1960)).

[172] Stump, *The Geography of Religion* at 4–5 (cited in note 8).

[173] Id at 6.

[174] Id at 5.

[175] Mead, *The Lively Experiment* at 13 (cited in note 6).

[176] Id at 7, 14–15.

different models of religious and political coexistence, so different individuals, groups, and sects reacted differently to the opportunities and challenges that this vast new space represented. The result was "a strange mingling of attitudes toward the predominant conception of [religious] freedom"[177]—a *variety*, not a unity, of conceptions of American religious freedom. In the years since Mead wrote, a substantial literature has engaged those questions.[178] This literature studies the historical importance of American "religious geography":[179] the ways in which Americans' religious practices, and their social and legal structures, were shaped and reshaped in response to the physical and political landscapes they inhabited.

Religious geography and its effects on American religious pluralism are visible at a number of levels, or "geographical scales."[180] This part focuses on developments in American religious geography at two levels: regional and local. Both help shed light on the various opinions in *Galloway*.

A. REGIONALISM AND COMPETING MODELS OF AMERICAN
RELIGIOUS PLURALISM

The use of regions has been a linchpin of studies in American religious geography since the 1960s.[181] Their usefulness as a measure of American religious life has been questioned from the outset.[182]

---

[177] Id at 15.

[178] See, for example, Shelby M. Balik, *Rally the Scattered Believers: Northern New England's Religious Geography* (Indiana, 2014); Gaustad and Barlow, *New Historical Atlas of Religion in America* (cited in note 1); Bret E. Carroll, *The Routledge Historical Atlas of Religion in America* (Routledge, 2000); David Chidester and Edward T. Linenthal, *American Sacred Space* (Indiana, 1995); Robert Orsi, ed, *Gods of the City: Religion and the American Urban Landscape* (Indiana, 1999).

[179] Balik, *Rally the Scattered Believers* (cited in note 178).

[180] Stump, *The Geography of Religion* at 223–24 (cited in note 8); see also Lily Kong, *Mapping "New" Geographies of Religion: Politics and Poetics in Modernity*, 25 Progress Hum Geog 211, 226 (2001); Tracy Neal Leavelle, *Geographies of Encounter: Religion and Contested Spaces in Colonial North America*, 56 Am Q 913, 928 (2004); Carroll, 80 J Am Acad Religion at 317 (cited in note 167).

[181] See Bret E. Carroll, *Reflections on Regionalism and U.S. Religious History*, 71 Church Hist 120, 120 (2002); Carroll, 80 J Am Acad Religion at 318 (cited in note 167). The subject is generally traced back to an article by the American cultural geographer Wilbur Zelinsky, and a historical atlas by the American religious historian Edwin Scott Gaustad. See Wilbur Zelinsky, *An Approach to the Religious Geography of the United States: Patterns of Church Membership in 1952*, 51 Annals Ass'n Am Geographers 139 (1961); Edwin Scott Gaustad, *Historical Atlas of Religion in America* (Harper & Row, 1962).

[182] See generally Laurie F. Maffly-Kipp, *Putting Religion on the Map*, 94 J Am Hist 522 (2007).

People move in and out of these regions constantly; religious traditions themselves evolve, and wax and wane in popularity. The
nature and number of faiths and cultures in the United States has
exploded since the elimination of national origin quotas in the Immigration and Nationality Act of 1965.[183] Some argue that even if
American geographical regions were once culturally distinct, they
have been smoothed over by a "national cultural convergence" that has
blurred the distinctions between different regions.[184]

   The notion of American religious regionalism is thus imprecise
and imperfect, and should be approached with caution. Its creators
admitted this, warning that any geographical schema that attempts
to represent "the enormous complexity of U.S. religious history" involves a significant, even dangerous, degree of generalization.[185] Nevertheless, regionalism remains a popular device among scholars of
the history and geography of American religious pluralism, and has
picked up subsequent empirical support.[186]

   The picture of American religious regions has also been filled out
significantly by a multiyear project conducted by the Leonard E.
Greenberg Center for the Study of Religion in Public Life at Trinity
College, in Hartford, Connecticut. Aided by the empirical work of
the American Religious Identification Survey, this project, called
"Religion by Region," has resulted in a series of edited collections
that provide a deep statistical, demographic, and cultural analysis
of American religious life at a regional level.[187] The Religion by Re-

---

[183] Pub L No 89-236, 79 Stat 911, amending INA § 201 et seq, codified as amended 8 USC
§ 1151 et seq.

[184] William M. Newman and Peter L. Halvorson, *Atlas of American Religion: The Denominational Era, 1776–1990* 30 (AltaMira, 2000).

[185] Carroll, 71 Church Hist at 121 (cited in note 181), quoting Gaustad, *Historical Atlas of
Religion in America* at x (cited in note 181).

[186] See Carroll, 71 Church Hist at 122–26 (cited in note 181).

[187] See Andrew Walsh and Mark Silk, eds, *Religion and Public Life in New England: Steady
Habits, Changing Slowly* (AltaMira, 2004); Randall Balmer and Mark Silk, eds, *Religion and
Public Life in the Middle Atlantic Region: The Fount of Diversity* (AltaMira, 2006); Philip Barlow
and Mark Silk, eds, *Religion and Public Life in the Midwest: America's Common Denominator?*
(AltaMira, 2004); Jan Shipps and Mark Silk, eds, *Religion and Public Life in the Mountain West:
Sacred Landscapes in Transition* (AltaMira, 2004); Patricia O'Connell Killen and Mark Silk, eds,
Religion and Public Life in the Pacific Northwest: The None Zone (AltaMira, 2004); Wade Clark
Roof and Mark Silk, eds, *Religion and Public Life in the Pacific Region: Fluid Identities* (AltaMira,
2005); Charles Reagan Wilson and Mark Silk, eds, *Religion and Public Life in the South: In the
Evangelical Mode* (AltaMira, 2005); William Lindsey and Mark Silk, eds, *Religion and Public
Life in the Southern Crossroads: Showdown States* (AltaMira, 2005). The work is summarized in a
helpful additional volume by the project's director and associate director. See Mark Silk and

gion project is highly relevant to an analysis of the Court's decision in *Town of Greece v Galloway*. It suggests, Bret Carroll writes, that

> the nation's religious regions are definable not only by their demographic profiles but by distinct, geographically and culturally conditioned styles of *pluralism*—characteristic kinds of alliances and tensions among the worlds occupying the regional spaces.[188]

Below, I summarize the standard picture of American religious regions, and each region's model of American religious pluralism. The reader is again duly cautioned that these regions, although useful, are neither precise nor scientific. Another important aspect of religious geography—the distinction between different localities, such as cities, suburbs, and towns—is elided here, although I take it up below. I then consider the implications of the regional picture of American religious pluralism for the main opinions in *Galloway*.

The *Middle Atlantic* region consists of New York, New Jersey, Pennsylvania, Delaware, Maryland, and the District of Columbia. It is home to a greater proportion of Catholics and Jews than the nation as a whole. Its Christian population is composed largely of mainline denominations; only here and in New England do mainline Protestants significantly outnumber evangelical denominations. It is marked by "strong links between religious and ethnic identity." Its characteristic form of religious pluralism is one of negotiated coexistence between ethnocultural groups: a "functioning ecology in which each community finds its niche under an umbrella of shared values." It features "a tradition of ecumenical cooperation and interfaith undertakings" between the major groups. The classic mid-century description of "tri-faith" American religious pluralism, made famous by Will Herberg's book *Protestant-Catholic-Jew*, is really just the Middle Atlantic model writ large.[189]

New England consists of Connecticut, Rhode Island, Massachusetts, Vermont, New Hampshire, and Maine. Once the base of strict

---

Andrew Walsh, *One Nation, Divisible: How Regional Religious Differences Shape American Politics*, paperback ed. (Rowman & Littlefield, 2011). I draw heavily on that book, as well as the descriptions in Bret Carroll's superb article on American religious geography, in this section. See Carroll, 80 J Am Acad Religion at 318–27 (cited in note 167). For the sake of economy, I have tried to keep footnotes to a minimum and to corral them at the end of each paragraph.

[188] Carroll, 80 J Am Acad Religion at 319 (emphasis added) (cited in note 167).

[189] See Silk and Walsh, *One Nation, Divisible* at 2–3, 15–40 (cited in note 187); Will Herberg, *Protestant-Catholic-Jew* (Doubleday, 1960); Carroll, 80 J Am Acad Religion at 319–20 (cited in note 167).

Puritan Christianity, it is now "the least Protestant region of the country." More important than its Puritan past is the Protestant-Catholic tension that burst onto the scene in the nineteenth century as a result of Irish immigration to the region. That tension produced this region's own model of religious pluralism: not the mid-Atlantic regime of intercultural cooperation, but the establishment of "geographically parallel religious worlds," separate enclaves with duplicate sets of social institutions. Under this regime, religion belongs "at the level of the individual, the family, and the voluntary religious community." Within the "democratic public realm, . . . citizens [do] not impose sectarian demands on one another[,] in order to preserve civic peace." This is the pluralism of the 1960 presidential election, and John F. Kennedy's half-sincere, half-strategic insistence that religion play no role in public life. It is the same vision that led the Supreme Court in the early 1960s to strike down school prayer.[190]

The *South* consists of Virginia, West Virginia, Kentucky, the Carolinas, Georgia, Florida, Alabama, and Mississippi. It is heavily evangelical in orientation; even mainline Protestantism tends to adopt a more evangelical tilt in this region. It is a region of self-declared culture warriors, defenders of "traditional religious values" against the forces of secularism and cultural change. Perceived as a powerful threat by secularists and liberals, from its own perspective it is culturally, religiously, and "spatially on the defensive."[191]

"The *Southern Crossroads*—Louisiana, Texas, Arkansas, Oklahoma, and Missouri—looks like the South plus Roman Catholics." Its Catholic population is twice that of the South. Much of the remainder is evangelical, including Pentecostal, Holiness, and Charismatic denominations. It is the region with the fewest members of minority faiths. Historically a region of "political and religious clashes of pronounced intensity," it retains that intensity today across a range of social and religious issues, including a fierce attachment to the lowering of the wall between church and state. It shares the South's political and social views. But it lacks the South's gentility and approaches flashpoint issues, including church-state conflicts, with the gloves off. Its

---

[190] See Silk and Walsh, *One Nation, Divisible* at 3–4, 41–62, 211–12 (cited in note 187); Carroll, 80 J Am Acad Religion at 326 (cited in note 167); *Engel v Vitale*, 370 US 421 (1962); *Abington School District v Schempp*, 374 US 203 (1963).

[191] See Silk and Walsh, *One Nation, Divisible* at 5–6, 63–84 (cited in note 187); Carroll, 80 J Am Acad Religion at 324–25 (cited in note 167).

"harder-edged culture-warriors," in both religion and politics—figures like James Dobson of Louisiana and Tom DeLay of Texas—spearheaded much of the national culture war of the 1990s and 2000s.[192]

California, Hawaii, and Nevada comprise the *Pacific*. Its religious mix is unique in many respects. For example, survey data suggest that "more residents of the Pacific identify with Eastern religions than with any of the mainline Protestant denominations," although the number of both is still relatively small. It is the region with the second highest proportion of the population that identifies with no religion at all. It is a region of "loosened" and "eclectic" religious commitments, in which many individuals freely adopt aspects of various faiths in a piecemeal fashion, or simply create views and practices of their own. Particularly in the last several decades, it has been home to an increasing number of committed conservative Protestants. But there is no dominant faith in the region, and no historical tradition of a dominant faith. (In the 1950s, only 3 percent of the public schools in western states engaged in "Bible readings and devotional practices," compared to 77 percent in the South.) The Pacific culture is one of "liquid modernity": of fluidity and "obligatory tolerance and individualism."[193]

Even more visibly than regions like New England, the approach to religious pluralism of the other two western regions is deeply dependent on the land—in this case, the land's *natural* features as well as its social characteristics. These regions thus provide a different and important approach to religious pluralism.

The *Pacific Northwest*—Oregon, Washington, and Alaska—is vast and variegated. Its religious makeup is noteworthy for the large number of "unchurched" individuals claiming no affiliation to a particular denomination, and for containing the largest number of Americans claiming no religious affiliations of *any* kind. This has earned it the sobriquet "the None Zone." It has a substantial Catholic population and a substantial number of evangelical Christians.

---

[192] See Silk and Walsh, *One Nation, Divisible* at 6–7, 85–108, 214–15 (cited in note 187); Carroll, 80 J Am Acad Religion at 325–26 (cited in note 167).

[193] See Silk and Walsh, *One Nation, Divisible* at 7–9, 109–34 (cited in note 187); Carroll, 80 J Am Acad Religion at 321–22 (cited in note 167); Wade Clark Roof, *Pluralism as a Culture: Religion and Civility in Southern California*, 612 Annals Am Acad Polit & Soc Sci 82 (2007). The phrase "liquid modernity" comes from Zygmunt Bauman, *Liquid Modernity* (Blackwell, 2000).

Unlike in the South, however, they are more likely to be Pentecostal or nondenominational Christians than Baptists. These demographic and physical attributes have led to two particularly noteworthy responses. First, the "fragility of the individual sectarian enterprises" has led to a tradition of "ecumenical and interfaith cooperation," a necessary "pooling [of] moral and financial resources." Second, there is a substantial regional divide between the urbane "nones" in the western parts of the region and the more religious, conservative, traditionalist Christians on the eastern side. These religious dissenters from the norms of cities like Seattle or Portland comprise a kind of "evangelical counterculture." One writer has suggested that it should be seen not as a "separate sectarian world in permanent confrontation with the surrounding culture," but as "a dissenting parallel community" of its own.[194]

The *Mountain West*—Arizona, New Mexico, Utah, Idaho, Colorado, Wyoming, and Montana—is the nation's "preeminent oasis, or archipelago, region." It features a few urban communities, isolated within vast unpopulated spaces. Other regions, such as the Middle Atlantic, require modes of pluralism that allow different faiths to coexist in the same small space. The different communities in the Mountain West do not, and have come up with three different models of pluralism instead. Taken together, they constitute a "'libertarian' variety [of pluralism] in which each spiritual community stak[es] out its own turf."[195]

The "Catholic heartland" of Arizona and New Mexico experienced conflicts over control of public institutions like the schools—controlled here by Catholics. After court rulings mandated strict separationism within the public schools, it responded by developing rival private school systems. It has also been the site of repeated conflicts with Native American tribes over access to sacred sites. The mountainous regions of Colorado, Wyoming, and Montana, rather than being characterized by any particular faith *or* any form of interfaith cooperation, are the sites of multiple "scattered enclaves."

---

[194] See Silk and Walsh, *One Nation, Divisible* at 9–10, 135–55 (cited in note 187); Carroll, 80 J Am Acad Religion at 324 (cited in note 167). For further discussion of the evangelical counterculture of the Pacific Northwest, see James K. Wellman, Jr., *Evangelical vs. Liberal: The Clash of Christian Cultures in the Pacific Northwest* (Oxford, 2008).

[195] Carroll, 80 J Am Acad Religion at 322 (cited in note 167) (quoting Mark Silk, *Defining Religious Pluralism in America: A Regional Analysis*, 612 Annals Am Acad Polit & Social Sci 64, 78 (2007)).

Those include both Native American reservations and non-native enclaves. Prominent examples include Boulder and Colorado Springs, "two cities separated by less than 100 miles but spiritually worlds apart": the first awash in both secularism and Eastern or syncretic spirituality, the second a hub for conservative evangelical groups such as Focus on the Family. Finally and most famously, there is the "Mormon corridor" of Utah and Idaho, dominated by the Church of Jesus Christ of Latter-day Saints. It is arguably "the only part of the United states that today possesses a de facto if not a de jure religious establishment."[196]

The *Midwest*, a sort of common denominator for the nation as a whole, may "provid[e] the model for religion in American public life in the twenty-first century." It consists of a large number of states—Ohio, Michigan, Indiana, Illinois, Wisconsin, Minnesota, Iowa, the Dakotas, Kansas, and Nebraska—lacking the common ties of other regions. It is as religiously and ethnically diverse as the Middle Atlantic region, but "different geographic conditions have generated differences of both religious demography and pluralistic style." It is a "[s]olidly pluralistic" region, lacking either a single dominant faith or deep rivalries between different faiths. At the same time, it is not subject to the privatizing impulses of New England politics. It features "a tradition of tolerant religious pluralism, high rates of religious adherence, and folkways that place considerable stress on the public value of religion." It favors a state that is religiously neutral; unlike New England, however, it is favorably disposed toward religiosity *in* public. This partly reflects the greater presence of evangelical Christianity in the Midwest, with an accompanying focus on common, publicly pronounced values and virtues. But Midwestern evangelicals are more moderate in their public expressions of faith than their southern co-religionists.[197]

Two key observations emerge from this account of the "array of geographically defined pluralisms" that help define American life.[198] These observations apply across what might be called social, geographical, political, and historical space. They not only help reveal the

---

[196] For this and the previous paragraph, see Silk and Walsh, *One Nation, Divisible* at 10–11, 157–79 (cited in note 187); Carroll, 80 J Am Acad Religion at 322–25 (cited in note 167).

[197] See Silk and Walsh, *One Nation, Divisible* at 11–12, 181–204, 224–32 (cited in note 187); Carroll, 80 J Am Acad Religion at 320–21 (cited in note 167).

[198] Carroll, 80 J Am Acad Religion at 327 (cited in note 167).

nature of current conditions in American religious and public life. They also reflect changing legal and political arrangements concerning church-state relations over the past several decades, roughly since the Supreme Court incorporated the Establishment Clause against the states.[199] These observations fill in this article's analysis of *Galloway*. They help explain why the primary contending opinions in that case come off as thin, unsatisfactory, and unlikely to achieve lasting consensus in American church-state relations.

The first point should be obvious from the preceding regional survey. Nevertheless, it is routinely overlooked in American church-state scholarship. That field focuses heavily on the decisions of federal courts, especially the Supreme Court.[200] Those heavily nationalist, centralized sources are supplemented by slices of founding-era history, and by abstract theorizing about religious liberty.[201] The literature tends toward generalized statements about "American religious pluralism" that treat the nation and its religious and political culture as a single, unparticularized whole.[202] Although law and religion scholars are aware that different American colonies "developed distinctive patterns of dealing with difference,"[203] they view the historical narrative as moving toward a single, final rule or regime of American pluralism. They have been incurious about the extent to which those distinctive approaches, while evolving considerably, remain in place today. This is precisely the conclusion that the regional account of American religious pluralism suggests.

---

[199] See *Everson v Bd. of Education*, 330 US 1 (1947).

[200] This is a general problem in constitutional law scholarship. See, e.g., Richard A. Posner, *Against the Law Reviews*, Legal Affairs, Nov/Dec 2004, online at http://legalaffairs.org/issues/November-December-2004/review_posner_novdec04.msp (lamenting the undue focus in the law reviews on the Supreme Court and the relatively few decisions it issues each year, and legal scholarship's comparative neglect of lower court decisions). I acknowledge the irony of saying so in this particular venue.

[201] See Paul Horwitz, *Freedom of the Church Without Romance*, 21 J Contemp Legal Issues 59, 92–93 (2013) ("[M]ost scholarship on law and religion, including much of the best of it, privileges ideas over interests. It invokes history, but it tends to emphasize intellectual history rather than a more jaundiced and institutionally focused historical analysis. It is also top-heavy with theory. In our field, a page of Rawls often outweighs a volume of financial or demographic data.").

[202] See Paul Horwitz, *Demographics and Distrust: The Eleventh Circuit on Graduation Prayer in Duval v. Adler County*, 63 U Miami L Rev 835, 881–87 (2009); Schragger, 117 Harv L Rev at 1813–19 (cited in note 12).

[203] Diana L. Eck, *A New Religious America: How a "Christian Country" Has Now Become the World's Most Religiously Diverse Nation* 37 (HarperOne, 2001).

The regional account also says something important about the variety and nature of those versions of pluralism. They tend to take a number of specific forms, adapted to the demographic, denominational, and political mix of each region, its history, and its landscape. They include the religious pluralism regimes, such as those of the Middle Atlantic or New England, that we are most familiar with and that form the basis of standard judicial and scholarly accounts of religious pluralism in the context of the Establishment Clause. The Middle Atlantic's regime involves peaceful coexistence, with openly religious language permitted and welcomed. New England's consists of peaceful coexistence under a rule discouraging or forbidding religious language in the public square.

As our regional survey suggests, however, there are other regimes. One we might call a "sorting" approach to religious pluralism.[204] The Mormon corridor offers an example: the use of migration (and expulsion) and "geographical distance" to establish a distinctive "society in the west that actualized [the Mormons'] highest theology and governed their everyday lives."[205] Another is the "enclave" strategy, as in Oregon or Colorado: the establishment of separate communities, each reflecting the religious views and social preferences of its residents. Still another we might call, drawing on the Dutch experience, "pillarization": the creation of parallel sets of institutions serving different religious and other communities, living side by side in the same larger community.[206] At one time, this was New England's answer to religious conflict.

The second observation comes from the conclusion to Silk and Walsh's summary of the Religion by Region project. There, they argue that our understanding of the "national narrative" of American church-state relations may be altered and enriched by what we have learned about American religious regionalism.[207]

On this view, the various "postwar dispensations" that have characterized American attempts to come to terms with religious diver-

---

[204] See Samaha, 2005 Supreme Court Review 135 (cited in note 12).

[205] Silk and Walsh, *One Nation, Divisible* at 164 (cited in note 187).

[206] See, for example, Stephen V. Monsma and J. Christopher Soper, *The Challenge of Pluralism: Church and State in Five Democracies* 56–60, 84–85 (Rowman & Littlefield, 2d ed 2009).

[207] Silk and Walsh, *One Nation, Divisible* at 205 (cited in note 187).

sity, and establish rules and norms (political and legal) to manage our pluralism, did not come about by happenstance. Nor did they come directly from early American history, by way of some oracle sitting on the Supreme Court,[208] or from some effort to obtain "constitutional meaning . . . by interpreting the materials in accordance with the best available political-moral theory."[209] Rather, and by whatever mechanism, those dispensations have come from, or bear a remarkable resemblance to, our regional models of pluralism. Some of those models have been influential mostly at a political or cultural level. At other times, they have been expressed more directly in the legal regimes that defined the Establishment Clause in different postwar periods.

The 1950s regime, for example, has been characterized as one of relative religious unity and peacefulness. Its spirit was captured in Herberg's *Protestant-Catholic-Jew*, a classic picture of a "tri-faith America"[210] that was publicly pious without being riven by sectarian division, largely because of its focus on "Judeo-Christianity."[211] This settlement manifested in various legal actions formalizing an openly, if thinly, religious American creed—in the amended Pledge of Allegiance, in the insistence that "In God We Trust" be stamped on our coins, and in the placement of Ten Commandments dis-

---

[208] See, for example, *Everson*, 330 US at 8–15 (offering a stylized picture of the "background and environment of the period in which [the] constitutional language [of the Establishment Clause] was fashioned and adopted," replete with references to "freedom-loving colonials," "abhorren[t]" practices, and the "dramatic climax" of the Virginia legislative debate over the tax levy for the support of religious ministers).

[209] Steven D. Smith, *Discourse in the Dusk: The Twilight of Religious Freedom?*, 122 Harv L Rev 1869, 1901 (2009) (book review).

[210] See Kevin M. Schultz, *Tri-Faith America: How Catholics and Jews Held Postwar America to Its Protestant Promise* (Oxford, 2011).

[211] See, for example, Anna Su, *Separation Anxiety: The End of American Religious Freedom?*, 30 Const Comm 127, 138–39 (2015) (book review). Eisenhower's famous statement, "Our government has no sense unless it is founded in a deeply felt religious faith, and I don't care what it is," comes from this period. As Andrew Koppelman observes, the line that followed this one is less remembered, but it is fully consistent with the equation of religious pluralism with the dominant Judeo-Christian triumvirate: "With us of course it is the Judeo-Christian concept[,] but it must be a religion that all men are created equal." Andrew Koppelman, *Corruption of Religion and the Establishment Clause*, 50 Wm & Mary L Rev 1831, 1885 (2009) (quoting Mark Silk, *Spiritual Politics: Religion and America Since World War II* 40 (Touchstone, 1988)). See also Silk, 612 Annals Am Acad Polit & Soc Sci at 67 (cited in note 195) (noting that the phrase "Judeo-Christian" was popularized in a series of conferences held at Columbia University, of which Eisenhower later served as president, and that Eisenhower's famous remarks were delivered in an address to the Manhattan-based Freedoms Foundation).

plays on government property.[212] Those actions would pose doctrinal dilemmas for future Courts.[213] At the time, however, they were simply the accepted religious, political, *and* legal landscape of the era.

As Silk and Walsh point out, the vision of American religious pluralism that undergirded these practices was strikingly similar, if not identical, to the Middle Atlantic approach to pluralism. The trifaith settlement was not equally relevant or applicable everywhere in the nation. To the contrary, it little resembled demographic or political conditions in many parts of the country. Nevertheless, the Middle Atlantic settlement defined the culturally and politically dominant themes of the era at a national level. Its model of "distinct ethnoreligious communities[,] minding their own business in reasonable harmony" with one another, provided a useful "image of the several separate but equal tribes of American religion pulling together against the common Communist foe."[214]

When this regime gave way, it was succeeded by the modern New England approach to pluralism: the view that "religion should be kept clear of the political fray, that the civic order functions best when religion is confined to the private sphere of individuals and faith communities."[215] The nation's demographic makeup had not changed overnight. But the New England dispensation suited the times. In particular, it suited a presidential candidate, John Kennedy (himself a New Englander), who needed to convince Protestants that his Catholicism was irrelevant to his role as president.[216] In addition to political and cultural dominance, this settlement became dominant on the Supreme Court. Beginning with its rulings

---

[212] See Frederick Mark Gedicks and Roger Hendrix, *Uncivil Religion: Judeo-Christianity and the Ten Commandments*, 110 W Va L Rev 275, 282–83 (2007).

[213] See, for example, *Van Orden v Perry*, 545 US 677 (2005) (examining a challenge to a Ten Commandments display on state property); *Newdow*, 542 US 1 (getting rid of a challenge to the requirement that schoolchildren say the Pledge of Allegiance, including the "under God" language). As I suggested above, this is the difficulty that Justice Kennedy attempts to dispel for good in *Galloway*, by giving the Court's advance blessing to any public religious practice that it adjudges to be sufficiently long-standing to form part of our "heritage and tradition." *Galloway*, 134 S Ct at 1825 ("As a practice that has long endured, legislative prayer has become part of our heritage and tradition, part of our expressive idiom, similar to the Pledge of Allegiance, inaugural prayer, or the recitation of 'God save the United States and this honorable Court' at the opening of this Court's sessions.").

[214] Silk and Walsh, *One Nation, Divisible* at 211 (cited in note 187).

[215] Id.

[216] Id; see also Horwitz, 39 U Memphis L Rev at 978–95 (cited in note 67).

striking down school prayer,[217] the Court struck down a number of pietistic public practices compatible with the earlier, Middle Atlantic–oriented approach to pluralism but incompatible with the New England regime.[218] "[T]he ideology of church-state separationism in fact reached its high-water mark during the Kennedy era."[219]

Other regional approaches to American religious pluralism have corresponded to changing views and trends in other periods of postwar history. For example, the rise of the Religious Right from the mid-1970s through today, with an accompanying increase in confrontationalism over religion and its public role,[220] suggests a challenge to the prior pluralism regimes from a Southern, and ultimately a more aggressive Southern Crossroads, perspective.[221] The Southern Crossroads approach continues to influence American political culture. But Silk and Walsh argue that the election of Barack Obama, who is more openly religious than a figure like Kennedy but less insistently sectarian than some of his opponents or predecessors, indicates the national ascendancy of the Midwestern model of religious pluralism.[222] Despite the strictures she would place on legislative prayer, it may be that Justice Kagan's eagerness to affirm it, rather than reject it as earlier liberal Justices did, buttresses this thesis.

Clearly, one should not accept this analysis unskeptically or apply it too mechanically. Among other things, Silk and Walsh do not explain clearly how and why particular regional settlements came to the fore in particular eras. The story they offer is arguably too neat, too cute. Nevertheless, they provide a compelling case for the conclusion that there is "an abiding geography of American religion."[223] It manifests itself in particular regional cultures and ap-

---

[217] See *Engel*, 370 US 421; *Schempp*, 374 US 203.

[218] See Gedicks and Hendrix, 110 W Va L Rev at 283 & n 53 (cited in note 212) (citing other examples).

[219] Silk and Walsh, *One Nation, Divisible* at 212 (cited in note 187).

[220] See generally Steven P. Miller, *The Age of Evangelicalism: America's Born-Again Years* (Oxford, 2014).

[221] See Silk and Walsh, *One Nation, Divisible* at 215 (cited in note 187) (noting the ultimate passage of leadership roles in politics and within politically active religious organizations from Southerners to individuals from states within the Southern Crossroads region).

[222] Id at 226.

[223] Gaustad, 30 J Bible & Religion at 38 (cited in note 171).

proaches to pluralism that move in and out of prominence at the national level.

Many writers, including legal scholars, think about religious pluralism only at the national level. They treat the various regimes that have characterized national culture and politics—the separationist model, the civil religion model, the forceful "Christian nation" model, and so on—as representing a *unitary* form of American pluralism, rooted in American history but unrooted from particular places. Each model has its champions; each champion assumes that the goal is the triumph of the "right" model of American religious pluralism. The regional story of American religious pluralism that we have examined here, and the fact that each transient national regime has corresponded to a particular regional model of pluralism, casts doubt on the entire enterprise, and on this entire way of thinking about American religious pluralism.

In short, it is a mistake to conclude that any given regime that has been hailed as *the* correct form of American religious pluralism is the final, definitive answer to the American church-state dilemma. It is also wrong to conclude that any such regime draws its authority directly from Founding-era historical sources, or from abstract theories of religious liberty. Rather, we should see each proposed model of American religious pluralism or church-state relations as just one of many *regional* regimes. Each is likely to come in and out of national prominence, briefly appearing to be *the* solution to American church-state relations but eventually being challenged or supplanted by some other region's approach.

This lesson applies directly to the Supreme Court's decision in *Galloway*. It suggests that there is a significant obstacle to the monistic, nationalizing project pursued, albeit with different results, by both Justice Kennedy and Justice Kagan and their brethren in *Galloway*, with the customary—and solitary—exception of Justice Thomas.

In their own way, both Kennedy and Kagan seek to present and entrench a single vision of American pluralism, one that results in a single correct model of legislative prayer. Each one, as it turns out, resembles one or more of the regional regimes that have competed for national prominence. In his confidence that legislative prayer—even if it turns out to be primarily Christian—will help "lawmakers to transcend petty differences in pursuit of a higher purpose," and that sectarian but generic religious language can "provide particular means to universal ends,"[224] Justice Kennedy draws heavily on the language and ideas of the Middle Atlantic settlement. In his statement that "willing participation in civic affairs can be consistent with a brief acknowledgment of [ ] belief in a higher power,"[225] he sounds like a latter-day Eisenhower, insisting on the importance of a vague but essentially Judeo-Christian "deeply felt religious faith" in public life.[226]

Justice Kagan's approach resembles a combination of the Midwestern and New England settlements. Her apparent endorsement of legislative prayer evokes the Midwestern faith in the importance of public religiosity in expressing our common values. At the same time, the stringent rules she would impose on legislative prayer suggest a deeper fear that public religiosity will inevitably "divide [Americans] along religious lines."[227] That is the New England strain in her dissent.

The point is not that one or the other approach is right or wrong. Each has its share of wisdom. It is that each represents just one of many possible church-state settlements. A regional examination of American religious life leads inexorably to the conclusion that "American religious pluralism can be understood as in fact consisting of *an array* of geographically defined *pluralisms*."[228] As long as these different pluralisms are ingrained in the history and culture of different regions, there is little chance that any one of them will command the permanent allegiance of all Americans. On the ground, American religious pluralism is too varied—by history, geography, culture, and circumstances—for all Americans, whatever their region, to subscribe to a single, final solution to the problem of American religious diversity and church-state conflict.[229] It is un-

---

[224] *Galloway*, 134 S Ct at 1818, 1823.

[225] Id at 1827–28.

[226] Horwitz, 39 U Memphis L Rev at 978 (cited in note 67).

[227] *Galloway*, 134 S Ct at 1854 (Kagan, J, dissenting).

[228] Carroll, 80 J Am Acad Religion at 327 (cited in note 167) (emphasis added).

[229] Consider Marty, *Religion and Republic* at 247 (cited in note 2) ("Whatever happens, however, it seems clear that not all human needs can be met by secular interpretation and private faith, by tri-faith or conventional denominational life, or by a common national religion. New particularisms will no doubt continue to arise, to embody the hopes of this 'people of peoples.'").

surprising that both Kennedy and Kagan's proposals, despite the confidence with which each is put forward, come off as thin, incomplete, and unconvincing.

B. LOCAL AMERICAN RELIGIOUS PLURALISM: URBANITY, HOMOGENEITY, AND BORDERS

Our geographical account of *Galloway* now shifts from the regional to the local: to "the cities, towns, and neighborhoods where interreligious encounters are most immediate," and where "what is at stake in the pluralist dynamic is felt most directly."[230] Here, religious geography's lesson is simple, subtle, and essential: "[R]eligious groups do not simply exist in space; they also imagine and construct space in terms related to their faith."[231] The legal lesson is similar: "[Religiously] identified space interacts with [religion]-neutral legal doctrine and public policy to enforce" religious dominance and its exclusionary effects.[232]

Figuratively and literally, these lessons intersect with *Galloway* at an imaginary line on a map: the line dividing the town of Greece, as a political jurisdiction, from the places where *some* of its people— an identifiable religious minority—worship. That imaginary line is crucial for the outcome in *Galloway*.

We begin with a preliminary point, one that is well known but often overlooked.[233] As I have argued, discussions of American religious diversity are often highly general in nature. They describe the United States as a whole as religiously diverse, without delving much into how those faiths are distributed.[234] The story is quite different on the ground. Some locales *are* incredibly religiously diverse. Elsewhere, a single religion—or even a denomination—dominates, with only a few members of minority faiths present.[235]

---

[230] Carroll, 80 J Am Acad Religion at 327 (cited in note 167); see also John C. Blakeman, *The Religious Geography of Religious Expression: Local Governments, Courts, and the First Amendment*, 48 J Church & St 399, 399–401 (2006).

[231] Stump, *The Geography of Religion* at 23 (cited in note 8).

[232] Richard Thompson Ford, *The Boundaries of Race: Political Geography in Legal Analysis*, 107 Harv L Rev 1841, 1845 (1994).

[233] For previous efforts to address it, see Horwitz, 63 U Miami L Rev at 881–92 (cited in note 202); Paul Horwitz, *Of Football, "Footnote One," and the Counter-Jurisdictional Establishment Clause: The Story of Santa Fe Independent School District v. Doe*, in Richard W. Garnett and Andew Koppelman, eds, *First Amendment Stories* at 481, 500–10 (Foundation, 2011).

[234] Horwitz, 63 U Miami L Rev at 882 (cited in note 202).

[235] See id at 886.

In the former condition, which represents the condition of urbanity in places like New York, Los Angeles, or Chicago, religious diversity may produce tension and conflict.[236] But it is also more likely to lead to cooperation and negotiation.[237] There will always be exceptions.[238] But the more religiously diverse a locality is, the less likely it is that any single faith will be politically dominant. Rather, it is far more likely that all religious (and nonreligious) stakeholders will broker an inclusive compromise. In areas that are *completely* homogeneous, peace may be achievable for the opposite reason: with no minorities to be dissatisfied or disadvantaged, the local practice will satisfy everyone.

Still, the former state of affairs only applies in the metropolis, and the latter is almost entirely hypothetical. The reality is that many locations are neither completely heterogeneous nor completely homogeneous. Rather, they are *overwhelmingly* religiously homogeneous, dominated by one faith but always with *some* religious minorities.

Religious minorities in such locales may find that they live in the worst of all possible worlds. They will be confronted by practices that exclude or disadvantage them, and subject to both legal and extralegal harassment if they dare come forward and object.[239] Courts may step in when such conduct occurs—*if* a plaintiff can be found and convinced to step forward—ending the harassment and halting the offending public religious practice. But doing so may in turn leave the majority with its own sense of injury, and further exacerbate existing conditions of religious conflict.[240]

The solution is unclear as a matter of first principles. Some favor a decentralized approach that would allow each jurisdiction to

---

[236] See Schragger, 117 Harv L Rev at 1814 (cited in note 12) (arguing that "the American experiment in pluralism is only truly tested under conditions of urbanity").

[237] See Roof, 612 Annals Am Acad Polit & Soc Sci at 93 (cited in note 193) (noting that religious leaders serving the immigrant communities of southern California are "well-educated urban leaders who appreciate diversity, openness, and the necessity of cooperation").

[238] See, e.g., *Bronx Household of Faith v Board of Educ. of City of New York*, 750 F 3d 184,188–89 (2nd Cir 2014) (recounting "long-running litigation" in which the New York City Board of Education repeatedly refused to accommodate a religious group seeking equal access to school facilities on weekends); Douglas Laycock, *Voting with Your Feet Is No Substitute for Constitutional Rights*, 32 Harv J L & Pub Pol 29, 41–42 (2009) (discussing this case and noting that the litigation had been in progress for some fifteen years as of the date of publication of that article).

[239] See, for example, Horwitz, 63 U Miami L Rev at 887–88 (cited in note 202) (offering examples); Horwitz, *The Story of Santa Fe Independent School District* at 488, 495, 502, 504 (same) (cited in note 233).

[240] See, for example, Samaha, 2005 Supreme Court Review at 147 (cited in note 12).

establish its own practices.[241] Others argue that the Establishment Clause should be read to favor an "anti-sorting" principle, under which the goal is to encourage the dispersal rather than the concentration of religious faiths in any particular jurisdiction. On this view, "national standards for religious liberty would be better than local political discretion and the resulting policy variance."[242] In contrast to both of these options, I have argued that, despite the resurgence of the view that the Establishment Clause forbids *federal* religious establishments but not state or local ones,[243] conditions on the ground suggest that "the Establishment Clause might be better understood, at least in the modern era, as being more properly concerned with state and local establishments of religion than with federal establishments of religion."[244]

For now, the answer to that question is unimportant. What *is* important is that Establishment Clause doctrine does not formally recognize the problem. Doctrine in this area is indifferent to the "institutional scale" and location of government action. As Richard Schragger has observed, it assumes that the same rule applies, no matter the size, scale, or nature of the governmental actor involved.[245]

The result is cases like *Galloway*. The Court paid lip service to the notion that the Establishment Clause inquiry must be "fact-sensitive," giving attention to "both the setting in which the prayer arises and the audience to whom it is directed."[246] In reality, it showed little interest in the question whether a town board ought to be treated differently than Congress or a state legislature for purposes of a challenge to legislative prayer. Any curiosity it had on this question was satisfied by the citation of a scintilla of evidence that legislative prayer by local governmental bodies also "has historical precedent."[247] Nor was it curious to discover what the nature and effect of these practices has been for religious minorities, whether it has eased or pro-

---

[241] See, for example, Schragger, 117 Harv L Rev at 1815–16 (cited in note 12).

[242] Samaha, 2005 Supreme Court Review at 138 (cited in note 12).

[243] In *Galloway*, that argument is advanced (as usual) by Justice Thomas, writing alone on this point. See *Galloway*, 134 S Ct at 1835 (Thomas, J, concurring in part and concurring in the judgment).

[244] Horwitz, 63 U Miami L Rev at 891 (cited in note 202); see also Horwitz, *The Story of Santa Fe Independent School District* at 504–08 (cited in note 233).

[245] See Schragger, 117 Harv L Rev at 1813, 1816–17 (cited in note 12).

[246] *Galloway*, 134 S Ct at 1825.

[247] Id at 1819.

voked local political division along religious lines, or anything else. Neither Justice Kennedy's majority opinion nor Justice Kagan's principal dissent, moreover, so much as *mention* Justice Thomas's opinion, which at least discussed the issue, albeit strictly on originalist and federalist grounds. Whatever the answer to the question how to address "the role of the local in the doctrine and discourse of religious liberty"[248] should be, it must at least be acknowledged and addressed directly.

Town of Greece v Galloway poses another interesting issue at the level of the local in religious and political geography. This issue concerns the boundaries of the town of Greece itself. The resources for analyzing this issue do not come from religious geography. They come from the field of legal and political geography more generally.[249] In particular, scholarly treatments of the relationship between religious geography and Establishment Clause doctrine may learn a great deal from the study of the relationship between geography and race. A number of scholars have recognized the importance of the similarities and differences between race and religion, although that work has been mostly intermittent and preliminary in nature.[250] Here, I draw primarily on the work of Richard Thompson Ford, who has employed the political geography literature to examine the relationship between race and the drawing of political boundaries.[251]

One of Ford's central points is that legal boundaries, like the lines that demarcate a political jurisdiction such as the town of Greece, are often taken as givens—as natural, necessary, or both. We must organize our affairs somehow, after all. We do so by drawing lines, and then assigning votes, representation, responsibility for providing

---

[248] Schragger, 117 Harv L Rev at 1813 (cited in note 12).

[249] For useful resources, see Blomley, Delaney, and Ford, eds, *Legal Geographies Reader* (cited in note 10); Braverman et al, eds, *Expanding Spaces of Law* (cited in note 10).

[250] See, for example, Joy Milligan, *Religion and Race: On Duality and Entrenchment*, 87 NYU L Rev 393 (2012); Pamela S. Karlan, *Taking Politics Religiously: Can Free Exercise and Establishment Clause Cases Illuminate the Law of Democracy?*, 83 Ind L J 1 (2008); Mary Anne Case, *Lessons for the Future of Affirmative Action from the Past of the Religion Clauses?*, 2000 Supreme Court Review 325; Tseming Yang, *Race, Religion, and Cultural Identity: Reconciling the Jurisprudence of Race and Religion*, 73 Ind L J 119 (1997); Thomas C. Berg, *Religion, Race, Segregation, and Districting: Comparing Kiryas Joel with Shaw/Miller*, 26 Cumb L Rev 365 (1996); Eugene Volokh, *Diversity, Race as Proxy, and Religion as Proxy*, 43 UCLA L Rev 2059 (1996); Jesse H. Choper, *Religion and Race Under the Constitution: Similarities and Differences*, 79 Cornell L Rev 491 (1994); Kenneth L. Karst, *Law's Promise, Law's Expression: Visions of Power in the Politics of Race, Gender, and Religion* (Yale, 1993).

[251] See especially Ford, 107 Harv L Rev 1841 (cited in note 232).

public services, and other markers of legal and political rights and duties according to those lines. Sometimes we treat those boundaries as mere creations—as "'governmental technique[s]'"[252]—albeit valuable ones.[253] At other times, we treat boundaries as *real* things, not arbitrary creations but necessary consequences of the land and our place in it: "We imagine that the boundaries that define local governments . . . are a natural and inevitable function of geography and of a commitment to self-government or private property."[254]

Where race is concerned, Ford writes, these views of political geography, and the ability to toggle between them, can "justify [political or] judicial failures to consider the effect of boundaries and space on racial segregation."[255] *Milliken v Bradley*[256] provides a useful illustration. There, the Supreme Court held that a district court school busing remedy designed to address de jure racial segregation in Detroit's public schools could not extend to the predominantly white suburban school districts ringing the city. It achieved this outcome by treating those political boundaries as demarcating two entirely separate, autonomous political units, and the suburban districts as thus being disconnected from the de jure segregation that had occurred in Detroit itself.

But those lines were not drawn by accident or as a result of the demands of physical space. They were a product of deliberate white flight from Detroit, and of the willingness of government to draw political lines in a way that would reflect, if not actively accommodate, that phenomenon. A single governmental entity—the state of Michigan—was ultimately behind the drawing of jurisdictional lines in this manner. By "fail[ing] to examine the motivation for the position of local jurisdictional boundaries," the Court allowed—even encouraged—the entrenchment of segregation in both communities.[257]

Galloway, too, involves an invisible line, a political boundary, that turns out to be significant—or, in another sense, oddly insignifi-

---

[252] Richard T. Ford, *Law's Territory (a History of Jurisdiction)*, 97 Mich L Rev 843, 846 (1999), quoting *Holt Civic Club v City of Tuscaloosa*, 439 US 60, 72 (1978).

[253] See Ford, 107 Harv L Rev at 1857 (cited in note 232) ("Legal boundaries are . . . [often] imagined to be either the product of aggregated individual choices or the administratively necessary segmentation of centralized governmental power.").

[254] Id.

[255] Id.

[256] 418 US 717 (1974).

[257] See id at 1875–76.

cant—to the outcome in the case. One of the plaintiffs in *Galloway* was Jewish,[258] and it is unquestioned that Greece had Jewish residents. But the town never invited any representatives of local synagogues to give the invocation. Instead, the invocations remained almost uniformly, explicitly Christian.[259] A number of Jewish synagogues were located just outside the boundaries of the town, in Rochester.[260] Although the town argued that the overwhelmingly Christian nature of the invocations was simply "the result of a random selection process," it was obvious to the Second Circuit that limiting invitations to pray to individuals and groups within the town's borders was hardly "random," given the certainty that the town's residents might "hold religious beliefs that are not represented by a place of worship within the town."[261]

That conclusion is surely correct. But it did not detain the Court in *Galloway*. For Justice Kennedy, it sufficed that the town "made reasonable efforts to identify [and invite] all of the congregations located within its borders."[262] The Constitution, he said, as if the matter were obvious, "does not require [the town] to search beyond its borders for non-Christian prayer givers in an effort to achieve religious balancing."[263]

As with *Milliken*, this begs the question. Why, given the facts, was it "reasonable" to treat the town's official boundaries as an acceptable limit for issuing invitations to prayer-givers? Even if one takes for granted that a line must be drawn somewhere, why treat this *particular* line on the map as the stopping point? The town's jurisdictional lines are significant, to be sure. But they are not natural. They were drawn; they could be redrawn. The *Galloway* Court invests the political boundary of Greece with a disproportionate constitu-

---

[258] *Galloway*, 732 F Supp 2d at 196.

[259] After the plaintiffs had begun complaining and taken legal action, the town eventually invited a "Jewish layman" to deliver an invocation. See id at 219 n 41. As it turns out, the plaintiffs also found that prayer objectionable. See id at 209.

[260] See, for example, *Galloway*, 681 F3d at 24. A MapQuest search for local synagogues, combined with an examination of the official boundaries of the town of Greece, available online at http://greeceny.gov/files/Ward%20Map/2014%20Town%20of%20Greece%20Ward%20Map.pdf, confirms the presence of local synagogues and suggests that two local synagogues were located a mere four and a half miles outside the town lines.

[261] *Galloway*, 681 F3d at 31.

[262] *Galloway*, 134 S Ct at 1824.

[263] Id.

tional significance. Other local facts, like the location of the synagogues where Greece's Jews worship and the resulting failure to invite any rabbis to give the invocation, are treated as unfortunate but necessary casualties of this invisible jurisdictional line. It may not be a wholly arbitrary line. But that does not make it the *right* line.

For that matter, it is not *necessarily* an innocent one. As Alan Brownstein has observed, it is common "[o]utside of large urban and suburban centers" for religious minorities to build a house of worship in one town, "with the understanding that this congregation will serve the religious needs of adherents who live in neighboring communities as well."[264] That practice may simply reflect the need to find a geographically central location for a synagogue or other house of worship in a region in which religious minorities will find themselves dispersed in small numbers throughout the villages, towns, and suburbs that dot that area. In other cases, it may be an artifact of an older tradition of residential segregation, which at one time was aimed at religious and ethnic groups such as Jews, as well as racial groups.[265] Justice Kennedy displays no doubt whatsoever of the constitutional sufficiency of the town's jurisdictional lines as the basis for its decision whom to invite to give the invocation. He should.

The most interesting and thoughtful discussion of political boundaries in *Galloway* comes not from Kennedy, but from Justice Alito's concurrence. Alito is especially concerned with ensuring that the practice of holding opening prayers at town meetings not be derailed by the "informal, imprecise way" in which "small and medium-sized units of local government" conduct their operations.[266] Requiring more care and greater "exactitude," he complains, would "pressure towns to forswear altogether the practice of having a prayer before meetings of the town council."[267] The fact that the synagogues in the

[264] Alan Brownstein, *Town of Greece v. Galloway: Constitutional Challenges to State-Sponsored Prayers at Local Government Meetings*, 47 UC Davis L Rev 1521, 1532 (2014).

[265] See, for example, Garrett Power, *The Residential Segregation of Baltimore's Jews: Restrictive Covenant or Gentleman's Agreement?*, Generations, Fall 1996, at 5. In a brief blog post, Mark Tushnet has wondered whether a similar phenomenon might have been at work in that corner of New York state at one time. See Mark Tushnet, *An Unexplored Fact in Galloway*, Balkinization, May 7, 2014, online at http://balkin.blogspot.com/2014/05/an-unexplored-fact-in-galloway.html.

[266] *Galloway*, 134 S Ct at 1831 (Alito, J, concurring).

[267] Id.

area were located across the town line in Rochester sufficed, in his view, to explain the town's failure to issue invitations to those houses of worship. It should not "be held to have violated the First Amendment" simply because it did not "comply in all respects with what might be termed a 'best practices' standard."[268]

This is a fascinating passage. Alito's basic point—small towns do not have all the resources, staff, or experience that larger governmental units, certainly including Congress and the state legislatures, have—is surely correct. Why this fact demands the abandonment of rigorous constitutional standards is quite another matter. But that, in essence, is Alito's conclusion. Anything less than a deliberate attempt to discriminate should be forgiven, lest a town be required to forgo the practice of having sectarian legislative prayers.[269]

Of all the Justices writing in *Galloway*, Alito is the most sensitive to "the scale of government action and to the fact that local governments and state and federal governments are differently situated with respect to their citizens."[270] In the end, however, the tail wags the dog in his opinion. He is far more concerned about maintaining sectarian legislative prayer in small and medium-sized towns than he is interested in considering the problems involved in doing so. He disdains the imposition of "best practices," lest they interfere with those towns' prayer practices; but he says little or nothing about what, in the circumstances, might constitute good practices, or even reasonable ones.

If he had, he might have considered the possibility—one that is bound to be common across the United States—that a town's political boundaries may have nothing to do with its religious makeup, and that many communities may be ringed by houses of worship that

---

[268] Id.

[269] See id (noting that the town's manner of putting together a list of invitees "was at worst careless, and it was not done with a discriminatory intent").

[270] Schragger, 117 Harv L Rev at 1892 (cited in note 12). Justice Thomas's concurrence argues for the importance of federalism considerations in Establishment Clause jurisprudence, but his approach is rather a blunt instrument that is not especially well suited to showing genuine sensitivity to the truly "local." See id at 1817–18. And, of course, Justice Kagan's dissent is concerned with the specific nature of the proceedings before the town board in Greece, where citizens are more likely to interact directly with, and sometimes petition, members on matters of individual concern. See *Galloway*, 134 S Ct at 1847 (Kagan, J, dissenting). Apart from an interest in the nature of the town board's *proceedings*, however, she is not otherwise especially interested in its location, or in its potentially limited capacity to marshal the same resources in planning its prayer practices that Congress or a state legislature might have. She is, in short, more interested in the *what* than the *where* of different governmental bodies.

serve a community but lie outside its political boundaries. Indeed, it might have occurred to him that sometimes, however innocent the current actors may be, this phenomenon might be an artifact of past efforts to keep religious minorities, or their houses of worship, outside those jurisdictional lines.

What might this phenomenon demand in practice? Should it have required the Court to reject altogether the possibility of local legislative prayer, or to impose on local communities the kinds of demanding tests that Justice Alito fears could never be satisfied? Although I personally believe that a proper reading of the Establishment Clause casts doubt on the propriety of legislative prayer at any level of government,[271] I think that, assuming that legislative prayer continues to exist, it is possible to come up with standards for its exercise that do not render it impossible for local governmental bodies to maintain such a practice. The answer is not the extreme deference—almost indifference—that Alito's concurrence suggests should govern in such cases. Nor is it the rather blunt binary choice that Justice Kagan's dissent offers, in which legislative prayer must remain rigidly nonsectarian, or government can allow sectarian invocations only if it ensures an unspecified degree of religious diversity as the *outcome* of its prayer practices.[272]

Rather, the solution to the dilemma of local religious pluralism is exactly what one would expect from a geographically aware approach, one that is "attentive to the local quality of church-state relations," as Richard Schragger has urged.[273] In judging the constitutionality of particular local legislative prayer practices, courts— and, more importantly, the governments that craft these policies in the first instance—should rely on actual local conditions and demographics, not on political boundaries. In deciding whom to invite to

---

[271] See Horwitz, *The Agnostic Age* at 233–34 (cited in note 50).

[272] Indeed, it is not clear that Kagan's binary solution is an especially appropriate remedy to the problem outlined in the text. Imagine a community, somewhat like Greece, in which the religious minority is not invited to give the invocation because its houses of worship are located outside the town's boundaries, but the invocations that *are* given—always by members of the majority religion in that community—are resolutely nonsectarian. This state of affairs would appear to be permissible under Kagan's dissent. But it would not address the real problem, and I doubt that the nonsectarian nature of the prayers would wholly mitigate the justified sense of exclusion on the part of the religious minority in that community.

[273] Schragger, 117 Harv L Rev at 1892 (cited in note 12).

give invocations, local governmental bodies should look to what its citizens actually *believe*, not to the location of their houses of worship (if any). Most obviously, if a substantial number of houses of worship are located just outside its official boundaries, it should recognize the obvious significance of that fact and invite someone from those groups to give the invocation. It should not treat their location as a basis for excluding them from consideration altogether. It need not require all invocations to be nonsectarian; indeed, a policy that did so, but that failed to ask anyone other than representatives of the local majority faith to give those invocations, would be just as indifferent to local conditions as the town of Greece's policy was. What it *must* do is make some effort to actually ascertain the religious makeup of the community and spread its invitations to a wide swath of those faiths, as well as those who are not religious believers at all.

This is a simple enough prescription. On a superficial level, it may appear to raise Justice Alito's concern that it would demand greater resources than many local communities have. On closer examination, however, I do not believe it does. To the contrary, such a standard relies on precisely the resource that local governments, which stand in a closer, more intimate relation to their citizens, most possess: local knowledge. A genuinely small political community need not look to surveys or census data to determine the backgrounds and preferences of its people; whatever resources it lacks, it ought to have this kind of knowledge in spades. A larger community, on the other hand—recall that Greece's population was close to 100,000 people—can be expected to have less local knowledge than that, but greater resources. It has a larger number of representatives and a greater number of employees. It is not beyond their capacity to call around; to ask those local ministers that they *do* know for contacts in the interfaith community; or for representatives to seek constituent input. And even the knowledge that one lives in a bedroom community with close to a hundred thousand residents, one that lies just outside a larger city, is a form of local knowledge in itself. That fact alone counsels doing more than relying on hand-me-down lists or depending on the local jurisdictional boundaries. It suggests that the presence of synagogues or other houses of worship just a few miles away is a good reason to issue an invitation to those places. At a minimum, it suggests that when a community is too large to rely on local individual knowledge, *some* form of public notice or outreach may be required to achieve a properly diverse list of invitees. Greece did not even do that.[274]

Contrary to Justice Alito's fears, the kinds of things that a community may do to ensure that the nature of its own religious population is reflected in its public practices are not necessarily costly, demanding, or resource-intensive. They truly do simply require local knowledge. What is not allowed is utter indifference to local conditions, or—which is much the same thing—a reliance on political boundaries that local residents know are not truly representative of the demographics of the community. It should be relatively easy, and certainly not impossible, for a community to meet such standards. That the town of Greece did not should be treated as evidence that it was, at the least, less than properly concerned to reflect the town's religious diversity. In those circumstances, and for reasons having less to do with the sectarian nature of the prayers that resulted than from the fact that it was so careless about putting together a policy that reflected the actual religious identity of the town, Greece's prayer policy was rightly subject to a serious constitutional challenge.

As it is, one may conclude that Justice Alito's opinion, of all the opinions in *Galloway*, most clearly addresses "the role of the local" with respect to the constitutional permissibility of legislative prayer— and that, for all the reasons he gives, the Court should have reached the opposite conclusion in the case.

IV. Conclusion

The outcome of *Town of Greece v Galloway* was unfortunate, in my view, but not surprising. It is hardly a shock that a majority of the current Court is willing to affirm the constitutionality of legislative prayer at different levels of government. Certainly *Marsh*'s fate was never in doubt—although it is striking that, where it was once possible to muster three votes on the Court to hold that legislative prayer is unconstitutional, now even the dissenters in *Galloway* are unwilling to challenge that practice. If there is an important doctrinal move in the opinion, it has less to do with this particular controversy than with what Justice Kennedy's opinion, with its reliance on history and its statement embracing a wide range of prac-

---

[274] See *Galloway*, 681 F3d at 23 (noting that the town acknowledged its failure to publicize to town residents the existence of the opportunity to give invocations at board meetings).

tices, such as the Pledge of Allegiance and inaugural prayer, as "part of our expressive idiom," says about the chances of future challenges to American civil religious practices.[275] Many of those practices are nowhere near as ancient as legislative prayer. Nevertheless, *Galloway* suggests that none of them is going anywhere. That's not really much of a surprise.

Viewed through a geographical lens, however, *Galloway* is more interesting. A look at the religious geography of the United States— at both a regional and a local level, both as a historical matter and within contemporary American life—says more than mere doctrine can about both American religious pluralism and our attempts to deal with it at a political and legal level.

It conveys at least three lessons. It suggests that we might do better to think not of *one* single American church-state settlement, one definitive nationally applicable approach to questions of religious pluralism, but rather in terms of an array of American religious *pluralisms*. It urges us to think more carefully about the role of local jurisdictions in Establishment Clause law: to recognize the many salient social and geographical differences between towns, cities, states, and other subunits of government, and not to rely too heavily on jurisdictional lines to resolve Establishment Clause cases, when the circumstances make clear that there is sometimes little correspondence between jurisdictional lines and the lived reality of religious pluralism. Finally and more broadly, it suggests that law and religion scholarship should ease up on its obsession with Founding-era history or abstract theory, stripped in both cases of geographical context, and take more account of the role played by space and place in American religious pluralism. If we continue to take the conventional approach, we "risk missing something crucially important" about our subject.[276] Law and religion, like American religious history and religious studies before it, could benefit from a spatial turn.

---

[275] *Galloway*, 134 S Ct at 1825.

[276] Gaustad and Barlow, *New Historical Atlas of Religion in America* at xxii (cited in note 1).

LAURA M. WEINRIB

CIVIL LIBERTIES OUTSIDE THE COURTS

When critics of a countermajoritarian judiciary agonize over the cost to civil liberties of deference to the elected branches, they proceed on a false historical premise. They assume that courts were inextricably tied to the American tradition of expressive freedom and minority rights that emerged in the aftermath of the First World War. In fact, even the staunchest interwar advocates of civil liberties shared deep misgivings about judicial power. Many imagined and administered alternative regimes for civil liberties enforcement—methods that marshaled state power to counteract distortions in the marketplace of ideas and to advance substantive rights. Surprisingly, these early proponents of civil liberties linked the term, above all, to workers' rights to organize, picket, and strike. As partisans of organized labor, they were profoundly skeptical of judicial intervention. The court-centered strategy that ultimately prevailed was fiercely contested throughout the New Deal, well after the foundational First Amendment victories.

Laura M. Weinrib is Assistant Professor of Law, The University of Chicago.

AUTHOR'S NOTE: For helpful suggestions and conversations, I am indebted to Emily Buss, Mary Anne Case, Daniel Ernst, William Forbath, Risa Goluboff, Alexander Gourevitch, Hendrik Hartog, Aziz Huq, Jeremy Kessler, Sophia Lee, Jessica Lowe, Martha Nussbaum, James Gray Pope, Christopher Schmidt, Geoffrey Stone, and David Strauss. The article benefited from comments by workshop participants at the University of Chicago, American Bar Foundation, Emory Law School Thrower Symposium, Yale Law School Freedom of Expression Scholars Conference, American Society for Legal History, University of Virginia Legal History Workshop, and Watson Institute for International Studies at Brown University. Casey Prusher and Paxton Williams provided invaluable assistance with citations. I am grateful for support from the Legal History Fund.

Reconstructing these competing visions of civil liberties and the corresponding experiments in civil liberties enforcement before and after the "Constitutional Revolution" of the New Deal provides an important corrective to contemporary debates over court-based constitutionalism. In areas ranging from same-sex marriage to racial equality, recent decades have witnessed a resurgence of interest in extrajudicial approaches to advancing civil rights. Endorsements of popular constitutionalism and calls for constitutional amendment and judicial restraint manifest a growing aversion to the court-centered rights mobilization that dominated legal academia and the liberal imagination for almost half a century.[1]

Even in the domain of First Amendment protection for free speech—long considered an unassailable case for robust judicial review—the Warren Court consensus has begun to crumble. From the Second World War until the Rehnquist Court, it was an article of faith among activists and academics that a strong First Amendment would preserve a platform for transformative political ideas. In an era when state and federal actors targeted radical agitators, civil rights protestors, and antiwar demonstrators, the Supreme Court was comparatively (if unevenly) friendly to the rights of dissenters. In the 1980s and 1990s, however, a growing chorus of legal scholars described a shift in First Amendment law from the protection of disfavored minorities against state suppression to the insulation of industrial interests against government regulation.[2]

---

[1] The vast literature includes works from a variety of disciplinary and methodological perspectives, including Gerald N. Rosenberg, *The Hollow Hope: Can Courts Bring About Social Change?* (Chicago, 1991); William E. Forbath, *Law and the Shaping of the American Labor Movement* (Harvard, 1991); Michael W. McCann, *Rights at Work: Pay Equity Reform and the Politics of Legal Mobilization* (Chicago, 1994); Cass R. Sunstein, *One Case at a Time: Judicial Minimalism on the Supreme Court* (Harvard, 1999); Mark Tushnet, *Taking the Constitution Away from the Courts* (Princeton, 1999); Jack M. Balkin and Sanford Levinson, *Understanding the Constitutional Revolution*, 87 Va L Rev 1045 (2001); Michael Klarman, *From Jim Crow to Civil Rights: The Supreme Court and the Struggle for Racial Equality* (Oxford, 2004); Larry D. Kramer, *The People Themselves: Popular Constitutionalism and Judicial Review* (Oxford, 2004); Catherine Albiston, *The Dark Side of Litigation as a Social Movement Strategy*, 96 Iowa L Rev B 61 (2011); John Paul Stevens, *Six Amendments: How and Why We Should Change the Constitution* (Little, Brown, 2014). On the relationship between adjudication and popular constitutionalism, see Robert Post and Reva Siegel, *Roe Rage: Democratic Constitutionalism and Backlash*, 42 Harv CR-CL L Rev 373 (2007). The various critiques are addressed in Part III.

[2] See, for example, Owen M. Fiss, *Liberalism Divided: Freedom of Speech and the Many Uses of State Power* (Westview, 1996); Cass R. Sunstein, *Democracy and the Problem of Free Speech* (Free Press, 1993); Mark A. Graber, *Transforming Free Speech: The Ambiguous Legacy of Civil Libertarianism* (California, 1991); Morton Horwitz, *Foreword: The Constitution of Change*, 107 Harv L Rev 30 (1993); id at 109 (section on "The Lochnerization of the First Amendment").

Over time, such appraisals have become more prevalent and more frenzied. Today, a broad range of legal scholars and cultural critics decry the Court's "Lochnerization" of the First Amendment: its persistent invalidation of legislative and administrative efforts to temper alleged corporate dominance, and its use of the First Amendment to undermine federal programs or to qualify public sector collective bargaining agreements.[3] They lament its simultaneous retreat from involvement in mitigating poverty, expanding equality, and securing economic justice.[4] They have urged judicial deference toward democratic efforts to balance competing constitutional values, within and outside the First Amendment context.

Students of the First Amendment may be surprised to discover well developed antecedents of such critiques in the modern history of free speech.[5] They have accepted two basic premises that have distorted their historical understanding and colored their consideration of potential paths forward. First, they have presupposed a well established tradition of progressive support for free speech, at least after the First World War demonstrated the dangers of gov-

---

Commentators have lamented the tendency of the Supreme Court to uphold and extend unfettered participation in the marketplace of ideas at the expense of meaningful access for underfunded and underrepresented speakers. John C. Coates, IV, *Corporate Speech and the First Amendment: History, Data, and Implications* (Feb 2015), online at http://ssrn.com/abstract=2566785.

[3] In addition to the campaign finance cases, see *Burwell v Hobby Lobby Stores, Inc.*, 134 S Ct 2751 (2014); *National Ass'n of Mfrs v SEC*, 748 F3d 359 (DC Cir 2014), overruled in *American Meat Institute v US Dept of Agriculture*, 760 F3d 18 (DC Cir 2014); and especially *Harris v Quinn*, 134 S Ct 2618 (2014).

[4] Scholars from a variety of disciplines have highlighted the tendency of the judiciary to impede state efforts to mitigate inequality. For example, Stephen Skowronek, *Building a New American State: The Expansion of National Administrative Capacities, 1877–1920* (Cambridge, 1982); Howard Gillman, *The Constitution Besieged: The Rise and Demise of Lochner Era Police Powers Jurisprudence* (Duke, 1993); Forbath, *Law and the Shaping of the American Labor Movement* (cited in note 1); Karen Orren, *Belated Feudalism: Labor, the Law, and Liberal Development in the United States* (Cambridge, 1991); Theda Skocpol, *Protecting Soldiers and Mothers: The Political Origins of Social Policy in the United States* (Harvard, 1992).

[5] The extensive literature on constitutionalism outside the courts has largely neglected the First Amendment. The principal exception is Paul Horwitz, *First Amendment Institutions* (Harvard, 2013), which focuses on nonstate institutions. Cf. Frederick Schauer, *Towards an Institutional First Amendment*, 89 Minn L Rev 1256 (2005) (arguing for greater judicial attention to institutional difference in First Amendment analysis). Work on civil liberties and congressional constitutionalism has focused on the Speech or Debate Clause or has regarded the First Amendment as a potential barrier to congressional activity in other domains. For example, Josh Chafetz, *Congress's Constitution*, 160 U Pa L Rev 715 (2012); David P. Currie, *The Constitution in Congress* (Chicago, 1997). In the administrative context, Reuel Schiller has argued that agency interpretations have informed judicial doctrine. Reuel E. Schiller, *Free Speech and Expertise: Administrative Censorship and the Birth of the Modern First Amendment*, 86 Va L Rev 1, 3–4, 101 (2000).

ernment censorship.[6] That is, they have imagined the expansion of First Amendment protections beginning with the famous Holmes and Brandeis dissents as a victory for advocates of oppressed groups. Second, and relatedly, they have assumed that conservatives resisted free speech claims in the late 1930s, as they had during World War I and as they would during the Cold War. Because the judiciary's retreat from judicial review in economic cases corresponded to a new vigilance with respect to free speech and "discrete and insular minorities," they regard both halves of the New Deal Settlement as repudiations of the Right.

Both of those assumptions are incomplete. In other work, I argue that conservatives were a key constituency of the New Deal coalition responsible for securing strong First Amendment rights in the courts.[7] In this article, I address the corresponding lack of enthusiasm for a court-centered First Amendment strategy among a substantial subset of liberal New Dealers. Then, as now, many critics of a comparatively conservative Court preferred to pursue their agenda outside the judiciary.

Moreover, faith in the First Amendment during the New Deal did not necessarily entail a preference for judicial enforcement. Some New Dealers who advocated state protection of social and economic rights perceived a strong First Amendment as a threat to their legislative agenda and thus opposed free speech as a constitutional value altogether. Others, however, regarded unfettered deliberation as a normatively and constitutionally necessary prerequisite for democratic rights but nonetheless rejected the courts as the primary institution for implementing the First Amendment. Still others turned to the judiciary for validation of free speech claims, but in a manner quite foreign to today's defensive practices. Rather than invoking the First Amendment as a shield against government infringement, they urged and secured federal prosecution of local officials and even private actors who curtailed expressive freedom.

These disparate approaches have been forgotten largely because of a terminological misunderstanding. Between the Second New

---

[6] The observation that progressives were skeptical of First Amendment claims by pacifists and radicals during World War I is a distinct claim. David M. Rabban, *Free Speech in Its Forgotten Years, 1870–1920* (Cambridge, 1997); Graber, *Transforming Free Speech* (cited in note 2); Laura Weinrib, *From Public Interest to Private Rights: Free Speech, Liberal Individualism, and the Making of Modern Tort Law,* 34 L & Soc Inq 187 (2009).

[7] See Laura Weinrib, *The Constitutional Compromise of 1937: Ideological Convergence and the Civil Liberties Consensus* (working paper on file with author), and Laura Weinrib, *The Taming of Free Speech* (book manuscript on file with author).

Deal and the Second World War, the courts emerged as the legitimate locus of interpretive authority in the domain of rights that
eventually occupied the category "civil liberties." Although it has no
specific doctrinal significance, that phrase has come to encompass
a recognizable and distinctive set of legal rights. Those rights ordinarily include the freedom of speech and religion, the procedural
rights of criminal defendants, perhaps reproductive rights or the
right to bear arms. Such rights, as they are conventionally understood, are asserted to block the state. They are invoked in court by
private actors—individuals and their representatives—often in the
course of a criminal prosecution. They are routinely described, albeit contentiously, as "negative" rather than "positive."[8] Health care,
old-age security, or a living wage may be desirable policy goals, but
they are not now considered civil liberties.[9]

---

[8] On the "controversy surrounding the positive-negative distinction," see Emily Zackin,
*Looking for Rights in All the Wrong Places: Why State Constitutions Contain America's Positive
Rights* 42–47 (Princeton, 2013). While acknowledging the role of government in enforcing
"negative" rights and in shaping putatively private relationships, Zackin provides a compelling argument for the use of the terms "positive" and "negative" in the context of American
constitutional history: "[A]t the level of their lived experiences, the activists who shaped state
constitutions perceived an important difference between governmental action and restraint.
They also distinguished between threats posed directly by government itself and dangers that
stemmed from other sources." Id at 45. The same might be said of the civil liberties advocates
described in this article. In 1935, David J. Saposs drew on the terms to describe AFL-style
labor voluntarism. He explained: "The workers were especially tutored to eschew becoming
the 'wards of the state' by shunning legislation and other forms of government intervention
in labor matters. Only legislation of a negative intent was to be acceptable." With the exception of legislation affecting women and children, "positive legislation," which included
social insurance as well as wage and hour laws, was "bound to corrupt and weaken the
workers' reliance upon their voluntary economic organizations, the unions." David J. Saposs,
The American Labor Movement Since the War, 49 Q J Econ 236, 237 (1935). Similarly, in a
1937 letter, Roger Baldwin described the Bill of Rights as "a defensive document guaranteeing the citizen protection against the invasion of his rights by the government." By
contrast, "the more positive program for civil rights [was] to be found in the Labor Relations
Acts and the other guarantees under which democratic organization in industry becomes not
only a defensive but a positive force." Roger Baldwin to Mrs. John Rogers Jr., Dec 28, 1937,
in American Civil Liberties Union Records, the Roger Baldwin Years, 1917–50, Seeley G.
Mudd Manuscript Library, Public Policy Papers, Princeton University, Princeton, NJ
(hereafter ACLU Papers), reel 142, vol 967. New Deal civil liberties advocates grappled with
what Hendrik Hartog has called "[t]he problem of dependency" that plagued the "eman-
cipatory project identified with constitutional rights consciousness"; that is, they agonized
over "the appropriate quantity of protection that the federal government, as well as other
structures of authority, ought to provide." See Hendrik Hartog, *The Constitution of Aspiration
and "The Rights that Belong to Us All,"* 74 J Am Hist 1013, 1019–20 (1987).

[9] The Court's reluctance to protect socioeconomic rights has been a distinguishing feature
of American constitutionalism. See, for example, Martha Nussbaum, *Foreword: Constitutions
and Capabilities: "Perception" Against Lofty Formalism*, 121 Harv L Rev 4, 57 (2007); Frank I.
Michelman, *Socioeconomic Rights in Constitutional Law: Explaining America Away*, Intl J Const L
6, 3–4 (2008); Cass R. Sunstein, *Why Does the American Constitution Lack Social and Economic
Guarantees?*, Syracuse L Rev 56, 1 (2005). In the First Amendment context, a socioeconomic

During the New Deal, by contrast, the designation was capacious enough to encompass all these rights and more. Progressives, conservatives, radicals, and liberals espoused antithetical views of state power, social and economic ordering, and individual rights. And yet all framed their programs in civil liberties terms. When scholars today see endorsements of "civil liberties" in judicial opinions, administrative records, and congressional debates, they assume that New Deal actors meant to invoke a basically compatible set of constitutional principles. Occasionally, contemporaneous observers made the same mistake.

In reality, celebrants of civil liberties were advancing distinct positions, even when they shared a set of overarching social and economic goals. There was only one legal and policy commitment that all placed squarely under the label they championed: the right of workers to engage in "peaceful" picketing.[10] The subsequent relegation of labor activity to second-class status under the First Amendment renders that single commonality almost inconceivable in retrospect.[11] During the 1920s, however, an unlikely coalition of lawyers and activists led by the American Civil Liberties Union had made the right to organize central to the definition of civil liberties. For a variety of reasons—some theoretical, some opportunistic—all embraced what Justice Frank Murphy called "the right to discuss freely industrial relations which are matters of public concern."[12] There was marked disagreement over the ideological justification for that conclusion, as well as the larger bundle of rights from which the rights of labor derived.

When New Deal liberals spoke in terms of civil liberties, they were laying claim to a label that had recently come to be viewed as normatively desirable and central to American governance. The

---

view has been particularly disfavored. See, for example, Frederick Schauer, *The Exceptional First Amendment*, in Michael Ignatieff, ed, *American Exceptionalism and Human Rights* (Princeton, 2005), 46 ("The Constitution of the United States is a strongly negative constitution, and viewing a constitution as the vehicle for ensuring social rights, community rights, or positive citizen entitlements of any kind is, for better or for worse, highly disfavored. . . . [T]his skepticism about the ability of any governmental institution reliably to distinguish the good from the bad, the true from the false, and the sound from the unsound finds its most comfortable home in the First Amendment").

[10] Participants defined "peaceful" in a variety of ways. For some, the term excluded mass picketing and methods considered as coercive under the common law.

[11] See, for example, Kenneth G. Dau-Schmidt et al, *Labor Law in the Contemporary Workplace* 711 (West, 2d ed 2014) ("[L]abor union speech receives less First Amendment protection than that of other activists").

[12] *Thornhill v Alabama*, 310 US 88 (1940).

content of that category remained ambiguous, but for much of the decade, among most of the groups who invoked it, it was linked to economic justice. Disparate competencies and areas of focus led competing advocates and institutions to envision the evils of modern society in different ways. In claiming to be the true defenders of civil liberties, and in defining the optimal enforcement of those rights, those actors wrestled over the contours of constitutional democracy in the United States. They expressed their clashing conceptions through a common vocabulary, but they voiced opposing judgments about which rights took priority and how they should be secured.

The vision of civil liberties that prevailed in the late New Deal established the judiciary as a check on majoritarian democracy and administrative discretion. State action was its target, not its engine. Civil liberties enforcement was a species of judicial review that closely resembled substantive due process—that is, it curtailed government's power to interfere with "private" behavior, without disturbing the legal framework through which market power was allocated and preserved—a feature that industry understood and quickly endorsed. I describe this constellation of commitments as the liberal vision of civil liberties. Its central pillar was the First Amendment.

But this narrow adherence to a state-constraining Bill of Rights was the terminus of the New Deal interpretive struggle rather than its origin. The goal of this article is to recover an earlier, more capacious moment, when the meaning of "civil liberties" was fluid and porous. Understanding how particular objectives and ideas were excluded from its purview yields important insights into the perceived advantages and limitations of the modern First Amendment, as well as the larger universe of strategies for social and constitutional change outside the courts. Many of the approaches advanced and tested during the New Deal resonate with current proposals. Others are scarcely recognizable as theoretical possibilities.

In this unfamiliar account of the articulation and enforcement of civil liberties during the 1930s, the major players are government actors and private organizations. The ACLU, whose deep state skepticism initially stemmed from the tenets of radical trade unionism, framed popular and judicial understandings of civil liberties in the interwar period and after. The account of civil liberties that the organization espoused and the Court eventually accepted reflected a strategic partnership with such unlikely entities as the

American Bar Association and the American Liberty League. Meanwhile, many of the ACLU's liberal and labor allies broke with the organization over its increasing reliance on judicial review. The labor movement, after all, had railed for more than a century at its ill treatment by the courts.[13] For their part, the New Deal reformers who called for active intervention in the economy also demanded active intervention on behalf of disfavored ideas. They advocated adjustments in the marketplace of ideas to correct distortions stemming from inequality of access or relative power. And many sought to implement that vision in spite of, rather than through, the courts.

Part I identifies four discrete visions of civil liberties in circulation among advocates and government actors during the New Deal: a radical, state-skeptical vision rooted in the "direct action" of militant trade unionism; a progressive vision premised on deliberative openness in the formulation of public policy; a conservative vision that linked economic liberty to the Bill of Rights; and a labor interventionist vision that regarded state support of collective bargaining as instrumental to achieving material social and economic goals. By the late New Deal, these competing understandings yielded to a synthetic, liberal vision that privileged judicial enforcement.

Part II then takes up, in turn, the practice of civil liberties enforcement within four New Deal institutions that vied for interpretive power. The Supreme Court was sympathetic to state efforts to effectuate labor's rights even while it constrained the government's ability to target the coercive effects of workers' (and eventually, employers') concerted activity. The Senate Civil Liberties Committee sponsored legislation to safeguard labor's organizational activity against intervention by both government and employers. The National Labor Relations Board subordinated free speech to the right to organize and legitimated state prohibitions on expression that unduly pressured workers due to disparities in bargaining power. Finally, the Civil Liberties Unit within the Department of Justice treated workers' associational rights as part of a broader

---

[13] See, for example, Forbath, *Law and the Shaping of the American Labor Movement* (cited in note 1); Christopher L. Tomlins, *Law, Labor, and Ideology in the Early American Republic* (Cambridge, 1993); Victoria C. Hattam, *Labor Visions and State Power: The Origins of Business Unionism in the United States* (Princeton, 1993); Daniel R. Ernst, *Lawyers Against Labor: From Individual Rights to Corporate Liberalism* (Illinois, 1995).

constellation of freedoms enforceable, with state assistance, against recalcitrant employers and the local officials who countenanced their illegal practices. For the administrative actors discussed in this article, the modal civil liberties were workers' rights to organize, boycott, and strike. The labor-centric view contended with other possibilities, however, which foregrounded individual autonomy in place of group rights.

In Part III, I draw several tentative conclusions from these historical materials with respect to the relationship between institutional constraints and the pursuit of particular rights. Sometimes, the institutional actors featured in this article operated at cross purposes. Often, their efforts overlapped. All proved to be responsive to popular pressures and yet capable of resisting public opinion to protect disfavored rights claimants against both government and private repression. And yet, it is possible to identify some salient differences between them, including, most notably, their respective attitudes toward state power.

As a matter of historical circumstance, the theory of civil liberties that prevailed during the New Deal foregrounded the courts as a check on state abuses. During the 1930s, the judiciary emerged for the first time as a potential guardian and even emblem of personal freedom. Reconstructing the alternative visions of civil liberties and their optimal enforcement reveals the anticipated advantages of the judicial strategy as well as its costs. That undertaking should matter to constitutional theorists as much as historians.

I. Visions of Civil Liberties During the New Deal

In May 1937, just one month after the Supreme Court upheld the constitutionality of the National Labor Relations Act,[14] the American Civil Liberties Union issued a report on the merits of judicial review. Its subject was only incidentally the Court's persistent invalidation of New Deal economic legislation, which prompted President Franklin D. Roosevelt's ill-fated Judicial Procedures Reform Bill.[15] Instead, the ACLU's report on the Court-packing plan—

---

[14] *NLRB v Jones & Laughlin Steel Corporation*, 301 US 1 (1937).

[15] On the constitutional revolution, see William E. Leuchtenburg, *The Supreme Court Reborn: The Constitutional Revolution in the Age of Roosevelt* (Oxford, 1995); Barry Cushman, *Rethinking the New Deal Court: The Structure of a Constitutional Revolution* (Oxford, 1998); Richard A. Maidment, *The Judicial Response to the New Deal: The United States Supreme Court*

prepared by Osmond Fraenkel, a member of the Board of Directors and the ACLU's Supreme Court litigator—addressed the question "how far the Court has been a defender of civil liberties." To
that end, it evaluated the Court's record since the nineteenth century.[16] It concluded that the Court had "more often failed to protect the Bill of Rights than preserve it," and that those decisions
favorable to civil liberties involved "less important issues." Still, the
Court had begun to protect "personal rights" (a term encompassing
privacy, bodily integrity, and expressive freedom) more vigilantly
as a result of its "widening conception" of the Due Process Clause.[17]
As Fraenkel reflected in comments to the ACLU board, "so long
as we believe in safeguarding the rights of minorities, the power of
review is essential to protect these rights."[18]

The ACLU's report is a striking document. It represents the
organization's effort to grapple with one of the most divisive questions facing social movements and sympathetic government officials during the 1930s: whether efforts to defend political minorities
and facilitate economic change should proceed through the legislature, government agencies, or the courts. That question was intimately bound up with an equally fundamental debate over how civil
liberties should be defined and what goals and values they served.[19]

---

and Economic Regulation, 1934–1936 (St. Martin's, 1991); Alan Brinkley, *The End of Reform:
New Deal Liberalism in Recession and War* (Knopf, 1995).

[16] It tallied the Court's decisions in such far-ranging areas as military trials, slavery or
peonage, searches and seizures, freedom of religion, education, aliens and citizenship, freedom of speech, and labor relations.

[17] ACLU Press Release, May 21, 1937, ACLU Papers, reel 143, vol 978. According to
Fraenkel, the Supreme Court had "spoken strongly against federal laws restricting civil lib-
erties" only once, in *Ex parte Milligan*, 71 US 2 (1866). Felix Cohen went further. By his
interpretation of the case law, "No person deprived of any civil liberty by an oppressive act of
Congress has ever received any help from the Supreme Court. On the other hand, when
Congress has extended aid to those deprived of civil liberties, the Supreme Court, in five
cases out of seven, has nullified the aid that Congress tendered." Felix Cohen to Osmond
Fraenkel, April 24, 1937, ACLU Papers, reel 143, vol 978.

[18] Preliminary Report of the American Civil Liberties Union Temporary Committee
Concerning the Supreme Court, ACLU Papers, reel 143, vol 978.

[19] See Laura Weinrib, *The Liberal Compromise: Civil Liberties, Labor, and the Limits of State
Power, 1917–1940* (PhD diss, Princeton University, 2011); Emily Zackin, *Popular Constitutionalism's Hard When You're Not Very Popular: Why the ACLU Turned to Courts*, 42 L & Soc
Rev 367 (2008). In the wake of the First World War, the nascent civil liberties movement had
sought unsuccessfully to secure its agenda through propaganda and popular persuasion. Its
constituents subsequently experimented with a range of top-down methods for cabining state
repression—including, but not limited to, a court-based approach—despite conflicting con-

To assess the field, the ACLU administered a survey to prominent legal authorities, soliciting their views on the implications for civil liberties (without defining that term) of various proposals to limit judicial review. Walter Gellhorn, an administrative law scholar who was then serving as regional attorney for the Social Security system, believed the courts could be constrained without significant danger to civil liberties. Lloyd Garrison, dean of the University of Wisconsin Law School and the first chair of the original NLRB, was somewhat friendlier to judicial involvement, and he cautioned against "giving majorities too much say over minorities."[20] Edwin Borchard, a law professor at Yale, thought it "apparent that the current danger is an expansion of the executive power into dictatorship"—and he considered the Supreme Court to be "the greatest safeguard we have against executive arbitrariness."[21] The socialist leader and Presbyterian minister Norman Thomas favored a constitutional amendment clarifying congressional power to legislate in "economic and social matters" and restricting judicial review exclusively in those domains.[22] These respondents and others uniformly endorsed civil liberties, but they differed profoundly with respect to the content of the rights they defended, the source of the threat to those rights, and the best means of preserving them.

In contrast to liberals' ambivalence, mainstream conservatives and the American Bar Association publicly celebrated the Supreme Court's recent decisions upholding (if tepidly) free speech and the rights of criminal defendants—decisions, that is, in cases argued by Fraenkel and the ACLU, which most members of the bar had staunchly opposed when they were handed down. Newly converted, the ABA proclaimed to radio audiences that the Supreme Court had proven its worth by defending personal and property rights alike. To Fraenkel, that was precisely the problem. "Since property can defend itself more effectively," he cautioned, "administrative officials and lower courts follow the Supreme Court more consistently in

---

ceptions of government's appropriate reach. Even in the domain of legal argument, its early victories were rarely decided on constitutional grounds; rather, civil liberties advocates counseled prosecutorial restraint and, in court, argued that criminal statutes and the common law contained safe harbors for dissenting views. By the end of the 1920s, however, civil liberties advocates increasingly pressed, and occasionally won, constitutional claims.

[20] Preliminary Report (cited in note 18).

[21] Edwin Borchard to Osmond Fraenkel, February 4, 1937, ACLU Papers, reel 143, vol 978.

[22] Norman Thomas to Roger Baldwin, February 25, 1937, ACLU Papers, reel 142, vol 969.

protecting property than personal rights." The result was that "the fight for personal rights has constantly to be fought over."[23]

Historians and constitutional scholars have approached New Deal perspectives on the First Amendment through an unduly narrow lens—a focus shaped by the state-skeptical and court-centered vision of civil liberties that ultimately prevailed. They have looked for struggles over the appropriate scope of state power to curb advocacy and expression, framed as a contest between national security or the public interest, on the one hand, and individual autonomy or deliberative openness on the other. They have found them in the seminal First Amendment cases that populate the pages of constitutional law casebooks.

Certainly these familiar battles over seditious speech were understood by many New Dealers as important civil liberties concerns. To cabin "civil liberties" in this way, however, is anachronistic. During the 1930s, the meaning of civil liberties was in flux. More to the point, it was vehemently contested. Whatever their underlying objectives, advocates across the political spectrum defended them in civil liberties terms. To some, civil liberties were constraints on state power; to others, they served as a basis for state intervention against private abuses or economic inequality. Civil liberties might undercut administrative discretion or justify government intrusions. By the end of the decade, even constituencies that had long decried free speech as a cover for subversive activity claimed the mantle of civil liberties as their own.

This convergence reflects a common engagement with (if not a shared solution to) a basic New Deal problem, namely, the appropriate balance between state power and individual rights in a period of rapid government growth. Under the rubric of civil liberties, New Deal insiders and sympathizers debated such far-ranging issues as antilynching legislation, tribal autonomy for American Indians, expansion of political asylum, transfer of colonial possessions from naval to civilian rule, and the rights of the unemployed. At an ACLU-sponsored conference on Civil Liberties Under the New Deal in 1934, representatives from such groups as the International Labor Defense, the National Urban League, and the NAACP discussed legislative proposals to expand asylum for political refugees, provide jury trials in postal censorship cases, and criminalize lynch-

---

[23] ACLU Press Release, May 21, 1937, ACLU Papers, reel 143, vol 978.

ing under federal law.[24] Although they "showed surprising unanimity of opinion on fundamentals,"[25] delegates clashed over the desirability of federal regulation of radio content—including a requirement to allocate equal radio airtime to all sides of controversial questions— and the trade-offs between private and public control.[26] Over the course of the decade, self-described civil liberties advocates would split over antifascist security measures, the extension of free speech to Nazi marches, and the propriety of racial discrimination in public accommodations.

If there was a single issue, however, that most poignantly foregrounded the costs and benefits of an interventionist state vis-à-vis personal rights, it was the labor question.[27] Between the First World War and the New Deal, the modern civil liberties movement evolved from a radical fringe group espousing labor's right of revolution to a mainstream exponent of widely held (if inconsistently enforced) principles of constitutional democracy. The primary architect of that feat was the ACLU. After an unsuccessful stint as a "frankly partisan[ ]" labor adjunct,[28] the organization had extended its operations into such areas as academic freedom, artistic expression, and sex education, in which broad-based consensus was feasible.[29] When it solicited assistance in labor cases during the 1920s, it was careful to emphasize the neutrality of its principles. And yet, for the radical

[24] Memorandum of Bills Proposed for Discussion, Conference on Civil Liberties under the New Deal, ACLU Papers, reel 110, vol 719.

[25] ACLU Press Bulletin 643, December 14, 1934, ACLU Papers, reel 110, vol 721.

[26] For example, Louis G. Caldwell, "Excerpts from 'Freedom on the Air,'" Conference on Civil Liberties and the New Deal, ACLU Papers, reel 110, vol 721.

[27] Although historians have largely neglected the labor history of the modern civil liberties movement, there is an extensive bibliography on efforts by the labor movement to mobilize constitutional rights, including free speech, during earlier periods (especially before World War I). The best-known examples are the IWW's Free Speech Fights and the AFL's boycott campaign. See, for example, Rabban, *Forgotten Years* (cited in note 6); John Wertheimer, *Free Speech Fights: The Roots of Modern Free-Expression Litigation in the United States* (PhD diss, Princeton University, 1992); Melvyn Dubofsky, *We Shall Be All: A History of the Industrial Workers of the World* 98–113 (Quadrangle, 1969); Philip S. Foner, *History of the Labor Movement*, vol 9, *The T.U.E.L. to The End of the Gompers Era* (International Publishers, 1991); Philip S. Foner, ed, *Fellow Workers and Friends: IWW Free Speech Fights as Told by Participants* (Greenwood, 1981); Glen J. Broyles, *The Spokane Free-Speech Fight, 1909–1910: A Study in IWW Tactics*, 19 Labor Hist 238 (1978); Stewart Bird, Dan Georgakas, and Deborah Shaffer, *Solidarity Forever: An Oral History of the IWW* (Lake View, 1985).

[28] Walter Nelles, Suggestions for Reorganization of the National Civil Liberties Bureau (undated), ACLU Papers, reel 16, vol 120.

[29] Laura M. Weinrib, *The Sex Side of Civil Liberties: United States v. Dennett and the Changing Face of Free Speech*, 30 L & Hist Rev 325 (2012).

core of the ACLU leadership, civil liberties were synonymous with the "right of agitation"—roughly, a right of private actors to marshal persuasion, propaganda, and collective power in the arena of political and economic struggle, without intervention by the state.

Needless to say, theirs was not the only view. While conservatives were marginal in the 1920s civil liberties coalition, some were sympathetic to expanding the scope of private autonomy.[30] Progressives, meanwhile, played a central part. For many of them, civil liberties served to buttress rather than undermine state power. When they endorsed the rights of workers to organize or disseminate their views, they emphasized the marketplace of ideas and disavowed radical ends. Their defense of labor radicals echoed Justice Holmes's dissenting pronouncement in *Gitlow v New York*: "If in the long run the beliefs expressed in proletarian dictatorship are destined to be accepted by the dominant forces of the community, the only meaning of free speech is that they should be given their chance and have their way."[31]

As long as civil liberties were primarily aspirational, disagreements within the civil liberties campaign were relatively inconsequential. In the 1930s, by contrast, aspiration stood to become reality. As a result, seemingly small differences took on immense proportions. And the most important fracture in the civil liberties alliance occurred over New Deal labor policy. Put simply, when New Dealers argued over the appropriate scope of government involvement in securing civil liberties, they were far more concerned about protections for unions and collective bargaining than adjustments in the marketplace of ideas. Indeed, their attitudes toward the latter were often mere applications of theories they developed in the labor context.

The core of the conflict involved competing attitudes toward state power and the federal courts. The various efforts to regulate labor relations during the New Deal prescribed a strong role for the state in

---

[30] See David E. Bernstein, *Rehabilitating Lochner: Defending Individual Rights Against Progressive Reform* 90–107 (Chicago, 2011). Cf. Ken I. Kersch, *Constructing Civil Liberties: Discontinuities in the Development of American Constitutional Law* (Cambridge, 2004) (arguing that the Court's "landmark education decisions of the 1920s . . . represented acts of resistance to progressive state building and nation building initiatives aimed at gaining increased national bureaucratic control over the lives of children, families, and schools, in the service of constructing a new 'American liberty,' a stand that—along with protection for 'economic rights'—the Supreme Court would abandon in reaching an accommodation with the New American State and the New Constitutional Nation").

[31] *Gitlow v New York*, 268 US 652 (1925).

brokering disputes between workers and their employers. This development marked a substantial departure from labor's long-standing skepticism toward state involvement, most familiarly expressed in the American Federation of Labor's commitment to labor voluntarism. Although they had often endorsed political candidates and welcomed government support in return, AFL unions had vehemently opposed compulsory arbitration and favored collective bargaining over government protections for workers' rights. As for radical trade unionists, while they anticipated the eventuality of a proletarian state, in the short term many promoted nonstate "direct action." Consistent with American labor leaders' deep distrust of the state, previous measures to protect labor's rights—most famously, the 1933 Norris-LaGuardia Act, which the ACLU had helped to draft[32]—had sought to shield the struggle between workers and industry from government (understood to include the courts) intervention, not to invite the state in. Indeed, in the early interwar period, insulating the instruments of direct action had been the civil liberties movement's most pressing goal. When it invoked First Amendment protection for labor activity, it was pursuing something very like the constitutionalization of the Norris-LaGuardia Act.[33]

Against this trajectory, the New Deal's state-centered labor policy reflected an ironic reversal of the civil liberties movement's founding assumptions. New Deal legislation explicitly recognized the "right of employees to organize" and preserved the "right to strike." In the National Labor Relations Act (NLRA), Congress eventually declared its intention to protect "the exercise by workers of full free-

---

[32] In 1931, its National Committee on Labor Injunctions managed to produce a draft anti-injunction measure agreeable to the AFL, labor lawyers, law professors, and interested organizations. Monthly Bulletin for Action, January 1931, ACLU Papers, reel 79, vol 444. The bill eliminated ex parte hearings, ensured that all violations of injunctions would be tried by juries, limited punishment of contempt, abolished yellow dog contracts, and ensured that no acts "which involve only workers' rights to meet, speak, [or] circulate literature" would be enjoined. Memorandum on the Proposed Injunction Bill, January 1932, ACLU Papers, reel 90, vol 536. Once the federal bill was passed, William Green, president of the AFL, arranged for the ACLU to assist in the preparation of state anti-injunction bills, as well. William Green to Roger Baldwin, December 29, 1933, ACLU Papers, reel 99, vol 615D.

[33] The extension of this principle beyond the labor context might have been understood in similar terms. To the architects of the civil liberties movement, the labor injunction was functionally equivalent to an injunction against publication, *Near v Minnesota*, 283 US 697 (1931), or even a postal ban, *Masses Publishing Company v Patten*, 244 F 535, 538 (SDNY 1917), reversed, 246 F 24 (2d Cir 1917). By the same token, historic convictions for criminal conspiracy, for example, *Commonwealth v Pullis* (Philadelphia Mayor's Court, 1806), resembled the seminal free speech cases of the World War I period.

dom of association, self organization, and designation of representatives of their own choosing."[34] Importantly, it accomplished these
objectives not merely by preventing *state* incursions on workers' organizing efforts, but employer interference as well. That is, it marshaled the power of the state to facilitate labor activity. In the process,
it sharply limited employers' common law prerogatives, including
some—such as freedom of contract—that had long been accorded
constitutional status.

From the perspective of state involvement, the NLRA reflected
a compromise. The statute employed state power to shield workers from employer retaliation for concerted activity and to force
employers to the bargaining table. But it was equally central to the
statutory framework that the parties would negotiate and police their
own substantive contractual terms. The NLRA sought to equalize
bargaining power by removing legal and economic obstacles to worker
power. The role of the NLRB was to ensure that employers played by
the rules.

The new approach satisfied most, but not all, proponents of labor's rights. Within the mainstream labor movement, the dissenters
were committed voluntarists representing established craft unions.
Their relatively strong bargaining power rendered government assistance unnecessary; in their view, the risks of administrative med-
dling outweighed the benefits.[35] By contrast, the industrial unionists
who sought to organize unskilled workers overwhelmingly favored
affirmative protections in part because they had more to gain.[36]

But there were critics on the Left, as well—and the Communists
and other radicals who opposed the Wagner Act framed their objections as civil liberties concerns.[37] Influenced by their formula-
tions, the ACLU informed Senators Wagner and Walsh in a letter
that the organization would not support the Wagner Act because
no federal agency could be trusted "to fairly determine the issues
of labor's rights." It expressed several concrete objections, including

---

[34] National Labor Relations Act (NLRA), 29 USC §§ 151, 163 (1935).

[35] James Gray Pope, *The Thirteenth Amendment versus the Commerce Clause: Labor and the Shaping of American Constitutional Law, 1921–1958*, 102 Colum L Rev 1, 7–17, 61–65 (2002).

[36] Forbath, *Law and the Shaping of the American Labor Movement* at 17 (cited in note 1).

[37] In addition to the concerns described below, Communists worried that exclusive representation (coupled with the closed shop) would interfere with organizing efforts by radical
unions.

the bill's exclusion of agricultural workers and its failure to prohibit "discrimination on account of sex, race, color or political convictions."[38] In later years, these would become major civil liberties issues.[39] For the time being, however, the ACLU emphasized other defects, including the ability of the board to act on its own initiative. To ACLU cofounder Roger Baldwin, who authored the letter, any governmental intervention in the labor struggle was an independent and fundamental incursion on civil liberties.[40]

Baldwin considered the contest between labor and capital to be the "central struggle involving civil liberties," and he believed that administrative intervention would inevitably undermine labor's cause. He acknowledged that his continuing state skepticism was increasingly out of line with mainstream opinion. Opposition to administrative power emanated from two principal sources, he explained: "employers still wedded to laissez-faire economics," and their unlikely allies, those "radicals who oppose state capitalism as a form of economic fascism, denying to the working class a chance to develop its power."[41] Baldwin was in the latter camp, and he believed that government could not be trusted to safeguard labor's interests. The workers who accomplished most were the ones who struck hardest. "The real fight is on the job," he said, "not in Washington."[42]

---

[38] Wagner declined to address the objections in light of Baldwin's "frank statement that [he was] philosophically against any legislation that might set up a government agency as one of the areas within which the industrial struggle might be waged." Robert Wagner to Roger Baldwin, April 5, 1935, ACLU Papers, reel 116, vol 780. In general, those advocates of the Wagner Act who were concerned with racial discrimination thought that "racial discrimination, etc. will only be eliminated after economic injustices are corrected." John W. Edelman to Roger Baldwin, ACLU Papers, reel 116, vol 780; John P. Davis to Roger Baldwin, January 25, 1935, in Gardner Jackson Papers, 1912–65, Franklin D. Roosevelt Presidential Library, Hyde Park, NY (hereafter Jackson Papers), General Correspondence, box 3, folder ACLU: Labor (advising against a prohibition on racial discrimination in trade unions because "such promises, even if enacted into law would be unenforceable in any real sense" and would in any case "be used by the industry as another weapon to defeat the solidarity of the trade-union movement," and urging the ACLU instead to enlist the support of the union rank and file in defeating segregation).

[39] See Sophia Lee, *The Workplace Constitution from the New Deal to the New Right* 11–34 (Cambridge, 2014).

[40] Roger Baldwin to Robert Wagner, April 1, 1935, ACLU Papers, reel 116, vol 780; Roger Baldwin to David I. Walsh, March 30, 1935, Jackson Papers, General Correspondence, box 3, folder ACLU: Labor.

[41] Speech of Roger Baldwin, Annual Meeting of the ACLU, February 19, 1934, ACLU Papers, reel 105, vol 678.

[42] Id. According to Baldwin, this principle was responsible for the particularly disfavored plight of "Negro workers" in the current administrative scheme. "Exploited by the employers

Where Baldwin saw violence and compulsion, others saw the potential for buttressing labor's strength. Wagner was disappointed at Baldwin's position and considered it shortsighted. In his view, which many progressives shared, government regulation was the only feasible means of countering powerful private interests. According to Wagner, appropriate state policies would facilitate organizing, not quash it.[43] As it turned out, the ACLU's national membership sided with Wagner rather than Baldwin, and the organization eventually rescinded its opposition to the bill.[44]

Historians who have noticed the ACLU's engagement with New Deal labor policy have regarded it as an aberration—a diversion from the organization's true and abiding concerns. In so doing, they have missed or misconstrued the organization's core commitments before and during the New Deal. Civil liberties, in the 1930s, were not reducible to the Bill of Rights.

What, then, are we to make of the fact that arguments about New Deal labor legislation were framed as civil liberties concerns? The NLRA created concrete, state-supported rights of a kind typically absent in accounts of American constitutionalism, much less civil liberties. These rights sometimes sounded in constitutional language, and they often intersected with claims to freedom of speech. Did the Wagner Act's proponents stake out an alternative constitutional vision, or did they reject constitutionalism altogether? Relatedly, what was the connection between their substantive commitments and the architecture they established for civil liberties enforcement? How did their new sympathy toward state solutions to the labor problem translate to more familiar aspects of the civil liberties agenda, such as the expressive freedom of political dissenters?

---

in the hardest and lowest-paid jobs, they are also excluded from most unions. They cannot organize and fight in independent unions, Negro Workers' rights—N.R.A. or no N.R.A.—are pretty near zero."

[43] Robert F. Wagner to Roger Baldwin, April 5, 1935, ACLU Papers, reel 116, vol 780.

[44] For example, John W. Edelman, David S. Schick, and Isadore Katz to Roger Baldwin, May 3, 1935, ACLU Papers, reel 116, vol 780; John W. Edelman to Roger Baldwin, ACLU Papers, reel 116, vol 780 ("Trade unionists who know 'what it's all about' realize well enough that the Labor Disputes Bill has many weaknesses and will not bring about social justice, but they also know that the passage of some such legislation is essential to enable the organization drive in the unorganized industries to continue. . . . The Civil Liberties [Union] functions usually for the alleged radical unions who are so weak that they are licked before getting started with or without a Labor Disputes Bill. In fact the Communist led unions don't really want to settle strikes and you know that is the case. But some of us are connected with really militant-acting unions who do things and who want to settle strikes. We have used the government mechanisms and the arbitration technique very effectively to that end.").

In discussions over the Wagner Act, advocates for workers' "civil liberties" were up against fundamentals. For the first time, the progressive project for the affirmative protection of labor's rights was a realistic possibility. The modern civil liberties movement had been founded on resistance to state power. When the state appeared ready to come genuinely to its aid, much of the labor movement set aside its reservations (which, in any case, had always been qualified) and embraced government action.

But for some civil libertarians, resistance to state authority had become a core unifying ideology, even outside the labor context. In such cases as *Pierce v Society of Sisters*, the *Scopes* trial, and *United States v Dennett*, they had denounced the governmental oversight of ideas as dangerous and misguided.[45] Over the course of the 1920s, they had expanded from a skeptical stance toward state intervention in labor disputes to a general aversion to state interference with minority viewpoints, personal morality, and private life.

The instigators of the interwar civil liberties movement were victims of their own success. To keep the state out of labor relations, they had hitched the right of agitation to the First Amendment. They emphasized a neutral commitment to freedom of speech and association consistent with government oversight of the economy, rather than a revolutionary right to restructure government and the economy through collective power. Strikes were legitimate not because the proletariat retained the right to reconstitute the state, but because picketing communicated workers' views.

The result was a fundamental reshuffling of the civil liberties lineup. The loose coalition of the 1920s was destined to dissolve. In its place, at least four competing visions of civil liberties emerged. The first was the *radical vision*, which Baldwin and some labor radicals continued to espouse. On this account, which foregrounded the right of agitation, state regulation of labor slid inevitably into fascism. To be sure, state suppression of artistic expression and sexual freedom was also ill-advised. But the true civil liberties threat was the institutionalization and consequent vitiation of labor's collective,

---

[45] *Pierce v Society of Sisters*, 268 US 510 (1925) (invalidating an Oregon compulsory public education law); *Scopes v Tennessee*, 152 Tenn 424 (Tenn 1925) (involving academic freedom, among other issues); *United States v Dennett*, 39 F2d 564 (2d Cir 1930) (overturning a criminal conviction for distribution of a sex education pamphlet). On these cases, see Weinrib, 30 L & Hist Rev at 336–39 (cited in note 29).

revolutionary power. These radicals did not regard civil liberties as bounded by the Bill of Rights. On the contrary, as they often emphasized, civil liberty preexisted the Constitution. The right of agitation mapped almost fully onto the labor struggle, and it was broad enough to encompass all of workers' tools.

The second view was a *progressive vision* of civil liberties that is still familiar to us today. For many New Dealers, the rights to organize, picket, and strike were derivative of a constitutional commitment to expressive freedom. Theirs was the understanding associated—in distinct but basically compatible forms—with Justices Holmes and Brandeis as well as influential First Amendment theorists such as Zechariah Chafee and Alexander Meiklejohn. Thus, in his capacity as a member of the ACLU's National Committee, Meiklejohn wrote to register his support for the NLRA, lamenting "the tendency of the [ACLU] Board to engage in industrial disputes instead of fighting for the maintaining of civil liberties in connection with them."[46]

The progressives had never entirely accepted the notion of a right of agitation as an independent revolutionary force, productive of (rather than protected by) the marketplace of ideas. More to the point, they never were opposed to state power as such, merely to the intrusion of the state into the realms of democratic decision making and private conduct. As a result, they were willing to bracket labor relations as an appropriate subject for regulation—even if the result was ameliorative and counterrevolutionary—as long as rights derived from the First Amendment were preserved. In other words, for progressives, transformation of the economic system might be accomplished through the exercise of civil liberties, but it was not a civil liberty in and of itself.[47]

It bears emphasis that the progressive understanding was, as yet, neither negative nor necessarily tied to the courts. It was, however, a constitutional vision. An earlier generation of progressives had understood civil liberties (though they did not yet use that phrase) as a

---

[46] Alexander Meiklejohn to Roger Baldwin, May 22, 1935, ACLU Papers, reel 116, vol 780.

[47] For some, however, the definition remained capacious. Letter from Arthur Garfield Hays, May 7, 1935, ACLU Papers, reel 116, vol 780 ("From the point of view of civil liberties the subject of unionism should be confined to the rights of free press, free speech, free assemblage, the right to organize, strike, picket and demonstrate, the right to be free from unfair injunctive processes and cognate matters.").

thumb on the scale, not a constitutional right. Often, civil liberties served simply as a background condition for the exercise of state authority, hardly distinguishable from good policy. Wherever possible, they argued, it was advisable to tolerate dissent rather than suppress it. Police commissioners, prosecutors, and administrative agencies exercised their discretion to accommodate minority interests and unpopular views—on occasion, disregarding explicit legislative directives in the process.[48] They did so because they believed that open discussion enhanced democratic legitimacy, defused violent conflict by avoiding the production of martyrs, and facilitated social and scientific progress. During the interwar period, they constitutionalized those commitments, and the progressive vision of civil liberties was born.

Progressives were not sanguine about state power. They acknowledged that administrative discretion posed a threat to unpopular minorities and views; postal censorship under the wartime Espionage Act and a wide array of invasive state practices thereafter had made that conclusion unavoidable. In their view, however, insulating unpopular ideas against state interference served to legitimate rather than undermine state power; as an ACLU-commissioned treatise had prematurely opined a decade earlier, the courts had abandoned their reliance on "natural rights" in favor of the "modern idea that grants liberty to men . . . for the sake of the state."[49]

Just as they believed that civil liberties might justify government power, the progressives believed that government power was a necessary prerequisite for civil liberties. Their reasoning is succinctly captured by philosopher and longtime ACLU member John Dewey: "social control, especially of economic forces, is necessary in order to render secure the liberties of the individual, including civil liberties."[50] Even as they called for limits on state power in the domain of ex-

---

[48] Rabban, *Forgotten Years* at 100–07 (cited in note 6). Jeremy Kessler has carefully reconstructed the efforts by President Wilson's War Department to accommodate conscientious objectors during World War I, with particular emphasis on Felix Frankfurter's exercise of administrative discretion to expand protections for freedom of conscience. For Frankfurter, as for earlier Progressives, such claims were best resolved at the level of legislative drafting and administrative interpretation, not by courts. Jeremy Kessler, *The Administrative Origins of Modern Civil Liberties Law*, 114 Colum L Rev 1083 (2014).

[49] Leon Whipple, *Our Ancient Liberties: The Story of the Origin and Meaning of Civil and Religious Liberty in the United States* (De Capo, 1972) (originally published 1927).

[50] John Dewey, *Liberalism and Civil Liberties*, Social Frontier 137 (February 1936).

pressive freedom, they extolled the state's unique capacity to protect important rights. Accordingly, the First Amendment test they endorsed was deferential to government efforts to correct market asymmetries, whether economic or ideational. Notably, that was a battle they lost in the courts, notwithstanding the strong purchase of their views in legal scholarship.

A third defense of civil liberties would emerge during the 1930s. Rooted in a commitment to individual autonomy, the *conservative vision* regarded the Bill of Rights as a bulwark against an intrusive state. Although antecedents of this idea appear in nineteenth-century treatises and in classical liberal thought, conservatives had typically opposed civil liberties claims, distinguishing between "liberty and license" and relegating disfavored speech to the latter, unprotected category. During the 1920s, the organized bar had opposed ACLU efforts to defend radical speech. In the 1930s, however, shifting political winds prompted a reevaluation of conservative ideals. The New Deal posed an unprecedented threat to the speech and association of conservative groups. Equally important, a vigorous defense of personal rights was poised to counter claims of judicial hypocrisy and buttress the case for judicial review.

Progressives were quick to note the resonances between the radical and conservative understandings. The notion that labor relations should be isolated from state intervention smacked of the *Lochner*-era tradition of economic liberty, which they had unequivocally repudiated.[51] The radicals registered the objection. In opposing state labor policy, Roger Baldwin was hesitant "to use so misunderstood a word as 'liberty,' invoked today so loudly by those rugged defenders of property rights" who understood liberty as a "right to exploit the American people without governmental interference."[52] He took great pains to distinguish the position of the ACLU leadership, emphasizing that "the historic conception of liberty" was "the freedom to agitate for social change without restraint";[53] although both groups opposed the NLRA, their reluctance was justified on

[51] Francis Biddle, chair of the NLRB created under Public Resolution No. 44, accused Baldwin of sounding like the Liberty League; Francis Biddle to Roger Baldwin, April 17, 1935, ACLU Papers, reel 116, vol 780.

[52] Roger Baldwin, "Civil Liberties under the New Deal," October 24, 1934, ACLU Papers, reel 109, vol 717.

[53] Id. He added: "Practically today that means freedom for the working-class to organize and of minorities to conduct their propaganda."

"diametrically opposite grounds."[54] The radical concern was "human rights," which were expressed collectively rather than as individual rights.[55] Like the radicals, conservatives linked civil liberties to labor relations, but in place of the radicals' abolition of wage labor or the progressives' social welfare, they privileged *Lochner*-style individual autonomy, including the freedom to sell one's labor under conditions that progressives and radicals deemed coercive.

Finally, debates over the Wagner Act hinted at a fourth conception of civil liberties that would take root within the NLRB and its congressional counterpart over the coming years. Like the radical understanding, the *labor interventionist vision* evinced unabashed support for labor's cause. Unlike the radicals, however, proponents of the interventionist view—like the progressives—imagined a strong role for the state in enforcing civil liberties.[56] They insisted, in the words of NLRB chairman J. Warren Madden, that "the most effective opposition to the organization of working people has been, not that of governments and their agents, but that of private interests."[57] Their aspirations for the administrative enforcement of civil liber-

---

[54] Roger Baldwin to Robert Wagner, April 1, 1935, ACLU Papers, reel 116, vol 780. See also Joseph Schlossberg to Roger Baldwin, May 14, 1935, ACLU Papers, reel 116, vol 780 ("Rightly or wrongly the American Federation of Labor is committed to the Wagner Bill. By your opposition to the bill you unwillingly lined up with the employers and all reactionaries who opposed the bill. . . . This is one case in which the Civil Liberties Union can well afford to take no official position.").

[55] Roger Baldwin, "The Main Issues of Civil Liberties under the New Deal," December 8, 1934, ACLU Papers, reel 110, vol 721; Roger Baldwin, "Coming Struggle for Freedom," November 12, 1934, ACLU Papers, reel 109, vol 717 ("[The American Liberty League and Americans First] are the dying gladiators of individualism in [the] business of laissez faire economics. But the landslide has buried their straw man of liberty. Collectivism has come to stay.").

[56] I borrow the emphasis on "interventionism" from David Saposs's classic 1935 account of the demise of voluntarism. According to Saposs, who served as chief economist of the NLRB from 1935 to 1940, organized labor had been most successful during "periods of widespread government intervention in industrial relations." He considered the NRA to be a "continuation, with a painful interlude, of government intervention in industrial relations first introduced during the war." He explained: "[I]n a modern industrial country voluntarism is an archaic philosophy. Furthermore, the conclusion is inevitable that a strong trade union movement is only possible when aided by the government. The capitalistic interests are so powerfully entrenched that the unions are at a tremendous disadvantage in a bare handed economic struggle." David J. Saposs, *The American Labor Movement Since the War*, Q J Econ 49, 239 (1935).

[57] Address of J. Warren Madden to National Conference on Civil Liberties, October 13, 1939, in the Papers of Grenville Clark in the Dartmouth College Library, ML-7, Rauner Special Collection Library, Hanover, NH (hereafter Clark Papers), Series VIII (ABA Committee on the Bill of Rights), box 10 (Cases): NLRB Address of J. Warren Madden, 10/13/39 (box 86, folder 41) (box numbers are given according to original and revised numbering system).

ties were intimately bound up with their antagonistic relationship to the judicial construction of constitutional rights. Importantly, the civil liberties they defended encompassed not only the rights to picket, boycott, and strike, but also a stronger position at the bargaining table. They believed affirmative state support for labor organizing would best serve the end goals of labor activity, including higher wages and better working conditions. Indeed, to Madden, it was the state's role to enforce as "fundamental" the liberty of the workers "to emerge from a condition of economic helplessness, and dependence upon the will of another, to a status of having one's chosen representative received as an equal at the bargaining conference table."[58] This liberty was prior to all other rights—including the rights of speech, press, and assembly—which might benefit the workers only after their right of collective bargaining was realized.[59]

These categories are, of course, ideal types. Many of the figures discussed in this article flitted between these commitments, drawing on strains of each in service of legal and political goals. Few would have drawn the lines between them so starkly. Indeed, the permeability of the boundaries rendered the categories unstable and susceptible to revision. In the late 1930s, these competing accounts of civil liberties attained a rough equilibrium. A fifth, *liberal vision* of civil liberties embraced a broad spectrum of the earlier views but, in finding common ground, fundamentally transformed them.

II. Civil Liberties in the New Deal State

Ultimately, consensus emerged around a state-skeptical and judicially enforceable conception of the First Amendment that developed during the interwar period and culminated in the New Deal settlement commonly associated with *Carolene Products'* footnote 4.[60] Before the new constitutional framework crystallized, however, the

---

[58] Radio address by Warren Madden, January 29, 1939, quoted in Brief for Respondent, *NLRB v Ford Motor Company*, No 8399, 54 (6th Cir, filed April 2, 1940) ("Respondent Sixth Circuit Brief"), in Ford Motor Company Legal Papers, Ford Motor Company and UAW Before the NLRB, Seventh Region, Benson Ford Research Center, Dearborn, MI (hereafter Ford Legal Papers), acc. 51 (NLRB Suits, Ford Motor Company Legal Department), box 4.

[59] Id.

[60] *United States v Carolene Products Company*, 304 US 144, 152 n 4 (1938). Footnote 4, which provided the basis for the most familiar civil-rights victories of the twentieth century, was initially invoked far more frequently in First Amendment cases than in race cases.

competing understandings of civil liberties contended for dominance in the various institutions that had been designated for their enforcement.[61]

What follows are snapshots of the four principal New Deal institutions in which ideological contestation over civil liberties took place. They are not comprehensive histories of these institutions or of the mundane administration of rights claims within their respective domains. Rather, they focus on discrete examples of legal and political conflict. They foreground clashes over labor policy because of its central significance to the actors who articulated the contours of civil liberties during the New Deal.[62]

A. THE JUDICIAL ENFORCEMENT OF CIVIL LIBERTIES

Strong judicial enforcement of the Bill of Rights is properly regarded as a keystone of the New Deal settlement. The transformation in constitutional law during the late 1930s is conventionally understood to contain two distinct but interconnected parts: first, a relaxation of structural constraints on Congress's control over the economy, entailing the complete revision of Commerce Clause and federalism doctrine, in addition to the abrogation of freedom of contract and property rights; and, second, an invigoration of constitutional protections for "discrete and insular minorities" along with free speech.[63] The latter is said to ensure the democratic legitimacy of the former. That is, judicial deference to the outcomes of

---

[61] I explore the process by which this ideological convergence occurred in Weinrib, *Constitutional Compromise of 1937* (cited in note 7), and Weinrib, *Taming of Free Speech* (cited in note 7).

[62] In elucidating these ideas, I refer to specific concepts, such as free speech or the right to organize, where feasible. Where I use the more general term "civil liberties," either I intend to draw attention to its fluidity, or I link it to one of the four visions described above in Part II. In the latter case, I mean it to encompass the bundle of rights and policy preferences that adherents of a particular vision ascribed to it.

[63] See, for example, Kramer, *People Themselves* at 122 (cited in note 1); Bruce Ackerman, *We the People* 105–30 (Harvard, 1991); Barry Friedman, *The History of the Counter-Majoritarian Difficulty, Part Four: Law's Politics*, 148 U Pa L Rev 971, 974 (2000); Jack M. Balkin, *The Footnote*, 83 Nw U L Rev 275 (1989); Richard A. Epstein, *How Progressives Rewrote the Constitution* 7–9, 52–83 (Cato Institute, 2006); G. Edward White, *The Constitution and the New Deal* 128–64, 227–32 (Harvard, 2000). The expansion of personal rights was associated with the "incorporation" of the First Amendment into the Fourteenth Amendment, which extended the protections of the former to incursions by state and local governments. Over the ensuing decades, many of the remaining provisions of the Bill of Rights would be incorporated as well.

democratic processes requires robust debate, with ample protection for minority interests, as state policy is formulated and implemented.[64]

However sensible the new arrangement appears in hindsight, however, few contemporaries understood judicial review as susceptible to decoupling in this way. On the contrary, most critics, as well as conservative opponents of the Court-packing plan, assumed that judicial review came as a package, and that in the absence of constitutional amendment, expansion of the First and Fourteenth Amendments to protect expressive freedom would buttress the Court's economic due process doctrine as well. That was a trade-off few were willing to make. Accordingly, many New Dealers were willing to forgo judicial enforcement of the Bill of Rights, and some actively resisted it. They insisted that the stewardship of personal liberties belonged in the political branches. Any other path, they assumed, would facilitate the judicial dismantling of the New Deal economic program.

As events unfolded, the judiciary's antiregulatory constitutionalism evolved along less predictable lines. The Supreme Court definitively abandoned its aggressive defense of property and economic liberty. And yet, industry rapidly assimilated free speech as a second-best alternative to *Lochner*-era economic rights. By 1940, the First Amendment stood in for substantive due process as a shield against government regulation of industry.[65] Labor's rights to picket and boycott would largely be written out of the First Amendment, even while the rights of corporations to circularize their employees and to influence political elections were written in.[66]

In 1937, however, the disaggregation of personal and property rights still harbored radical potential—and an account of civil liberties that is true to historical circumstances has to evaluate civil liberties claims as they were framed, not as they have been remembered. Such an approach necessitates a reassessment of the line between the two halves of the New Deal settlement. In the late 1930s, the

---

[64] See Graber, *Transforming Free Speech* (cited in note 2).

[65] See Weinrib, *Constitutional Compromise of 1937* (cited in note 7), and Weinrib, *Taming of Free Speech* (cited in note 7).

[66] This process is still unfolding. Notably, the First Amendment has recently been used to undermine union security agreements, particularly in the public sector. On the inconsistent treatment of corporate speech and labor unions under the First Amendment, see Catherine L. Fisk and Erwin Chemerinsky, *Political Speech and Association Rights After Knox v. SEIU, Local 1000*, 98 Cornell L Rev 1023 (2013); Benjamin I. Sachs, *Unions, Corporations, and Political Opt-Out Rights After Citizens United*, 112 Colum L Rev 800 (2012).

Court's vigorous enforcement of "preferred freedoms" and its new-found deference toward labor and economic legislation were of a single civil liberties piece. Both advanced that crucial segment where the various civil liberties visions intersected: the protection of workers' rights to organize, bargain collectively, and strike.

Of the many institutions that construed and enforced civil liberties during the New Deal, the Supreme Court is undoubtedly the most familiar. Constitutional law scholars have painstakingly traced the Court's evolving understanding of expressive freedom between the world wars: its dismissal of the Holmes and Brandeis dissents; its tepid incorporation of the First Amendment into the Fourteenth beginning with *Gitlow v New York*; its rejection of "prior restraint" in *Near v Minnesota*; its bold extension of First Amendment protection to freedom of assembly and religious proselytizing in *DeJonge v Oregon* and *Lovell v City of Griffin*.[67]

Sometimes, accounts of the Supreme Court's early First Amendment jurisprudence observe that the interwar cases disproportionately involved labor speech. They assume, however, that the Court's inquiry pertained only to the freedom of radicals and revolutionaries to disseminate their subversive views. In these respects, the constitutional law canon has fallen victim to winners' history. That is, it has been distorted by the near total dominance in the postwar era of a liberal vision of civil liberties premised on judicially enforceable constitutional rights. Given the wide circulation and high salience of alternative understandings of civil liberties during the New Deal, it is unsurprising that the liberal conception was not the only one to reach the Supreme Court.

The better place to begin is not with the well-worn First Amendment cases, but rather their Commerce Clause and freedom of contract counterparts. Two features of the "Constitutional Revolution" are often elided in discussion of the best-known cases. First, insofar as the Wagner Act advanced the rights of labor, *Jones and Laughlin Steel* was not a complement to the Supreme Court's civil liberties decisions; it was itself a civil liberties decision.[68] To be sure, the Supreme Court upheld the NLRA as an exercise of Congress's power

---

[67] *Gitlow v New York*, 268 US 652 (1925); *Near v Minnesota*, 283 US 697 (1931); *DeJonge v Oregon*, 299 US 353 (1937); *Lovell v City of Griffin*, 303 US 444 (1938).

[68] *NLRB v Jones & Laughlin Steel Corporation*, 301 US 1 (1937); *NLRB v Fruehauf Trailer Company*, 301 US 49 (1937); *NLRB v Friedman-Harry Marks Clothing Company*, 301 US 58 (1937).

under the Commerce Clause,[69] not as a means of enforcing the constitutional rights of employees to organize under either the Thirteenth Amendment (an argument advanced by Andrew Furuseth and other conservative trade unionists) or the First.[70] It does not follow, however, that the Justices were blind to the labor interventionist vision of civil liberties that motivated the NLRB. Given how dominant that understanding was in public rhetoric and political debate, it would have been hard to miss.[71]

Guided by past experience, the NLRB was reluctant to frame its legal claims in terms of constitutional rights for fear that the Court would cabin those rights.[72] The courts were understood to hold an interpretive monopoly in the domain of constitutional rights, and labor advocates were all too aware of their past biases. New Deal lawmakers believed the Wagner Act vindicated substantive rights—even constitutional rights—and they loudly proclaimed as much outside the courtroom.[73] Their legal arguments, however, emphasized neutral principles and congressional prerogatives, in a poignant parallel to the debates over free speech.

It is therefore striking that the labor interventionist vision of civil liberties found its way into the majority opinion in *Jones and Laughlin Steel*, even if the Court did not rely on it.[74] Notwithstand-

---

[69] William Forbath stresses that the Court's embrace of social rights constitutionalism was limited, in part due to the exclusion and disenfranchisement of African Americans in the South. William E. Forbath, *Caste, Class, and Equal Citizenship*, 98 Mich L Rev 1 (1999). For a response emphasizing the achievements rather than limitations of the New Deal revolution, see Bruce Ackerman, *Revolution on a Human Scale*, 108 Yale L J 2279, 2336–40 (1999).

[70] Pope, 102 Colum L Rev (cited in note 35); William E. Forbath, *The New Deal Constitution in Exile*, 51 Duke L J 165 (2001).

[71] William Forbath has extensively documented Wagner and Roosevelt's promotion of "social citizenship." Forbath, 51 Duke L J (cited in note 70); Forbath, *Law and the Shaping of the American Labor Movement* (cited in note 1); Forbath, 98 Mich L Rev (cited in note 69).

[72] Forbath, 51 Duke L J at 182 (cited in note 70) ("In public political discourse, New Dealers cast the changes they sought as fundamental rights reinvigorating the Constitution's promise of equal citizenship by reinterpreting it. Yet, as a matter of statutory drafting and litigation strategy, they consistently relied on congressional power clauses, not on rights-affirming clauses of the Constitution. The New Deal Constitution took this odd and, from today's perspective, lamentable form not for lack of constitutional commitment, but because of a specific conception of the rights at issue and the appropriate allocation of interpretive and enforcement authority regarding them, combined with a strategic concern about judicial interpretation and enforcement.").

[73] Id at 176.

[74] Pope, 102 Colum L Rev (cited in note 35), argues that the Court adopted a narrow, Commerce Clause approach because it wanted to empower administrators rather than the working class.

ing the NLRB's cautious approach, Hughes described "the right of employees to self-organization" as a "fundamental right."[75] No less an authority on constitutional interpretation than Edward Corwin recognized the sweep of Hughes's language. In summer of 1937, Corwin reflected that American constitutional law had "undergone a number of revolutions, but none so radical, so swift, so altogether dramatic as that witnessed by the term of Court just ended."[76] What was revolutionary about the Court's decision in *Jones and Laughlin Steel*—far more than its newfound deference to congressional priorities—was its reconceptualization of liberty to entail an obligation on the state to act against private parties.[77] As Corwin understood it, the Court had recognized "'liberty' . . . as something that may be infringed by other forces as well as by those of government; indeed, something that may require the positive intervention of government against those other forces." In short, the United States Supreme Court had recognized the labor interventionist vision of civil liberties. And "this recognition," according to Corwin, "mark[ed] a development of profound significance in our constitutional history."

---

[75] *Jones & Laughlin Steel*, 301 US at 33. Justices Hughes's surprising opinion merits lengthy quotation: "In its present application, the [NLRA] goes no further than to safeguard the right of employees to self-organization and to select representatives of their own choosing for collective bargaining or other mutual protection without restraint or coercion by their employer. That is a fundamental right. Employees have as clear a right to organize and select their representatives for lawful purposes as the respondent has to organize its business and select its own officers and agents. Discrimination and coercion to prevent the free exercise of the right of employees to self-organization and representation is a proper subject for condemnation by competent legislative authority. Long ago we stated the reason for labor organizations. We said that they were organized out of the necessities of the situation; that a single employee was helpless in dealing with an employer; that he was dependent ordinarily on his daily wage for the maintenance of himself and family; that, if the employer refused to pay him the wages that he thought fair, he was nevertheless unable to leave the employ and resist arbitrary and unfair treatment; that union was essential to give laborers opportunity to deal on an equality with their employer. We reiterated these views when we had under consideration the Railway Labor Act of 1926. Fully recognizing the legality of collective action on the part of employees in order to safeguard their proper interests, we said that Congress was not required to ignore this right, but could safeguard it. Congress could seek to make appropriate collective action of employees an instrument of peace, rather than of strife. We said that such collective action would be a mockery if representation were made futile by interference with freedom of choice. Hence, the prohibition by Congress of interference with the selection of representatives for the purpose of negotiation and conference between employers and employees, 'instead of being an invasion of the constitutional right of either, was based on the recognition of the rights of both.'"

[76] Edward S. Corwin, *The Court Sees a New Light*, New Republic 354 (August 4, 1937).

[77] That the so-called "revolution" proved to be less radical than Corwin anticipated and many subsequent commentators have assumed is bound up with the pullback from that interventionist promise. This trajectory is developed in Weinrib, *Constitutional Compromise of 1937* (cited in note 7).

Of course, the NLRA was designed to eliminate *employer* interference with labor organizing. It was not directed at state suppression of the right to picket or strike, and justifying it explicitly on First Amendment grounds would have required a radically new conception of state action and the scope of the Bill of Rights.[78] Such an approach was not unthinkable, but New Deal officials and NLRB brief-writers had good reason to doubt it would succeed. In other contexts, however, the federal courts had ample opportunity to evaluate labor activity under constitutional provisions. In cases involving suppression with strikes and pickets by state or local officials, sometimes as a direct result of state legislation or city ordinances, they faced the question whether labor activity was constitutionally protected head on.

Thus, the second important corrective to the conventional account of the Constitutional Revolution stems from the observation that labor cases and First Amendment cases often overlapped in unfamiliar ways. For example, the Court's 1937 decision in *Senn v Tile Layers Protective Union* is well known by labor scholars for upholding a state statute authorizing labor picketing and withholding injunctive relief. The ACLU filed an amicus brief in the case, but it nowhere mentioned the First Amendment, instead invoking the "right to organize" to buttress the legitimacy of the labor bill it had helped to secure.[79] Notwithstanding the organization's framing of the issues, Justice Brandeis's opinion for the Court presumed that "members of a union might . . . make known the facts of a labor dispute, for freedom of speech is guaranteed by the Federal Constitution."[80]

Indeed, the foundational labor and speech cases often involved the same parties, the same lawyers, and the same underlying activity. Take *Associated Press v NLRB*, decided the same day as *Jones*

---

[78] For this reason, the Thirteenth Amendment appeared to some contemporaries to be a stronger alternative. Pope, 102 Colum L Rev (cited in note 35).

[79] Brief on Behalf of American Civil Liberties Union and International Juridical Association, Amici Curiae, *Senn v Tile Layers Protection Union*, No 658, 17–18 (US, filed Mar 29, 1937). The brief explained: "The complaint which has been heard so continuously in legislative halls, and to which so-called anti-injunction legislation was a response, stems from the basic contention by working men that recognition of labor's abstract right to organize necessarily implies recognition and sanction of labor's concrete right to use, among other economic measures, the appeal for public support in its controversies with employers."

[80] *Senn v Tile Layers Protection Union*, 301 US 468, 478 (1937).

and Laughlin Steel.[81] In a world divided between newly deferential economic review and preferred personal freedoms, the case falls squarely on the economic side of the line. After all, it was among the five foundational cases upholding the constitutionality of the Wagner Act. The Supreme Court concluded that the Associated Press was involved in interstate commerce and therefore validly within the reach of the statute. In a surprising twist, the AP had also asserted a First Amendment claim premised on the conservative civil liberties vision ("Freedom of expression," it concluded, "is as precious as either due process or the equal protection of law"[82]). Citing recent First Amendment victories for radical defendants, among other cases,[83] the AP argued that the compulsory employment of unionized workers would undermine its control of editorial content. "Freedom of the press and freedom of speech, as guaranteed by the First Amendment, means more than freedom from censorship by government," the AP's brief argued, albeit unsuccessfully.[84] "[I]t means that freedom of expression must be jealously protected from any form of governmental control or influence."[85]

In another context, those words might have been warmly endorsed by the ACLU—but in *Associated Press v NLRB*, they engendered fierce resistance. Indeed, the attorney for the American Newspaper Guild was none other than ACLU co-counsel Morris

---

[81] *Associated Press v NLRB*, 301 US 103 (1937). On *AP v NLRB*, see Jeremy Kessler, *The Civil Libertarian Conditions of Conscription* (unpublished manuscript, Jan 2014); Sam Lebovic, *The Failure of New Deal Press Reform and the Emergence of the Laissez-Faire First Amendment* (unpublished manuscript, Sept 2014) (on file with author).

[82] Brief on Behalf of Petitioner the Associated Press, *Associated Press v NLRB*, No 365, 101 (US, filed Feb 5, 1937) ("AP Brief").

[83] For example, *Stromberg v California*, 283 US 359 (1931); *De Jonge v Oregon*, 299 US 353 (1937).

[84] AP Brief at 100. In a dissenting opinion, the conservative Justices embraced the First Amendment argument. Justice Sutherland wrote: "No one can read the long history which records the stern and often bloody struggles by which these cardinal rights were secured, without realizing how necessary it is to preserve them against any infringement, however slight." He continued, more dramatically: "Do the people of this land—in the providence of God, favored, as they sometimes boast, above all others in the plenitude of their liberties—desire to preserve those so carefully protected by the First Amendment? . . . If so, let them withstand all beginnings of encroachment. For the saddest epitaph which can be carved in memory of a vanished liberty is that it was lost because its possessors failed to stretch forth a saving hand while yet there was time." *Associated Press*, 301 US at 135, 141 (Sutherland, J, dissenting).

[85] AP Brief at 100.

Ernst. In an amicus brief for the guild, he squarely rejected the AP's reasoning. The First Amendment, he argued, did not license the press to discriminate against unionized employees. On the contrary, nonenforcement of editors' organizing rights posed the graver threat to the First Amendment. "Non-action of a governmental agency may be far more destructive of a fundamental guarantee than positive legislation," Ernst asserted. That Congress could not abridge the freedom of the press did not preclude it from combating "an evil which threatens of itself to nullify that freedom." Labor unrest was an impediment to the free flow of information and liberty of thought; the key to a free press was a strong union.[86]

Notably, Ernst also served as counsel in a seminal First Amendment case, *Hague v CIO*.[87] The case stemmed from the suppression of CIO organizing activities in Jersey City, across the Hudson River from New York. By the time it was decided, the Supreme Court's hands-off approach to economic legislation was firmly entrenched, and the NLRA was secure against judicial invalidation. The trouble in Jersey City was not recalcitrant employers, though they played a role. Rather, the principal obstacle to organizing in Jersey City was the town's powerful mayor, Frank Hague.

Boss Hague, as he was known to his political foes, was determined to keep the CIO out of Jersey City. Facing a fiscal crisis owing as much to mismanagement as the Great Depression, he had launched a campaign to attract New York businesses to Jersey City by keeping unions at bay. Hague's police force harassed, beat, and arrested agitators and shut down all picketing, meetings, and leafleting by organized labor—and by the ACLU observers who endeavored to defend them. When organizers began provoking arrests in order to challenge local ordinances and police practices in the courts, Hague simply had them deported across city lines.

---

[86] Brief on Behalf of the American Newspaper Guild as Amicus Curiae, *Associated Press v NLRB*, No 365, 26–27 (US, filed Jan 22, 1937). As in *Jones and Laughlin Steel*, the NLRB characterized the right to organize as a "recognized and essential liberty." Brief for the National Labor Relations Board, No 365, 93 (US, filing date illegible). Justice Sutherland, by contrast, squarely embraced the conservative civil liberties view. He wrote: "We may as well deny at once the right of the press freely to adopt a policy and pursue it, as to concede that right and deny the liberty to exercise an uncensored judgment in respect of the employment and discharge of the agents through whom the policy is to be effectuated." *Associated Press*, 301 US at 137 (Sutherland, J, dissenting).

[87] *Hague v Committee for Industrial Organization*, 307 US 496 (1939).

Hague, then, involved civil liberties violations in recognizable guise. As Jersey City officials, Hague and his henchmen were unmistakable state actors, and the Supreme Court had signaled that they were within the reach of the First Amendment. The Court of Appeals, substantially affirming the District Court's decree in favor of the plaintiffs, insisted that the city was obligated to open space for public discussion, and if private violence threatened, it was the function of the police to "preserve order while they speak."[88] Mere noninterference would not suffice. That is, the Constitution required the government to act to promote expression. In a fragmented 1939 decision, the Supreme Court upheld the right to picket and hold meetings in Jersey City's public spaces, subject to reasonable limitations to maintain order in the public interest. It is notable that Justice Roberts's plurality opinion, which rested on the Privileges or Immunities Clause of the Fourteenth Amendment rather than the Due Process Clause, concluded that it is a privilege inherent in United States citizenship to discuss the "full freedom of association and self-organization of workers" conferred by the NLRA.[89]

In the face of international totalitarianism, the ACLU secured broad-based support for its legal and publicity campaigns in *Hague*. It even managed to solicit an amicus brief from the American Bar Association's newly formed Committee on the Bill of Rights—a development that marked the ascent of the conservative vision of civil liberties in the wake of the Court-packing plan. The wide consensus gratified the ACLU, but the CIO leadership was more ambivalent. On the one hand, the *Hague* decision was an unmistakable "go signal" (as California's state bar journal put it) for labor organizing in Jersey City and elsewhere.[90] On the other, public enthusiasm for free speech was supplanting support for labor activity per se. The *Yale Law Journal* reflected that "when practically every shade of public opinion became outraged at what appeared to be a blatant denial of fundamental rights, emphasis shifted from specific attempts by one group at raising abnormally low Jersey City working conditions to the more basic issue of whether constitutional guaranties of free

---

[88] *Hague v Committee for Industrial Organization*, 101 F2d 774, 784 (3d Cir 1939).

[89] *Hague*, 307 US at 513.

[90] Harry Graham Balter, *Recent Civil Rights Decision Discussion*, Cal Bar J 14, 200–04 (June 1939).

speech, free press, and free assembly apply to union sympathizers as well as to other citizens."[91] In other words, civil liberties claims were shifting markedly away from labor interventionist demands.

The transition took some time. As late as 1940, the Supreme Court handed down two monumental decisions on labor and free speech that also advanced labor interventionist goals. In *Thornhill v Alabama*, the Court (invoking footnote 4 of *Carolene Products*) upheld the right to picket as an expression of ideas.[92] The decision established that "the dissemination of information concerning the facts of a labor dispute" was within the realm of "free discussion" protected by the Constitution.[93] As in *Senn v Tile Layers Protection Union*, the Court stressed the public communicative function of picketing. Even if its effect was to induce action in others, picketing was speech.[94] The Court observed: "Free discussion concerning the conditions in industry and the causes of labor disputes appears to us indispensable to the effective and intelligent use of the processes of popular government to shape the destiny of modern industrial society." In *Thornhill*'s lesser-known companion case, *Carlson v California*, the Court declared that "publicizing the facts of a labor dispute in a peaceful way" was likewise entitled to constitutional protection against abridgment by a state.[95] Here was the vindication of long-standing radical and labor interventionist goals, cloaked in the language of expressive freedom.

Thornhill and *Carlson* were argued in the Supreme Court by, respectively, Joseph Padway, AFL general counsel and a member of the ABA's Committee on the Bill of Rights, and Lee Pressman, CIO general counsel. Padway, who had argued *Senn*, had good reason to be optimistic about vindicating labor's rights in the judiciary. Pressman had long expressed skepticism toward the courts, but he had come to believe that the First Amendment might offer a counterbalance to its protection of property rights.[96] In his brief, he cited *Hague* for the proposition that "danger to the state arises not from the picket line but from the vigilantes who would suppress

---

[91] *The Hague Injunction Proceedings*, 48 Yale L J 257 (1938).

[92] *Thornhill v Alabama*, 310 US 88, 95, 102–03 (1940).

[93] Id at 102.

[94] Id at 104.

[95] *Carlson v California*, 310 US 106 (1940).

[96] Lee Pressman to Arthur Garfield Hays, February 10, 1939, ACLU Papers, reel 169, vol 2080.

the picket line by force and violence."[97] Despite his general antipathy toward a "legal approach to labor action," he saw great potential in "the growing realization and acceptance of the fact that labor action is nothing more or less than the exercise of constitutional rights" to freedom of speech and assembly.[98]

The constitutional status of labor's most effective methods—including mass picketing and the secondary boycott—was, however, far from secure. A rapid contraction of First Amendment protection for labor activity followed on the heels of *Thornhill* and *Carlson*. In its 1941 decision in *Milk Wagon Drivers Union v Meadowmoor Dairies*, the Supreme Court upheld a state-court injunction against picketing by a union that had engaged in violence and destruction of property, explaining that "utterance in a contest of violence can lose its significance as an appeal to reason and become part of an instrument of force."[99] Under such circumstances even peaceful expression could be constitutionally curtailed, Justice Frankfurter explained for the Court. To the extent that labor doubted that judicial review would reliably serve its interests, its fears were well founded. Indeed, from the perspective of the ACLU's foundational goals, the modern First Amendment turned out to be an abject failure. Radical propaganda retained its protected status, but the right to organize quickly fell out of the realm of ideas.

B. THE CONGRESSIONAL ENFORCEMENT OF CIVIL LIBERTIES

In the years between passage of the Wagner Act and its validation by the Supreme Court in *Jones and Laughlin Steel*, employers flagrantly resisted compliance with the new legislation. Indeed, they continued to engage in blatant antilabor practices, including industrial espionage, strikebreaking, and the use of munitions and private police forces.[100] Although these methods were clear violations of workers' new statutory rights, employers' lawyers advised that the Wagner Act was unconstitutional and would shortly be declared so

---

[97] Brief for the Appellant, *Carlson v California*, No 667, 36 (US, filed Feb 29, 1940).

[98] Quoted in Gilbert J. Gall, *Pursuing Justice: Lee Pressman, the New Deal, and the CIO* 108 (SUNY, 1999). He was optimistic that the "simple protection of these constitutional rights will solve many of the complicated legal problems that are involved in the exercise of labor's right to picket and to boycott." Gall traces the use of the civil rights statutes by the DOJ's Civil Liberties Unit to Pressman's urging. Id at 109.

[99] *Milk Wagon Drivers Union v Meadowmoor Dairies, Inc.*, 312 US 287 (1941).

[100] Jerold S. Auerbach, *The La Follette Committee: Labor and Civil Liberties in the New Deal*, J Am Hist 51, 443 (1964).

by the Supreme Court. True to form, employers mobilized around a legal campaign, supported most visibly by the American Liberty League's National Lawyers Committee, a collection of corporate lawyers who believed that the Wagner Act was incompatible with *Lochner*-era values. The threat of an adverse decision was so menacing that the NLRB devoted much of its energy during 1935 and 1936 to formulating its own legal strategy.

Congress did not leave the beleaguered NLRB without recourse. In the spring of 1936—prompted by the suppression of the Southern Tenant Farmers Union, an organization of tenant farmers and sharecroppers in northeastern Arkansas, and by the ineffectuality of the NLRB—Senator Robert La Follette Jr. (whose famous father had begun his career as a law partner of the Free Speech League's Gilbert Roe) submitted a Senate resolution authorizing the investigation of "violations of the rights of free speech and assembly and undue interference with the right of labor to organize and bargain collectively."[101] La Follette initially doubted that the Senate would act on his proposal, but after effective preliminary hearings, the resolution was approved in June with significant public support.[102] La Follette went on to chair the subcommittee, which was organized within the Senate's Committee on Education and Labor.[103]

Known as the La Follette Civil Liberties Committee, the new body was an early and powerful voice for the labor interventionist vision of civil liberties. As its title suggests, the committee regarded the rights of labor, whether statutory or constitutional, as core civil liberties issues. It set out to investigate the activities of detective agencies, employer associations, corporations, and individual employers "in so far as these activities result in interference with the rights of labor such as the formation of outside unions, collective bargaining, rights of assemblage and other liberties guaranteed by

---

[101] See generally Jerold S. Auerbach, *Labor and Liberty: The La Follette Committee and the New Deal* (Bobbs-Merrill, 1966).

[102] Gardner Jackson to Roger Baldwin, April 9, 1936, Jackson Papers, box 42, folder La Follette Civil Liberties. See also Robert Wohlforth to Senator Elbert D. Thomas, October 6, 1936, in Violations of Free Speech and Rights of Labor, General Data and Information, Sen 78A-F9, Record Group 46 (Records of the United States Senate), National Archives and Records Administration, Washington, DC (hereafter La Follette Committee Papers), 10.25, box 4, folder October 1936 (enclosing nine editorials from New York and Washington papers and commenting that "nearly all of the editorials, with few exceptions, are favorable").

[103] The committee also included Elbert Thomas, a Utah Democrat, and Louis Murphy, who died soon after his appointment.

the Constitution."[104] No one bothered to explain how employers, as private actors, might infringe upon constitutional rights.

Prominent members of the ACLU were instrumental in engineering the new measure, which they had first proposed at the Conference on Civil Liberties under the New Deal. Roger Baldwin, newly reconciled to state involvement in labor relations,[105] was convinced that "the worst evil which should be investigated is the mounting rise of force and violence by employers against the organization of labor," which threatened "rights presumably guaranteed by federal legislation."[106] He thought a successful inquiry would justify a full slate of federal laws protecting the rights of labor against public and private curtailment.[107] At first, the ACLU urged the committee to investigate government abuses in other contexts as well.[108] It soon became evident, however, that the La Follette Committee would confine its inquiry to labor relations. At the preliminary hearings, NLRB chair J. Warren Madden was the first witness. He tellingly declared, "The right of workmen to organize themselves into unions has become an important civil liberty."[109] The connection between the two bodies was not merely ideological; much of the La Follette Committee's staff was borrowed from the NLRB.

The La Follette Committee aimed to eliminate all interference with workers' right to organize, whether perpetrated by local law

---

[104] Felix Frazer (investigator) to James A. Kinkead, October 9, 1936, La Follette Committee Papers, 10.25, box 4, folder October 1936.

[105] It bears emphasis that Communists, too, abandoned their resistance to the NLRA in 1935. At the height of the so-called Popular Front, many CIO organizers identified with or were sympathetic toward the Communist Party.

[106] Roger Baldwin to Robert La Follette Jr., April 16, 1936, ACLU Papers, reel 131, vol 887.

[107] Id. In particular, he recommended legislation involving an amendment to the Civil Rights statute; the federal licensing of detective agencies engaged in interstate business; the relation of federal aid to state troops used in strikes; the importation of strike-breakers; and the relation of the federal government to local interference with the rights of the unemployed.

[108] Morris Ernst to Roger Baldwin, April 9, 1936, ACLU Papers, reel 131, vol 887. At the preliminary hearings, Arthur Garfield Hays and Morris Ernst were prepared to testify regarding postal and radio censorship, sedition and criminal syndicalism laws, and alien laws, as well as the operation of the federal civil rights statute, the use of state troops against strikers in relation to the federal government's aid to the national guard, and other issues. Memorandum Re: La Follette Investigation, April 20, 1936, ACLU Papers, reel 131, vol 887. La Follette declined their offer. Robert La Follette Jr. to Roger Baldwin, April 22, 1936, ACLU Papers, reel 131, vol 887.

[109] Quoted in Auerbach, *Labor and Liberty* at 65 (cited in note 101).

enforcement or by employers themselves. Its supporters, however, were seasoned and savvy politicians. They sought to generate approval by invoking the specter of totalitarianism—"We are unquestionably the most powerful agency against Fascism in this country," one staff member wrote—and the corresponding collapse of American democracy.[110] In his testimony at the hearings, NLRB member Edwin Smith recited the civil liberties movement's well-worn argument that unchecked abuses would lead to violent revolt. He denounced "entrenched interests" and "alleged patriotic organizations" for arguing that repression was the only means of saving America from the radicals. "You cannot suppress freedom of expression," he cautioned, "without rapidly undermining democracy itself."[111]

La Follette and his staff were policymakers, not scholars or theorists. There was much slippage in their characterization of civil liberties. Still, some salient features emerge from their public defenses of the committee and from their private communications. First, the true goal of the committee was something more than expressive freedom or individual rights. As Edwin Smith put it, "civil liberties are not abstractions which hover above the passions of contending groups and can be successfully brought to earth to promote the general welfare."[112] Robert La Follette Jr. was adamant that "the right of workers to speak freely and assemble peacefully is immediate and practical, a right which translates itself into the concrete terms of job security, fair wages and decent living conditions."[113] Progressives and conservatives increasingly were casting civil liberties in neutral terms—as a commitment to deliberative openness rather than particular values. The La Follette Committee, by contrast, was most focused on economic security.

---

[110] Felix Frazer to Byron Scott, February 3, 1937, La Follette Committee Papers, 10.25, box 5, folder February 1937.

[111] Statement by Edwin S. Smith before Hearings of Subcommittee on Senate Resolution 266, April 23, 1936, ACLU Papers, reel 131, vol 887. The committee was careful to maintain an air of impartiality to maintain its credibility. See, for example, Robert Wohlforth to Harold Cranefield, March 9, 1937, La Follette Committee Papers, 10.25, box 5, folder March 1937 ("Under no condition should you or any members of this Committee try to address any union meetings. However well intentioned this may be, it is providing ammunition for those opposed to the Committee to give us a terrific smear.").

[112] Edwin S. Smith, *Civil Rights for Labor*, before Washington, DC branch of ACLU, January 1938, ACLU Papers, reel 156, vol 1078.

[113] Robert M. La Follette Jr., *Management, Too, Must be Responsible*, Natl Law Guild Q 1, 4 (Dec 1937).

Second, and relatedly, threats to civil liberties did not emanate exclusively, or even primarily, from the state. The committee was determined to introduce new, affirmative protections for labor's organizing efforts, many of which were directed against private action. These rights would be established by statute and enforceable through administrative actors—namely, the NLRB—as well as the state and federal courts.

The La Follette Committee did not clarify the relationship between its operations and the Constitution, but NLRB chair J. Warren Madden addressed the definitional question head on in a 1939 address to the ACLU-sponsored National Conference on Civil Liberties. The Wagner Act, he explained, "gave to employees the right to organize and took away the legal privilege of employers to destroy their organization." In evaluating what to label the "new right," he observed that it was conferred by a statute that "restrains the private interests which formerly could and did prevent unionization, rather than by an act of self-denial on the part of the government itself, pledged in the text of the Constitution." He continued:

> Is it, for that reason, inaccurate to call it a civil liberty? I should suppose that the year 1935 was as propitious a year for the birth of a civil liberty as the year 1789. . . . In each of these years 1789 and 1935 the Federal Government placed in the body of its law the guarantee of the aspirations of multitudes of its citizens, for which they had struggled for decades. But let us not quibble about names. However it may be classified it is a new right which millions of Americans are exercising who never did so before. They have joined A.F. of L. unions, C.I.O. unions and unaffiliated unions. No one longer denies that they have a moral right to do so. And no one can successfully deny that they needed the protection of the government in order to be free to exercise this moral right.[114]

Whatever their title, the tools of union organizing had attained the status of rights. This was a classification distinct from the government largesse of the Progressive Era. It imposed an obligation on the state to exercise its power on behalf of labor and at the expense of private interests.

The La Follette Committee was similarly noncommittal in articulating the nature of the rights it defended, and similarly focused on the functional obligations its authority entailed. In common usage,

---

[114] Address of J. Warren Madden to National Conference on Civil Liberties, October 13, 1939, Clark Papers, Series VIII (ABA Committee on the Bill of Rights), box 10 (Cases): NLRB Address of J. Warren Madden, 10/13/39 (box 86, folder 41).

civil liberties were increasingly associated with the Bill of Rights, and defenses of the committee's work often capitalized on the cachet of the American constitutional tradition. Certainly the La Follette Committee considered its recommendations to be consistent with the Constitution, even important extensions of its underlying goals. To justify incursions on employers' property rights and managerial discretion as constitutional mandates, however, would require a revision of constitutional thought more radical than the so-called Constitutional Revolution.

A changing political climate made any such claim untenable before it could be tested. In spring 1937, the same season in which the Supreme Court upheld the constitutionality of the NLRA, the tide began to turn against labor's demands for state support. Following a major CIO organizing effort involving a wave of powerful sit-down strikes, employers' groups organized to foment public opinion against workers' unruliness and to pressure local police and administrators to enforce the law. Some specifically used the language of "civil rights" to describe the unvindicated personal and property interests of employers.[115] Increasingly, public and political figures expressed concern at unions' aggressive attitude, and momentum seeped from the congressional labor agenda. The economy had contracted sharply as a result of Roosevelt's fiscal policy, fueling frustration and desperation by industry and workers alike.[116]

The Wagner Act, newly secured by the Supreme Court from constitutional attack, was suddenly open to legislative challenge. Republican opponents of the New Deal reached out to Southern Democrats, who feared that active intervention in labor disputes would open the door to federal interference with Jim Crow. To make matters worse, the AFL attacked the NLRB for favoring the CIO and undermining labor voluntarism. New Deal Democrats responded by citing the violent and unlawful suppression of labor by employers, relying heavily on the findings of the La Follette Civil Liberties Committee.

---

[115] *Partial Report of Proceedings, Meeting, Organization Committee, National Committee of One Thousand on Civil Rights,* La Follette Committee Papers, 50.25, box 86, folder March 1937. Archibald Stevenson, best known for his role in the New York State legislature's Lusk Committee after World War I, helped organize the National Committee of One Thousand on Civil Rights to combat sit-down strikes.

[116] On "Roosevelt's Depression," see Richard Polenberg, *Reorganizing Roosevelt's Government: The Controversy over Executive Reorganization, 1936–1939,* 149 (Harvard, 1966).

By the summer of 1938, however, neither Congress nor the public considered the committee to be a credible source. The staff was regularly fielding demands that it investigate labor unions in addition to employers. One outraged citizen, voicing widely shared anti-union sentiments, insisted that "people read the News Papers and know that if strikers did not attack men hired to protect plants, there would be no fighting."[117] Another, who claimed to have known the elder Senator La Follette as well as Samuel Gompers, lamented the nation's decline into "anarchy" and urged the committee to present a "true picture of all sides."[118] In a move that captures the growing incompatibility between the labor interventionist vision of civil liberties and its alternatives, one correspondent suggested that the committee investigate President Roosevelt for his court-packing plan.[119]

In March 1939, the work of the La Follette Civil Liberties Committee drew to a close. Its extensive findings over years of congressional hearings culminated in a bill "to eliminate certain oppressive labor practices affecting interstate and foreign commerce." Had it passed, it would have made antilabor espionage, munitions, private police, and strikebreaking punishable by fine or imprisonment. William Green and John L. Lewis both supported the bill.[120] So, "heartily," did Attorney General Murphy, who believed "that the Federal Government has a definite role to play in the preservation of civil liberties."[121] By 1939, however, a sweeping congressional endorsement of the labor interventionist vision of civil liberties was bound to fail. Instead, the La Follette Committee yielded the spot-

---

[117] J. C. Pinkney to Robert La Follette Jr., February 2, 1937, La Follette Committee Papers, 50.25, box 85.

[118] George Porter to Robert La Follette Jr., February 5, 1937, La Follette Committee Papers, 50.25, box 85.

[119] J. D. Fidler to Robert La Follette Jr., February 25, 1937, La Follette Committee Papers, 50.25, box 85.

[120] Debate on S. 1970 centered on the supposed Communist threat to American industry. Amendments proposed by North Carolina Senator Robert R. Reynolds prohibited all companies from hiring aliens in excess of 10 percent of their workforces or from employing "any Communist or member of any Nazi Bund organization." The Senate bill, thus amended, passed by a vote of 47 to 20. The House version was buried in committee. Auerbach, *Labor and Liberty* at 454 (cited in note 101).

[121] Statement of Attorney General Murphy Before the Senate Committee of Education and Labor, re: Bill S 1970, in National Archives and Records Administration, College Park, MD, Record Group 60, General Records of the United States Department of Justice, Records of the Special Executive Assistant to the Attorney General, 1933–40, Subject Files, 1933–40 (hereafter Attorney General Papers), box 6, entry 132.

light to Martin Dies Jr.'s House Committee on Un-American Activity. Among the many insinuations made by that committee was that the La Follette Committee's civil liberties work was corrupted by Communist influence.[122]

C. THE ADMINISTRATIVE ENFORCEMENT OF CIVIL LIBERTIES

Consistent with the La Follette Committee's labor interventionist vision of civil liberties, the early NLRB considered the rights of labor to be independent rights deserving of state protection. NLRB member Edwin Smith put the point bluntly. In his view, organized labor was the only force capable of preserving democracy. To survive, it must "receive from the government firm protection against those who have the power and will to destroy it."[123]

In its enforcement of the Wagner Act, the NLRB sought to implement this ideal. The early operations of the NLRB have been documented in tremendous depth and detail. On the whole, its members were unexpectedly aggressive in advancing labor's interests. Whether state support energized organized labor or instead deradicalized it is a much debated question. So too is the effect of the NLRB's preference for CIO-style industrial unionism over the established craft model of the AFL. These inquiries have important implications with respect to the effects of institutional differences on civil liberties enforcement, and I will briefly address them in Part III. For now, I want to stress that the NLRB often spoke in terms of civil liberties when it administered the NLRA.

For much of the 1930s, civil liberties advocates within and outside the NLRB assumed they were defending the same ideals. Labor interventionists at the NLRB proclaimed their commitment to protecting the civil liberties of workers. Proponents of the progressive civil liberties vision celebrated the agency's service on behalf of labor but regarded its operations as economic regulation

---

[122] The hearings of the Special Committee on Un-American Activities were convened on August 12, 1938 by Representative Martin Dies of Texas. On the relationship between the Dies Committee and civil liberties, see Auerbach, *Labor and Liberty* at 450 (cited in note 101) ("The Dies Committee, more than any single institution, abetted the charge that the La Follette Committee's origins, composition, and direction evidenced affinity for communism.").

[123] Address by Edwin S. Smith Before the Carolina Political Union, March 30, 1938, quoted in *Memorandum in Support of Proposal to Confine the National Labor Relations Board to the Functions of Accusing and Prosecuting and to Transfer Its Judicial Functions to a Separate Administrative Body Similar to the Board of Tax Appeals*, 15, Ford Legal Papers, box 3, vol 3.

outside the sweep of civil liberties concerns. In early 1939, however, the two visions clashed head on. Building on mounting hostility toward CIO organizing tactics and the perceived partisanship of the NLRB, a congressional coalition of Republicans and Southern Democrats introduced a host of amendments designed to curb the board's authority. Concurrently, Massachusetts Democrat David I. Walsh proposed a more moderate bill, which was backed by the AFL and commanded considerable support.

Two provisions in the Walsh bill were particularly divisive among civil liberties advocates. The first provided for more robust judicial review of NLRB decisions. Although progressive civil libertarians opposed the measure because it singled out the NLRB for special treatment, they were beginning to regard administrative agencies as incipient civil liberties threats. In other words, the progressive civil liberties vision was in transition. One of its long-standing pillars— confidence in unfettered administrative regulation of economic relations, if not free speech—had begun to crumble. In response to the bill, ACLU attorney Arthur Garfield Hays called for enhanced procedural protections in "trial by commission" and convened a committee to study quasi-judicial boards.[124] Hays thought the commissions were censoring business, "which [was] just as bad as a censorship over literature."

Another of Senator Walsh's suggestions was even more pressing: a provision guaranteeing an employer's right to free speech in the context of union organizing efforts. During the late 1930s, the NLRB had aggressively policed the employer distribution of antiunion materials on the theory that it coerced employees in the exercise of their right to organize under the NLRA. In response, the ACLU reluctantly defended the right of such notorious antilabor employers as Henry Ford to circulate antiunion propaganda—a position that polarized the ACLU and coincided with the expulsion or resignation of its board's Communists and fellow travelers.[125]

Testimony by J. Warren Madden before the Senate Committee on Education and Labor captures the NLRB's understanding. Madden told the committee that an employer's accurate statement that the leaders of a union were Communists might dissuade an employee

[124] Board Minutes, January 30, 1939, ACLU Papers, reel 189, vol 2233; Arthur Garfield Hays to ACLU, January 26, 1939, ACLU Papers, reel 169, vol 2080.

[125] See Weinrib, *Liberal Compromise* at 457–557 (cited in note 19).

from joining and would therefore constitute coercion. "The fact that it is true," he insisted, "does not keep it from being coercive." Citing labor injunctions, he argued that "there is no privilege against being enjoined from telling the truth if you state it at such times or under such circumstances that you destroy somebody else's rights."[126] Madden was weighing employers' speech rights against the rights of workers to organize. Both were arguably grounded in the Constitution. For Madden, that the suppression of workers' rights stemmed from private power rather than state action was not dispositive. Acknowledging that rights claims involve trade-offs, he argued that the state was best positioned to make the necessary calculations and intervene on behalf of the weaker party. If free speech was incompatible with economic justice, the former would have to give way.

From the progressive perspective, "Brother Madden['s]" reasoning threatened to undercut a decade of civil liberties gains.[127] Indeed, labor activity had often been regulated for precisely the reasons Madden was endorsing; the Supreme Court had long denied First Amendment protection to labor picketing in light of its coercive effect. Despite "violent[] oppos[ition]" to the free speech amendment from longtime labor allies,[128] many progressives thought some sort of legislative reformulation was desirable.[129] The ACLU ultimately opposed the free speech amendment, along with the other amend-

---

[126] The question, he suggested, was one of parity. "If there were any constitutional doctrine that people could go about the world speaking the truth or speaking their opinions under any and all circumstances, and regardless of its destructive consequences, we of course would follow it. The courts do not follow any such doctrine when they are protecting property or when they are protecting employers against picketing and that kind of thing." Any other decision, he concluded, would amount to class discrimination. Testimony of J. Warren Madden, Hearings Before the Senate Committee on Education and Labor, April 19, 1939, ACLU Papers, reel 169, vol 2080.

[127] John Haynes Holmes to Roger Baldwin, April 20, 1939, ACLU Papers, reel 169, vol 2080.

[128] Lee Pressman to Arthur Garfield Hays, February 10, 1939, ACLU Papers, reel 169, vol 2080. CIO General Counsel Lee Pressman told Arthur Garfield Hays that the CIO was "violently opposed" to the amendment. The CIO had explained its position in an earlier pamphlet (in which it implicitly compared the proposed curtailment of the board's powers to Roosevelt's judiciary reorganization plan). Committee for Industrial Organization, *Why the Wagner Act Should NOT Be Amended*, October 1938, ACLU Papers, reel 156, vol 1078 ("[It is] useless to pretend that constitutional rights of free speech are being invaded. There are many kinds of speech which are unlawful. . . . Society is entitled to impose such reasonable limitations upon freedom of speech and press as may be necessary to its own protection. It has always done so and always will.").

[129] The 1938 Annual Report had still celebrated the NLRA as "in substance a civil liberties document." American Civil Liberties Union, *Eternal Vigilance!: The Story of Civil Liberty*,

ments, as "either unnecessary or dangerous to the fundamental purpose of the act."[130] The organization did not, however, endorse the
NLRB's view of employer speech. Instead, it argued that existing
limitations on the board's authority were sufficient—that the abridgment of employer speech was inconsistent with the NLRA as well
as unconstitutional.[131]

In this, the progressive and conservative visions of civil liberties
aligned. The demise of economic due process had made civil liberties
all the more appealing: the dispute over employer speech demonstrated that the First Amendment might succeed where freedom of
contract had failed. The ACLU's position on employer speech was
warmly celebrated by the United States Chamber of Commerce and
the ABA.

D. THE EXECUTIVE ENFORCEMENT OF CIVIL LIBERTIES

Enforcement of constitutional rights through the courts is often reduced to the practice of judicial review. During the New Deal,
however, a different strategy emerged for advancing those rights
through litigation—one that entailed vindicating rather than invalidating government interests. Over the course of 1930, the state began to pursue civil liberties through its prosecutorial arm, by bringing
transgressors to justice in the federal courts.

On January 3, 1939, Frank Murphy succeeded Homer Cummings
as Attorney General of the United States. As mayor of Detroit from
1930 to 1933, Murphy had been a strong advocate for the unemployed. In 1937, he was elected governor of Michigan. Shortly after

---

1937–1938, 25 (ACLU, 1938). John Haynes Holmes thought Madden's interpretation was
sufficiently troubling to justify removal of Madden as chair or amendment of the NLRA.
Even Arthur Garfield Hays thought the Ford case had demonstrated the necessity for an
amendment like the one Walsh had proposed. Arthur Garfield Hays to ACLU, February 14,
1939, ACLU Papers, reel 169, vol 2080 (arguing that the Ford case indicated that a free
speech amendment was necessary). William Fennell also favored the free speech amendment.
William Fennel to Osmond Fraenkel, January 28, 1939, ACLU Papers, reel 169, vol 2080.

[130] ACLU Press Release, April 24, 1939, ACLU Papers, reel 176, vol 2130; *Statement on
Proposed Amendments to the NLRA* (adopted by the board on January 30, 1939), ACLU Papers,
reel 168, vol 2080.

[131] The board was not unwilling to adapt in the face of public concern, even if it regarded
change as unwarranted. For example, in June the NLRB obviated a particularly popular
amendment proposal by announcing that it had amended its rules to permit employers to
petition the board for an election in cases where two or more bona fide labor organizations
were claiming a majority. NLRB Press Release, June 21, 1939, ACLU Papers, reel 169,
vol 2080.

he took office, he refused to call in state troops to break a sit-down strike by the fledgling UAW. That decision was influential in the subsequent rise of the CIO. As Murphy explained the affair, workers in Michigan had been angry at the failure of employers to abide by the Wagner Act, as well as the prevalent use of industrial espionage to defeat unionization. In seizing control of industrial property, thousands of misguided but "honest citizens" had acted to "defend[] their own rights against what they believed to be the lawless refusal of their employers to recognize their unions." Murphy emphasized that he had never condoned sit-down strikes, and he had advised union representatives that they were illegal and imprudent. He nonetheless believed that in the face of widespread disobedience, it was necessary to "weed out the cause," not merely to "enforce the law."[132]

Murphy brought the same sensibilities to his duties as Attorney General. He was intimately familiar with the work of the La Follette Committee in his home state and elsewhere, and he was convinced that the abridgment of workers' civil liberties by employers and their government collaborators was a major source of class strife. But Murphy's commitment was not limited to workers' rights. He considered civil liberties to be essential to every part of life, "social, political, and economic." They extended to such far-ranging ideals as "the right of self-government, the right of every man to speak his thoughts freely, the opportunity to express his individual nature in his daily life and work, [and] the privilege of believing in the religion that his own conscience tells him is right." The American model of civil liberties represented a crucial compromise between governmental regulation, which was "necessary for an orderly society," and the unbounded freedom of nature. More basically, the rights to speak freely, to practice one's religion, to assemble peaceably, and to petition government for the redress of grievances were essential to a functioning democracy. They applied with equal force to "the business man and the laborer."[133] Here, then, was the progressive vision

---

[132] Statement of Honorable Frank Murphy, Attorney General of the United States, Before a Sub-Committee of the Committee on the Judiciary of the United States Senate, Attorney General Papers, box 5, entry 132, folder Murphy (Attorney General—Items about Him).

[133] Frank Murphy, *Civil Liberties*, radio address, National Radio Forum, March 27, 1939, Attorney General Papers, box 5, entry 132, folder Civil Liberties.

of civil liberties, grafted onto a prosecutorial model of civil liberties enforcement.

From his first day in office, it was clear that Murphy would make civil liberties a priority. Shortly after his confirmation, his special assistant in charge of public relations helped him arrange a radio program on the protection of civil liberties by the federal government.[134] He told Roger Baldwin that the subject was "one of the things that interest[ed him] most keenly," and that the opportunity to pursue it was one of the "great satisfactions" of his service as Attorney General. Indeed, he was "anxious that the weight and influence of the Department of Justice should be a force for the preservation of the people's liberties."[135]

On February 3, one month after he was sworn in, Murphy's office made an announcement. Within the Criminal Division of the Department of Justice, a new entity had been established, to be known as the Civil Liberties Unit. Its principal function was to prosecute violations of the constitutional and statutory provisions "guaranteeing civil rights to individuals."[136] In particular, it would pursue cases of beatings and violence, denial of workers' rights under the NLRA, and deprivation of freedom of speech and assembly.[137] Murphy explained that in a democracy, the enforcement of law entailed the "aggressive protection of the fundamental rights inherent in a free people." The Civil Liberties Unit, consistent with the recommendations of the La Follette Committee, would undertake "vigilant action" in ensuring that those rights were respected.[138] For the first time, it would throw the "full weight of the Department" behind the "blessings of liberty, the spirit of tolerance, and the fundamental principles of democracy." In Murphy's estimation, the creation of

---

[134] Gordon Dean, Memorandum for the Attorney General, January 27, 1939, Attorney General Papers, box 5, entry 132, folder Murphy (Attorney General—Items about Him) (suggesting Murphy speak with the director of America's Town Meeting of the Air); Gordon Dean, Memorandum for Miss Bumgarnder, January 27, 1939, Attorney General Papers, box 5, entry 132, folder Murphy (Attorney General—Items about Him) ("The Attorney General knows all about the Lawyers Guild and that it is the liberal national lawyers' group.").

[135] Frank Murphy to Roger Baldwin, February 3, 1939, ACLU Papers, reel 168, vol 2070.

[136] Order No 3204, Office of the Attorney General, February 3, 1939, Attorney General Papers, box 22, entry 132, folder Civil Liberties.

[137] *"Civil Rights" Unit Set Up by Murphy*, New York Times (Feb 4, 1939).

[138] Press Release, February 3, 1939, Attorney General Papers, box 22, entry 132, folder Civil Liberties.

the Civil Liberties Unit was "one of the most significant happenings in American legal history."[139]

At the first nationwide gathering of U.S. attorneys in Washington, D.C., Murphy enjoined federal prosecutors to wield their power responsibly—to enforce the civil rights statutes "not just for some of the people but for all of them," "no matter how humble."[140] Civil liberties, he told them, were more important than at any previous time in history. The Depression had brought with it "the usual demands for repression of minorities," and it was up to the federal government to stave off the rampant incursions.[141]

Murphy's plans for the Civil Liberties Unit were ambitious. Among other functions, it would alert local officials that the federal government would not tolerate arbitrary and abusive conduct, alone or in conjunction with private interests.[142] It would also raise awareness and influence public opinion. Murphy was adamant that the federal government could "take the initiative," but it could not "do the whole job." The problem was partly jurisdictional; some rights inhered in individuals as residents of the separate states, and they could not be vindicated by federal authorities. The threats to American freedom came not only from city ordinances and the arbitrary exercise of state power, but from mob murder, lynchings, and vigilante violence. More basically, however, "the great protector of civil liberty, the final source of its enforcement" was the "invincible power of public opinion."[143] The courts could provide a remedy for lawlessness, but they could not prevent its taking hold.

In the immediate term, the Civil Liberties Unit had a concrete program. It would study and evaluate (and eventually prosecute under) the potential constitutional and statutory provisions applicable to civil rights enforcement, including laws prohibiting kidnapping, peonage, and mail fraud.[144] The most important of the potential causes of action, at least for the time being, were under the Recon-

---

[139] Frank Murphy to Franklin D. Roosevelt, July 7, 1939, Attorney General Papers, box 5, entry 132, folder Murphy: 6 Months Report.

[140] *Murphy Sworn in at the White House*, New York Times (Jan 3, 1939).

[141] *Murphy Tells Aides to Guard Civil Rights*, Washington Post (April 20, 1939).

[142] In 1940, Solicitor General Francis Biddle told the Junior Bar Conference that this deterrent effect was the most important function of the Civil Liberties Unit. *Civil Rights Protection*, Buffalo Daily Law Journal (Sept 14, 1940).

[143] Murphy, *Civil Liberties* (cited in note 133).

[144] Order No 3204, Office of the Attorney General, February 3, 1939, Attorney General Papers, box 22, entry 132, folder Civil Liberties.

struction era civil rights statutes, Title 18, Sections 51 and 52 of the criminal code.[145] The department expected to employ the statutes regularly, though it recognized their limitations. Section 52 was applicable only to deprivations of civil liberties under color of state laws. It also suffered "from the malady of old age"; after many years of disuse, it was likely to face significant resistance. Section 51 was similarly limited in its applicability. It was passed to rein in the Ku Klux Klan, "and by reason of that fact, together with its severe punishment, it [was] a somewhat difficult statute, for psychological reasons, to prosecute under." Moreover, although it permitted prosecution for violation of constitutional rights, few constitutional provisions could be construed to limit private action. Finally, both sections faced an additional obstacle, in that both criminalized conduct in violation of rights "secured by" the Constitution or federal statutes. Defendants were apt to argue that Section 51 applied only to rights "created," not "guaranteed," by the Constitution, and that the rights of free speech and assembly preexisted the federal government.[146] In light of these obstacles, the Civil Liberties Unit expected to make recommendations for "some modern legislation on civil rights."[147]

Within its first month of operation several hundred complaints were referred to the Civil Liberties Unit, including lynchings, interference with meetings, illegal police practices, deportations, and voting rights violations.[148] The department also contemplated prosecutions under Section 51 for violations by employers of the Wagner Act.[149] That program seemingly received judicial sanction with the Supreme Court's decision in *Hague v CIO*, which the department

---

[145] Those provisions are now codified at 18 USC §§ 241–42. The peonage laws would in fact prove more useful, in light of the state action requirements of Sections 51 and 52. See Risa Lauren Goluboff, *The Lost Promise of Civil Rights* 142–52 (Harvard, 2007).

[146] Memorandum for Mr. Dean, Attorney General Papers, box 22, entry 132, folder Civil Liberties. On the origins and implications of this interpretation of "secured by" in the Civil Rights Acts of 1870 and 1871, see Lynda G. Dodd, *Constitutional Torts in the Forgotten Years: Retracing the Winding Road to Monroe v. Pape* (unpublished manuscript) (on file with author).

[147] Gordon Dean to Leigh Danenberg, March 6, 1939, Attorney General Papers, box 22, entry 132, folder Civil Liberties. For example, the unit was considering recommending legislation that would allow the federal government to seek injunctive relief as an alternative to criminal action. "This would overcome the difficulties pointed out above and would also free the case of local prejudice on the part of citizenry from which jurors must be selected." Memorandum for Mr. Dean, Attorney General Papers, box 22, entry 132, Folder Civil Liberties.

[148] Gordon Dean to Leigh Danenberg, March 6, 1939, Attorney General Papers, box 22, entry 132, folder Civil Liberties.

[149] Joseph Matan, Memorandum to Assistant Attorney General Brien McMahon, May 14, 1937, Attorney General Papers, box 22, entry 132, folder Civil Rights.

regarded as a strong endorsement of the Civil Rights Act.[150] The Court's interpretation of the jurisdictional and private-action provisions was an apparent invitation for criminal prosecutions under Sections 51 and 52.[151] The Department of Justice read the Court's decision in *Hague* to mean that "if a Federal statute otherwise constitutional gives a private right to a citizen, Section 51 will serve for prosecution of any group of persons who attempt to take it away from him." This reasoning arguably applied to private acts of violence affecting statutory rights "under the recently extended commerce clause." The NLRA was the most prominent such example,[152] and the CIO quickly announced that it would "request the Department of Justice to take steps for criminal prosecution of all who interfere with its organizing activities by violating the civil rights of workers."[153] For a time, the department vigorously pursued the new strategy, albeit with uneven results.[154]

Within a few years, however, the department abandoned its ambitious program in favor of a more manageable task. In 1941, the Civil Liberties Unit was renamed the Civil Rights Section. Although the terms "civil liberties" and "civil rights" were often used interchangeably during this period, the new nomenclature reflected a shift in the unit's priorities from industrial labor to race. During the 1940s, the CRS focused on economic justice for African Americans, eschewing the type of formal equality arguments that would mark the

---

[150] Lewis Wood, *Hague Ban on CIO Voided by the Supreme Court, 5–2, on Free Assemblage Right*, New York Times (June 6, 1939).

[151] Justice Stone's opinion implicitly rejected the narrow interpretation of Section 51 in *United States v Cruikshank*, 92 US 542 (1876), an 1876 case growing out of the mob murder of more than a hundred black Republicans in Reconstruction Louisiana. The defendants were convicted of conspiracy to deprive citizens of the United States of their rights to assemble and bear arms, among other charges. The Supreme Court reversed the convictions on the theory that such rights were not protected by the Fourteenth Amendment. Justice Stone's opinion suggested that *Cruikshank* was no longer good law. *Hague*, 307 US at 526.

[152] Id (citing *Hague* as well as the Pennsylvania System case, which arose under the 1930 Transportation Act). Its curtailment by employers was the theory of the Harlan County case. The Harlan case itself never reached the court, because it was nolled as part of a negotiated settlement.

[153] Wood, *Hague Ban* (cited in note 150) (quoting Lee Pressman).

[154] Annual Report of the Attorney General of the United States for the Fiscal Year 1939, 63, Attorney General Papers, box 30, HM 1994 (reporting cases prosecuted by the Civil Liberties unit in 1939 and 1940); see also *Recent Development: Conspiracy to Coerce Employees into Union Activity Not Indictable Under 18 USC § 241*, 55 Colum L Rev 103 (1955); Tom C. Clark, *A Federal Prosecutor Looks at the Civil Rights Statutes*, 47 Colum L Rev 175 (1947); *The Press: In Mobile*, Time (May 22, 1939) (describing use of Section 51).

NAACP's litigation strategy in the run-up to *Brown v Board of Education*.[155] Still, the claims the CRS took up were those of desperate black farmworkers, not the powerful unions of the new labor regime. Rescuing the country's most vulnerable workers from conditions close to slavery threatened America's racial hierarchy, a goal of patent historical importance. Nonetheless, the CRS considered its new commitments, like its new name, to be less "radical" and more politically palatable than its earlier path.[156]

In any case, the continued validity of the state action doctrine made earlier proposals to pursue claims against individual employers for interference with labor activity unfeasible. The Fourteenth Amendment did not reach individual action, as the CRS well understood.[157] The state action requirement expressed in such cases as *Cruikshank* and *Wheeler* meant that Section 51 was inapplicable to "the great mass of civil liberties cases" the department would otherwise have pursued. In 1939, Assistant Attorney General O. John Rogge reported that the Criminal Division was evaluating those cases to determine whether they represented "sound law." If they did not, the Civil Liberties Unit would have "no hesitation" in asking the Supreme Court to overrule them.[158] The Supreme Court, however, declined the offer, and a legislative solution was by that time off the table.[159] Even if authorization were possible, CRS reservations may have stood in the way. Robert Jackson, Murphy's successor as Attorney General (and his future colleague on the Supreme Court), was skeptical of a state-centered approach. "Compared with [the] rather narrow powers to advance civil rights," he reflected, "the

---

[155] Notably, its project was premised on the Thirteenth Amendment, not the Equal Protection Clause of the Fourteenth.

[156] Goluboff, *Lost Promise* at 112 (cited in note 145). Goluboff's work on the Civil Rights Section is crucial here. See also Richard D. McKinzie, Oral History Interview with Eleanor Bontecou, Washington, D.C., June 5, 1973, Harry S. Truman Library, Independence, Missouri (explaining that the peonage cases were successful because they were in line with public opinion).

[157] As Assistant Attorney General O. John Rogge told the ACLU's National Conference on Civil Liberties in October 1939: "No matter how much the content of the due process clause has been expanded, rights under the due process clause are not protected against mere individual action, on the standard interpretation of the Fourteenth Amendment as a restriction on State action only." *Civil Rights Conference*, Civil Liberties Q (September 1939), 1, ACLU Papers, reel 167, vol 2061.

[158] Address by O. John Rogge, National Conference on Civil Liberties, October 14, 1939, Attorney General Papers, box 22, entry 132, folder Civil Rights.

[159] See *Screws v United States*, 325 US 91 (1945).

possibilities that the Department of Justice by misuse of power will invade civil rights really gives me more concern."[160]

III. The Uncertain Stakes of Civil Liberties Enforcement

During the late New Deal, a broad range of government actors and private organizations openly endorsed civil liberties. Indeed, the federal government contained multiple entities explicitly committed to securing them, including a Senate committee and Department of Justice unit with the term "civil liberties" in their names. There were, however, essential differences in the ways that the various actors understood their underlying objectives. That is, congruence at the level of rhetoric belies a growing distance between competing conceptions of civil liberties' substantive sweep, as well as methods of civil liberties enforcement. The question for this part is the extent to which those variations tracked institutional lines.

Scholars of legal change have long asked which institutions are best suited to advancing particular rights.[161] Judicial enthusiasts cite the ability of courts and constitutional victories to reshape cultural understandings, resist popular pressures, and energize potential supporters at relatively low cost.[162] Critics counter that court-based constitutionalism privileges individual over collective rights, dera-

---

[160] Robert H. Jackson, *Messages on the Launching of the Bill of Rights Review*, 1 Bill of Rights Rev 34 (1940).

[161] Often this question is addressed explicitly and through a theoretical lens, as in the Law and Society and American Political Development literatures. For helpful overviews of the former, see Albiston, 96 Iowa L Rev (cited in note 1); Douglas Nejaime, *Constitutional Change, Courts, and Social Movements*, 111 Mich L Rev 877 (2013); on the latter, see Paul Frymer, *Law and American Political Development*, 33 L & Social Inquiry 779 (2008). Sometimes, it is the implicit question motivating historical work on social movements, litigation, and constitutional change. Legal scholars, too, have grappled extensively with the political and institutional constraints on the courts. For an effort to integrate the various analytic approaches to this issue, see Michael McCann, *How the Supreme Court Matters in American Politics: New Institutionalist Perspectives*, in Howard Gillman and Cornell Clayton, eds, *The Supreme Court in American Politics* (Kansas, 1999).

[162] Much of legal scholarship seeks to defend particular normative visions of the judiciary as essential to American governance. For some representative defenses of judicial review from competing political and ideological orientations, see John Hart Ely, *Democracy and Distrust: A Theory of Judicial Review* (Harvard, 1980); Morton Horwitz, *The Warren Court and the Pursuit of Justice: A Critical Issue* (Hill and Wang, 1998); Erwin Chemerinsky, *In Defense of Judicial Review: The Perils of Popular Constitutionalism*, 2004 U Ill L Rev 673; Christopher L. Eisgruber, *Constitutional Self-Government* (Harvard, 2001); Ronald Dworkin, *Law's Empire* (Belknap, 1986).

dicalizes social movements, and alienates the organizational base.[163] Champions of grass-roots organizing, political activism, and interest-group pluralism charge that resources devoted to litigation could be spent more productively on mobilizing, lobbying, or influencing administrative actors on behalf of broader goals.[164]

Meanwhile, accounts of popular constitutionalism evaluate the influence of public opinion on judicial decisions construing constitutional rights.[165] In doing so, they assume—often implicitly, and sometimes explicitly—that legislative and administrative actors are inherently more responsive to popular pressures.[166] Similarly, the countermajoritarian difficulty presumes that the laws and policies subjected to judicial review more closely approximate democratic consensus than the decisions that strike them down.[167] Above all,

---

[163] For example, Derrick A. Bell Jr., *Serving Two Masters: Integration Ideals and Client Interests in School Desegregation Litigation*, 85 Yale L J 470 (1976); Michael W. McCann, *Taking Reform Seriously: Perspectives on Public Interest Liberalism* (Cornell, 1986); Robert W. Gordon, *Critical Legal Histories*, 36 Stan L Rev 57 (1984); Janet Rifkin, *Toward a Theory of Law and Patriarchy*, in Piers Beirne and Richard Quinney, eds, *Marxism and Law* 295 (Wiley, 1982); Marc Galanter, *Why the "Haves" Come Out Ahead: Speculations on the Limits of Legal Change*, 9 L & Society Rev 95 (1974). For an early overview and critique of these binary positions, see Stuart A. Scheingold, *The Politics of Rights: Lawyers, Public Policy, and Political Change* (Yale, 1974).

[164] For example, Michael W. McCann and Helena Silverstein, *Rethinking Law's Allurements: A Relational Analysis of Social Movement Lawyers in the United States*, in Austin Sarat and Stuart Scheingold, eds, *Cause Lawyering: Political Commitments and Professional Responsibilities* 261 (Oxford, 1998); Scheingold, *Politics of Rights* (cited in note 163).

[165] Scholars of popular constitutionalism argue that constitutional decisions should in fact reflect popular preferences, for example, Kramer, *People Themselves* (cited in note 1); Richard D. Parker, *"Here, the People Rule": A Constitutional Populist Manifesto* (Harvard, 1994); Mark Tushnet, *Taking the Constitution Away from the Courts* (Harvard, 1999). For the idea that popular constitutionalism is better suited to constitutional theories that limit rather than expand state power, see Christopher W. Schmidt, *Popular Constitutionalism on the Right: Lessons from the Tea Party*, 88 Denver U L Rev 523 (2011).

[166] There is, of course, a substantial literature arguing that judicial decisions typically reflect broader political and cultural norms, without necessarily embracing that claim as a normative matter. See, for example, Klarman, *From Jim Crow to Civil Rights* (cited in note 1); Barry Friedman, *The Will of the People: How Public Opinion Has Influenced the Supreme Court and Shaped the Meaning of the Constitution* (Farrar, Straus and Giroux, 2009); Jeffrey Rosen, *The Most Democratic Branch: How the Courts Serve America* (Oxford, 2006). For a critique of this position, see Justin Driver, *The Consensus Constitution*, 89 Tex L Rev 755 (2011). There is also abundant evidence that judges' personal and political preferences influence judicial outcomes. For example, Lawrence Baum, *Measuring Policy Change in the U.S. Supreme Court*, 82 Amer Pol Sci Rev 905 (1988); Jeffrey A. Segal and Harold J. Spaeth, *The Supreme Court and the Attitudinal Model* (Cambridge, 1993).

[167] Alexander Bickel, *The Least Dangerous Branch: The Supreme Court at the Bar of Politics* 16–23 (Bobbs-Merrill, 1962); Ackerman, *We the People* 8–16 (cited in note 63).

there is broad agreement that constitutional interpretation in the federal courts restrains the state, in contrast to a reliance on government power in the political branches.[168]

The history of civil liberties during the New Deal presents something of a natural experiment with respect to these claims. In this moment of profound uncertainty and possibility, meaningful alternatives to judicial review were proposed and tested. Institutions formulated their own distinctive approaches to defining and enforcing civil liberties commitments. Observers debated which were best.

Unsurprisingly, those who favored a labor interventionist view of civil liberties were relatively hostile to the courts. Even as he championed the Senate Civil Liberties Committee, Robert La Follette Jr. endorsed a constitutional amendment to curtail judicial review. He argued that "no kind of legal guaranty has ever been able to protect minorities from the hatreds and intolerances let loose when an economic system breaks down."[169] That assessment diverged increasingly from the progressive civil liberties vision. It found echoes in a statement by the leftist International Juridical Association (and reproduced as a pamphlet by the National Lawyers Guild), which concluded that "there can be no true enforcement of the Bill of Rights in the interests of persons instead of wealth, except by the elected representatives of the people."[170]

Many New Dealers regarded Congress as the institution most responsive to majoritarian impulses and the judiciary as the most insulated, with administrative agencies somewhere in between.[171] They doubted the will or power of the courts to create labor rights,

---

[168] For example, Cass Sunstein has argued that the legislative and executive branches are better suited to implement positive rights. Cass R. Sunstein, *The Partial Constitution* 9–10, 131–49 (Harvard, 1993). For accounts that emphasize the role of courts in buttressing rather than constraining regulatory power, see Novak, People's Welfare; Paul Frymer, *Acting When Elected Officials Won't: Federal Courts and Civil Rights Enforcement in U.S. Labor Unions, 1935–1985*, 97 Amer Pol Sci Rev 483; John Fabian Witt, *The Accidental Republic: Crippled Workingmen, Destitute Widows, and the Remaking of American Law* (Harvard, 2004).

[169] He continued: "Liberals, be realists; do not let a lot of professional legalists, paid to do the job, bind you to the woods while they are showing you the trees." Radio Address by Hon. Robert M. La Follette Jr., February 13, 1937, ACLU Papers, reel 143, vol 978.

[170] International Juridical Association, *Curbing the Courts* (1937), in William Gorham Rice Papers, Wisconsin Historical Society Archives, Madison, WI, box 19, folder 7.

[171] By contrast, the ACLU believed that judicial tenure insulated judges against lobbying from strong special interests. That is, judges were freer than legislators to follow public opinion. Accordingly, the ACLU often organized efforts to influence judges through letter-writing campaigns by prominent citizens.

and they assumed that administrative actors were more apt to invoke state power on behalf of rights claimants against private abuse. In the face of contending constitutional claims, they called upon Congress to curtail employers' use of economic weapons, with the hope of tipping the constitutional balance from property to speech and association and from the rights of employers to the rights of labor. While these assumptions and aspirations were based in part on prevailing political alignments, it may be that some have wider significance.

To be sure, it is always dangerous to extrapolate from historical cases. At the level of discrete institutions, there is simply too much noise: strong personalities, budget constraints, idiosyncratic preferences. In short, there are too many shocks and too much contingency to justify generalization. That problem is all the more acute where, as here, the interval of observation is short; in light of rapid political retrenchment, opportunities for experimentation were quickly foreclosed.

Take the NLRB. Although Congress justified the Wagner Act on the basis of industrial stability as well as workers' rights, the historical evidence points strongly to the primacy of the latter in early understandings. The principal threat to labor's civil liberties came from private sources, that is, employers. In combating private abuses, industrial unions hitched themselves to the enforcement powers of the state. Notwithstanding their caution in court, they routinely cloaked their demands in constitutional language. If any institution held out the promise of a distinct, extracourt constitutionalism this was it.

By the late 1930s, however, it was evident that the agency's partiality toward labor—and, by extension, its aggressive enforcement of labor's rights—would not last. The NLRB never fully realized the vision of civil liberties that its early leadership espoused. On some accounts, that failure flowed from institutional constraints. In stark contrast to the sympathetic treatment of legislation and regulation securing civil rights, labor scholars have often argued that a state-centered approach is inherently accommodationist. They have reasoned that agencies are subject to regulatory capture, and that within a capitalist economy, the NLRB was bound to capitulate to industrial interests.

If one takes seriously the NLRB's conception of its mandate as a civil liberties project, then its treatment of workers' rights during the 1940s makes a neat counterpoint to the liberal civil liberties vision. After all, the courts assumed a largely deferential stance toward the NLRB in the 1940s. Certainly the members of the NLRB were acutely aware of the Administrative Procedure Act, along with the ever-present and increasing threat of judicial review.[172] Still, labor historians have amply documented the board's hasty retreat from its early ambitions. In place of fundamental rights, the new NLRB emphasized industrial pluralism. The strike quickly gave way to collective bargaining.[173] The NLRB of the 1940s put more stock in stabilizing production than in equalizing the bargaining power between workers and their employers.

After a wave of powerful labor activity in the wake of World War II, Congress passed the Taft-Hartley Act in 1947 over President Truman's veto. By then, there was broad-based agreement that the labor movement had grown too strong and too reckless. A rare holdout, the ACLU denounced Taft-Hartley as a "direct violation of labor's rights" and cautioned that the act's provisions were "fraught with peril to the maintenance of civil liberties in labor disputes."[174] It lamented the popular desire, expressed in the 1946 elections, to break free of the "irritating shackles" of state control and to reinstate "the presumably sound leadership of private business." The statute accomplished that goal in part by altering the substantive provisions of the NLRA, and in part by buttressing the supervisory role of the courts. The new skepticism toward state economic regulation had "produced an atmosphere increasingly hostile to the liberties of organized labor, the political left and many minorities."[175] In other

---

[172] That the board's new leadership enhanced procedural protections for parties to NLRB proceedings was likely essential to judicial deference. See Daniel R. Ernst, *Tocqueville's Nightmare: The Administrative State Emerges in America, 1900–1940* (Oxford, 2014), 97–105.

[173] Christopher L. Tomlins, *The New Deal, Collective Bargaining, and the Triumph of Industrial Pluralism*, 39 Indust Labor Rel Rev 19 (1985). Historians and labor scholars have emphasized that the mature NLRB validated the strike only as a response to employer interference with collective bargaining, consistent with the regulatory framework of the NLRA. See, for example, Karl E. Klare, *Labor Law as Ideology: Toward a New Historiography of Collective Bargaining Law*, 4 Berkeley J Emp & Lab L 450, 454–56 (1981); Peter H. Irons, *The New Deal Lawyers* 295–96 (Princeton, 1982).

[174] *Civil Liberties Union Condemns Labor Bill*, New York Times (June 16, 1947).

[175] *Setback Reported for Civil Liberties*, New York Times (Sept 3, 1947). Ironically, Congress was reintroducing by statute some of the very same restraints on labor's rights to strike and picket that the Supreme Court, before 1937, had imposed on constitutional grounds.

words, Americans had forgotten that curbing state power might undermine, rather than buttress, constitutional rights.

Historians have characterized Taft-Hartley as little more than an afterthought. Perhaps the NLRB's state-centered approach dulled organized labor's radical edge, as critics have alleged.[176] No doubt politics played a part as well. Even before the Second World War, the rightward shift within Congress and in public opinion led to changes in personnel at the NLRB, which in turn tempered the agency's pro-labor stance. Certainly the NLRB continued to police employers' unfair labor practices, and the right to organize was firmly entrenched. Union density would not peak until the 1950s, and it would take decades for labor to register the depth of its subsequent decline. Still, by 1947, the labor interventionist vision of civil liberties had long since lost its bite, within Congress and the NLRB just as much as the courts.

In fact, it was arguably in the judiciary—where decision makers enjoyed judicial tenure and were most insulated from rapidly shifting politics—that the progressive, labor interventionist, and radical visions of civil liberties coexisted longest.[177] Even as they clashed in the legislative and administrative arenas, the various civil liberties constituencies made common ground in the courts. For a time, robust First Amendment protection for labor activity seemed plausible. *Thornhill* and *Carlson* all but collapsed the radical, labor interventionist, and progressive visions into a unitary celebration of labor's rights. Just as quickly, however, the Supreme Court pulled back from the transformative potential of such decisions. By the 1940s, it read civil liberties through a liberal lens that privileged the Bill of Rights.

By the early 1940s, then, a new, liberal vision of civil liberties commanded substantial, though not absolute, consensus across institutions. That vision regarded the state as hostile and valorized the checking power of the courts. It shared the radicals' call for a neutral state. It shared the progressives' concern for robust policy debate.

---

[176] Christopher L. Tomlins, *The State and the Unions: Labor Relations, Law, and the Organized Labor Movement in America, 1880–1960* (Cambridge, 1985).

[177] Such effects, however, are necessarily time-limited. As Robert Dahl observed at mid-century, political control over the judicial appointments process constrains significant divergence from mainstream views. Robert A. Dahl, *Decision-Making in a Democracy: The Supreme Court as a National Policy-Maker*, 6 J Pub L 279 (1957).

It shared the conservatives' reliance on judicially enforceable rights. Only the labor interventionists were excluded from its domain.

It is impossible fully to disentangle institutional explanations from external political pressures. It is likely that the two were closely linked. I argue elsewhere that the new liberal commitment was a compromise among competing constituencies and advocacy groups, all of whom shared an aversion to state power in the realm of expressive freedom, and all of whom mobilized legal professionals to frame their claims in the political branches as well as the courts.[178] Joint briefing by labor lawyers, the ACLU, and the ABA in foundational First Amendment cases steered the Supreme Court toward a vision of civil liberties compatible with a long-standing constitutional principle, namely, judicial constraint on government power. Radicals feared and predicted that the state would turn against them before long. Progressives valued deliberative openness in formulating and legitimating social and economic policy. Conservatives, for the first time, had reason to fear that the state suppression of speech would undermine their prerogatives, and that a laissez-faire approach to the First Amendment would redound to their benefit. Legislators and administrators, in addition to judges, proved receptive to their collective appeal for judicial policing of the Bill of Rights. Whatever the causal chain, the moment for experimentation quickly passed. Less than five years after the ACLU issued its equivocal assessment of judicial review, the organization declared resolutely that its "battleground [was] chiefly in the courts."[179] Its volunteer attorneys had carried "scores of civil liberties issues" to the Supreme Court of the United States, "where decisions in case after case [had] firmly established the interpretations of the Bill of Rights which the Union supports."[180]

---

[178] On the key role played by lawyers and legal advocacy groups in institutionalizing legal claims, see Marc Galanter, *Why the "Haves" Come Out Ahead: Speculations on the Limits of Legal Change*, 9 L & Society Rev 95 (1974); Robert A. Kagan, *Adversarial Legalism: The American Way of Law* (Harvard, 2001); William N. Eskridge Jr., *Some Effects of Identity-Based Social Movements on Constitutional Law in the Twentieth Century*, 100 Mich L Rev 2062 (2002). On social movements and constitutional compromise, see Jack M. Balkin, *Constitutional Redemption: Political Faith in an Unjust World* (Harvard, 2011).

[179] American Civil Liberties Union, *Presenting the American Civil Liberties Union, Inc., November 1941* (1941).

[180] American Civil Liberties Union, *Presenting the American Civil Liberties Union, April 1947* (1947), 5.

Given the rapidity of this shift and the copious confounding variables, what lessons can we derive from the proliferation of institutional mechanisms for the enforcement of civil liberties before the new consensus crystallized? The first is the basic historical insight that alternative paths existed. The liberal vision of civil liberties familiar to us today was not the only or, necessarily, the preferable possibility. Some New Deal officials rejected state-constraining constitutionalism in favor of legislative or administrative efforts to secure labor's rights. Others accepted a central role for the Bill of Rights but resisted the premise that courts were best suited to enforce its provisions. In investigating, legislating, and litigating, they understood themselves to be legitimate stewards of First Amendment freedoms.

Second, regardless of their substantive views, New Deal actors had a capacious understanding of the opportunities for collaboration across institutions. In framing its prosecutorial program, the Civil Liberties Unit of the Department of Justice responded to and pushed the limits of state action doctrine as construed by the courts. The NLRB looked to the La Follette Committee to expand and vindicate its power. And the judiciary acknowledged legislative and administrative priorities in assessing the appropriate scope of First Amendment rights. Sometimes that meant accommodating civil liberties to political judgments about public safety or national security, as it does today.[181] Sometimes the Court invoked changing legislative priorities in expanding the First Amendment to admit new activity, like labor picketing, into the ambit of First Amendment protection.[182] There was no bright line between constitutionalism within and outside the courts.

Third, and relatedly, it is a crucial feature of this period that extrajudicial judgments about civil liberties were not consigned to the shadows of court decisions. In other words, when the NLRB rea-

---

[181] For example, *Korematsu v United States*, 323 US 214 (1944); *Minersville School District v Gobitis*, 310 US 586 (1940).

[182] For example, *Thornhill v Alabama*, 310 US 88, 102–03 (1940) ("In the circumstances of our times the dissemination of information concerning the facts of a labor dispute must be regarded as within that area of free discussion that is guaranteed by the Constitution. . . . The merest glance at State and Federal legislation on the subject demonstrates the force of the argument that labor relations are not matters of mere local or private concern. Free discussion concerning the conditions in industry and the causes of labor disputes appears to us indispensable to the effective and intelligent use of the processes of popular government to shape the destiny of modern industrial society.").

soned that the right of workers to organize trumped the right of
employers to distribute antiunion literature, it was not operating
strictly in the interstices of existing doctrine, nor was it merely attempting to influence judicial reasoning.[183] Rather, in a moment of
profound constitutional change, it imagined itself as a coequal partner in the New Deal realignment of powers and rights. Not only
had the Supreme Court signaled a new deference to the political
branches, but President Roosevelt had proven willing to challenge
the entire enterprise of judicial review. And despite the failure of the
court-packing plan, there was still considerable support for alternative proposals, including jurisdiction stripping and constitutional
amendment to eliminate judicial review, if circumstances so required.
Even after the President's bill failed, defenders of judicial independence worried that a single decision invalidating New Deal legislation "might mean that the President would return to the attack."[184]
Constitutionalism outside the courts was never unconstrained, but
nonjudicial actors in the late New Deal operated at a level of autonomy unprecedented at the time and unparalleled since. How they
exercised their perceived power offers a glimpse of what an unme-
diated extracourt constitutionalism might accomplish, at least in the
First Amendment context.

Fourth, the vulnerability of judicial review during the New Deal
serves as a reminder that judicial outcomes help to shape institutional features in addition to reflecting them. There is a tendency in
the literature to assume that institutional parameters are relatively
fixed—the culmination of evolving customary practices or the man-
ifestation of constitutional commands. The broad appeal of court-
curbing measures during the 1930s suggests that a judiciary too far

---

[183] On the ways in which noncourt actors account for the Constitution, see, for example,
Jerry L. Mashaw, *Norms, Practices, and the Paradox of Deference: A Preliminary Inquiry into
Agency Statutory Interpretation*, 57 Admin L Rev 501 (2005); David A. Strauss, *Presidential
Interpretation of the Constitution*, 15 Cardozo L Rev 113, 113–14 (1993). On constitutional
interpretation within administrative agencies, see Gillian E. Metzger, *Ordinary Administrative
Law as Constitutional Common Law*, 110 Colum L Rev 479 (2010); Reuel E. Schiller, *The Ad-
ministrative State, Front and Center: Studying Law and Administration in Postwar America*, 26 L
& Hist Rev 415, 422–23 (2008); and Sophia Lee, *Race, Sex, and Rulemaking: Administrative
Constitutionalism and the Workplace, 1960 to the Present*, 96 Va L Rev 799 (2010).

[184] Grenville Clark, Memorandum for Messrs. Burlingham, Arant, and Marbury, August 31,
1937, Clark Papers, Series VIII (National Committee for Independent Courts), box 1, folder
Burlingham, Charles C. (box 70, folder 11 under prior numbering system).

out of step with popular pressures or political demands risks institutional overhaul.[185] That is, the political branches may favor an independent judiciary under ordinary circumstances, but pushed too far they will elevate their immediate policy objectives over long-term institutional concerns.[186] Conversely, vested actors—in this case, the organized bar—may choose to privilege institutional stability over substantive law.

The generalized commitment to expressive freedom during the New Deal was a new and momentous development. It was not that earlier government actors were autocratic in their suppression of dissent. On the contrary, they had often exercised their discretion to accommodate disfavored speakers and views. Congress had considered free speech in debating such measures as the Espionage and Sedition Acts, and it had expressly avoided provisions that were perceived to go too far.[187] Occasionally, the Department of Justice had declined prosecution in cases involving political agitation.[188] Various federal agencies, including the post office, the customs service, and the War Department, had considered constitutional and policy constraints in formulating and administering their policies.[189]

By the same token, the federal government of the 1930s garnered its share of criticism with respect to the Bill of Rights. The Roosevelt administration was responsible for a massive expansion of secret surveillance by the FBI, and Frank Murphy's justice depart-

---

[185] By the same token, during the 1910s, the ABA reacted to the campaign for judicial recall by introducing procedural reforms. See Weinrib, *Taming of Free Speech* ch 1 (cited in note 7).

[186] Deference to the judiciary on contentious issues can advance legislators' priorities while preserving electoral support. Mark A. Graber, *The Non-Majoritarian Difficulty: Legislative Deference to the Judiciary*, 7 Studies in Am Pol Development 35 (1993). It may also serve institutional interests shared by the political branches. Keith E. Whittington, *Political Foundations of Judicial Supremacy: The Presidency, the Supreme Court, and Constitutional Leadership in U.S. History* (2007). George Lovell has argued that the NLRA's drafters intentionally deferred controversial political decisions about labor to the judiciary. George I. Lovell, *Legislative Deferrals: Statutory Ambiguity, Judicial Power, and American Democracy* (Cambridge, 2003).

[187] Geoffrey R. Stone, *The Origins of the "Bad Tendency" Test: Free Speech in Wartime*, 2002 Supreme Court Review 411 (2002); Rabban, *Forgotten Years* at 250–55 (cited in note 6).

[188] For instance, Attorney General George Wickersham declined to prosecute the IWW under federal law, despite encouragement from local law enforcement and President Taft. For this and other examples, see Rabban, *Forgotten Years* (cited in note 6); see also Dubofsky, *We Shall Be All* 195 (cited in note 27).

[189] Weinrib, *Liberal Compromise* (cited in note 19); Kessler, 114 Colum L Rev (cited in note 48).

ment authorized spurious prosecutions of radical dissenters.[190] As for Congress, the Smith Act prohibitions on "subversive activities" and the House Committee on Un-American Activities quickly supplanted the LaFollette Civil Liberties Committee and its legislative program as the signature contributions of the prewar period.

Such qualifications notwithstanding, the New Deal ushered in a thoroughgoing revision of the relationship between state power and the Bill of Rights. In previous decades, that relationship had been primarily oppositional. Free Speech League founder Theodore Schroeder expressed the point forcefully to the federal Commission on Industrial Relations when he complained in 1915 that there were tens of thousands of statutes and ordinances "enacted to defend property" but, to his knowledge, "not one law anywhere in the United States which even remotely squints at an attempt to protect by law [the] constitutional guarantee as to freedom of speech and press."[191] Schroeder's assessment captured a state of affairs that persisted well into the interwar period. When the federal government entertained civil liberties claims, it was to constrain executive discretion or moderate repressive laws, not to curb abuses by local governments or private actors. Put differently, state actors operated in the shadow of the Constitution, as they ordinarily do today.[192] Sometimes, they expressly limited or altered their policies to avoid running afoul of the First Amendment; constitutional interpretation, to the extent they engaged in it, served to cabin instead of empower them.

In the 1930s, in a marked departure from its historic practices, the state marshaled its resources to protect rather than suppress the rights of unpopular minorities as well as the channels of protest and dissent.[193] In all reaches of government, administrators and policymakers professed allegiance to civil liberties as a central value

---

[190] Samuel Walker, *Presidents and Civil Liberties from Wilson to Obama: A Story of Poor Custodians* 96–97 (Cambridge, 2012).

[191] United States Commission on Industrial Relations, Final Report and Testimony Submitted to Congress by the Commission on Industrial Relations, 11 vols, 64th Cong, 1st sess (Government Printing Office, 1916), vol 11, 10845.

[192] This is the interpretive process ordinarily addressed in the literature on constitutionalism outside the courts.

[193] During Reconstruction, the federal government had endeavored (unevenly) to protect the rights of African Americans in the South. The New Deal efforts expanded on that precedent in creating an institutional structure to promote the dissemination of unorthodox views and to insulate dissent more broadly.

of American democracy, and they deployed state power to effectuate civil libertarian ends.

The short window of experimentation and the swift ideological reconfiguration have obscured the significance of these alternative enforcement regimes. Their influence, however, persisted for decades. Perhaps there is no better example than the brief for the United States as amicus curiae in *Brown v Board of Education*. "Few Americans believe that the government should pursue a laissez-faire policy in the field of civil rights, or that it adequately discharges its duty to the people so long as it does not itself intrude on their civil liberties," the brief declared in language strongly reminiscent of New Deal civil liberties enforcement. In pursuit of racial justice, the brief invoked popular support for a principle that seems incongruous with civil liberties claims today: a "general acceptance of an affirmative government obligation to insure respect for fundamental human rights."[194]

Finally, it is worth underscoring that the liberal civil liberties vision that prevailed across institutions by the early 1940s unequivocally privileged the courts. Whether the courts, in turn, favored the liberal vision remains an open question. On one reading, the Supreme Court's endorsement of workers' concerted activity as a "fundamental right" in upholding New Deal legislation, remarkable as it was at the time, served also to legitimate the Court's commitment to a rights-based constitution.[195] The Court was not deferring to discretion writ large. Rather, it was permitting the political branches to prioritize one set of rights over another, a formula that facilitated the rapid retrenchment of the postwar period.

Put simply, it is unclear whether the judiciary embraced the antistate, court-centered approach because it was most consistent with its institutional interests and competencies, or whether the courts, like their administrative and legislative counterparts, were channeling broader developments.[196] The answer is elusive, just as it is

---

[194] Brief for the United States as Amicus Curiae, *Brown v Board of Education*, Nos 1–5, 2 (US, filed Dec 2, 1952). On the persistence during the Cold War of state-centered enforcement on behalf of racial equality, but not free speech, see Christopher W. Schmidt, *The Civil Rights-Civil Liberties Divide*, 12 Stan J C R & C L (forthcoming 2016).

[195] *Jones & Laughlin Steel*, 301 US at 33. See footnote 72 and accompanying text.

[196] Compare Ajay K. Mehrotra, *Making the Modern American Fiscal State: Law, Politics, and the Rise of Progressive Taxation, 1877–1929*, 24–25 (Cambridge, 2013); James T. Kloppenberg, *Institutionalism, Rational Choice, and Historical Analysis*, 28 Polity 1 (1995).

difficult to discern from the historical record whether the Constitutional Revolution flowed from jurisprudential or doctrinal concerns as opposed to court-packing pressures or popular demand. In the late New Deal, economic contraction, hostility toward labor, and the rise of totalitarianism abroad all abetted the liberal civil liberties vision. So did the legal advocates whose opinions mattered most to the New Deal Court. But it is telling, at the very least, that so many actors across the political spectrum believed—some optimistically, some with real trepidation—that the judiciary was bound to serve a checking function on state power and labor rights.

IV. Conclusion

That the architects of the liberal civil liberties vision were deeply ambivalent about the institutional mechanisms for rights enforcement has largely been forgotten. It is an observation with important implications for debates about extracourt constitutionalism and the scope of the First Amendment today. As scholars and advocates contemplate the allocation of institutional authority to define and defend constitutional rights, they would do well to consider the anticipated advantages and limitations of the court-based constitutionalism that prevailed.

I do not mean to overstate this claim. The transinstitutional convergence on the liberal vision of civil liberties challenges the assumption that the judicial forum is altogether distinctive in its conception of rights, or that the trade-offs entailed in constitutional litigation are limited to its purview. There was more ideological variation within institutions and less ideological variation across institutions than contemporaries predicted and modern scholars might suppose. Indeed, a capacious account of civil liberties lasted longest in the judiciary. Today, even as some First Amendment scholars lament the judiciary's stubborn adherence to a free marketplace of ideas, labor law scholars query whether unions would not have fared better in the courts.[197]

But if institutional distinctions in civil liberties enforcement were less apparent than New Dealers might have expected, neither were they inconsequential. The effects of domestic economic conditions and an imminent World War on civil liberties advocacy and doc-

---

[197] See, for example, Cynthia L. Estlund, *The Ossification of American Labor Law*, 102 Colum L Rev 1527, 1584–87 (2002).

trine no doubt dwarfed the impact of institutional distinctions. Still, especially outside the labor context, tangible differences emerged.

In the years after the Constitutional Revolution of the New Deal, the federal government sought out ways to increase access to competing ideas without favoring particular outcomes. That is, government actors developed methods to promote and secure a forum for expressive contestation—just as they had created a framework for collective bargaining, without prescribing particular results, through the NLRA. In 1938, President Roosevelt introduced a discounted postage rate to facilitate the circulation of printed matter. ACLU Attorney Morris Ernst, who persuaded Roosevelt to adopt the program, proclaimed that it "permitted a flow into the market place of great additional diversity of points of view."[198] In 1946, the FCC adopted new standards for granting and renewing radio licenses, which required stations to allocate time for the discussion of "important public questions" and to cover all sides of controversial issues. In practice, of course, such requirements served to increase access by disfavored and marginal speakers; popular and commercial speakers were likely already to have ample coverage. The radio industry denounced the measures as censorship, but the ACLU disagreed. If the government sought to withhold radio licenses based on its assessment of the *content* of programming, it explained, the station owners had recourse to the courts. As things stood, "[t]he standards fixed provide[d] for more speech, not less."[199] Such developments emerged directly out of the New Deal's more ambitious experimentation in civil liberties enforcement.[200]

---

[198] See Fred Rodell, *Morris Ernst, New York's Unlawyerlike Liberal Lawyer Is the Censor's Enemy, the President's Friend*, Life (Feb 21, 1944). The measure was justified on the basis that "in this democracy of ours, unlike the dictatorship lands, we are dedicated to the ever increasing extension of a free market in thought as a means to the perpetuation of our national ideals. As they burn books abroad, we extend their distribution." Announcement by National Committee to Abolish Postal Discrimination Against Books, 5–6, Oscar Cox Papers, Franklin D. Roosevelt Presidential Library, Hyde Park, NY, Alphabetical File, Douglas–Ernst, box 9, folder Ernst, Morris; Memorandum by Morris Ernst Prepared at the Request of the [ACLU] Board of Directors at the Special Meeting, 9 October 1941, Lowell Mellett Papers, 1938–1944, Franklin D. Roosevelt Presidential Library, Hyde Park, NY, gr 60, box 11, folder Morris Ernst.

[199] American Civil Liberties Union, *Radio Programs in the Public Interest* (American Civil Liberties Union, July 1946). Compare *Red Lion Broadcasting Company v Federal Communications Commission*, 395 US 367 (1969).

[200] Even here, institutional distinctions are murky. Notably, 1946 was the same year that the Supreme Court issued its aberrational decision requiring a private actor to open its property to public discussion. *Marsh v Alabama*, 326 US 401 (1946).

In an era when radical revolution seemed possible—when the goal of labor activity was the general strike, not a union contract—minor differences like these would have seemed inconsequential. Proponents of the radical civil liberties vision naively hoped that a naked right to agitate would pave the way to substantive change. Implicit in their position was the confidence that even in an unfettered marketplace, their agenda would prevail. By the 1940s, employers understood that no free exchange in ideas existed. They understood that a right to free speech would almost invariably favor those with superior resources. As Nathan Greene (coauthor with Felix Frankfurter of *The Labor Injunction*) cautioned in relation to antiunion propaganda, employer speech amounts to "a *protected* commodity in a *monopoly* market."[201] On this view, it was not that New Deal institutions deradicalized the labor-friendly civil liberties visions; it was the liberal civil liberties vision that deradicalized the New Deal state. That is, what was determinative was ideological contestation and compromise, not institutional enforcement.

Then again, a young Roger Baldwin might have suggested that the radicals' mistake was to trust in state institutions at all. The story of civil liberties between the Depression and World War II conforms to a truism of labor advocacy during the Progressive Era: namely, that courts, no less than administrators or legislatures, are creatures of the state. Indeed, the notion that the Supreme Court could have stretched the First Amendment to encompass labor's most coercive tactics seems fanciful in retrospect. Even prospectively, many within the labor movement considered the judicial strategy to be misguided. At the dawn of the New Deal, the architects of the modern civil liberties movement eschewed the administrative enforcement of civil liberties. The alternative that they favored was labor's collective power, not the courts. Theirs was not liberal constitutionalism, administrative constitutionalism, or even popular constitutionalism. They defended civil liberties as rights prior to the Constitution, enforceable by "economic power and organized pressure alone."[202]

---

[201] *Civil Liberties and the NLRB*, 5, International Juridical Association, reprinted from speech by Nathan Greene, March 8, 1940, Sugar Papers, folder 54:17 (emphasis in original).

[202] Resolutions, Conference on Civil Liberties under the New Deal, December 9, 1934, ACLU Papers, reel 110, vol 721.